The Rights of Children

Reprint
Series
No. 9

Harvard Educational Review

THIRD PRINTING, 1982. Library of Congress Card Number 74-79545. ISBN 0-916690. Printed by Capital City Press, Montpelier, Vt. 05602. Cover design by Cyndy Brady.

Photo Credits — Eric Olson, cover; Marsha Hirano, p. ii; Shari Ostrow, p. 45; Alex Packer, pp. 46, 48, 352, 386; Shelley Rotner, pp. 47, 105, 346, 351, 388; Leigh F. Palmer, pp. 55, 58, 61, 65; Ellen Foscue Johnson, pp. 104, 345, 353, 354; Karin Rosenthal, pp. 106, 347, 350, 387, 392.

PUBLISHED BY HARVARD EDUCATIONAL REVIEW, LONGFELLOW HALL, 13 Appian Way, Cambridge, Massachusetts 02138

The Rights of Children

SOCIAL POLICY FOR CHILDREN

BOOK REVIEWS

Preface

The *Harvard Educational Review* has always been interested in children, but we have usually seen them as subjects for research, objects of pedagogy, or products of the schools. We have been more curious about the impact of the educational process than about the group it presumably serves. While this approach has helped structure academic inquiry, often it has not helped us understand what it is like to be a child growing up in America or how various social institutions, among them the schools, affect children's lives.

Until recently, the discussion of children has been at once too broad and too narrow. In 1957 the United Nations ratified a Declaration of the Rights of the Child and in 1970 the White House Conference on Children endorsed a children's Bill of Rights. Each proclaimed a set of rights to which all children are entitled, but neither helped much to show what it meant as a practical matter to fulfill these rights. No one can argue, for instance, with the right to be born a wanted child. But what does that tell a physician treating an abused child or an administrator of a foster care program? Likewise, most people can agree with a child's right to an education. But how does a teacher or principal translate that into a program? On the other hand, in trying to be specific, we have asked questions as if they had one best answer. For example, we have tried to do research on cognitive development as if it could be separated from emotional or psychological events; we have looked at the array of adult outcomes in life and tried to explain it solely on the basis of differences in educational opportunity in schools; or we have seen a family's trouble damaging a child and have removed the child from the home to end the source of the trouble. None of these approaches adequately describes reality. Our strategy has not been sufficiently inclusive.

This collection of articles is an attempt to restructure the inquiry to take into account the standpoint of the child. From birth to adulthood, what are the institutions, policies, and professionals a child encounters? How do these shape children's lives, curtail freedoms, delineate rights? Should we continue to presume children's incompetence in making decisions which affect their future? Should we still accept the premise that adults—parents and the state—act in the child's best interests? What kinds of research and reforms are needed to make the world fairer from the child's point of view?

Certainly children have equal rights to the freedoms and services that the nation provides. But children often are not capable of fulfilling the responsibilities that go along with rights because they are dependent. They need the love of their caretakers, and they benefit from the actions adults take to ensure their safety, health, and development. Adults, recognizing this, perhaps err too far on the side of protection, deciding that children's needs are more important than their rights. Margaret Mead has noted a pattern in this country's history to remove children from situations where they are endangered or their needs are not being met, rather than to correct the situation and allow children to remain. She believes this has the effect of removing a humanizing influence from the institutions in question, while at the same time preventing general standards of fairness from applying to children. Shut away in their own institutions, safe from adult excesses, children sometimes benefit, but they may also suffer the adverse consequences of unlimited adult discretion in the name of children's special needs.

Our traditional paternalistic stance is not surprising when children's status in society is viewed historically. To have rights, subjects of the state must be considered persons. But as Philippe Aries has argued in his *Centuries of Childhood,* the conception of children as a distinct group of citizens is unique to modern western culture. Before the Middle Ages, infant mortality was so high that parents could not afford to become psychologically attached to their children. Until they reached seven or eight years of age, children were not regarded as persons. If they survived past that age, they joined adult society and had no unique privileges or tasks, no distinctive clothing, toys, psychology or institutions. Over the centuries children have been seen as playtoys for adults, souls to be saved, private property of their fathers, natural resources to be used efficiently, raw material to be molded wisely, human capital to be invested. To think about children as persons is a new conception that is only beginning to influence our laws and institutions.

In order to make explicit the notion of children as equal persons under the law, more and more advocates speak of children's rights rather than their needs. Symbolically the two words have very different meanings, with potentially different policy implications. A need and a right both may refer to the same phenomenon, such as adequate nutrition or education of high quality. But a need connotes dependency, and it is not clear whose responsibility it is to correct the situation, the individual's or the state's. A right, on the other hand, implies equality, as in the equal protection of those whose inalienable rights are guaranteed by the Constitution. If a right is abridged, this is an injustice which the institutions of the state must correct. Thus, if reading is treated as a skill or need, widespread inability to read is a problem which may or may not merit society's benevolent concern. But if reading is a right, then schools must protect each child's ability to fulfill that right and the society's responsibility is unambiguous.

The shift in thinking of children's needs as rights has also been influenced by the civil rights and the women's liberation movements. When racial minorities or women were not considered people with equal stature under the law and when their political power was insufficient to enforce basic rights, their freedoms were ignored and their needs were unrepresented. Children are a minority group in the most literal sense. Unless they achieve equal stature under the law and use the political process on their own behalf, infringements of their rights will be allowed to continue. Analogies between human or civil rights and children's rights should not, of course, be used to gloss over the many real problems which would arise if we always treated children and adults alike under the Constitution, the law, or the political process. Equality, or blind impartiality, may not in all cases benefit children. In thinking about changes in law and policy affecting children, we must combine a respect for their rights with a sensitivity to their emerging capacities.

We were concerned when we solicited material for our two special issues on the Rights of Children that our authors have a broad understanding of children's place in society and yet be concrete in their analyses and recommendations. We looked for articles in three areas. First, we wanted to explore and further establish the foundations of children's rights. Part I of this Reprint includes an article on children and the law, and one on the philosophical justifications for the rights of children. Secondly, we wanted to explore the politics of children. What is the best balance between the interests of the state, the family, and the child? Should children continue to be shielded from politics, or is political advocacy their best protection? Part II includes four articles dealing with these and related issues. Finally, we asked authors to look at specific institutions and services for children. Part III deals with various social agencies and the impact of their policies on children.

Unfortunately, some important topics have gone untreated. We regret not having an article on formal and informal child care arrangements, one on child health care delivery, and one on the politics of providing adequate nutrition for all children. We also would have welcomed an article lending cross-cultural perspectives, and a general sociological overview of the role of childhood in America today. Perhaps most of all, we regret not having more insights from children themselves. Many of our authors point out that children should have a stronger voice in defining their own interests. But institutions and most journals are not organized to facilitate children's participation. We, too, have fallen into a familiar trap; we are adults speaking for children.

Current thinking on children's rights is clearly at the stage where we are closer to asking good questions than to finding final solutions. But many of our authors have advanced the discussion in their fields considerably by their contributions. Legislation, hearings, litigation, advocacy, administrative reform, and basic research all are approached with a new concern for the viewpoint of the child. Our authors also stress that public and professional attitudes toward children must change before new policies and practices will take effect. We hope this process has been advanced in the pages of the *Review* and will continue.

ROCHELLE BECK
HEATHER BASTOW WEISS
Issue Editors

Children Under the Law

HILLARY RODHAM

Children's Defense Fund

The author examines the changing status of children under the law. Traditionally, the law has reflected a social consensus that children's best interests are synonymous with those of their parents, except under the few circumstances where the state is authorized to intervene in family life under the doctrine of parens patriae. *Little consideration has been given to the substantive and procedural rights of children as a discrete interest group. At present, law reform is moving to change children's legal status in two ways: by extending more adult rights to children and by recognizing certain unique needs and interests of children as legally enforceable rights. Ms. Rodham summarizes recent Supreme Court decisions which will influence changes of both kinds, and suggests specific directions reform might take.*

The phrase "children's rights" is a slogan in search of definition. Invoked to support such disparate causes as world peace, constitutional guarantees for delinquents, affection for infants, and lowering the voting age, it does not yet reflect any coherent doctrine regarding the status of children as political beings. Asserting that children are entitled to rights and enumerating their needs does not clarify the difficult issues surrounding children's legal status. These issues of family autonomy and privacy, state responsibility, and children's independence are complex, but they determine how children are treated by the nation's legislatures, courts, and administrative agencies.

This paper briefly sets out the legal conception of children's status underlying American public policy and case law, and suggests various ways in which this conception needs major revision. There are important new themes emerging in the

Harvard Educational Review Vol. 43 No. 4 November 1973, 487–514

1

interpretation of children's status under the law, and several new directions which future litigation and legislation in the interest of children might take. Of particular interest in the trend toward recognizing children's needs and interests as rights under the law.

Attributing a right to a person may involve describing an existing relationship or prescribing the formation of a new one. The prescriptive aspect of right represents a moral judgment about how particular interests should be ordered so that certain ones will be given priority over others. The recent literature on children's rights is filled with such prescriptions, based on arguments from political, legal, and moral philosophy. Rarely, however, do the writers mention the important differences between an existing legal right and other claims of right. A legal right is an enforceable claim to the possession of property or authority, or to the enjoyment of privileges or immunities.[1] Moral prescriptions and political demands, on the other hand, are not formally recognized by the law and have the status of needs or interests, not rights. Adult Americans enjoy the legal rights set forth in the Constitution, statutes, regulations, and the common law of the federal and state governments.[2] Child citizens, although their needs and interests may be greater than those of adults, have far fewer legal rights (and duties). Indeed, the special needs and interests which distinguish them from adults have served as the basis for not granting them rights and duties, and for entrusting enforcement of the few rights they have to institutional decision-makers.

Current Legal Status of Children

"Children" is sometimes a term of legal classification, but it is more common to find the legal categories of "infancy" or "minority" describing people under twenty-one, or under eighteen for some purposes. The status of infancy, or minority, large-

[1] Defining "right" apart from the general usage which the term enjoys is difficult. The best attempt to unravel the jurisprudence of rights and to elucidate the various meanings which it has acquired in the law is Wesley Newcomb Hohfeld's analysis in *Fundamental Legal Conceptions* (New Haven: Yale University Press, 1919). The definition used here is drawn from the Compact Edition of *Oxford English Dictionary*, v. II, pp. 2546-2547 (New York: Oxford University Press, 1971).

[2] As one commentator described adult rights: ". . . today liberty has been extended so far as *the law alone* may extend it to all adults, white or black, male or female, rich or poor, intelligent or stupid; subordinate relations to private persons must be consensual relations and probably cannot, under the Thirteenth Amendment and common law limitations on the freedom to contract, be total." Andrew Jay Kleinfeld, "The Balance of Power Among Infants, Their Parents and the State, Part II," *Family Law Quarterly*, 4 (December 1970), 409, 410.

ly determines the rights and duties of a child before the law regardless of his or her actual age or particular circumstances. Justifications for such a broad, chronologically determined classification rely on the physical and intellectual differences between adults and children.

There is obviously some sense to this rationale except that the dividing point at twenty-one or eighteen years is artificial and simplistic; it obscures the dramatic differences among children of different ages and the striking similarities between older children and adults. The capacities and the needs of a child of six months differ substantially from those of a child of six or sixteen years.

In eighteenth century English common law, the term children's rights would have been a nonsequitur. Children were regarded as chattels of the family and wards of the state, with no recognized political character or power and few legal rights. Blackstone wrote little about children's rights, instead stressing the duties owed by "prized possessions" to their fathers.[3] Early American courts accepted this view.[4] In this country children have long had certain rights resulting from their attainment of some other legal status, such as parties injured by tortfeasors, legatees under wills, or intestate successors. Even these rights, however, can be exercised only vicariously through adult representatives. Older children have a few additional legal rights, granted by statutes which reflect some legal recognition of their increased competence. Examples include the right to drive a motor vehicle, the right to drop out of school, the right to vote, the right to work, and the right to marry (although before a certain age marriage can be voided in the absence of parental consent). The doctrines of emancipation and implied emancipation release a child from parental control following his or her marriage, after entering military service, or after achieving economic independence or meeting another statutory definition of maturity. Finally, the Supreme Court has held on a few occasions, and with greater frequency in recent years, that the Constitution requires recognition of particular rights of children, among them the right to certain procedural protections in juvenile courts,[5] the right to refuse to salute the flag in the

---

[3] William Blackstone, *Commentaries on the Laws of England*, Vol. I, 12th ed. (London: A. Strahen and W. Wordfall for T. Caddell, 1700-1795).

[4] See, e.g., James Kent, *Commentaries on American Law*, Vol. I, 14th ed. (Boston: Little Brown, O. W. Holmes ed., 1873).

[5] *Haley v. Ohio*, 332 US 596 (1948) (protection of Fourteenth Amendment against coerced confession extended to fifteen year old boy in state criminal trial); *Kent v. US*, 383 US 541 (1966) (waiver from juvenile court to adult court has to meet minimum requirements of due process); *In re Gault*, 387 US 1 (1967) (adult procedural protections in criminal trial extended to delinquency proceedings); *In re Winship*, 397 US 358 (1970) (quantum of proof necessary for conviction in juvenile court raised to reasonable doubt standard).

public schools when doing so would violate religious beliefs,[6] and the right to don a black armband to protest the Vietnam war.[7]

Beyond such instances, the law's concern with children has been confined to those occasions when the state may limit parental control in the interest of necessary protection or justifiable punishment of the child, or in the name of some overriding state interest. The theory of benevolent intrusion into families by the state seems to embody a contradiction. On the one hand, it operates within the context of a powerful social consensus that the proper relationship between parents and the state in their joint exercise of control over a child's life favors parental dominance. On the other hand, the doctrine of *parens patriae* has long justified state interference with parental prerogatives and even termination of all parental rights.

The social consensus that forms the first half of this apparent contradiction includes the following assumptions: a) America is a familial, child-centered society in which parents are responsible for their own children and have primary control over them; b) the community of adults, usually represented by the state, will not assume responsibility for the child unless the parents are unable to do so or will not do so, or until the child breaks a law; c) because ours is a child-loving society, non-parents and other adults representing the state want to and will do what is in the child's "best interests"; and d) children need not or should not be participants with the family and the state in making decisions which affect their lives. The tenets of this consensus, legitimized in the rules of law governing children's affairs, have represented outer limits beyond which child-oriented reforms cannot be effected. The other half of the apparent contradiction, however, involves regular challenges to family authority by state representatives. Certain social norms are enforced at the expense of family privacy, in the name of a child's best interests.

The most striking characteristic of children's law is the large degree of discretion permitted decision-makers in enforcing community norms. When intervention must occur, bureaucratic discretion replaces familial discretion. The statutes authorizing state intervention implicitly accept that the state's representative will know what children need and should not be straight-jacketed by legal technicalities. For example, laws against child neglect or abuse represent a community's decision to intervene in a parent-child relationship. Although the legislative decision favoring intervention may be widely supported, it proves difficult to specify the condi-

---

[6] *Board of Education v. Barnette*, 319 US 624 (1943).
[7] *Tinker v. Des Moines School District*, 393 US 503 (1969).

4

tions under which it should occur. Our pluralistic beliefs about child-rearing do not lead to a uniform interpretation of the best interests standard. The allowance of some degree of discretion is necessary for any legal system to operate, especially one presumed to deal with the specialized needs of its subjects. When few standards guide the exercise of discretion, however, and when there rarely are careful reviews of the judgments it produces, the legal system will not only be likely to treat individuals capriciously, but will also subject members of social minorities to the prejudices and beliefs of the dominant sector of the community.[8] This is especially true in children's law, where reservations against state intervention are most easily overcome in cases involving poor, non-white, and unconventional families. Children of these families are perceived as bearers of the sins and disabilities of their fathers, and as burdens which an "enlightened" society must bear.[9] This attitude is especially prominent in regard to the labelling of certain behavior as delinquent. In addition to acts which are criminal for adults (e.g. armed robbery), children may be accused of delinquency for misbehavior that is not criminal for adults. The so-called status offenses, incorrigibility, truancy, running away, sexual precociousness, represent a confused mixture of social control and preventive care that has resulted in the confinement of thousands of children for the crime of having trouble growing up.

In practice, therefore, powerlessness of a family, because of political, psychological, or economic reasons, renders it susceptible to benevolent intrusion. Unfortunately, the state has not proved an adequate substitute parent in many of the cases where intrusion has resulted in the removal of a child from his home. In many instances, states have been guilty of neglect according to their own statutory standards. Fears about arbitrary and harmful state intervention have led to increased rights of parents and custodians so that they are now entitled to certain procedural guarantees before the state may remove their children.[10] Only recently, however, has attention focused on the rights of the children who are the subjects of state intervention, both against their parents and against the state when it assumes the parenting responsibility. This attention is struggling for legal recognition against the

[8] The amount of discretion necessary in a legal system handling children's needs is very difficult to determine, especially because the options for the exercise of any discretion are so limited by inadequate resources. But the abuses of discretion are well documented. See, e.g. Sanford N. Katz, *When Parents Fail* (Boston: Beacon Press, 1971).

[9] See, e.g., Ten Broek, "California's Dual System of Family Law: Its Origins, Development and Present State," *Stanford Law Review*, 16 (1964), 257; Anthony Platt, *The Child Savers* (Chicago: University of Chicago Press, 1961), pp. 176-181.

[10] See, e.g., *Stanley v. Illinois*, 405 US 645 (1972).

prevailing assumption in children's law that a child's interests are identical to those of his parents. Even when a child cannot or will not recognize the identity of his interests with his parents', the law ordinarily does so, confident that children usually do not know what is best for themselves. Necessarily, the law must presume that parents or the state as parent do know what is best. The force of this position is weakened by the fact that adults consistently refuse to support programs designed to meet the needs and interests of children either when they are still in their homes or when they are in the state's charge. As a recent history of the White House Conference on Children points out, this country has a "cultural recalcitrance toward assuming public responsibility for children's needs."[11]

Rewriting laws has not substantially altered the long dominant consensus or dissipated public recalcitrance. The thrust of most reforms, amply supported by demonstrations of children's needs has been to persuade adult society to treat children better, but has not changed the position of children within society or made them capable of securing such treatment for themselves.[12]

Claims of Right

The needs and interests of a powerless individual must be asserted as rights if they are to be considered and eventually accepted as enforceable claims against other persons or institutions. The advocacy of rights for children, coming as it does on the heels of adult rights movements, highlights the political nature of questions about children's status. That children's issues are political may seem obvious. Political theorists from Plato onward have sought to specify proper child-rearing practices and have discussed the proper position of children within society, often coming to conclusions inconsistent with the prevailing American ones.[13] In the United States, the problems of children have usually been explained without any consideration of children's proper political status. Accordingly, the obstructionist role of the unstated consensus and the laws reflecting it has seldom been appreci-

[11] Shelley Kessler, unpublished paper on the past White House Conferences on Children (New Haven, Conn.: Carnegie Council on Children, 1972).
[12] For histories of various child-saving reforms, see Platt, *The Child Savers*; Robert M. Mennell, *Thorns and Thistles* (Hanover, N.H.: University Press of New England, 1973); Robert J. Pickett, *House of Refuge* (Syracuse: Syracuse University Press, 1969); Sanford Fox, "Juvenile Justice Reform: An Historical Perspective," *Stanford Law Review*, 22 (1970), 1187.
[13] Plato, *The Republic*, 235-264 (New York: Oxford University Press, 1945); Aristotle, *Politics*, 32-33, 316 (Sherman ed.; New York: Oxford University Press, 1962); J. Locke, *Treatise on Civil Government*, 34-50 (Sherman ed.; New York and London: Appleton Century, 1937); J. S. Mill, *On Liberty* (Chicago: Henry Regnery, 1955).

ated. The pretense that children's issues are somehow above or beyond politics endures and is reinforced by the belief that families are private, non-political units whose interests subsume those of children.[14] There is also an abiding belief that any official's failure to do what is best by a child is the exception, not the rule, and is due solely to occasional errors of judgment.[15] Moreover, nothing countervails against this pattern, since children are almost powerless to articulate their own interests or to organize themselves into a self-interested constituency and adults allied with them have seldom exerted an appreciable influence within the political system.

The basic rationale for depriving people of rights in a dependency relationship is that certain individuals are incapable or undeserving of the right to take care of themselves and consequently need social institutions specifically designed to safeguard their position. It is presumed that under the circumstances society is doing what is best for the individuals. Along with the family, past and present examples of such arrangements include marriage, slavery, and the Indian reservation system. The relative powerlessness of children makes them uniquely vulnerable to this rationale. Except for the institutionalized, who live in a state of enforced childishness, no other group is so totally dependent for its well-being on choices made by others. Obviously this dependency can be explained to a significant degree by the physical, intellectual, and psychological incapacities of (some) children which render them weaker than (some) older persons. But the phenomenon must also be seen as part of the organization and ideology of the political system itself.[16] Lacking even the basic power to vote, children are not able to exercise normal constituency powers, articulating self-interests to politicians and working toward specific goals. Young children in particular are probably not capable of organizing themselves into a political group; they must always be represented either by their parents or by established governmental or community groups organized to lobby, litigate, and exhort on their behalf. The causes of younger children have not fared well, partly because these representatives have loyalties diluted by conflicts between children's rights and their own institutional and professional goals. Older children have organized themselves politically with some success, especially on the issues of the eigh-

---

[14] For a discussion of the reasons why the family, as one of society's private units, is not properly a subject for political analysis, see Sheldon Wolin, *Politics and Vision* (Boston: Little Brown, 1960).

[15] For the argument that the exception is the rule, see Justine Wise Polier, "Problems Involving Family and Child," *Columbia Law Review*, 66 (1966), 305, 306.

[16] Dean Roscoe Pound suggested in a 1916 article, "Individual Interests in the Domestic Relations," *Michigan Law Review*, 14 (1916), 177, 186-87, that the law deprived children of their bargaining power so as to promote social values, like family unity.

teen-year-old vote, civil liberties of school students, and anti-war activities, but they too have relied heavily on the support of adults. "Successful" reforms on behalf of children—the establishment of juvenile courts, the institution of public schooling, the passage of child labor laws—were effected only after vigorous political struggles.

While these legal reforms may now seem, in the light of revisionist histories,[17] to have been catalyzed by questionable motives, they did give children certain legally enforceable rights not previously held. Moreover, these reforms signalled some change in general public attitudes about children.

Whenever reforms have been enacted, however, the rights they provide are those which the state decides are in the best interests of the public and the child. Age and ability differences have not been entirely ignored, but the use of chronological dividing lines to mark legal distinctions has continued. Nor has the child been given any choice in the exercise of his rights; they are compulsory, not susceptible to waiver. Thus all children below a certain age are forbidden to work, regardless of individual desire, aptitude, and need.[18] Similarly, all children below a certain age are required to attend school.[19] Finally, the institutions created to embody and enforce these rights are endowed with essentially unchecked discretion. Therefore, even though special juvenile proceedings, exemption from work, and compulsory attendance are all rights in the strict sense of legally enforceable claims against the state or third persons, neither their rationales nor their implementation provide models for the rights movement.

Present claims of right follow two general approaches: advocating the extension of adult rights to children and seeking legally enforceable recognition of children's special needs and interests. The first approach is exemplified by proposals for extending all the rights of adult criminal defendants to accused delinquents, proposals for empowering children to request medical care without parental consent, and proposals for providing a child with legal representation in any situation where his interests are affected. Such rights may either be extended in the precise form exercised by adults, as in recent legislation lowering the voting age, or they

[17] See footnote 12.

[18] In *Prince v. Massachusetts,* 321 US 158 (1944), the Supreme Court held that the application to Jehovah's Witnesses of a state statute providing that no boy under twelve and girl under eighteen should sell periodicals on the street was constitutional. The child involved in the case, a nine-year-old girl, had been selling religious literature with her guardian; both were members of the sect; the child testified as to her religious beliefs; and the guardian was convicted of violating the state Child Labor Law.

[19] On November 20, 1959, when the United Nations General Assembly promulgated the right of every child to a compulsory education in its *Declaration of the Rights of the Child,* a delegate reportedly asked how a person could be given a right that he was compelled to exercise.

may be tailored to special characteristics of children. Tailoring is found in court decisions holding that children have rights of freedom of expression under the First Amendment while at the same time taking children's immaturity and dependent status into account in defining the scope of those rights. Tailored standards are used to regulate exposure to obscenity,[20] authorize medical treatment without parental consent,[21] and determine circumstances under which a child's contract may be binding.[22] Even rights which appear to be extended whole cloth to children, with the exception of the right to vote, do not seem to escape modification in practice.

Modification apparently occurs not only because of the actual physical and psychological differences between children and adults, but also because of the discretion in legal proceedings involving children and because adults finally determine what seems best. These practical constraints on extending adult rights to children are illustrated by the experience of the juvenile court system in guaranteeing the right to counsel, as granted by the Supreme Court in *In re Gault*. A study of the actual implementation of *Gault* revealed:

The views of lawyers about the rights of children differ quite fundamentally from those expressed by the Supreme Court and academics. Lawyers apply different standards to juvenile clients, because they are children, not necessarily because lawyers have been constrained by the courts' welfare orientation. A lawyer typically has conscientious reservations about helping a juvenile to 'beat a case,' and, if a case is won on a technicality, he feels obliged personally to warn his client against the danger of future misconduct.[23]

Thus, even the child's own lawyer will likely go beyond the scope of his professional responsibility in determining for himself and for the child where the child's best interests lie.

The second approach to children's rights begins with the belief that even if all adult rights were granted to children and were strictly enforced, this would not

[20] See, e.g., *Ginsberg v. New York*, 390 US 629 (1968).

[21] In many states children are allowed to seek treatment for venereal disease and drug addiction without parental permission or knowledge.

[22] Although the general rule remains that a child is not liable for his contracts, it is riddled with exceptions; e.g., when the contract is for "necessaries."

[23] This quote is from the summary of two studies that Anthony Platt participated in as reported in his book, *The Child Savers*, p. 167; footnote 108 on page 166. See also, the discussion in *Handbook for New Juvenile Court Judges*, 23 (Winter 1972), pp. 14-15, as to whether or not a juvenile judge has to strictly follow the rulings of the Supreme Court. Even though disregard of Court rulings is not uncommon in adult proceedings, it is there accomplished informally and less visibly, rarely dignified by the professional journals, and confined mostly to critiques of the law, not invitations and rationales for ignoring it.

guarantee that certain critical needs unique to children would be met. This line of reasoning is reflected in the various bills of rights which have been proposed for children, each unveiling a blueprint for the child's fullest development.[24] These "need manifestos" proclaim the rights of children to adequate nutrition,[25] a healthy environment,[26] continuous loving care,[27] a sympathetic community,[28] intellectual and emotional stimulation,[29] and other prerequisites for healthy adulthood. Although a child may be entitled to such rights under theories of natural law or moral philosophy, most claims based on psychological and even physical needs are not yet considered legal rights by our system. Even though such rights are beginning to achieve some recognition, particularly in judicial decisions concerning education and psychological treatment, their scope and content raise troublesome questions.[30] Given the great difficulty of specifying psychological prerequisites and devising workable governmental responses for meeting them, a distinction should perhaps be made between claims focusing on psychological needs and those specifying physical ones, because the latter are more easily defined. Many of us might agree that a child should have the right to "grow up in a world free of war,"[31] or to live in a "reconstituted society,"[32] but who should the law hold responsible for seeing that those rights are enforced? Or, how should a "right to be wanted" be defined and enforced? Doubtless there are definitions of these socio-psychological rights,[33] but if the law attempted to incorporate them, the necessarily broad and vague enforcement guidelines could recreate the hazards of current laws, again requiring the state to make broad discretionary judgments about the quality of a child's life. Moreover, the limits of the legal process itself would tend to undermine the integrity and effectiveness of such laws. These limits are rarely appreciated.

[24] See generally, Mary Kohler, "The Rights of Children," Social Policy, 39 (March/April, 1971); Paul Adams et al., Children's Rights: Toward the Liberation of the Child (New York: Praeger, 1971); Henry H. Foster and Doris Jonas Freed, "A Bill of Rights for Children," Family Law Quarterly, 6 (1972), 343.

[25] WHERE, April 1971, publication of Advisory Centre for Education in Cambridge, England.

[26] Joint Commission on Mental Health of Children, Crisis in Child Mental Health: Challenge for the 1970's (New York: Harper & Row, 1969, 1970), pp. 3-4.

[27] Crisis in Child Mental Health.

[28] 1930 White House Conference on Child Health and Protection.

[29] Crisis in Child Mental Health, pp. 3-4.

[30] For examples of right to education and treatment cases, see: Pennsylvania Association for Retarded Children v. Pennsylvania, 343 F. Supp. 279 (E.D. Pa. 1972); Mills v. Board of Education, 348 F. Supp. 866 (D.D.C. 1972); Wyatt v. Stickney, 325 F. Supp. 781 (1971); 334 F. Supp. 1341 (1972).

[31] Adams, et al., Children's Rights, p. 41.

[32] See Joseph Goldstein, Anna Freud, Albert J. Solnit, Beyond the Best Interests of the Child (New York: The Free Press, 1973), for a thoughtful discussion of the concept of a "wanted" child and suggestions for incorporating it into the law.

[33] Crisis in Child Mental Health, pp. 3-4.

There is attributed to the law a magical power, a capacity to do what is far beyond its means. While the law may claim to establish relationships, it can, in fact, do little more than acknowledge them and give them recognition. It may be able to destroy human relationships, but it cannot compel them to develop.[34]

It is important to recognize the limited ability of the legal system to prescribe and enforce the quality of social arrangements.

Although many special claims of rights are far from legal recognition, some perhaps fundamentally unsuited for it, this does not mean they should be dismissed as "meaningless exhortations."[35] The law is not unresponsive to societal values, and decisions are frequently influenced by notions of conventional morality, occasionally reflecting acceptance of changing morality. In recent years, courts have become somewhat more willing to ask whether children should have additional rights, and if so, how might they be secured. The concept of right is constantly in ferment and Constitutional theory may eventually be expanded to include at least some quality of life claims as citizenship rights. New statutes with enforcement and review mechanisms aimed at limiting state abuses of power may also create such guarantees.

Exemplary Supreme Court Decisions

Judicial decisions concerned with questions of children's rights provide one means for examining relevant legal opinions and conclusions. Because the Supreme Court has been active in this regard and because it remains the final arbiter of the Constitution, it is valuable to review a few of its recent decisions in the field of children's rights. These opinions, sometimes holding with the children's movement, sometimes against, reveal to what extent a more favorable judicial view of children's rights is emerging. Consideration of children's rights before the Supreme Court has primarily been in the areas of education, child welfare, and juvenile court procedures. The Court has avoided "taking the easy way" with a flat holding that all rights constitutionally assured for adults may be extended to children.[36] Instead, it has carefully tried to carve out an area between parental dominion and state prerogatives, where certain adult rights can be extended to children under specific circumstances. The Court has also tried to fashion modified versions of other rights.

[34] Joseph S. Goldstein, "Finding the Least Detrimental Alternative," *Psychoanalytic Study of the Child* 628, at 637 (1972).
[35] *Juvenile Justice Standards Project,* Final Report Planning Phase, 1971-72 (New York: Institute of Judicial Administration, 1972), 72.
[36] *McKeiver v. Pennsylvania,* 403 US 528, 545 (1971).

This delicate operation of inserting new elements into the control-of-children equation began during the compulsory schooling controversy. From the first confrontations between parents and the state, education has been the subject of continuous and often bitter struggles, primarily over the proper social role of education and the proper treatment of children within the schools. In enforcing state schooling laws, the Supreme Court took care to reinforce the parental right of supervision over their children's education.[37] The education cases reaching the Supreme Court, including the desegregation cases, reflect this emphasis. The significance of early education cases in regard to children's rights, however, rests more on what the Court did *not* consider than what it did consider in its deliberations: "These cases never mention rights or interests of children involved. Since they rest entirely on a doctrine of parental right, the question whether the parent may not be loyal to the interests of his child is not discussed."[38] Neither, the author might have added, was any question about the state's loyalty to the interests of the child raised.

But one of the first specific children's rights precedents, *Brown v. Board of Education,* occurred in the area of education.[39] In *Brown,* the Court held that the constitutional rights of black school children were violated by segregated education and emphasized the critical importance of education both to children and to the general public:

Today education is perhaps the most important function of state and local government . . . it is a principal instrument in awakening the child to cultural values, in preparing him for later professional training, and in helping him to adjust professionally to his environment. In these days it is doubtful that any child may reasonably be expected to succeed in life if he is denied the opportunity of an education. Such an opportunity, where the state has undertaken to provide it, is a right which must be made available to all children.[40]

Brown's regard for rights in education and its willingness to enforce those rights with affirmative action mark it as a significant precedent.

Like the public education legislation, laws governing juveniles charged with violations of the law have assumed the benevolence of state action. For a long time these statutes and the case law interpreting them provided no substantive or procedural guarantees for the child. Before the 1960's only a few courts held that the Constitution required recognition of a child's right to procedural protections in

[37] See, e.g., *Meyer v. Nebraska,* 262 US 390 (1923); *Pierce v. Society of Sisters,* 268 US 510 (1925).
[38] Kleinfeld, Part II, 418.
[39] *Brown v. Board of Education,* 347 US 483 (1954).
[40] *Brown,* 493.
[41] *In re Gault,* 387 US 1 (1967).

any kind of case, civil or criminal. Most courts continued to follow the non-recognition rule implicitly sanctioned by the social consensus.

In 1967 the Supreme Court decided *In re Gault*,[41] the landmark case on procedural rights in juvenile court and still the most famous children's rights case. *Gault* held that children in juvenile court were constitutionally entitled to certain due process guarantees previously granted only to adults in criminal court: a) notice (to both parent and child) adequate to afford reasonable opportunity to prepare a defense, including a sufficient statement of the charge; b) right to counsel, and if the child is indigent, provision for the appointment of counsel; c) privilege against self-incrimination; and d) right to confrontation and cross-examination of witnesses. The Court restricted its holding to precisely these procedural guarantees and not others. It also limited the guarantees to those juveniles facing possible commitment to a state institution. But *Gault* declared, generally, that "neither the Fourteenth Amendment nor the Bill of Rights is for adults alone."[42] This and similar language in the opinion suggested future grounds for arguing the constitutional rights of children. In the six years since *Gault*, the Court has continued to hear children's rights cases with mixed and at times incongruous results. The Court has decided that children are "persons" under the Constitution[43]; it has removed some of the disabilities traditionally imposed upon illegitimate children[44]; it has protected the exercise of some First Amendment rights of students in the public schools[45]; and it has upheld the constitutionality of the eighteen-year-old vote.[46] On the other hand, during this same short span, the Court has denied that jury trials for alleged delinquents in juvenile court are Constitutionally required[47]; it has declined to review a lower court decision upholding the right of school systems to use corporal punishment for disciplinary purposes[48]; it has rejected the claim, *Brown* notwithstanding, that there is a fundamental, personal right to education under the Constitution[49]; and it has generally revealed an unwillingness to pursue the broad promise of *Gault*.

The Court's present reluctant mood is reflected in Justice Blackmun's plurality

[41] *Gault*, 13.

[43] *Tinker v. Des Moines School District*, 393 US 503, 515 (1969).

[44] See, *Levy v. Louisiana*, 391 US 68 (1968); *Weber v. Aetna Casualty and Surety Company*, 406 US 164 (1972).

[45] *Tinker*.

[46] *Oregon v. Mitchell*, 400 US 112 (1970).

[47] *McKeiver v. Pennsylvania*, 403 US 528 (1971).

[48] *Ware v. Estes*, 328 F. Supp., 657 (N. I. Tex. 1971), *cert. den.* in 409 U.S. 1027.

[49] *San Antonio Independent School District v. Rodriguez*, 93 S. Ct. 1278 (1973).

opinion in *McKeiver v. Pennsylvania,*[50] in which the Court refused to hold that jury trials for juveniles are constitutionally required. Justice Blackmun acknowledged the many defects of the juvenile court system, but denied that they were of "constitutional dimension."[51] He gave the Court's sanction to the juvenile court's rehabilitative goals:

The juvenile court concept held high promise. We are reluctant to say that, despite disappointments of grave dimensions, it still does not hold promise, and we are particularly reluctant to say, as do the Pennsylvania petitioners here, that the system cannot accomplish its rehabilitative goals.[52]

The present inability of the system to realize its goals was attributed by the plurality to inadequate resources, rather than to any inherent unfairness in the juvenile court system. As one commentator noted:

To say that these shortcomings resulted from lack of resources rather than inherent unfairness seemed irrelevant to those who realized that until such shortcomings were rectified, regardless of their source or cause, there could be no justification for failing to afford juveniles facing incarceration and stigma the same procedural rights accorded adults accused of crime.[53]

The plurality's answer to that criticism again indicates the Court's reluctance:

If the formalities of the criminal adjudicative process are to be superimposed upon the juvenile court system, there is little need for its separate existence. Perhaps *ultimate disillusionment* will come one day, but for the moment we are disinclined to give impetus to it.[54]

Thus the present Supreme Court appears to have "limited efforts toward the 'constitutional domestication' of juvenile procedures begun during the Warren Court years."[55] This same post-*Gault* restraint can be found in the areas of welfare law and education.

In a 1972 Supreme Court case, *Jefferson v. Hackney,* Justice Rehnquist, writing for the majority, held it consistent with both the Constitution and the Social Security Act that the state of Texas could provide a lower standard of welfare benefits

[50] *McKeiver v. Pennsylvania,* 403 US 528 (1971).
[51] *Id.,* 547-48.
[52] *Id.,* 547.
[53] Note: "Parens Patriae and Statutory Vagueness in the Juvenile Court," *Yale Law Journal* 82 (1973), 745, 753.
[54] *McKeiver,* 550-551.
[55] Note, 82 Yale L.J., 745, 746.

to recipients of AFDC than to eligible or disabled persons receiving welfare assistance under the Act.[56] The federal program for Aid to Families with Dependent Children is this country's most comprehensive child welfare legislation. Under the program, the care and protection of needy children has been entrusted to states and localities, who in turn have usually relied heavily on private voluntarism. The rights and duties of children under resulting programs have been adjudicated primarily by state courts, with patchwork results. Consequently, to evaluate the status of dependent children the laws and court decisions of fifty states must be examined. A less exhaustive but more manageable approach is to explore congressional and Supreme Court reactions to the problems of dependency, also complex but at least enabling certain generalizations. In passing AFDC legislation the Congress admitted that some children needed assistance because of their family's financial status. They have periodically qualified that admission, however, with a number of value judgments about reasons for a family's poverty. State governments have been given considerable discretion in screening potential welfare recipients and in policing their conduct. The Supreme Court has brought constitutional standards into the process. One result of the Court's decision has been to ensure that irrational state rules against parental behavior would not be allowed to interfere with the rights of dependent children to minimum financial security.

In *Jefferson v. Hackney* the Burger Court refused to "second guess" state officials charged with the difficult task of administering welfare and brushed aside the argument that children might suffer irreparable harm from insufficient welfare benefits.

Applying the traditional standard of review under that [14th] Amendment, we cannot say that Texas' decision to provide somewhat lower benefits for AFDC recipients is invidious or irrational. Since budgetary restraints do not allow the payment of the full standard of need for all welfare recipients, the state may have concluded that the aged and infirmed are the least able of the categorical grant recipients to bear the hardships of an inadequate standard of living. While different policy judgments are of course possible, it is not irrational for the state to believe that the young are more adaptable than the sick and elderly, especially because the latter have less hope of improving their situation in the years remaining to them. Whether or not one agrees with this state determination there is nothing in the Constitution which forbids it.[57]

Setting aside issues of constitutional and statutory interpretation, Justice Rehn-

---

[56] *Jefferson v. Hackney,* 406 US 535 (1971).
[57] *Id.,* 549.

quist's view that the state's decision to provide needy and eligible children an inadequate standard of living was "not irrational" reveals a grim adherence to the convention that the authorities know what they are doing and will not harm the children whose needs they are charged with meeting. In this opinion there is also a heavy dose of the old-time belief that for the young, however poor, survival is only a bootstrap away. Justice Marshall, in a vigorous dissent, asserted that the Texas policy was inconsistent with a congressional finding in the legislative history of the AFDC Act: "Many of these children will be seriously handicapped as adults because as children they are not receiving proper and sufficient food, clothing, medical attention, and the other bare necessities of life."[58]

The logic of *Jefferson v. Hackney* was extended in the recent education case, *San Antonio Independent School District v. Rodriguez.*[59] That case arose out of the claim that the Texas method of financing public education through the property tax, which resulted in widely varying per pupil expenditures, violated the constitutional rights of students in San Antonio's poorest, lowest tax base district to equal protection of the laws and to education itself. The Supreme Court denied the claim, reversing a three-judge Texas district court. Writing for the majority, Justice Powell held first that the students of the school district in question were not a suspect class under the Equal Protection Clause, and thus were not entitled to a strict judicial review of the Texas financing scheme, and second that the Constitution provides no explicit right to education, nor can education be construed as an implicit, fundamental right under the Constitution, "essential to the effective exercise of First Amendment freedoms and to the intelligent utilization of the right to vote."[60] Instead, the majority held that the importance of education for the effective exercise of rights is arguably less than the significance of adequate food, clothing, and housing, none of which are constitutionally protected rights.[61] Thus the Court declined to invalidate the Texas scheme, leaving the matter of educational finance to the discretion of the state:

The very complexity of the problems of financing and managing a statewide public school system suggest that 'there will be more than one constitutionally permissible method of solving them,' and that, within the limits of rationality, 'the legislature's efforts to tackle the problems' should be entitled to respect.[62]

[58] *Id.,* 581.
[59] *San Antonio Independent School District v. Rodriguez,* 93 S.Ct. 1278 (1973).
[60] *Id.,* 1298.
[61] *Id.,* 1299.

Justices White, Brennan, Marshall, and Douglas dissented, asserting that invalidation of the Texas scheme was compelled. They each gave somewhat different reasons for disagreeing with the majority opinion, but four reasons predominated. First, some took direct issue with the argument that education is not a fundamental, Constitutionally recognized interest, "inextricably linked to the right to participate in the electoral process and the rights of free speech and free association guaranteed by the First Amendment." Instead, it was argued that "any classification affecting education must be subjected to strict judicial scrutiny,"[63] i.e., the state must prove that the financing system does *not* discriminate against poorer students and their parents. Second, the school children in poorer districts and their parents are indeed a suspect class under the Fourteenth Amendment because they are allocated school funds under the Texas law on the basis of wealth, and therefore the strict scrutiny standard applies.[64] Third, regardless of whether a fundamental right to education exists, there are rights in education, once the state has undertaken to provide it, which, under *Brown*, "must be made available to all on equal terms."[65] Finally, even if plaintiffs are not a suspect class, education not a fundamental right, and the *Brown* test not controlling on the issue of educational finance, the Texas law must meet the rationality test of the Fourteenth Amendment. While Texas's objective in preserving local control over the public schools is a constitutionally permissible one, the financing scheme is not rationally related to it because it accords " 'different treatment . . . to persons placed by a statute into different classes on the basis of criteria wholly unrelated to the objective of that statute.' "[66]

In the *Rodriguez* case, the Court was unwilling to restrict the scope of the state's discretion by defining the educational needs and interests of children as rights. Even when the Court is prepared to limit state control, however, it often avoids formalizing the status of such needs and interests. Decisions are inclined to follow the traditional formula of balancing the state's interests with those of the parents, simply assuming that these reflect what is best for the child. This method was employed by the Court in *Wisconsin v. Yoder*,[67] even though in that case the children whose interests were at stake had the capacity to evaluate their interests for themselves. It was by no means evident that the interests of the children were identical

[63] *Id.*, 1301-2.
[63] *Id.*, 1312 (J. Brennan's dissent).
[64] *Id.*, 1336 (J. Marshall's dissent).
[65] *Id.*, 1339 (J. Marshall's dissent).
[66] *Id.*, 1314 (J. White's dissent).
[67] *Wisconsin v. Yoder*, 406 US 205 (1972).

17

to those of their parents. *Wisconsin v. Yoder* involved a challenge by several Old Order Amish parents to Wisconsin's statute which imposed an affirmative duty on parents to require their children to attend high school, and made violation of this duty a crime. Three parents, Mr. Yoder, Mr. Miller, and Mr. Yutzy, claimed that the compulsory school law violated their religious freedom and that of their children. Only one of the children, however, actually testified in court that she shared her parents' religious views and did not wish to continue to attend school. The other two children did not testify.

Chief Justice Burger, writing for the majority, upheld the right of the Amish parents to exemption from the statute. The opinion held that this exemption was necessary to promote free exercise of religion. The Chief Justice took pains to distinguish the genuine religious claims of the Amish from those of others who merely had unconventional life styles and might also be tempted to seek such a First Amendment exemption from compulsory schooling laws.[68] Having made this distinction, the majority opinion then reaffirmed the Amish parents' rights to control the upbringing of their children—to the point of depriving them of an advanced, worldly education.

Justice Douglas took a different and ground-breaking view of the case. He joined the Court's opinion only regarding the schooling of the child who had publicly subscribed to her parents' religious objections.[69] As to the children of the other two defendants, Justice Douglas dissented from the majority. He held that the majority opinion was inadequate because these defendants had raised their children's religious beliefs in defense but had not brought their children to testify. Reviewing various cases holding that "children themselves have constitutionally protectible interests,"[70] Douglas asserted first that the critical interests at stake were those of the children, not those of their parents, and second that the dispute could not be properly resolved until the children had represented their own interests in court.

I agree with the Court that the religious scruples of the Amish are opposed to the education of their children beyond the grade schools, yet I disagree with the Court's conclusion that the matter is within the dispensation of parents alone. The Court assumes that the only interests at stake in the case are those of the Amish parents on the one hand, and those of the State on the other. The difficulty with this approach is that, despite the Court's claim, the parents are seeking to vindicate not only their own free exercise claims, but also those of their high-school-age children. . . .

[68] *Id.,* 215-219.
[69] *Id.,* 243.
[70] *Id.,* 243.
[71] *Id.,* 241-42, 44-46.

On this important and vital matter of education, I think the children should be entitled to be heard. While the parents, absent dissent, normally speak for the entire family, the education of the child is a matter on which the child will often have decided views. He may want to be a pianist or an astronaut or an oceanographer. To do so, he will have to break from the Amish tradition.

It is the future of the student, not the future of the parents, that is imperilled in today's decision. . . . It is the student's judgment, not his parent's, that is essential if we are to give full meaning to what we have said about the Bill of Rights and of the right of students to be masters of their own destiny. If he is harnessed to the Amish way of life by those in authority over him and if his education is truncated, his entire life may be stunted and deformed. The child, therefore, should be given an opportunity to be heard before the State gives the exemption which we honor today.[71]

Douglas based his opinion not only on available legal precedents, but on psychological and sociological findings that children of the relevant ages possess the moral and intellectual judgment necessary for making responsible decisions on matters of religion and education. To rebut the presumption that children lack sufficient maturity to make such decisions, Douglas relied on the works of Piaget, Kohlberg, Kay, Gesell, and Ilg. He also argued that "the maturity of Amish youth, who identify with and assume adult roles from early childhood . . . is certainly not less than that of children in the general population."[72]

The majority opinion does not deal with the merits of Douglas' views; it only notes that the children are not parties to the litigation.[73] Only two justices, Brennan and Stewart, acknowledged in their concurring opinions that the issues raised by Douglas "are interesting and important."[74] They agreed with the majority, however, that these issues should not be before the Court because "there is no suggestion whatever in the record that the religious beliefs of the children here concerned differ in any way from those of their parents."[75] This statement reiterates the presumption of identity of interests between parent and child, and here the consequences of acting in accord with the family's religion may be quite different for children than for their parents.

Establishing the Rights of Children

These opinions illustrate two persistent, general problems of legal theory which children's rights advocates seek to overcome. First, legal policy is ambivalent about

[71] *Id.*, 245-246, footnote 3.
[73] *Id.*, 230-31.
[74] *Id.*, 237 (Justices Brennan and Stewart concurring).
[75] *Id.*, 237.

the limitation of parental control and the assertion of state control over children. There is an absence of fair, workable, and realistic standards for limiting parental discretion and guiding state intervention. Second, the state generally fails to evaluate a child's independent interests, giving a competent child the chance to articulate his interests for himself.

Ascribing rights to children will not immediately solve these problems, or undermine the consensus which perpetuates them. It will, however, force from the judiciary and the legislature institutional support for the child's point of view. As was once said, in another context: "rights to have any meaning must adhere to particular institutions: the rights of Englishmen are indeed, necessarily more secure than the 'Rights of Man.' "[76] Children's rights cannot be secured until some particular institution has recognized them and assumed responsibility for enforcing them. In the past, adult institutions have not performed this function, partly, as we have seen, because it was thought children had few rights to secure. Unfortunately, the institutions designed specifically for children also have failed to accomplish this aim, largely because they were established to safeguard interests, not to enforce rights, on the assumption that the former could be done without the latter.

Securing children's rights through the legislatures and the courts will include generating new lines of legal theory, grounded in past-precedent but building on it to more reasonable laws and legal interpretations for the future. Certain interesting legal theories have been introduced already, which are being utilized by children's rights advocates in pressing further claims, and which, if accepted, could resolve the theoretical problems outlined above. While the resolution of theoretical problems may not eliminate the main obstacles to the enforcement of children's legal rights or to the creation of services to meet their needs, it will at least strip away the legalistic camouflage surrounding the continuing problems of unchecked discretion, inadequate resources, and widespread public indifference.

As stated earlier, claims of rights for children fall into two broad categories: claims that the rights which adults enjoy be granted to children, and claims that the special needs and interests of children be recognized as rights. Legislation granting rights in either category probably is preferable to judicial opinions decreeing them, but both governmental branches should be pressed to reexamine and revise children's status under the law. Legal positions will contribute to a new social attitude toward children's rights.

Turning to the first strategy for obtaining new rights, the following three posi-

[76] Bernard Crick, *In Defense of Politics* (London: Penguin Books, 1962), p. 48.

tions focus attention on the independent status of children: a) the legal status of infancy, or minority, should be abolished and the presumption of incompetency reversed; b) all procedural rights guaranteed to adults under the Constitution should be granted to children whenever the state or a third party moves against them, judicially or administratively; and c) the presumption of identity of interests between parents and their children should be rejected whenever the child has interests demonstrably independent of those of his parents (as determined by the *consequences* to both of the action in question), and a competent child should be permitted to assert his or her own interests.

Devising acceptable arguments to support recognition of special rights based on physical and psychological needs is more difficult. Rather than specifying particular needs that the legal system could meet, the following suggestions concern a methodology for constitutionalizing such rights and a procedural device for overseeing the needs of children for whom the state assumes primary responsibility. The strictures of the new equal protection theory should apply to children, i. e., classifications of children *qua* children, or of certain classes of children, should be considered suspect, and needs which from a developmental standpoint are fundamental should be protected as fundamental interests under the Constitution. Also, in areas where decision makers will necessarily continue to exercise discretion they should no longer just be guided by the best interests of the child standard, but should be subjected to a review process which focuses not only on the child but also on the state's responsibility as a substitute parent.

These arguments will now be discussed more fully.

Abolition of minority status

Age may be a valid criterion for determining the distribution of legal benefits and burdens, but before it is used its application should be subjected to a test of rationality. Assessing the rationality of age classifications could be expedited by legislative abolition of the general status of minority and adoption of an area-by-area approach (as has already been done to a degree, for example, in the motor vehicle statutes). It could also be accomplished by judicial declaration that the present classification scheme is over-inclusive, after which the state would bear the burden of justifying its restrictions on infants. As Foster and Freed point out, ". . . the arguments for and against perpetuation of minority status have a familiar ring. In good measure they are the same arguments that were advanced over the issues of slavery and the emancipation of married women."[77] The abolition of slavery and the emancipation

---

[77] Foster and Freed, p. 343.

of married women did not automatically invest previously "inferior" persons with full adult citizenship rights, but the state at least had to begin to rationalize its treatment of those groups. The abolition of minority, more justifiably, need not mean that children become full-fledged miniature adults before the law. Their substantive and procedural rights could still be limited or modified on the basis of supportable findings about needs and capacities at various ages.

If the law were to abolish the status of minority and to reverse its underlying presumption of children's incompetency, the result would be an implicit presumption that children, like other persons, are capable of exercising rights and assuming responsibilities until it is proven otherwise. Empirical differences among children would then serve as the grounds for making exceptions to this presumption and for justifying rational state restrictions. For example, in his dissent in *Wisconsin v. Yoder*,[78] Justice Douglas presumed that the children involved in the case were intelligent and mature enough to express opinion when their interests were affected. In essence, Douglas reversed the presumption of incompetency. He then looked for evidence to contradict the presumption of competency and when he found none, he argued that the children should be given full rights as parties to a lawsuit. If the children involved had been younger, Douglas might have concluded that the presumption of competency should have been suspended. However, young children are known to possess strong opinions on some issues, and many such opinions may have a rational basis. In custody suits, for example, many states now require that the opinions of children over twelve be followed and that the opinions of younger children be accepted as evidence in a case. Feelings of the young should at least be recorded and weighed. This argument is reinforced by the fact that very young children have at times been found competent to give evidence in trials where adult interests are at stake.

The difference between a rebuttable presumption of incompetency and a presumption of competency is that the former places the burden of proof on children and their allies, while the latter shifts it to the opponents of changing children's status. Many legislatures now regard the presumption of incompetency as rebuttable and are legislatively removing some of children's legal disabilities. When Congress and the states extended the right to vote to eighteen-year-olds through the Voting Rights Act of 1970 and the Twenty-Sixth Amendment to the Constitution, they went through the process of reversing the presumption of incompetency regarding enfranchisement. Through hearings and other fact finding procedures, a

[78] See pp. 504-505 in text; *Wisconsin v. Yoder*, 406 US 205, 240-246.

majority of Congressmen and state legislators were persuaded by available evidence that the presumption should be rebutted, and voting rights granted in the same form enjoyed by adults.

Granting all procedural rights

The argument for this position is simple. A child is now considered a person under the Constitution. When the State moves against persons and threatens to take away their liberties or otherwise affect their interests adversely, they are entitled to the protective procedures of the Bill of Rights, as applied to the states through the Fourteenth Amendment. As the late Mr. Justice Black said, concurring in *In re Gault:*

> When a person, infant or adult, can be seized by the State, charged, and convicted for violating a state criminal law, and then ordered by the State to be confined for six years, I think the Constitution requires that he be tried in accordance with the guarantees of all the provisions of the Bill of Rights made applicable to the States by the Fourteenth Amendment. . . . Appellants are entitled to these rights not because 'fairness, impartiality, and orderliness—in short, the essentials of due process'—require them and not because they are 'the procedural rules which have been fashioned from the generality of due process,' but because they are specifically and unequivocally granted by provisions of the Fifth and Sixth Amendments which the Fourteenth Amendment makes applicable to the States.
>
> Undoubtedly this (entitlement to Constitutional guarantees) would be true of an adult defendant, and it would be a plain denial of equal protection of the laws—an invidious discrimination—to hold that others subject to heavier punishments could, *because they are children,* be denied these same constitutional safeguards.[79]

The only effective means for securing these Bill of Rights guarantees in our current legal system is by the provision of legal counsel. Although the introduction of the adversarial system into juvenile court proceedings is deplored by many, lawyers representing children should ensure three critical prerequisites for fairness. First, they can articulate and argue the child's position, even though filtered through their own adult and professional perspectives. Second, they can require that the law be strictly followed. And third, they can make new law in the area by appealing cases and lobbying for statutory changes. Independent counsel for children should not be restricted to children accused of delinquency, but should be required in any case where a child's interests are being adjudicated. The courts must become more

---

[79] *In re Gault,* 387 US 1, 61 (1967). Cf., also, J. Douglas's dissent joined by J. Black and J. Marshall in *McKeiver v. Pennsylvania* arguing the same point.

sensitive to such cases, recognizing that children in neglect or custody proceedings may have interests independent of their parents or the state.

Substitution of an evaluation of consequences for the implied identity of interests between parents and children

This point was treated clearly and at length by Justice Douglas in his opinion in *Wisconsin v. Yoder*.[80] Only one aspect of the arguments requires further stress. Justice Douglas chided the majority for subsuming the rights of school children under their parents' rights, and for not giving the children the opportunity to be heard. Justice Douglas might have added that the majority presumed an identity of religious opinions was the same as an identity of interests. In general, it is not clear whether the implied identity of interests operates as a legal presumption or only a permissible assumption in the absence of contrary evidence. Regardless, the values it represents should be treated only as an assumption, and in cases of potential conflict between parent and child the consequences to the child of parental action or inaction should be considered. Where the consequences appear irreversible, the assumption should be discarded in favor of an extrafamilial decision that takes into account the opinions of all interested parties. If the consequences seem reversible or insubstantial, the assumption that the parent knows best should probably continue to govern.

Application of the new equal protection theory

The Equal Protection Clause of the Fourteenth Amendment guarantees that all people similarly situated will be treated alike by the state. The Supreme Court and lower federal courts use two standards of judicial review for assessing the constitutionality of state action under this clause. Under traditional equal protection analysis, a state has broad discretion to classify persons, so long as the classification bears a reasonable relationship to a permissible state objective. The measure of reasonableness is "the degree of its success in treating similarly those similarly situated."[81] A classification, under this standard, is unreasonable if it is over- or under-inclusive or in some other way not rationally related to the achievement of a legitimate state objective. Under the so-called new equal protection analysis, the state bears the burden of justifying its classification on grounds of a "compelling state interest" whenever that classification is suspect because of its effects on the group of persons in the class or whenever it seems to be in conflict with a funda-

[80] See, pp. 504-505 in text.
[81] Tussman and Ten Broek, *The Equal Protection of the Laws, Selected Essays 1938-62*, 789 (1963).

24

mental personal interest. The Supreme Court has been restrained in its use of this strict form of judicial review.

The argument for defining various developmental needs of children as fundamental interests is well-stated, with respect to education and AFDC benefits, in the opinions of Justices Marshall and Brennan, quoted above.[82] Under their test of fundamentality, a child's need or interest only has to be shown to relate to "the effectuation of those rights which are in fact constitutionally guaranteed."[83] Thus, ". . . as the nexus between the specific constitutional guarantee and the non-constitutional interest draws closer, the non-constitutional interest becomes more fundamental and the degree of judicial scrutiny applied when the interest is infringed on a discriminatory basis must be adjusted accordingly."[84] The argument that certain types of children form suspect classifications is also made in the dissenting opinion of Justice Marshall in the *Rodriguez* case, with respect to poor children living in low tax base school districts.[85] The courts already recognize as suspect those classifications based on race,[86] national origin,[87] alienage,[88] indigency,[89] and illegitimacy.[90] Thus, application of the doctrine to poor school children is arguably within its traditional scope. The *Rodriguez* majority disagreed with this application, however, apparently on the theory that economic deprivation is suspect only when actual or functional indigency obtains and not when there is "comparative poverty vis-a-vis comparative affluence."[91] Some courts have found classes of retarded or handicapped children suspect, which supports strict judicial scrutiny of the state's treatment of them.[92]

There is less support for the contention that children *qua* children should be treated as a suspect class, but an argument may be constructed using the original rationale for suspect classifications. The suspect character of classifications based on racial or ethnic characteristics or wealth differentiations originated in the recog-

---

[82] See, pp. 502-503 in text.

[83] *Rodriguez*, 41 LW 4407, 4426.

[84] *Id.*, 4426.

[85] *Id.*, 4441.

[86] See, e.g., *Brown v. Board of Education*, 347 US 483 (1954); *McLaughlin v. Florida*, 379 US 184 (1964).

[87] See, e.g., *Oyama v. California*, 332 US 633 (1948).

[88] See, e.g., *Graham v. Richardson*, 403 US 365 (1971).

[89] See, e.g., *Griffin v. Illinois*, 351 US 12 (1956).

[90] *Weber v. Aetna Casualty & Surety Company*, 406 US 164 (1972).

[91] *Rodriguez*, 93 S. Ct. 1278, footnote 6, 1311 (Stewart, J. concurring); see the majority opinion discussion, 1290-94.

[92] See, e.g., *Colorado Association for Retarded Children v. Colorado*, C.A. No. C-4620 (N. Colo., filed Dec. 22, 1972).

nition that certain groups of persons comprise "discrete and insular"[93] minorities who are relatively powerless to protect their interests in the political process. The use of age as a classifying characteristic has rarely been questioned.

In his dissent to the Supreme Court case upholding the constitutionality of the eighteen-year-old vote in federal elections, Justice Stewart flatly asserts that: "The establishment of an age qualification is not state action aimed at any discrete and insular minority."[94] But age categories should be open to scrutiny for some of the same reasons well established suspect classifications are. The assumption that age qualifications are generally rational is not borne out by much of the evidence about the abilities of children at various ages and developmental stages before twenty-one. Thus, a group discriminated against on the basis of age could constitute a discrete and insular minority if their access to the political system were limited solely because they were young. They might possess the requisite rationality to participate, but be forbidden to do so. If this were the case, then they would be a suspect minority and state action affecting their interests should be required to demonstrate a compelling governmental interest in maintaining legal disabilities. If, however, some or all of the members of the age-defined minority were not rational or mature enough to participate in the political process, then state action affecting them should also be subjected to strict judicial scrutiny, because of their powerlessness. On the basis of either set of conclusions about children's abilities, the state should no longer be allowed to assume the rationality of regulations based on age, and should at least be required to justify its action on the basis of modern legislative or administrative findings. Under the new equal protection doctrine, it would additionally have to demonstrate a compelling state interest in its legislative objective.

Moving away from the "best interests" standard

The argument against the continued reliance on the "best interests" standard has particular reference to instances of state intervention when a child is "neglected," "dependent," "abused," "in need of supervision," or "wayward." The statutory descriptions fitting these labels are imprecise, often deliberately so, in order that concerned state agents will not be hampered in their efforts to free a child from an unhealthy or dangerous family environment. Some children, of course, do suffer incalculable harm while in the custody of their parents, and the community should protect these children from the harm which would result were

[93] The quote is from *United States v. Carolene Products Co.*, 304 US 144, 152, n. 4 (1938). See generally the discussions in *Serrano v. Priest*, 5 Cal. 3d 584, 487 P 2d. 1241, 1265 (1971); Note, "Developments in the Law-Equal Protection," *Harvard Law Review* 82 (1969) 1065, 1124-26; Merle McClung, "School Classification: Some Legal Approaches to Labels," *Inequality in Education*, 14 (July 1973), pp. 17-37.
[94] *Oregon v. Mitchell*, 400 US 112 (1970).

parental discretion left unchecked. But the unchecked discretion of the state has vices of its own. The best interests standard, initially followed in most state interventions and explicitly used as the standard for adjudicating children's interests in proceedings evaluating parental care, is not properly a standard. Instead, it is a rationalization by decision-makers justifying their judgments about a child's future, like an empty vessel into which adult perceptions and prejudices are poured. It does not offer guidelines for how adult powers should be exercised. Seductively, it implies that there is a best alternative for children deprived of their family. This implication prevents both the decision-maker and those to whom he is accountable from carefully weighing the possible negative impact of any decision.

Recognizing the weaknesses of the best interests standard, Professor Joseph Goldstein has suggested another guideline for decision-makers in custody cases: "that which is least detrimental among available alternatives for the child."[95] Although this guideline may appear only a semantic change, Goldstein argues that:

Introducing the idea of 'available alternatives' should force into focus from the child's vantage point consideration of the advantages and disadvantages of the actual real options to be measured in terms of that which is least likely to preclude the chances of the child becoming 'wanted.' The proposed standard is less awesome, more realistic, and thus more amenable to relevant data gathering than 'best interest.' No magic is to be attributed to the new formulation, but there is in any new set of guiding words an opportunity at least for courts and agencies to re-examine their tasks and thus possibly to force into view factors of low visibility which seem frequently to have resulted in decisions actually in conflict with 'the best interests of the child.'[96]

Goldstein's guideline may result in a new focus on the probable harm of state intervention into a parent-child relationship, but it still falls short because it does not specify the standards which should govern such intervention. The principles which compete whenever there are efforts to draft workable standards are not amenable to any comfortable resolution.

Sentiment against state intervention stems from the state's poor record in caring for children removed from their families. Restricting state intervention to instances where there is evidence of physical abuse would eliminate from judicial jurisdiction cases of emotional or psychological neglect. Ironically, reaction against state intervention in cases of non-physical abuse is consistent with consensus romanticism about the family, accepting as inevitable that families can deny children rights. Even though state interference with family privacy should be minimized because of the state's unwillingness, or inability, to care for children as well as most families

[95] Goldstein, "Finding the Least Detrimental Alternative," p. 633.
[96] Goldstein, "Finding the Least Detrimental Alternative," p. 637.

27

do, the state, representing the community of adults, has the responsibility to intervene in cases of severe emotional deprivation or psychological damage if it is likely that a child's development will be substantially harmed by his continued presence in the family. The state not only has the responsibility to intervene, but to nurture the child after intervention. The absence of a commitment to post-intervention care does not necessarily negate the reasons for the original intervention. Some children, even in these days of inadequate services, do benefit from a temporary or permanent removal from their families.

The principal challenge lies in determining which children could benefit from removal. Standards that limit the amount of discretion vested in decision-makers must be drafted. This will involve specifying acceptable reasons for intervention and providing workable review mechanisms for both the initial decision and the child's placement. Intervention should be allowed only after the state has attempted to provide services for the child and his parents aimed at ameliorating the conditions of neglect. Only medically justifiable reasons for intervention should be acceptable. Such reasons should include inadequate psychological care, as in cases of children presenting symptoms of maternal deprivation or severe emotional disturbance. Parental behavior that does not result in medically diagnosable harm to a child should not be allowed to trigger intervention, however offensive that behavior may be to the community.

A common complaint about the exercise of discretion in neglect cases is that alien values, usually middle-class, are used to judge a family's child-rearing practices. One way to answer that complaint is to entrust the discretion necessary for evaluating a child's needs to persons representing the milieu in which a family lives. Boards composed of citizens representing identifiable constituencies—racial, religious, ethnic, geographical—could make the initial decision regarding intervention or review judicial decisions. Additionally, they should be responsible for periodically reviewing placements and making recommendations about terminating parental rights. The board membership should include parent and professional representatives, perhaps children as well. Decisions to intervene and to terminate parental rights should require a three-fourths vote to overcome the presumption against intervention. Membership might be elected and should rotate often to avoid institutional calcification. Providing a check on judicial and bureaucratic discretion, this form of community involvement also might broaden the constituency of adults actively concerned about services for children. Without an increase in community involvement, the best drafted laws and most eloquent judicial opinions will merely recycle past disappointments.

A Philosophical Justification
For Children's Rights

VICTOR L. WORSFOLD

Harvard University

The author discusses the status of children's rights according to various philosophical conceptions of social justice. He describes three traditional paternalist views of children and concludes that, on the whole, they are discouraging in their implications for children. After analyzing some of the difficulties of previous philosophical attempts to create systems of justice ensuring children's rights, Worsfold sets forth three criteria which any adequate justification for children's rights must fulfill. He argues that these criteria are best met within the theory of justice proposed by John Rawls which, while still paternalistic, presents a more adequate framework for securing children's rights to fair treatment.

Historically, rights in society have been ascribed only to adults. Children have been treated paternally; their conduct has been controlled by parents or others in authority. Such control has been justified, in the paternalist view, by the need to protect children from themselves and others. It is argued that children cannot be responsible for their own welfare because by their nature they lack an adequate conception of their own present and future interests.[1] They are said to want instant gratification and to be incapable of fully rational decisions.

Well-intentioned though this view may be, its implicit claim that adults *do* have

I wish to thank Robert W. O'Connor for his kind advice and encouragement in the course of my writing this paper.

[1] Gerald Dworkin, "Paternalism," in *Morality and the Law*, ed. R. A. Wasserstrom (Belmont, Cal.: Wadsworth, 1971), p. 119.

Harvard Educational Review   Vol. 44   No. 1   February 1974, 142–157

an adequate conception of children's interests, and that they are always willing to act upon this conception, is open to serious question. In fact, parents often do not know what is best for their children, and children often can make sensible decisions for themselves about their own lives. In addition, the parents, however wise, may have interests and preferences which do not coincide with those of the child.

It will be the task of this article to challenge the paternalist view in its simplest and most common variants, demonstrating that these do not guarantee acceptable treatment of children. I will maintain that although some of the tenets of the paternalist view are unavoidable, they should not commit us to a political or ethical philosophy in which children have no rights of their own. I will also argue that there is one philosophical framework, John Rawls's theory of justice, which, while still paternalist, does provide a justification for according children rights to fair treatment. To assert rights to fair treatment, as Rawls does, is to assert an obligation on the part of adults to acknowledge the just claims of children. A claim which is just in Rawls's scheme is one which is consistent with the procedural principles of justice on which society should be founded, principles which should extend to children as well as adults. In Rawls's theory, the exercise of children's rights may not always be left to the children themselves, but children are presumed to be able to exercise their own rights unless all of society agrees that someone else should make decisions for them.

This article does not talk about which rights as a practical matter should be exercised by children themselves. It also does not discuss the ages at which the exercise of various rights should be permitted, or the realm of duties and obligations which should fall to children of various ages. What the article sets out to do is more basic: to challenge well-established philosophical preconceptions about a system of fair treatment for children, and to outline the basis for a new philosophical structure under which children can be regarded as full participants in society.

The Paternalism of Hobbes, Locke, and Mill

Thomas Hobbes, writing in the seventeenth century, offered one version of the paternalist view. Hobbes argued that children are cared for solely because they are capable of serving their fathers, and that the relationship between father and child must be founded on fear.[2] Children are assigned a position of complete de-

---

[2] This passage on Hobbes owes much to David P. Gauthier, *The Logic of Leviathan* (Oxford: Clarendon Press, 1965), p. 118.

pendence. Hobbes thought that "like the imbecile, the crazed and the beasts, over ... children ... there is no law."[3] Children have no natural rights and no rights by social contract because they lack the ability to make covenants with the other members of society and to understand the consequences of such contracts. Instead, children must acknowledge their fathers as sovereigns. Fathers have the power of life and death over children and "every man is supposed to promise obedience to him in whose power it is to save or destroy him."[4]

Hobbes's argument has an unfortunate flaw in that on the one hand it requires children to promise obedience, and on the other it assumes they are incapable of making such a promise and upholding its consequences. But the essence of the argument is clear. The relationship between father and child is seen as one of mutual benefit, in which in return for protection and livelihood the child must serve the father. Hobbes equates rights with powers. It follows that children cannot be granted rights, for the logic of the primary relationship between father and child does not permit it. Hobbes said, "There would be no reason why any man should desire to have children or to take care to nourish them if afterwards to have no other benefit from them than from other men."[5]

Writing later in the same century, John Locke took a somewhat different position. He asserted that children were to be under the jurisdiction of their parents "till they can be able to shift for themselves."[6] Until that time, the child lacks understanding, and therefore cannot exert his or her will. Locke compared this subjugation to wearing swaddling clothes, implying that children can cast off their dependency when they become adults and are rational enough to understand the principles by which they are governed. In Locke's view, there is an obligation for children to honor their parents. This obligation "ties up the child from anything that may ever injure or affront ... the happiness or life of those from whom he has received his."[7] But in direct contradiction to Hobbes, Locke argues that this obligation is "far from giving parents a power of command over their children, or an authority to make laws and dispose as they please of their lives and liberties."[8] Introducing the notion of natural rights, he attributed rights to individuals as though these rights were intrinsic properties, which no other claim could preempt. Chil-

---

[3] Thomas Hobbes, *Leviathan* (Molesworth ed., Vol. 3; London: J. Bohn, 1839-45), p. 257.

[4] Hobbes, p. 188.

[5] Hobbes, p. 329.

[6] John Locke, *The Second Treatise of Government* (New York: Bobbs Merrill, 1952), Sect. 60, p. 34.

[7] Locke, Sect. 66, p. 37.

[8] Locke, Sect. 66, p. 37.

dren, like adults, have natural rights which need to be protected. The development of the child's freedom is paramount, because that is God's will.

Locke did not address the objection that there might be conflicts between the natural rights of parents and children. Instead he espoused the doctrine that the child's good is the same as the parents'. Parental benevolence is sufficient to ensure the fulfillment of children's rights.

In both Hobbes's and Locke's views there is a clear demand that parents control the lives of children according to preconceived notions of the children's future welfare. In a Hobbesian society, this notion is that children are instruments, and must serve their parents in order to survive. In Locke's view, there is an emphasis on the emergent freedoms and responsibilities of the child. Locke, more than Hobbes, wants to constrain parental dominance of the child. But we must not sentimentalize Locke's thought, for well-meaning benevolence can be used to manage the affairs of children with the same effect as explicit force. Both involve the continued dependency of children on their parents. Each prevents children from making claims of their own and thereby hinders society from seeing them as worthy of respect as individuals.

In the nineteenth century, John Stuart Mill espoused another kind of paternalism. The libertarian persuasion usually associated with Mill does not extend to his thinking about children. In his discussion of the limits of society's authority over the individual, Mill declared that "the existing generation is master both of the training and the entire circumstances of the generation to come."[9] The power of society over children appears absolute. There is no sign of Mill's principle of individual liberty, which states that "[an individual] cannot rightfully be compelled to do or forbear because it will be better for him to do so, because it will make him happier, because in the opinions of others to do so would be wise or even right."[10] Mill is explicit that this doctrine of the ultimate value of personal choice does not extend to children: "We are not speaking of children, or of young persons below the age which the law may fix as that of manhood or womanhood."[11]

Mill's justification for this position is based in part on the need to protect children against the possibility of injury from themselves and others. He felt that freedom to make claims had no place until the child was capable of self-improvement as the result of rational discussion.[12] Mill also argued the case against children's

[9] John Stuart Mill, *On Liberty* (New York: Washington Square Press, 1963), p. 207.
[10] Mill, p. 135.
[11] Mill, p. 136.
[12] Mill, p. 136.

right to free choice from a strictly utilitarian standpoint. The need to maximize overall goodness in society dictates that children, unlike adults, should not be permitted the right to interpret their own good, for fear they will not act in accordance with the public good. He realized that the existing generation cannot make the next "perfectly wise and good," but he insisted that the existing generation is "well able to make the rising generation as a whole as good and a little better than itself."[13] In another passage, Mill extended this view, saying that "the uncultivated cannot be competent judges of cultivation. Those who most need to be made wiser and better usually desire it least, and if they desired it, would be incapable of finding the way to it by their own lights."[14] Paternalism, then, is acceptable in the case of children because they are incapable of deciding what is in their own and society's best interest.

Taken together, these three philosophers provide a coherent if somewhat negative attitude toward children. As we progress from Hobbes's thought through Locke's to Mill's, the strict paternalism of Hobbes is replaced by an emphasis on benevolence in the treatment of children. Despite this, all three philosophers regard the child as someone to be molded according to adult preconceptions. None of these philosophers would have considered seriously the perspective of children themselves in determining their own best interests. None accorded children rights of their own.

Inadequacies of Certain Traditional Justifications for Children's Rights

It is commonly thought that philosophers must justify the rights of children by demonstrating that children are part of a class of beings entitled to rights. The search for a philosophical justification of children's rights might begin, for instance, with the assertion that the right to fair treatment is based on some element of *human nature* which is common to both adults and children. By this line of reasoning, children's rights may be justified religiously, morally, or simply on grounds of biological fact. Once a common element is accepted as the philosophical basis of rights, then the rights of children become self-evident.

This approach has the appeal of resolving in a stroke what many would find problematic: that in their fundamental rights children and adults are the same.

[13] Mill, p. 207.
[14] Quoted by Dworkin, p. 116.

But it also raises problems. Even if we ignore the likely criticism that this position begs important questions, we must face the additional issues of precise definition of the shared attribute, on the one hand, and class inclusion on the other. Any common element of human nature we select must be operationally clear and must not err either by including too many beings in the category of those deserving rights, or by excluding some important classes of beings.

It has sometimes been argued that rationality is the common element among all humans. We are all human in that we are capable as rational animals of understanding the reasons for our choice of personal ends. But this criterion can readily be challenged. One philosopher, Henry David Aiken, has doubts, for instance, about including in the category of rational beings "babies, fetuses, [and] people who are becoming senile."[15] Others maintain that those who lack exposure to education or so-called civilization should be added to Aiken's list. Various additional categories of humans, such as the mentally ill, also might have to be excluded. Surely all of these groups are worthy of certain rights.

As a prior question, of course, it is also extremely difficult to ascertain exactly what is meant by rationality, and whether we can operationalize it precisely enough to determine whether an individual possesses the capacity or does not. This, it would seem, is a major problem with the criterion as it relates to children. Rationality can be thought of in a number of ways, as the capacity for willful action, the capacity to infer the possible consequences of a choice, as an ability to use the moral precepts of a community, as the possession of a certain level of measured intelligence on some standardized IQ test, and so forth. The possible characterizations are numerous, and in general tend to be too narrow to include all those to whom we would wish to accord rights.

Those of a religious persuasion propose another possible common element for adults and children: both are members of a class of beings capable of suffering. But this view is too broad. Its application results in the inclusion of prisoners, invalids, and mental incompetents, for instance, and even animals. It is also difficult to know what should count as true suffering.

Even the argument that all humans are worthy of rights because they are members of the same species presents a dilemma. The category of "human" again raises problems of definition and class inclusion, as for instance in the case of unborn fetuses.

Aiken has an interesting response to the lack of a well-defined common element

[15] Henry David Aiken, "Rights, Human and Otherwise," *The Monist*, 52 (October 1968), p. 513.

as a criterion for the ascription of rights to all persons. He construes human rights, and for our purposes children's rights, as belonging "normatively and ideally to persons to whom we, as moral beings, owe a certain kind of responsibility."[16] This shifts the argument for rights to a new position, making the ascription of one person's rights contingent on other people's moral obligations. But the position leads to a new set of difficulties. Consider a possible analogy between parents and colonialists. Imagine a developing country where a local political leader hopes he can convince the colonial authorities that, as moral persons, they have a responsibility to accord his countrymen respect, acknowledge their rights to fair treatment, and grant them nation status. Failure to do so, in the politicians' view, would indicate the failure of the colonialists to see the citizens of the developing country as their equals. The colonialists, on the other hand, might deny the developing country nationhood on the grounds of certain differences between themselves and the local people, like skin color, lack of maturity, and comparative poverty. Furthermore, they might insist that in recognizing the existence of these differences they were respecting the local people. By this familiar logic, if the developing country wants self-government later, then it is reasoned the country would be better under foreign rule now, since self-government demands a self-sufficiency and self-regulation the country presently could not sustain. This position, of course, ignores the possibility that the citizens of the developing country would in full cognizance prefer to be poor but independent *now*. Should their choice be respected, or should the colonialists continué to act as enlightened agents protecting their well-being?

Acting on Aiken's proposal, it may not be possible to address the developing country's point of view. His notion that we are to ascribe rights to persons because we ought to, that is, because such an ascription of rights is morally proper, will not provide a strong enough foundation against counter arguments. There are countervailing moral principles, and the colonialists need to be convinced of *why* they should yield control—that is, why self-governance is the developing country's right and why it is in the country's long-term self-interest. No argument can suffice which says that it is part of the colonialists' *duty* to accord nationhood. They might fervently believe that there are various classes of beings toward whom we have duties without owing them rights.

Children are in a situation analogous to that of the citizens of the developing country. The burden of proof is presently on them and on adults speaking in their behalf to demonstrate why they have a right to do what they prefer when it con-

---

[16] Aiken, p. 514.

flicts with what their parents or society prefer. Notions of morality which govern decisions of parents and society depend on how convincing their arguments can be. This example serves to illustrate why any entitlement to rights cannot be resolved without reference to some broader framework, a comprehensive theory of justice, to which all parties can agree. Without such a framework and such a consensus, moral claims will continue to be a matter of assertion and counter-assertion.

Necessary Features of Children's Rights

It is helpful to indicate briefly three features, first proposed by Maurice Cranston in justifying rights in general,[17] which are necessary in any scheme justifying children's rights. These will give a clear sense of why many previous attempts at justification have proved unsatisfactory, and why a rationale in the framework of a theory of justice may be more adequate.

Adopting the ideas of Cranston, the first necessary characteristic of children's rights is that they be *practicable*. By this Cranston means they must be theoretically possible, or acceptable within some larger conception of the good society. This meaning is grounded in statements prescribing or applying rules of fair treatment which are philosophically derived. Children's rights must cohere and be theoretically consistent within the society's conception of justice.

Children's rights can be theoretically possible or reasonable without being popular or practical to implement. In fact, it is hard to imagine any scheme which would significantly increase the domain of children's rights which would not raise objections in at least some small segment of the adult community. Moreover we need not expect children to exercise their rights well in society as we know it. Even if it is impossible in society as we know it to provide fair treatment for children, this does not make it wrong to claim fair treatment as a right. It only means that these rights must make sense within the framework of some reasonable conception of society.

A second necessary feature of children's rights is that they be genuinely *universal*, appropriate for all children everywhere. The idea, for instance, that only those who are white are to be accorded rights fails to take account of this feature. This criterion needs no great elaboration, except that there may be misunderstandings about its implications for different age groups. It might be objected, for instance, that preschoolers should not have rights while adolescents should, or that in any event the rights of the two groups should not be the same.

[17] Maurice Cranston, "Human Rights, Real and Supposed," in *Political Theory and the Rights of Man,* ed. David D. Raphael (Bloomington: Indiana University Press, 1967), pp. 55 ff.

Our concern with including this criterion is much more a concern with establishing a philosophical doctrine of *capacity*, the groundwork for a presumption that children have rights, than it is a concern with the particular practical domain in which these rights are routinely exercised by children themselves. To establish the foundations for rights, making an adequate philosophical argument that they should be accorded, is not the same as spelling out the actual scope and nature of their exercise for every age group. This distinction is analogous to the distinction between capacity and exercise of rights which is made in the narrower context of the legal system. All persons do not enjoy the same legal rights, but all are presumed to have the same capacity for rights and enjoy the presumption that treatment will not be different for them than for others. In the law, this is called the doctrine of impartiality, or equal consideration. The meaning of capacity for rights is simply that no individual, whatever his or her age, should be *without* the rights accorded others in society.

This criterion obviously does not take us far toward determining those areas where children of various ages should be allowed to make practical decisions for themselves. It merely lays down one necessary precondition of any adequate philosophical argument for children's rights.

The third and last feature of children's rights is that they be *of paramount importance*. When fair treatment is accorded children as a right, it must override all other considerations in society's conduct toward children, for example, consideration of children's fun. This feature may be less clear than the others. It serves to override the utilitarian objection that when we do what is in children's best interest we should be concerned less with their rights and more with their pleasure or satisfaction, or the aggregate short-term and long-term good achieved for them and others. If the utilitarian principle were pre-eminent, then we can imagine many situations where adults could justify depriving children of rights simply on the grounds that there was a prior importance of children's satisfaction or well-being which required that certain rights not be allowed them; or, more comprehensively, it could be maintained that when the total good of society is taken into consideration children must be deprived of rights because this leads to more sensible decisions for the whole society, leading to the greatest good for the greatest number, children included. We can also imagine many situations where a right to fair treatment for children would require them to become involved in painstaking deliberations or proceedings on their own behalf, which they might prefer to avoid if their own pleasure were of equal importance. Pleasure may be important in the lives of children, and so may the aggregate good of ends achieved for children, but neither should have the same importance as children's right to make just claims.

Children's Rights under John Rawls's Theory of Justice

An interesting and adequate framework for children's rights can be established in the context of John Rawls's theory of justice. Rawls bases his theory of the just society on a particular kind of social contract. A system of justice, for Rawls, requires that people "understand the need for, and they are prepared to affirm, a characteristic set of principles for assigning basic rights and duties and for determining what they take to be the proper distribution of the benefits and burdens of social cooperation."[18] His goal is to permit each individual to act according to a personal conception of his or her own best interests, but not at the expense of others.

In order to achieve Rawls's just society, individuals engage in a mutual process of evolving principles of fair treatment for everyone, present and future. His central idea is that everyone in the society must participate in choosing these principles, and that the principles are to be selected in a hypothetical state, or "original position," in which the individuals are ignorant of their own specific interests and circumstances in real life. All participants in society are self-interested in making their decisions. But ignorance of their station in life and of the particular configuration of their society guarantees for Rawls that the individuals will choose principles of justice impartially, with equality in mind, so that no one is made to serve as an instrument of the interests of others.

In the Rawlsian scheme, the only constraints on selfishness in choosing the principles of justice are that the individuals make their choices behind the original "veil of ignorance," that they be rational in choosing, and that they understand roughly what might constitute an adequate theory of justice. Assuming these conditions are met, Rawls argues that only one set of principles of justice will emerge. They will be agreed upon by everyone, because all participants in society will see it in their own personal interest to come to the same general conclusions about adequate rules for the system of justice.

In their condition of ignorance and self-interest, the individuals will choose two fundamental principles of justice. The first is that each person should have a personal liberty compatible with a like liberty for all others; no one should be any

---

[18] John Rawls, *A Theory of Justice* (Cambridge: Harvard University Press, 1972), p. 5.

freer than anyone else in society to pursue his or her own ends. The second is that societal inequalities are to be arranged such that all individuals must share whatever advantages and disadvantages the inequalities bring. This principle is intended to preclude discrimination against those who are born into poverty or natural deformity. Taken together, the two procedural principles provide the basis for the entire system of justice. Individuals agree to the principles because acting on them will best implement the individual's sense of his or her own good, as perceived in the original position of ignorance.

Rawls argues that in the original position, self-interested persons would want first to guarantee their own freedoms and would initially make the conservative assumption that others in society might want to curtail these freedoms. Thus their first motive would be to ensure that minimal guarantees of their own liberty were preserved. Rawls suggests that in everyone's case there is this kind of prior concern about preserving personal liberty. Assuming this minimal condition is met, individuals would then want to proceed with the fulfillment of other interests. Clearly the preservation of individual freedom is not without some cost to the individual, however, since in the initial state of ignorance it requires that an assurance of one's own freedom be made prior to knowledge of one's own practical identity and life circumstances. Thus, to ensure minimal personal freedom involves granting a like freedom to all others, and constraining one's own freedom as one would wish the freedom of others to be constrained.

Rawls also insists that when individuals engage in the mutually advantageous business of constructing a framework of justice, no individual would choose to submit to the restrictions of the society without expecting similar submission from others. And those who do submit to the restrictions would demand a just claim against all others in the society. Thus, all individuals would have a right to insist upon fair treatment at the hands of their fellows. The justification for this right does not depend on the moral convictions of the members of the society, or on any conditions of the individual, such as the capacity for suffering. Rather, the justification depends on the fact that all individuals in the society have freely agreed to make themselves subject to the claims of their fellow members. Each individual has rights against all others in the society.

In an interesting footnote, Rawls characterizes the rights granted under his scheme as "natural." By this Rawls means that the rights accorded to individuals "are assigned in the first instance to persons and that they are given special weight."[19] The principles of justice thus guarantee rights which are based on the

[19] Rawls, p. 506.

nature of individuals. To violate rights is to that extent to violate the nature of the person. These thoughts are reminiscent of Cranston's remarks in reference to the rights of men, when he writes, "such rights are not given us by anybody; we have them already. The only thing needful is that they be acknowledged, recognized, and respected."[20]

What, then, about children and others whom society must treat paternally? Rawls is quite explicit about implications of his theory for these groups, and his point of view, while not radical, seems to contain major implications for children's rights.

In Rawls's theory, children are participants in the formation of the initial social contract to the extent they are capable. In order to participate fully in this process one must be rational, and this, for Rawls, means among other things that one must have attained the "age of reason."[21] But there is no attempt to rigidly define this age, or to link it with a particular conception of rationality or a particular notion of prerequisite skills and understanding. Instead, Rawls seems to imply that as children's competencies develop, their participation should increase.

Rawls points out that it is the capacity for accepting the principle of fairness which matters when deciding who is to count as a member of society. He writes that "a being that has this capacity, whether or not it is yet developed, is to receive the full protection of the principles of justice."[22] Children are pre-eminently such beings, and therefore qualify as members of the society, with just claims to fair treatment. Clearly some individuals in society will be better at applying the principles of justice than others. Any advantage those people receive from the exercise of these principles, however, will be regulated by the second principle of justice: people are not to enjoy a special advantage as a result of natural ability or social status. The characteristic which defines the just individual is the *capacity* for a sense of justice rather than the immediate realization of this capacity.

But skeptics may not yet be satisfied. They may argue that if children cannot participate fully in generating the principles necessary for the just society, they should not be accorded rights. In the Rawlsian view, however, it is more reasonable to assume that children *are* competent to perform this initial task, at least in part, rather than risk the logical alternative to it; that they shall be denied the possibility of pursuing their own just ends. Rawls wants to take account of our intuitive sense that even quite young children often *do* know what they want, and are capable of

[20] Maurice Cranston, "Human Rights: A Reply to Professor Raphael," in Raphael, p. 96.
[21] Rawls, p. 209.
[22] Rawls, p. 509.

weighing alternatives and of acting on the decisions they make—precisely the kind of deliberation required of those choosing the original principles.

Consider, for instance, children participating in a family decision about where to live. To permit children to participate in making this kind of decision is to run the risk of allowing a wrong decision to emerge—a risk which our society is reluctant to take. But if children are to learn to make such decisions, then, as Aristotle pointed out, they must be allowed to act and to be responsible for the consequences of their actions. Adults may assist in making choices for children, even exert some influence. But there must be good reasons for children to accept the authority of the older generation. By analogy, as adults we sometimes relinquish personal exercise of rights because someone else's proven skills or special knowledge is sufficient to convince us we should allow that person to advise us and guide our actions. One example of this willingness is in our attitudes toward the expertise of the scientific community or the medical profession. But in such cases, authority is conditional on the way it promotes or inhibits the attainment of our goals, or the choice of wise goals. Likewise, for children the authority of adults depends upon the way it facilitates or prevents the achievement of personal ends.

For Rawls, lack of full participation by children in the original consensus does not lead to parental domination. In the hypothetical, original position of society, those choosing are choosing not merely for themselves but for all who are to come. This means that principles of fairness must be formulated in a temporal limbo as well as a spatial and social one. Participants must choose principles without knowing their age or generation, as well as not knowing their life situation. They must entertain the possibility of actually being children, or of not yet being born, and choices about principles of justice must be made with this contingency, among others, in mind.

Those selecting the principles of justice in the original position would probably consent to some form of paternalism. But they would be very reluctant to adopt any paternalism which did not protect them against abuses of authority by members of the older generation.

Others are authorized and sometimes required to act on our behalf and to do what we would do for ourselves if we were rational, this authorization coming into effect only when we cannot look after our own good. Paternalistic decisions are to be guided by the individual's own settled preferences and interests insofar as they are not irrational, or failing a knowledge of these, by the theory of primary goods. As we know less and less about a person, we act for him as we would act for ourselves from the standpoint of the original position. We try to get for him the things he presumably wants whatever else he wants.

We must be able to argue that with the development or the recovery of his rational powers the individual in question will accept our decision on his behalf and agree with us that we did the best thing for him.[23]

The conception of children's interests implicit here is already more adequate than that of the classical paternalist schemes explored earlier. For Rawls, children are entitled to rights of their own. Also, the interests of the child are not necessarily synonymous with those of parents or protectors.

Even though the scheme is more libertarian than its predecessors, however, it still has one possible problem. Whenever adults act on behalf of a child, doing for the child what they would wish done for them if they were in the child's place, they do so without any mechanism available for children to question their judgment or dispute the correctness of their decisions. There may be no recourse for the child who feels that decisions are being made wrongly in his behalf. This objection is wholly analogous to objections raised to the "best interests of the child" standard as it is applied in legal proceedings, for instance, where adults often act according to their own conception of the child's best interests without sufficient chance for children themselves to take issue with this conception or to participate in the decision-making process.

Rawls anticipates this objection, and addresses the problem directly. First, he makes it clear that adults cannot claim after the fact that they have treated children fairly simply on the grounds that the children are finally persuaded of the correctness of their decision. To illustrate the danger of permitting such a rationalization, Rawls gives an example:

. . . imagine two persons in full possession of their reason and will who affirm different religious or philosophical beliefs; and suppose that there is some psychological process that will convert each to the other's view, despite the fact that the process is imposed on them against their wishes. In due course, let us suppose, both will come to accept conscientiously their new beliefs. We are still not permitted to submit them to this treatment.[24]

The spectre of brainwashing raised here could readily be extended to various forms of socialization and education. The point of view of the child must be considered at the time any decision concerning his or her welfare is made, not later.

Rawls makes two additional stipulations. First, he states that "paternalistic intervention must be justified by the evident failure or absence of reason and will."[25]

[23] Rawls, p. 249.
[24] Rawls, pp. 249-250.
[25] Rawls, p. 250.

By this he means that there is a presumption of rationality, that is, of the full ability to decide for one's self. Only when it has been demonstrated that this presumption is unwarranted is it fair to act on another's behalf. This point has major implications for children's rights, shifting the burden of proof to those who would deny children the exercise of their own rights. Although there are no doubt many areas where children are justifiably denied the exercise of freedoms, the correctness of this denial is no longer taken for granted. On the contrary, it must be shown to be just.

Rawls also suggests that any paternalistic intervention must be "guided by the principles of justice and what is known about the subject's more permanent aims and preferences, or by the account of primary goods."[26] This suggests, at a minimum, that children should be consulted about their aims and preferences. While the information may not be perceived by the adult as pre-eminent in making decisions about the child's life, it should be weighed along with other information, and weighted more heavily to the extent the child is old enough to think rationally about the choices presented.

We can test the Rawlsian justification for children's rights against the three necessary characteristics outlined earlier: practicability, universality, and paramount importance. In general, all three features are taken into account by Rawls in setting out the principles of justice. In his procedural conception of justice, Rawls has provided a framework within which the granting of children's rights is practicable, that is, theoretically sound. It is consistent with the theory that children be granted rights, and that these rights be exercised by children themselves wherever possible. The society must acknowledge the just claims of children, even if it is not always advantageous for adults to do so.

By his insistence on the need for impartiality in the original position, Rawls also allows for the universal aspect of children's rights. Those who must live with the chosen principles are the same people who decide on the principles. The notion of impartiality ensures that all shall be considered equally in the division of societal advantages and disadvantages. This view is in conflict with a classical utilitarian conception, which would have as its end the greatest happiness for the greatest number. The utilitarian approach could lead to policies benefiting some people at the expense of others, perhaps leading, for example, to enforced child labor on the grounds that such labor was most advantageous for society. To make a utilitarian

[26] Rawls, p. 250.

argument of this sort is, as Rawls says, "to mistake impersonality for impartiality."[27] The utilitarian disregards the claims of those whose good is sacrificed.

The paramount importance of children's rights is also assured in Rawl's theory. The primacy of personal rights, as against some other conception of the highest good, is a central tenet of the theory. Children are individuals; hence this aspect of the framework extends to them as well as other members of society. To respect children by according them rights is to recognize that they possess "an inviolability"[28] which society cannot override.

The justification of children's rights under Rawls's theory has one major emphasis: children have a right to make just claims, and adults must be responsive to these claims. This conception of the just society, if widely accepted, would lead to a change in attitude on the part of adults. In according rights to children, the theory makes adults more accountable to children. They can no longer assume it is only at their pleasure that children are permitted to make claims and exercise freedoms. Adopting this new conception of children's rights would in itself be an important reform.

[27] Rawls, p. 190.
[28] Rawls, p. 586.

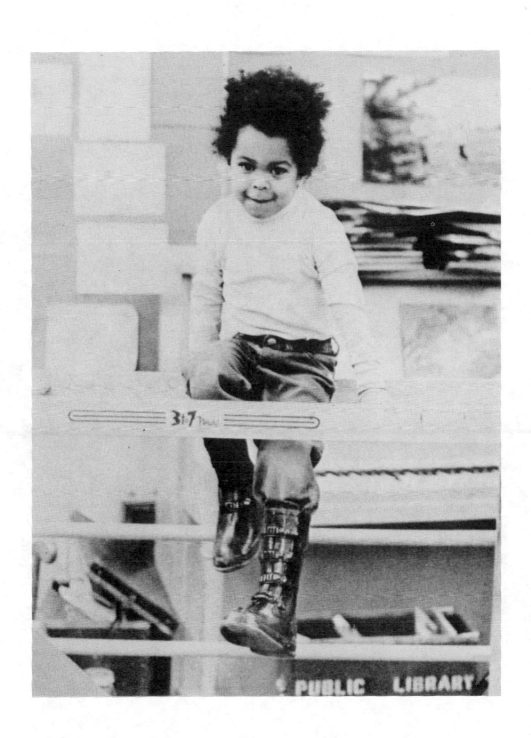

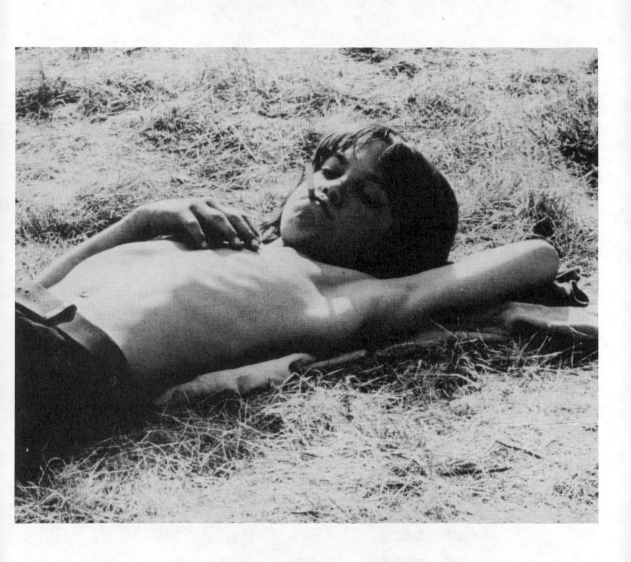

A Statement by
Senator Walter F. Mondale

Senator Mondale, a Democrat from Minnesota, is a leading congressional spokes-
man for children. He is a member of the Senate Subcommittees on Education,
on Poverty, and on Health. He also was a member of the now expired Subcom-
mittee on Indian Education, served as Chairman of the Select Committee on
Equal Educational Opportunity and the Migratory Labor Subcommittee, and is
currently chairman of the Subcommittee on Children and Youth.

During Senate hearings and investigations on large-scale social problems of hunger,
education, health, poverty, and migratory labor, several points have become clear.
First, as difficult as these problems are for all of the people they affect, they almost
always hit children the hardest. When they strike during early childhood, the
time of a child's greatest opportunity and greatest vulnerability, they may cause
irreversible damage. They have kept and continue to keep large numbers of disadvantaged children from entering society on the same footing as those born
into more fortunate circumstances. A second, almost equally disturbing realization
is that while we have made significant new investments in education, health care,
and nutrition programs for poor children, our ability to evaluate them has often
been disappointing. Our studies have tended to concentrate on the "cold" facts
of input variables, like amounts of money spent on schools or numbers of child
care slots available, and too often have been unable to measure the "hot" facts or
output variables like how, or to what degree, or with what permanence children
are actually benefitting from programs designed to help them. We are making
progress, but we still do not know enough about how federal and state programs
for the disadvantaged are assisting children to be healthier and better motivated,
or to learn to read, spell, and do basic math.

Harvard Educational Review Vol. 43 No. 4 November 1973, 483–486

My work on children's programs has convinced me that there is nothing more important for a child than a healthy family. Just as the ecology movement has sharpened our understanding that we cannot make policies and carry them out without considering their impact on the total environment, so we are beginning to recognize that we should not make decisions on taxes, transportation, housing, and welfare without considering their impact on families and children. Policies in these fields directly impinge on the stability and strength of the family and so directly affect the development of the next generation.

We should begin by trying to understand better some possible negative consequences of current social policies. For example, military personnel or young executives and their families often are required to move every two are three years. Maybe this makes good military and business sense, but we should stop for a moment and consider the possibility that such mobility could be harmful. Or think for a moment about tax policies. Corporations can write off the cost of $2,000,000 private jets, conferences in exotic places, or $50 business lunches as deductible expenses. The average working family, on the other hand, gets a tax saving of only $150 per year for all of the expenses involved in raising a child, an insignificant sum in comparison to the estimated $40,000 to $75,000 it costs to raise a child from birth through college. Many other countries, such as Canada, have a children's allowance to relieve some of the costs incurred in childbirth and childrearing. These financial burdens hit young couples the hardest, when total family income typically is at its lowest point. Contrary to the expectations of some, children's allowances have not encouraged families to have more children; instead they have helped young families and working-class families shoulder the expenses of raising their young. Perhaps we should consider shifting our tax structure to include increased support to families with young children. At the very least, we should begin considering the interests of children and the economic security of their families along with those of business and industry when we do our fiscal planning and review our tax laws.

Existing tax policies often have discriminatory or unintended outcomes contrary to their initial goals. As an example, we now provide assistance in the form of tax deductions for the cost of child care or preschool education when a mother works outside the home, and I support this concept. But we do not provide any preschool assistance if a mother stays home with her children. In addition, those child care deductions which are currently allowed under federal income tax regulations primarily benefit families with incomes between $10,000 and $20,000. They do little or nothing for the near poor. Another problem surrounds the incentives of the welfare system, which at present do not promote family stability. Over half the states require poor couples where the head of the household is unemployed to separate or get divorced in order to be eligible for welfare. Some of the so-called workfare proposals would have the same net effect. Under the guise of welfare reform women with preschool children would be forced to work regardless of how much they felt their children needed them at home.

It will not be easy to assess the impact of policies on families and children. Values, jobs, lifestyles, and needs vary widely. To envision a single model family, a single way to raise children, or a single solution to children's needs could produce rigid national policies as unappealing in their consequences as many current ones. We need to devise policies that provide *alternative* ways of strengthening families, with options and choices. For some families this might mean financial support to permit a mother to stay at home with her children; for others it might mean the provision of homemaker services. For still others, the strongest family might result if the mother could go to work, either for the family's economic benefit or her own fulfillment.

The options, however, must be real ones. For example, if we intend to give mothers with young children a choice of working full-time, part-time, or not at all, available child care must be of high enough quality so that a mother can leave her child in such a program and know the child will be treated well. I have seen the child care facilities presently available to poor families, working-class families, and even many middle-class families. Too often they are overcrowded, understaffed centers where bare custodial services are provided. As the number of working mothers continues to grow, the need for child care of high quality becomes imperative. That is why I sponsored the Comprehensive Child Development Act of 1971, which passed the Congress but was vetoed by President Nixon, and why I attempted to pass a revised form of that vetoed bill in the Senate last year. I will continue fighting for child development and child care legislation until we get a bill enacted.

One of the biggest barriers to informed judgments about policies for families and children is the low quality of available information. Policymakers rarely have sufficient funds or staff to discover how present policies affect family life, and the sums spent on social science research in this realm are not commensurate with those in other areas of government. I have recommended for some time and will continue to promote the establishment of a Council of Social Advisers, an institution similar to the Council of Economic Advisers but designed to concentrate on human programs. The Council would produce an annual report and refine the use of social indicators to give us a better idea of how human services can most effectively be provided. In addition, I would like to see the creation of a national social science foundation, established to concentrate on social science questions and coordinate social science research in the same way the National Science Foundation currently serves the natural sciences.

Evaluation of social programs requires sensitivity and understanding as well as the ability to analyze complex data. It is a difficult task, but one we must undertake. Serious appraisal of social policy toward the nation's children and their families deserves high priority in the Congress, the federal agency structure, and the country as a whole.

An Interview with Marian Wright Edelman*

Marian Wright Edelman, as Director of the Children's Defense Fund of the Washington Research Project, has added child advocacy to her agenda of action for social change. Beginning as an attorney in the civil rights movement, she directed Jackson, Mississippi's office of the NAACP Legal Defense and Education Fund, Inc. Headstart, children, and education were large issues for community development, and her involvement with the Child Development Group of Mississippi focused her concern on the welfare of poor and minority children. One of the principal architects of the Comprehensive Child Development Act of 1971, she has broadened her commitment to advocate the rights of all children. She has selected several specific areas on which to concentrate: the exclusion of children from school, labeling and treatment of children with special needs, the use of children in medical experimentation, their right to privacy with regard to school and juvenile court records, reform of the juvenile justice system, and children's right to day care of high quality. Ms. Edelman talked about these and other issues with HER.

Marian, you recently announced the formation of a new organization, the Children's Defense Fund. Can you tell us what it is and why it was created?

The Children's Defense Fund (CDF) is an attempt to create a viable, long-range institution to bring about reforms for children. If they are to receive fair treatment and recognition in this country, children require the same kind of planned, systematic, and sustained advocacy, legal and otherwise, that the NAACP Legal Defense

* Interviewers were Rochelle Beck and John Butler of the HER Editorial Board.

Harvard Educational Review Vol. 44 No. 1 February 1974. 53-73 and Education Fund, for example, instigated for blacks three decades or more ago. We hope to bridge two large gaps. One is between people in local communities and advocates at the federal level. The former care about kids but have no larger strategies into which they can fit their local action, and the latter may be politically savvy but need support from local groups to implement any kind of change. Professional child advocates may know a great deal about federal legislation and administrative processes, but unless we can transmit such knowledge to local groups who can educate their constituencies and provide the political muscle, we will continue to lose much of our effectiveness.

The second gap is among people in various disciplines. Researchers and academics have gone off in one direction and those of us who have been involved in policy have gone off in another. As a result, there is often no useful evidence on the particular issues policymakers need to make decisions about. I think there is a lack of understanding from the academic community of what we need to know and do for children with immediate needs. Similarly, lawyers have spent a lot of time filing suits and winning legal victories but have not paid adequate attention to the problems of remedy or the involvement of the community. For example, a right to a hearing is hollow unless people know they have it and are helped to take advantage of it.

CDF is attempting to cut down on the usual fragmentation of effort by molding a staff of people from various disciplines who will seek a unified approach to change. We have litigators and researchers, federal administrative monitors, and community liaison back-up people. We have contracted with local organizing groups like the American Friends Service Committee to provide us with eyes and ears sensitive to local people and problems. We are also retaining local attorneys whom we can use to help identify, where possible, those effective local action groups working in behalf of children.

There is also a separate national entity, the Washington Research Project Action Council, which has a legislative agenda and can lobby on behalf of children—with child development and child health legislation at the top of the list.

What are the specific issues CDF has chosen to pursue?

CDF is premised on the assumption that effective advocacy is specialized; global approaches to change on behalf of children are doomed. We have selected six priority issues for change which could affect broad numbers of children and which are easily understood by large segments of the public. They are: 1) the exclusion of children from school, 2) classification and treatment of children with special needs,

3) the use of children in medical, particularly drug, research and experimentation, 4) the child's right to privacy in the face of grow computerization and data banks, 5) reform of the juvenile justice system, and 6) child development and day care. These issues are subject to attack from a number of vantage points—local, state, and federal—as well as through a combination of strategies, such as litigation, monitoring, model legislation, or efforts at exposure which might in turn provoke congressional hearings, local organizing efforts, and so forth.

Why did you choose the exclusion problem and what have you found?

I got curious about the exclusion of students from school after reading the report of the Massachusetts Task Force on Children Out of School. The report did a splendid job of drawing profiles of children I identified and understood. I knew it was a problem in Mississippi and in Boston, but had no sense it was an epidemic of national proportions. Then one day a Puerto Rican legal group came to the

Harvard Center for Law and Education and said they had read the Task Force report and would like to bring a suit against the Boston schools on behalf of Puerto Rican kids out of school. They said, "We know the figures in that report," but they needed hard data for a lawsuit. The data were not available. But I began thinking about whether the problem of school exclusion which surfaced in Boston existed on a national basis and whether anyone knew the extent of the problem. I wrote to every state department of education in the country and to the relevant federal agencies to inquire about non-enrollment. It became plain quickly that no one had any reliable information or sense of how many children were not enrolled in school in America.

The federal government didn't have any hard figures on the number of excluded students?

They don't know anything about the number of kids out of school! We had to turn to 1970 census data. We did a state by state analysis using the conservative criteria of the census for non-enrollment, i.e., children who had no contact with school the three months prior to April. We found among children seven through fifteen years of age (which incorporates the compulsory education ages in most states), more than one million children were not in institutions and were not enrolled in either public or private schools. The problem of non-attendance or non-consecutive absenteeism is much greater and is not included in this census figure. Some states, like Kentucky, show almost 5 percent of the eligible children not enrolled in school. That's a lot. Certain county by county census nonenrollment breakdowns showed shocking percentages of children nonenrolled—some as high as 20, 30, and 40 percent. We selected nine states for on-site monitoring, designed a survey questionnaire and sampling technique, and went to every third or fourth door in selected census tracts to find out who the children were and why they were out of school. We tried to select a variety of tracts with different kinds of families, but focused on those which appeared to have a substantial non-enrollment problem. According to the census figures one county in Colorado has 48 percent of its seven- to twelve-year olds not enrolled. In Massachusetts, for example, Cambridge had an 18.1 percent non-enrollment figure for seven- to twelve-year-old black children. I wanted to know who in the world those kids are and why they are not in school.

Did you do any of the monitoring yourself?

Yes. Monitoring has taught me a lot. Some days it was so discouraging to see the problems between families and schools that you wanted to throw up your hands for lack of any sense about where to begin. The number of children out of school, not reading, or with unmet special needs seemed enormous. Children's and parents' distrust of schools and teachers made education seem impossible. And the entrenchment of attitudes and practices among certain school officials seemed to warrant the helplessness many parents felt about making things better. It's as if schools get rid of children as a first, not last, resort. Many discipline problems seem to me to be education problems. I wonder what would happen if schools were forbidden to exclude any child. Would they feel more responsibility for educating them? I would recommend denying schools the power to suspend children except in very narrowly defined emergencies—and then only on a temporary basis.

One of the striking things is that many of the problems I thought were found only in southern districts and districts with many minority students have turned out to be much more universal. The expulsion-suspension-disciplinary problems I'd associated largely with desegregation are severe everywhere and disproportionately affect lower class white as well as minority children. Arbitrary and unfair disciplinary processes are common. Holyoke, Massachusetts, though it has a substantial Spanish-speaking population—largely Puerto Rican—had not one Puerto Rican teacher at the time of our survey. The lack of minority faculty is more of a problem in some northern districts now than in many southern ones.

What do you think a good policy on student suspension from school would look like?

That question is the subject of a great deal of our time and thought, and the report on our study of exclusion will address this matter. I personally favor a policy that would almost never permit schools to suspend. I would completely forbid long-term or indefinite suspensions and expulsions. Since the courts now generally permit suspensions of three days or less without a hearing, some children are effectively expelled from school by a series of repeated three-day suspensions, without benefit of due process and often for unfair or arbitrary reasons. I would not permit this practice to continue.

Out and out suspensions and expulsions are not the only problem though. In addition, there are myriad informal and extra-legal ways of encouraging children to leave. These include disciplinary transfers, in-house suspensions, never bothering to enforce truancy laws, etc.

How do we get school people to change their view of their responsibility in these matters?

There has to be a re-examination of why we have schools, whom they are to serve, and what their responsibilities are to children. I think if we said that from now on no school can kick a student out for any reason, schools might be forced to educate. It is a complex problem, but one thing is clear: any recommendations in this area must go beyond simply establishing due process procedures and must deal with feasible substantive alternatives for children who find it difficult to function in traditional classrooms.

How do you define and propose to deal with the problem of functional exclusion?

Functional exclusion is having a Puerto Rican or Chinese child sit in class without understanding a word. It is permitting a child to be disturbed or hungry, and to go unrecognized as such. Since these children are unable to learn, they often become discipline problems. They are mislabeled mentally retarded or are put in a track that often is totally unresponsive to their needs. Further, I think a child is functionally excluded also if he or she is not liked, knows it, and is not expected to learn.

Such cases present a complicated question of strategy for CDF. We are very concerned with in-school failures, but tactically we see physical exclusion as the best wedge to initiate a public debate that can lead us into these more complex in-school issues. Nobody can argue much about a million children who are out of school. When you get into the more fuzzy areas of misclassification and educational programs unsuited to children's needs, you confront larger problems of definition and remedy.

The problems of tracking, suspension or expulsion may be indicative of the fact that the first priority of the system is the efficiency of the schools rather than the education and welfare of the kids. In the broadest sense there are three basic constituencies whose interests are often in conflict: children, their parents, and the society. Isn't it sometimes difficult to decide whom you will support, or what is in the best interests of the child?

I don't think these are three separate constituencies for all purposes and issues. Constituencies will vary depending on the issue, the place, and the time. But your question is difficult. For example, one of the interesting things we're discovering in talking with parents and kids with special needs is that parents like labels and children don't because parents tend to think labels may help their kids get more suitable placement and treatment. Parents are protective, and they often want their children in specialized schools. Children dislike labels because they separate them from their peers—stigmatize them. They seem more willing to risk the rough and tumble of normalcy.

You found that handicapped kids didn't want to go to a school for the handicapped, but their parents thought they should go there. What would you advocate in this situation?

I'm not sure I can make a firm general statement, although I begin with the presumption that it is better for children to be with other children—all kinds of other children. The world contains different kinds of people, and schools and classrooms should reflect that. I don't like people being put off in closets by virtue of their race, handicap, or anything else. Can institutions serving normal children provide those extra things required to meet the needs of special students? I often wonder if the quality of many specialized schools is comparable to the best that the children get from the better public schools. What are the aspirations fostered in special schools for the crippled, blind, or deaf? Are they encouraged to continue after they go through elementary school? Do they go on through secondary schools in any-where near as large numbers as "normal" children? To college? Are they all trained to weave baskets? It seems to me that by definition specialized schools will empha-size the handicap rather than the normal aspects of the children who happen to have a handicap.

Are you suggesting that there should be no specialized schools?

No. Rather that the harder question comes in deciding which children really can-not function in a regular or normal setting. I think, in the final analysis, that those requiring some kind of institutionalizing or segregation will probably constitute a very small percentage of children.

I visited Belchertown and Fernald (two residential schools for the handicapped in Massachusetts) not too long ago. The former had almost no programming that I could see, which meant hundreds of people were living like vegetables. Fernald struck me as somewhat better in terms of programming, and many of the patients seemed to have a more dignified existence. But I asked an official at Belchertown what percentage of the children who were there need not have been there if suitable alternatives had been available in the community. He responded that while it was difficult to state certainly how many should never have been institutionalized in the first place, he thought probably the majority. They have now stopped admitting children.

Would you advocate keeping children with special needs in their communities rather than in institutions?

While I have a basic bias in favor of deinstitutionalization, it is not a simple issue. I believe that there are some people for whom institutionalization may be neces-sary. But we have to be much more careful in determining who they are. We should start from the premise that, whenever possible, keeping people at home or in com-munities is preferable. Conversely, however, those who favor deinstitutionalization have a very heavy responsibility to create suitable and sufficient alternatives for placement. It is too easy to simply say we should close down institutions without having something equal or better for the occupants and their families. In some instances closing down institutions may result in fewer services for people who need them.

This raises the crucial question of whether enough funds will be made available to establish alternative treatments or initiate new programs for children. Why, in a world of competing priorities, should anyone be so interested in children at this point?

I think the question should be turned around. Why is it that we can't do much more for children? It's sinful that we prefer to spend billions on weapons of destruction rather than building human lives. We subsidize farmers not to grow food while we scream that child development legislation would be prohibitively expensive. I suspect we spend a lot more on annual contract overruns at the Pentagon than on Headstart. But priorities won't be changed until we change the poli-

tics. Child advocates simply have not molded themselves into a convincing enough political force to cause a congressman or senator to think as strongly about cutting an education appropriation as he or she does about cutting the military budget or voting on the oil depletion allowance. I also think child advocates could profitably adopt the environmentalists "dirty dozen" approach of analyzing congressmen's voting records, as a means of serving notice on legislators that we are serious about our cause. We can start by doing an analysis of voting records of congressmen on key issues affecting children and families and then ranking members. Congressmen who rank at the bottom will be targets for challenge. The Washington Research Project Action Council is preparing such an analysis for distribution.

What are the other priorities for CDF?

One is what we call the "Guinea Pig Project," where we are investigating the extent to which children, particularly institutionalized children, are used for medical experimentation without the provision of adequate informed consent procedures or other protections. It is an extremely interesting area. We have found it difficult for two reasons: first, medical research has been conducted largely in secrecy, without public knowledge or accountability, even while much of it is done with public funds; and second, doctors, like lawyers and other professionals, think that only they should regulate themselves—even in the face of information showing substantial abuse. The Tuskegee syphilis experiment and the South Carolina sterilization case dramatically illustrate the need for public attention in this area.

We recently won an important case in the Federal District Court of the District of Columbia under the federal Freedom of Information Act. This decision allowed us access to NIMH grant applications and research protocols, including so-called pink sheets and site visit reports, which contain the conclusions and comments of peer review groups whose approval is required of all federal research applicants. The Court also ordered HEW to revise its regulations and grant application procedures to assure that such materials are made available to the public in the future. This decision, if sustained on appeal, will go far in demystifying medical research and building some public accountability into federally funded research grants affecting children. Our investigation of the medical practices in this area will result in a report later this year.

It is a sad fact that there is a better government policy to protect animals than children from experimentation. It is only in the aftermath of blatant abuses that government panels have been assembled to discuss and draft more specific guidelines for human experimentation. I am especially concerned about preventing institutionalized children from being used for experimentation. It still remains to be seen when, and in what form, guidelines in this area will emerge. CDF has monitored the guideline drafting process carefully, and we have prepared and are advocating our own draft regulations.

How are the current guidelines for human experimentation insufficient to protect children?

The current guidelines governing human experimentation are inadequate on the informed consent issue. They completely ignore the problems of consent among the institutionalized. CDF's top priority in this area is to safeguard the child who is least protected—the orphan, the retarded, the neglected and dependent, the institutionalized and the poor—from being guinea pigs in the marketing of new drugs. The consent issue is different for adults and children, particularly children who are under the control of the state or third parties. I feel differently about an adult prisoner consenting to participating in a drug experiment than I do about such an experiment being performed on a child in an institution for the mentally retarded or in a home for the orphaned and neglected.

Isn't the notion of consent problematic with children anyway?

Yes. At what age should a child have to be involved in giving consent, rather than simply consulting the child's parent. Should institutions be permitted to give constructive consent for purposes of experimentation? I would not want any jailer in Alabama or elsewhere to have the right to consent on behalf of juvenile wards on such matters.

Whether protections and procedures are implemented is another crucial but difficult issue. Researchers may give lip-service to paper procedures but ignore them in reality. A substantial consent question was raised in an experiment conducted by a Dr. Dimascio through Boston State Hospital.

What was the experiment?

It involved administering drugs to school children in certain Boston public schools who supposedly reflected behavioral problems which were very broadly defined. The early proposal suggested the experiment was more an attempt to test the effect of the drugs rather than a treatment for specifically identified medical problems. The proposal described a potpourri of symptoms such as restlessness or inattentiveness that could have resulted from a variety of social causes like poverty or hunger, as well as from medical causes. Yet the approach in the proposal, apparently directed at poor children, first explored therapeutic rather than social solutions to the symptoms. If a child is restless because he's hungry, adequate nutrition ought to be the first level of inquiry and response—not the administration of some drug. Further, it was unclear just what the parents were told about the experiment or how the consent procedures worked. I know as a parent I would never have consented to my child participating in such a poorly designed experiment. But when we tried to find out more, we were turned down. It was to get this proposal and others that we sued NIMH under the Freedom of Information Act and which resulted in the decision I mentioned earlier.

We have met with a great deal of defensiveness and concern among some of our friends in the medical profession who fear that we are out to (or may inadvertently) destroy medical research. That is the farthest thing from our intentions. We do believe that it is important to enforce public accountability on these important issues. This is an issue which involves very complex judgments, but a total policy vacuum or reliance on self-regulation within the medical profession in the face of increasing evidence of abuse is not a desirable solution.

To give you a specific example, it is necessary, in my opinion, for more people to be aware of and question the frequency with which drugs like Ritalin are employed in the treatment of children's problems. The use of amphetamines on children is far more widespread and promiscuous than has been suspected or documented. And for imprecisely defined medical problems. What is a hyperactive child? How much misdiagnosis is involved? Who should diagnose the child? A physician? A teacher? A parent? What is the impact of long-term use of such drugs? Is the availability of drugs an incentive for easy, mabe incorrect, labels and treatments which serve as substitutes for more costly, complex, or demanding services for children?

You mentioned that a child's right to privacy in the face of growing use of computerization and data banks was a CDF interest. What are you doing in this area?

We have begun what we call our 1984 Project, which focuses on behavioral screening for the purpose of identifying and labeling children with alleged criminal or other behavioral problems and on exploring the use of computerized record keeping of information on children.

This project examines the crucial issues of privacy and classification, to say nothing of raising more fundamental issues about what kind of country we are or ought to be. I have very strong feelings about how much the government or other officials ought to be allowed to know about individuals. Indiscriminate data banking and careless sharing of information can subject those children who are most dis-

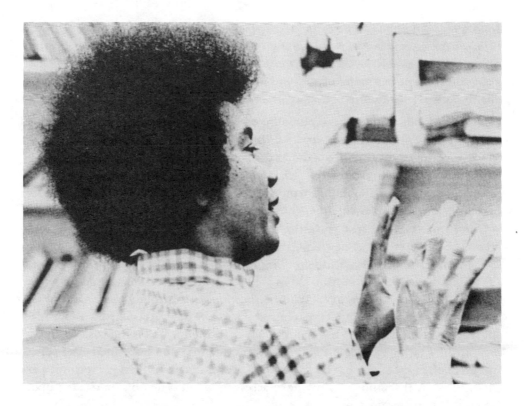

liked and most prone to be mislabeled—the poor child, the minority child, the neglected child—to unfair scapegoating by governmental authorities. Children may gain a stigma at a very early age that can never be shaken. For example, a young person picked up for speeding at sixteen might be checked through some centralized data bank and found to have a history of school problems or contacts with the juvenile court. He or she will, in all likelihood, be treated differently once this information is known.

Accessibility of school records also presents problems. Some information fed into a child's records (to which she or he may not have had access) may be of questionable nature. For example, suppose a principal or teacher thought the child was on drugs but could not prove it. Suppose this observation was included in a school file which was later turned over to the juvenile court when the child was picked up for truancy. This information might later go into a data bank accessible to police authorities. The ramifications of the unsubstantiated charges could go on and on and the child would never have the opportunity to refute them.

Some say that various kinds of specialists in the schools should have access to all information about the child and use it at their discretion. Others say that this kind of information should be withheld from school personnel and reserved for the parents, unless they want to divulge it, thus arguing for something more like a formal doctor-patient relationship between the specialist and the child. How do you see it?

It seems to me that if there is a counseling service at a school, the counselor should have access to the records necessary to do his or her job. This is true of any specialists attempting to deal with special problems. The information sought and collected, however, should be appropriate and necessary to the service being performed. None of the data should go outside the school, for any purpose, without the parents' or the child's consent (depending on age).

Unfortunately, it is still the practice in many places to deny parents and children access to school records. A new law giving parents access to their children's records was recently passed in Massachusetts. This right does not exist in many other states. Like welfare recipients' records, all files are confidential. Even the person on whom files are kept may not see them. Who is being protected from whom? One of the reasons it's so important to give parents and student access to their own files is to cut down on the hearsay evidence and rumor that often serves as the basis for labeling a child. In instances when a child is on trial, stands to be suspended or expelled from school, or otherwise has his status negatively altered in a serious way, his parents and counsel should certainly have access to all information or records upon which the charges were based.

You said "depending on age," implying there may be different levels of responsibility for children as they get older. Is CDF considering the developmental differences and competencies of kids at different age levels?

Sure. I ought to make clear that we are not a children's liberation operation. I'm not sure what children's liberation really means or whether it's a good thing. Children are not simply another oppressed minority group who could function independently if allowed to do so. As a parent, I know that a six-year-old and a twelve-year-old have very different capacities and that we should be flexible in designing remedies suitable to various levels of development. The issue of consent and access to records should differ depending on the child's age. While it's a difficult area, I personally would permit any children old enough to understand to have a say in whether they want to participate in a non-beneficial medical experiment where any discomfort or danger may be involved. Where the use of their bodies is involved for non-therapeutic purposes, children's opinions should be given great weight. I think parents and children *together* should decide about issues that affect them.

Why do you say you're not a children's liberation operation?

We don't yet have a sound enough conceptual framework to approach children's rights. That's one of the things we will become more wise about as we proceed. I think it is clearly incorrect to state that every child should be liberated. Similarly, the narrow legal approach of merely extending adult rights to children is not the answer. Children do have, in my view, special needs and require special protections in certain regards. Defining the working medium between the extremes must be done carefully.

I would like to see more systematic attention given to formulating policies for children. I'd like CDF to have one or two top-notch policy people who will begin thinking and talking about developing materials in the area of children's rights. We have an obligation to design a long-range framework for approaching children's issues while trying, in the meantime, to bring about specific reforms and immediate relief. We need to get lawyers, educators and parents to talk more to each other and begin to break down the narrow boxes from which we approach change and which result in ignoring the whole child.

Out of this kind of dialogue and examination of existing policies, we may be able to make thoughtful suggestions to policy makers about what should be done rather than sniping at what is being done, as most advocates do.

Looking at the Children's Defense Fund as it relates to your own recent history of involvement in efforts for social change, what are some consistent themes?

Well, in many ways the Children's Defense Fund is the natural next step for me. My interest in child development legislation, especially the 1971 Child Development Act, grew out of my work in the mid and late sixties with the Headstart program and the Child Development Group of Mississippi (CDGM). CDGM was the largest community based and operated Headstart program in the nation. This experience taught me the crucial importance of bridging the gap between local efforts and federal policy. The lack of a Washington-based advocate who could anticipate, police, and counter the hostile moves by Senator Stennis and others meant that the people who should have been concentrating on children spent inordinate amounts of time trying to survive political attacks. Moreover, as the politics of the poverty program began to change with the onset of increased war expenditures and the dissatisfaction of local governments with community action, the states began to gain more control. Funds were cut back, jobs in communities were whittled away, and the local and independent institutional bases for change in Mississippi were being eroded.

Regardless of what the evaluators have said about the effectivenss of Headstart generally, in Mississippi it was, after the summer project of 1964, perhaps *the* most important social catalyst for change in the state. It provided poor parents and children with a forum for learning together for the first time. It created new jobs not controlled by the state or plantation owners. It helped poor parents understand new ways of having an effect on their children's education. For example, they began to question why public schools were different from Headstart centers; why teachers didn't welcome parents into the school like the Headstart teachers did; why the texts did not show black as well as white kids as the centers' books did. They began to confront public school officials. And when they met with no response, they began to run for school boards. This process spread to other areas like health and welfare.

As Headstart's existence was increasingly threatened, those of us who felt the importance of these local institutions knew that Headstart's survival depended on broadening the base of its constituency. This meant identifying the need for child care services in the larger population. I had moved to Washington in early 1968, where I spent a lot of time trying to keep federal grants alive for local Mississippi community groups. Meanwhile child care proposals were introduced in the Congress that virtually would have turned over control of child care services to the states and, I feared, the public schools. In Mississippi and other southern states this action would have meant the end of parental involvement for the poor. With labor and civil rights help, we were able to oppose them. One thing became clear. If we were going to get the kind of legislation that would ensure quality comprehensive care to poor communities, it was necessary to take the initiative, to try to formulate what we wanted, and to see what kind of support we had.

Where did the support for child development legislation come from?

It's fascinating. We sent out a letter to various day care people: the Day Care and Child Development Council of America, the Child Welfare League, the National Association for Education of Young Children, and those kinds of groups. We wrote to people in the National Welfare Rights Organization, which had very interesting and conflicting positions on day care. Many in the group opposed day care because they saw it as a mechanism for forced work in the context of Nixon's repressive welfare policies. But they need child care services nonetheless, and were concerned about avoiding custodial and damaging care for their children.

We also set out to get as many labor groups involved as possible, and the AFL-CIO, ILGWU, the Amalgamated Clothing Workers and the UAW turned out to be our staunchest supporters. Their constituency of working-class people needed day care services almost as urgently as poor people.

What was the reaction of women's groups?

The women's movement was beginning to get a lot of publicity at that time and clearly was a force for good child care. They responded readily to our appeal, particularly the National Organization for Women. Our first meeting was amazing; you could not get in the room. Everyone who had been invited, plus many who had not, showed up, and they thought child development legislation was a terrific idea. The astonishing thing for me (which says a lot about why there has to be a Children's Defense Fund and some kind of systematic advocacy) is it never occurred to the day care establishment to draft their own bill. During the drafting session we fought fiercely over priorities. Welfare mothers almost came to blows with some of the middle-class women liberationists who thought they should have equal access to day care if they wanted time to go to an art gallery. But welfare mothers who have no choice but to work wanted their kids' needs to come first. After about a dozen sessions, we reached agreement on five issues: delivery systems, eligibility criteria, priorities for services, roles for parents, and funding levels. After drafting the bill, which drew considerably from earlier ones, the whole coalition's membership met with key congressmen it wanted to take the leadership.

Is there broad national support for day care, or do many women believe their place is in raising their own children?

Some women are interested in day care and some are not. It is clear that one of the major tasks facing proponents of quality child care legislation is to combat people's fears and misperceptions of day care and what we mean when we call for federal involvement in this area. There are a lot of fears, some justified, which Mr. Nixon so successfully appealed to in his veto message. Child care proposals challenge some of our traditionally held views of the family as the major child caring entity and raise fears about governmental interference in family affairs. Many are afraid that government sponsored child care will encourage even more mothers to work, or will result in the government supporting some groups who are too lazy and shiftless to take care of their own children. After all, they reason, if they were any good they would want and be able to take care of their own children. What these views ignore is that there are presently millions of working mothers with millions of young children who are forced to suffer custodial, inadequate, and sometimes damaging care for lack of viable, quality alternatives. Everyone should read the study of day care done by Mary Keyserling for the National Council of Jewish Women, *Windows on Day Care,* for evidence about this. In 1971, 42.6 percent of all persons in the labor force were women, leaving millions of preschool and older children in need of care. At the same time, there were less than a million licensed day care slots. Saddest is the fact that many thousands of children—some under six years of age—are left alone without any care at all.

How will you overcome these fears or traditional ideas about the family?

We must conduct a broad grassroots information and education campaign about the needs that we are attempting to address. We should emphasize that good child care must build on and respond to family needs, and that its objective is to keep families together. Many families are now forced to break up because of the outmoded and divisive policies typified by our welfare and foster care systems. I wonder how many neglected, dependent, and handicapped children who have been institutionalized or placed in foster care might have remained in their families if decent, supportive, temporary community group or home child care support had been available? Something is wrong, as Justine Polier points out, when a country chooses to pay least support for children who remain at home (AFDC payments are abysmally low) and most support to institutionalize them.

President Nixon said in his veto message that he thought the Child Development Bill would lead to communal child rearing and that it was against basic American family values. Do you think an increase in child care would undermine the family as a social institution?

Senator Ernest Hollings of South Carolina, hardly a flaming liberal, had a good response to these charges of communalism. In a debate over an amendment to cut appropriations to child care he said something like this: "Ask anybody at the country club where their kid is, and they will say 'at the kindergarten.' But, ask any poor folks and it is the day care center. But who argues communalism when you talk about public schools?" In that sense, our bill was far less communal and compulsory than compulsory public education. Participation was clearly voluntary, unlike Mr. Nixon's own program which would have eliminated choice and forced welfare mothers with young children to work. Our bill mandated parental control. It did not provide only group care, but allowed parents to choose between programs on a continuum from individual care in homes to center care, respecting diversity and pluralism. Given our insistence on voluntarism, parent control, flexibility and choice among types of care, I can't see how Mr. Nixon's rhetoric about communalism applies.

Do you think children have a right to quality child care?

Yes. The preamble of the Comprehensive Child Development bill put the nation on record as saying that children have certain rights: to basic nutrition, health care, education, and child developmental care in their early years. Fulfillment of these rights should not be contingent on families' ability to pay for them. I believe that the nation has an obligation to care for its children from birth. This makes sense in humane and self interest terms if we value our national future. The 1971 bill tried to address the entitlement of *all* children and sought not to make child care a class issue. We don't need any more singling out of poor kids.

Parent involvement is also crucial, because when you are dealing with children it seems to me to make sense to try to involve those individuals who have the most influence and responsibility in the child's life. Since much of the literature seems to say that what goes on in the home may be the most decisive factor in a child's development and school achievement, why not try to strengthen this home tie? Bronfenbrenner and others suggest that the programs with most lasting impact on children have involved some continuing interaction between children and their parents or caretaking adults. But this is very difficult. Many professionals don't trust parents. Many parents don't trust themselves. This must be combated. I think it unwise to have professionals assume exclusive or major responsibility for children's rearing. It seems best to temper their role with parental involvement in programs.

Do you mean parent involvement or parent control?

I want parents to have a major policy say in what kind of care they need in their community and who should provide that care. The 1971 bill gave local policy committees, with parents comprising half of the committees, a veto over major staffing and policy decisions. Since it is so crucial that children have a good early attitude toward learning, I'd like to equalize the options of poor parents with my options as a middle-class parent. If I don't like the teacher or the school, I can yell until I'm satisfied with a change, or I can take my children elsewhere. In many ways middle-class parents don't exercise much control over their children's schools. But we generally have more political clout and more choice about the kind of education and treatment our children will get. Poor parents have less of a choice in both areas.

I would like to see parent and family counseling in day care centers, to help parents understand more about the developmental needs of their children. As many activities as possible should involve families in the life of the center. Siblings and other young people should be employed to work with the younger children. Different kinds of parents will need different kinds of options for participation, ranging from working in centers on a paid or volunteer basis to simply dropping in. Building up participation is a hard and long-term effort. Child care workers must establish a relationship of trust and a basis for continuing outreach.

In the legislation you proposed, the federal government would provide funds for centers. Are there other ways to implement day care centers which might motivate parents to be more involved, a voucher scheme or a family allowance, for example?

I'm not presently in favor of vouchers. They reinforce existing patterns of class and racial segregation. They put the cart before the horse. What is there to buy? Who's going to get served? Start-up costs to build and begin day care programs are high; where will community groups and the poor get the funds to do this if government has withdrawn? Until there are more good services available, I'm not clear that giving individuals money means much. In many instances, we may be helping a lot of well-to-do parents buy more of what they're already buying. I'm not impressed with consumer effectiveness, Nader notwithstanding. Ensuring accountability in a tight market, from my experience, is not promising. I worry about the profit-making groups who could take advantage of a voucher arrangement, and I worry about mechanisms to foster racial and class integration which are missing from that scheme. I'm waiting to see the results of current voucher experiments. It could be that after a system is established, vouchers may be one alternative method of funding. They were not prohibited under the 1971 Bill (which encourages local community choice). Since we don't know what's going to work best we should be open to various approaches.

Marian, getting back to children's rights generally, what can people who are interested in this area do at the community level?

I think people can do a lot. For example, if, as we now know, the number of kids out of school is a major problem, any person can document the extent of this problem in her or his community. They can come to CDF for interview materials. We can help them learn what to look for, where to go, and what their rights are. We can give them the A through Z finding out if exclusion is a problem in their area.

The same thing is true in the human experimentation project and in our juvenile detention project. How many kids in your community are being held in adult jails? Does your state law or regulation forbid this? We are now conducting a study in eleven states looking at the extent to which children are still retained in adult facilities which are unsuitable and merely school them in crime. I'd like to see local groups help us ban this practice. We would be delighted to share with them our questionnaires and information on how we are going about discovering the extent of the problem. Ultimately, if children are going to be treated decently, it will be because of an informed and aroused citizenry in communities around the country.

And everyone can help to change their community's attitudes about what is possible. Children need caring communities, schools, teachers, and parents much more than great amounts of money or new legislation. Yet caring is the most difficult thing to give them. Without this, our other reforms will ring hollow. By exposing some of the sad and damaging experiences of too many children in America and by trying to provide ways that people in various positions can work to change these conditions, the Children's Defense Fund hopes to help create a more responsive and decent country for children to live in.

The Massachusetts Task Force Reports: Advocacy for Children

PETER B. EDELMAN
University of Massachusetts

This essay is not about what needs to be done for children, but about tactics, ways to go about trying to change public policy as it affects children. It focuses on one case, a citizen advocacy effort at the local level directed at remedying the exclusion of children from school, and then generalizes about the validity and pitfalls of a variety of advocacy tactics.

At the outset some general considerations might be in order for those who are just now setting sail on a course of changing the world for children. One such consideration is humility. Mistakes can be avoided, of course, by making no effort at all. Academia is well populated with people whose armchair analysis has produced no policy failure because it has produced no policy.

But those who truly labor at practical efforts to change public policy for children can do damage, and need, above all, to be aware of that. Today's institutions may be tomorrow's prisons. The dangers are both substantive and tactical. For example, is it right or wrong to close all large residential institutions for juvenile offenders? We may decide it is right, and push hard for it, but we had better watch for the backlash that could make things worse than they were to start. We had better be sure that those young people who need supervision and support if they are going to remain in the community are getting it, and that the groups who contract to deliver community-based services to the young people do so. We had better see to all these things, or in one way or another, the young

Harvard Educational Review Vol. 43 No. 4 November 1973, 639–652

74

people we were trying to help may end up in a worse position instead of a better one. If so, we will have given good intentions a bad name for some time to come.

It is well to be humble for another reason. More than once, unplanned and unforeseen changes have overrun the charted paths of reform. Within a generation after the advent of television, it became clear that children's attitudes and habits are formed perhaps more by thousands of viewing hours than by any other single force. Who can say, looking to the future, what will happen to children as a result of the smaller families and the more stable population size which birth control, abortion, and changing attitudes about population growth are going to bring? Will children get better schooling and social services in a society where next year's class will be smaller than this year's? Or will a stable population mean economic stagnation and limited resources to give to children?

But humility does not necessitate paralysis. One need not be so skeptical and tentative as to fall into the trap of those who say action is impossible until we know not only the direction we want to travel but also the road we want to take. Nor need one fall prey to the lure of those who call the solutions of the 1960's massive failures without so much as differentiating among them, distinguishing between inherent failure and remediable error, or examining the adequacy of the funding that was provided. Finally, one need not fall into the snare of those who analyze and re-analyze ten-year-old statistics to produce books that gasp for the fresh air of what is happening to real children a few miles away. Along with humility there must also be a willingness to take risks—to begin somewhere, using as much foresight and peripheral vision as possible, but nonetheless to begin.

There are many vantage points from which one might undertake to change public policy for children. Elected officials, both executive and legislative, sometimes try. Lawyers and media people, foundation staff and social service professionals, community organizers, charismatic leaders, and citizens sometimes try. Indeed, when any change does occur, it is the product of interaction among all or most of these people. In any given case, the initial impetus may come from any of these people and/or the institutions or organizations of which they are a part.

An additional impetus has come into existence in recent years in the form of the citizen-advocate, the person or small group which engages in advocacy tactics designed to involve others among those listed above in changing public policy. Ralph Nader is the most visible practitioner of this art, although his efforts have primarily been oriented to consumer issues. But there are others all over the country who have been at it for a long time on a wide variety of fronts. One such local group, relatively recent in its origin (1968), is a Boston effort called the Task Force on Children Out of School, known since 1972, when it received a sizeable Ford Foundation grant, as the Massachusetts Advocacy Center.

The story of the Task Force is a useful rubric within which to analyze some further guidelines for children's advocacy activity. The story begins with a remarkable man named Hubert E. Jones. Trained as a social worker, Hubie Jones was Director of the Roxbury Multi-Service Center from the mid-1960's until 1971. In that capacity he became aware that many of the families with whom his agency came into contact had children who were involuntarily out of school. The reasons were many and varied (pregnancy, disciplinary problems, physical handicap, mental retardation), but all led to exclusion. The non-English-speaking were also effectively excluded.

Hubie Jones saw what was there for all to see. Perhaps others saw it, too, but he was the only one who acted. In December of 1968 he convened a city-wide conference of social service workers, mental health personnel, and community leaders from thirty-five agencies all over Boston to discuss the problem. All agreed it was an emergency. Another meeting was held a month later, this time with the addition of people from the Boston school system, the State Education Department, and the State Department of Mental Health. They agreed to set up a task force to look into the scope of the exclusion problem.

Here, then, is rule number one for citizen advocacy: someone must identify the problem and set the process for action in motion. Indeed, someone or small group has to stay with the effort throughout, or those whose interest, however genuine, is only a secondary priority will not stay involved long. There is a word for it: leadership.

Corollary number one is: only certain kinds of issues can be addressed by small-group advocacy. The problem has to be small enough so that efforts for its solution do not turn into the naive pursuit of some all-encompassing agenda. The problem must be comprehensible to the public and capable of evoking the sort of strong emotion that attends the demonstration of a clear injustice. It must be manageable and packageable. And it must have specific remedies; there are many reasons why the Kerner Commission produced little change, but one, surely, is that there are no obvious, specific remedies for racism. In the problem must be the victimization of children in specific ways, as opposed to things as global as mental health or quality education.

Hubie Jones represented one essential form of leadership, but another essential ingredient is professional staff, those able, dedicated, persevering people who will pursue the problem on a day-to-day basis for as long as it takes to get results. Many a worthwhile advocacy idea has come to nothing for lack of such staff. The Massachusetts Task Force staff was organized by Larry Brown. He was just getting his doctorate in social welfare from Brandeis, and had written an article about the work of the Citizens' Board of Inquiry into Hunger and Malnutrition in the United States which had come to Hubie Jones' attention.[1] Larry Brown was hired to be staff director of the Task Force.

Not surprisingly, Brown had a model in mind, that of *Hunger, USA*, the report of the hunger inquiry group.[2] The model was fairly simple: elicit the interest of some key interest groups (in that case the UAW, the churches, and the civil rights-anti-poverty community), use that interest to raise some foundation money. and use those elements to attract a board of distinguished and representative citizens. Then hold hearings and conduct staff inquiries, issue a searing report with maximum media coverage, and, finally, figure out how to get action on the reports.[3]

If there was ever an issue that was tactically appropriate for a planned approach it was hunger. Whether people do or do not have enough to eat is reasonably ascertainable. If they do not, the public is capable of understanding and sympathizing deeply. If the fact of hunger is publicly clear, not only do specific remedies suggest themselves, but it is also hard to get away with arguing interminably about whether to give out food or food stamps or jobs or welfare.

Even so, there were millions of hungry people in America in the late 1960's, and no one had ever pointed that out in a way that received national attention. It took the dedicated efforts of a few people in Congress, in the media, in the foundation world, and in the world of anti-poverty "advocacy" to get the story told. The exclusion of children from school may be the hunger issue of the 1970's. The numbers are ascertainable, albeit with some effort. Preliminary census data indicate one and one-half to two million children between eight and fifteen are not enrolled in any school. While the remedy is not easy to see for all these children, it is for most; their reasons for being out of school are essentially the same as those of the children in Boston. Thus, it was probably no accident that Larry

[1] Larry Brown, "Hunger, USA: The Public Pushes Congress," *Journal of Health and Social Behavior*, 11 (June 1970), pp. 115-126.

[2] Citizens' Board of Inquiry into Hunger and Malnutrition in the United States, *Hunger, USA* (Washington, D.C.: The National Council on Hunger and Malnutrition and the Southern Regional Council, April 1968).

[3] The work of the hunger inquiry panel is described in more detail in Nick Kotz's excellent book, *Let Them Eat Promises* (Englewood Cliffs, N.J.: Prentice-Hall, 1969).

Brown undertook to apply the *Hunger, USA* approach to the problem of children out of school in Boston.

The next question was: who should serve on the Task Force? Constituting such bodies is always a delicate balancing effort.They should not be composed too heavily of people who are already on one's side, because the final report would have less weight with such a group. But one does not want to risk being outvoted. President Johnson's Presidential Commissions (e.g., those on crime, riots, and violence) suggest a pattern. Each had a few obvious liberals and fewer obvious conservatives. Then there were conservative-looking people on whom the constituting authorities were making a bet: when these establishment people saw the facts about the issue they were charged to examine, they would be radicalized.

That bet paid off on all of the LBJ Commissions, perhaps better than he wished. It worked for Hubie Jones and Larry Brown, with one added variation. Instead of looking for big-name, power structure citizens to radicalize, they went for middle-to-upper level professionals in the agencies which would have to respond to the report, and academic professionals with decent views but no particular street knowledge. These people were sufficiently within the mainstream to legitimize the work of the Task Force, and more likely to stay involved in the follow-up activities than bankers and business people would have been. The obvious liberals on the Task Force were people from the communities affected and from neighborhood level agencies which worked directly with those communities.

The result was what Jones and Brown hoped. When the Task Force members saw and heard what was really going on, they were all appalled. For many, if not most, the final report was a document they would not have dreamed of signing at the outset.

It should be clear that the composition of the Task Force, the definition of its agenda, the fund raising, and the location of staff all took time. Nine months passed from the January 1969 meeting until the first Task Force meeting. Typically, money is not easy to come by for an effort of this kind at the local or the national level. The Task Force had no track record. It was the classic chicken-and-egg situation. Money was needed to prove there was a problem, but money was not forthcoming in significant amounts until the proof had already been amassed.

Thus the whole Task Force operation was performed for something like $9,000, all the money that could be raised. After the report came out, was obviously good, and received major attention, money began to become available for implementation, culminating finally in the recent Ford grant and the institutionalization of the Task Force into Mass Advocacy. Here, then, is another rule:

do not expect to start big. Do not expect to walk into the Ford Foundation and say, "Give me money to investigate X." It is fair to say that unless some people work for nothing or next to nothing for a while, perhaps stealing time from other jobs (Larry Brown had a graduate fellowship at Brandeis), a local advocacy effort is not likely to get off the ground. Much of the work on the Task Force report was done by student volunteers.

Pursuing his application of the *Hunger, USA* model, Brown had the Task Force hold meetings in the neighborhoods around the city. Thirteen local meetings were held over the course of somewhat less than a year. At the same time the staff was occupied with research and interviews, but these meetings were crucial. The invited witnesses included both critics of the Boston schools and defenders, mainly school officials. Each meeting was designed to invite conflict in the testimony. Thus the process of the Task Force attracted attention even before the report was written, thereby building an audience. Similarly, the fact that the meetings were held in the neighborhoods, with open airing of the full dimensions of the argument, began building a constituency for follow-up action. These lively meetings were informative to the Task Force members and provided them an opportunity to compare and test the various points of view.

It is important to stress that the Task Force leaders did not know precisely what would happen when they began. They had defined the problem to their general satisfaction, and they had some idea of redress if not specific remedy. But they did not know what the dynamics of the Task Force operation would be, or what sort of report would ensue. While they were determined to follow up on the report, they had even less idea of the specific goals and tactics this would involve.

There are two significant points here. One is the importance of follow-up. Just doing a report is of limited use; if someone is not committed to implementation it is unlikely to occur. It is rare that anyone other than the drafters of a particular report has much of a stake in its implementation. It may be that the lack of follow-up on at least some of the Presidential Commission reports under LBJ, for example, was due at least as much to the fact that the people involved went away as it was to lack of agreement with the recommendations. Continuity of the people involved is essential.

If the determination to follow up is essential, so is an understanding that the battle plan cannot be drawn up in every detail at the outset. This is a subtle point. I do not mean to suggest that the process is even predominantly trial and error. Yet, even if adequate effort is made to define the problem and the tactics, one must be prepared for the agenda and the tactics to change in midstream, either because of success with some of the goals, definitive failure, or because times change.

George Wiley was a good example of the delicate combination of a sure hand and the ability to adapt; he taught many of us well. He began in the civil rights movement, but while many of his colleagues became successively more frustrated with the slowing pace of achievement, he saw the need for and value of an issue-oriented coalition of all the poor; the National Welfare Rights Organization was formed. While many lost hope as the modest successes of that effort brought an anti-welfare backlash, he saw the need and utility of trying to build a coalition among all who feel a lack of power in this country—hence the Movement for Economic Justice he was organizing when he died. He had a superb sense of organization and a brilliant grasp of substantive issues. But above all, his special quality was that he was almost always ahead of everyone else in sensing the need to adapt and change agendas.

The report of the Task Force came out in late 1970,[4] about a year after the group began functioning. Because the resources of the Task Force were so minimal, there is not much new or hard statistical data on the over-all numbers of excluded children, but in human terms the report is particularly moving. It begins with a gripping series of vignettes of individual excluded children, a human montage of the exclusion problem. The reader is introduced to the subject not with dry statistics or long recitations of bureaucratic evasion and obfuscation, but with pictures of children who have been pushed around and pushed out. It makes the report hard to put down, a singular achievement among commission reports.

The report includes a short chapter on each type of exclusion, with documentation of the meagre amount of financial and human resources the Boston school system devotes to each area and enough proof of the magnitude of each problem to show that tragedy is occurring daily. Neither the statistics nor the suggested remedies are detailed enough to enable a court to design a decree specifically ordering a level of service to a particular client group. But that is not a fair test of the report's value. Coupled with the ensuing follow-up, it more than sufficed to gain attention from the media, influential citizens, and elected and appointed officials.

[4] Task Force on Children Out of School, *The Way We Go to School: The Exclusion of Children in Boston* (Boston: Beacon Press, 1970, 1971).

A variety of tactics were and are being utilized in the follow-up effort, partly because the different aspects of the problem suggest differing approaches, and because there is not one magic approach. Effective tactics are a mosaic of differing efforts: the mix depends on the facts and politics of the situation at the particular time. Throughout, constant attention to the development of coalitions and constituencies is essential, although such alliances may need to change.

Use of the media is a key element. This means not only being able to get attention for one's own work but having media allies who will do timely articles and filmed reports of key issues on their own. Having media friends who will help on a day-to-day basis is extremely important. When trying to get a particular report released from a public agency, or opposing some new regulation which an agency is quietly trying to promote, it is particularly helpful to be able to get a newspaper story about this on a moment's notice. The publicity can do wonders for the agency's sense of what it can and cannot get away with. The Task Force has been very effective with this kind of tactic. But when the need for media assistance goes beyond day to day collaboration to require independent investigation things become more complicated.

It is remarkable how little investigative journalism there is on issues where words like powerlessness, exploitation, and discrimination are applicable. The print media are not nearly as bad as the electronic media on this score. Two of the handful of memorable television documentaries about poverty in the last five years, "CBS Reports on Hunger" and an "NBC White Paper on Migrants," were made by the same man, Martin Carr. After he made the hunger film, which aroused the ire of powerful congressmen and others, CBS gave him no further assignments for over a year until his contract ran out. This, by the way, is a technique which CBS is also alleged to have used in the case of Peter Davis, the man who made "The Selling of the Pentagon." Carr then went to NBC, where his problem was that his film pointed the finger too directly at the Coca-Cola Company's housing for migrant workers in connection with its Snow Crop and Minute Maid operations in Florida. Again, his contract was not renewed when it ran out, and this time he could not get further work in commercial television for some nineteen months. It should be added that the two documentaries in question won both Emmy and Peabody awards.

Media assistance is not always appropriate. Non-communication may be better when a desire not to alert potential opponents is of more weight than the need to attract support.

Litigation is a second element. The Task Force did not bring law suits even though it has lawyers on its staff, but instead developed alliances with other law-yers. It has worked with these mainly poverty lawyers repeatedly. A good example of the collaboration was a successful suit to force reinstatement of a pregnant girl to school, a result which effectively became law for the whole state.

Litigation, like publicity, can be either a short- or long-range tool. Sometimes a lawsuit or the threat of one is the best way to obtain withheld documents or thwart an administrative action. And sometimes litigation is the best way to force long-range policy change. Litigation, however, has its dangers, especially for long-range change. A badly conceived, badly prepared, or badly tried lawsuit can make matters much more difficult for others. A dismissal or a loss in one jurisdiction may be cited by a court elsewhere as the reason for an adverse ruling. Litigation without community or clientele awareness or involvement runs a double risk. It may be seeking relief which is not what the interest group involved wants, and it may gain relief which does no good because no one outside the courtroom knows that a right has been declared.

Legislation is a third element. The Task Force could not lobby because of its tax exemption, but it has done research at the request of key legislators and served as a technical resource to other advocacy groups which were free to lobby. Massachu-setts' new bilingual education and special education laws can be traced partially to the Task Force's report and subsequent research.

The final effort—and really the main business of the Task Force, and now Mass Advocacy—is in the area of administrative negotiation. The Task Force has spent a great deal of time working with others in the first three areas, but the process of advocacy with executive and administrative officials is at the heart of Mass Advocacy.

It is a sad fact that this is a relatively new kind of activity, at least insofar as those who might be termed "the powerless" are concerned. There is still a huge vacuum in place of such advocacy at every level, from federal on down and local on up. Large corporations have known for a long time how to get at elected executives and career officials, but others have not. The civil rights movement in the early '6o's, for example, was almost wholly oriented to legislation. There were contacts with non-legislative officials, but mainly in connection with getting legislation passed, and to some extent with the Department of Justice about its civil rights law enforcement activity. There was little or no contact with the Department of Health, Education and Welfare, or Labor, or with any other de-partment regarding the application and interpretation of federal law and pro-grams. There was little or no activity directed at influencing the promulgation of regulations in such agencies, ensuring that they were spending funds as Congress intended, or affecting the choice of people to administer the programs.

The Office of Economic Opportunity legal services lawyers took an interest in the activities of Executive Branch departments, but they did so by using the device of litigation and challenging the validity of regulations and administrative practices in court. Few people rolled up their sleeves to sit down and argue directly with the bureaucrats to pressure them just as a powerful corporation might.

Ralph Nader changed this to some extent with some of the follow-up activity to his reports. Advocates for the poor have now found they too can deal with executive branch agencies, and that middle-level officials can be as helpful as those higher up. This was first proven by the Poor People's Campaign (PPC). The style was movement politics, the use of masses of people as leverage, but the substance was administrative advocacy. While the failures of the PPC and the mud of Resurrection City were getting the publicity, agency after agency was meeting with PPC representatives to hear carefully drawn demands which included accomplishable items. And the agencies were responding.

The gains were not earthshaking, a regulatory liberalization here, a small program expansion there. But they were important, both intrinsically and because they opened a front for bureaucratic contact that is still partially operative even after five years of Richard Nixon. There were and are dozens, even hundreds, of career officials throughout the federal government who are delighted to feel pressure and be able to report to their superiors that there is a political reason to do the right thing. It turns out, too, that many officials are willing to pass along valuable information and make suggestions regarding tactics which might move their superiors or people in other agencies. It is terribly important to understand that the bureaucracy is not monolithic.

The Task Force staff began negotiation in many directions at once because different problems involved different agencies, and because the same problem often involved multiple sets of regulators. They went to the State Commissioner of Education to press him regarding the misclassification of children as retarded and the miseducation of children who are retarded. The Commissioner responded in a number of ways. He issued an order directing Boston to re-evaluate all 2,800 children assigned to classes for the retarded. He brought the State Department of Mental Health into the discussions, and new statewide regulations governing the education of all retarded children were the result. At Task Force instigation he issued statewide directives safeguarding the right of pregnant students to remain in school and regarding the rights of physically handicapped children to attend school.

The Task Force went to the Boston School Department and the School Committee about various things: bilingual education, classes for emotionally disturbed children, the pregnancy issue. The direct results of their advocacy were more limited here because the audience was not very friendly. Many of the subsequent gains on these subjects came because of statewide administrative directives, new state legislation, and court orders.

Why did they get in the door anywhere? First, because they had done the report and it was not only good but also had received a lot of attention. In addition, it appeared they had real staying power: they would not get tired and go away. Equally important, they were reliable and not ideological. Their work was well-written and solid, and their advocacy did not ring with hostile allegations of conspiracy and bad faith, however justified such allegations might have been. If they were asked to help draft a regulation or a directive, their product was sound and usable. If documentation was needed, it was forthcoming. These qualities are not merely virtues; they are absolute essentials. Overt radicalism may be all right for other kinds of strategies, but it is inappropriate for advocacy with administrative officials.

Such advocacy is hard enough without the burden of ideology. Administrative advocacy differs from litigation. In litigation there is at least a set, ritualized way to proceed, so that radical litigative lawyering may sometimes work. There is a formula for getting in the courthouse door, so that an openly radical position is not per se destructive of one's position. In administrative advocacy, however, there is no ritual, no guaranteed way of getting in the door, and an explicitly radical stance may make getting a hearing even more unlikely. Of course, desperation may dictate a more radical posture, and the existence of a strong, active, and large constituency willing to put their bodies on the line may permit tactics which are less polite.

The staff quickly learned the value of specificity. They went to the Boston School Committee with their views on bilingual education and the Committee was unimpressed, even hostile. Then they met with the chairman and produced a list of 600 specific children, with names and addresses, who were not in school because of the lack of a bilingual program. This time the chairman reacted, getting the School Committee to set up a special panel of School Committee members, professionals, and community people to look at the problems. Even before the new state bilingual legislation had passed, the Boston schools had doubled their number of bilingual classes.

The Task Force received the worst reception from the State Department of Mental Health. Months of very friendly conversation produced almost nothing by way of improvement of services to emotionally disturbed children. Here is an example of the need to be flexible about tactics as the problems change and reveal themselves. The Task Force decided it would have to do another report, about the politics of mental health services to children in Massachusetts. After almost a year of follow-up effort on this aspect of the first report, it was clear the Department of Mental Health would not be moved in any other way; so another report was done.[5]

The second report was another strong effort although not enough time has passed to judge its effects fully, it seems not quite as effective as the first report. The personal hostility between key Task Force people and the Commissioner of Mental Health is evident throughout, and this seems to detract from its objectivity. The tone of the first report is one of controlled anger; the second has more heat, with the consequent implication, fair or not, of passion overrunning reason. Nonetheless, the report had one key consequence. The Commissioner resigned a few months later. There were of course various reasons for his departure, but the work of the Task Force was certainly one. What will happen now is still an open question; a new Commissioner is beginning his work as this article is being written.

In all of the Task Force's administrative advocacy efforts its developing network of bureaucratic contacts was a significant factor. In the interplay between State and Boston school officials, the Task Force staff often received key facts and tactical suggestions from the State side. Much of the information in *Suffer the Children* came from sympathetic Department of Mental Health personnel.

One particularly instructive aspect of the follow-up to the first report was the formation of the Alliance for Coordinated Services. In one area of the city where the exclusion problem was particularly bad, the Task Force pushed for creation of a permanent interagency group with its own staff to see that service would be provided. Some sixty-three mental health and social agencies were drawn into a commitment to work through the Alliance in an area of some twenty-nine public schools serving 18,000 children. The formation of the Alliance teaches a key tactical lesson. The Task Force staff felt, as one of its members says, "We couldn't hit the School Committee over the head and work with them at the same time." So a separate service organization was created to help keep the Task Force free to continue its confrontational and advocacy efforts with less worry about undesirable side-effects.

[5] Task Force on Children Out of School, *Suffer the Children: The Politics of Mental Health in Massachusetts* (Boston: Task Force on Children Out of School, 1972).

It should be said that the work of the Task Force is not without its critics. There are some politicians and bureaucrats who regard it as raucous and rabble-rousing. There are commentators who think it has oversimplified the situation, particularly in failing to give credit to those sympathetic teachers and administrators who have tried to do the right thing. Others criticize it for having failed in four years to come up with hard numbers on the extent of exclusion from the Boston schools, arguing that without such evidence significant change will not occur. Another contention is that in trying to work with the Boston schools the Task Force is helping to shore up a failed set of institutions which reformers would affect more if they set out to develop alternative schools and programs. There are also those who say the Task Force has not sufficiently involved "community people" in its work and its decisions on strategy. And some feel that the Ford Foundation grant to enable the group to broaden its scope of activity was an act of manipulation by people in power to diffuse the effectiveness of the previous focus on exclusion.

The mix of agency pressure points and tactics which the Task Force has used was based on the specific situation in Massachusetts, where the state administration is liberal, the legislature is relatively liberal, and the local Boston School Committee is very conservative. It is a small state, and power is centralized in Boston. Therefore it made sense to use the responsiveness of the state as the central leverage in an effort to affect school policies in Boston. If the Governor had been Ronald Reagan and the chief state school officer Max Rafferty, the Task Force would have had to operate very differently if it could operate at all. Depending on the over-all political climate, foes like Reagan and Rafferty can make things impossible. Or because they become symbols of a widely deplored position, they can actually make things easier.

Apart from questions of political climate, a group seeking to operate in a situation where the state and local officials are of the Reagan-Rafferty ilk would have to proceed differently. It might rely much more on litigation against recalcitrant or discriminatory agencies and officials. It might try much harder to get Washington involved, by bringing in Congressional committees to help expose conditions or by trying to get unenforced HEW regulations applied properly. If local media were unresponsive, it might try for national media coverage. This is what happened in Mississippi in the 1960's. Long-time civil rights workers there were often heard to say they might as well move to Washington because anything good that they accomplished for Mississippi came out of Washington.

But this is not true in Massachusetts, and I suspect it is not true in most of

America in 1973. I am not suggesting Washington should be ignored, but rather that the model of the Task Force operating at the local level is one which is replicable in many places even though the tactics will differ from place to place. It may seem hard to believe sometimes, but there are elected and career officials in many states and localities who would do the right thing far more often if someone or some group on the outside were showing them the way and creating a political imperative for action.

The Task Force is of course just one approach to advocacy for children, and the effort here has been to generalize from it regarding various tactics. The most important generalization is that the effort to achieve social change for children has been hampered by a serious imbalance: too often the talk is about ends, with scant attention given to means. Hopefully, this essay has served to redress that imbalance just a bit.

The White House Conferences on Children: An Historical Perspective*

ROCHELLE BECK

Harvard University

> Sometimes when I get home at night in Washington I feel as though
> I had been in a great traffic jam. The jam is moving toward the Hill where
> Congress sits in judgment on all the administrative agencies of the
> Government. In that traffic jam are all kinds of vehicles . . . There are
> all kinds of conveyances, for example, that the Army can put into
> the street—tanks, gun carriages, trucks . . . There are the hayricks and
> the binders and the ploughs and all the other things that the Department
> of Agriculture manages to put into the streets . . . the handsome
> limousines in which the Department of Commerce rides . . . the barouches in
> which the Department of State rides in such dignity. It seems to me as I
> stand on the sidewalk watching it become more congested and more
> difficult, and then because the responsibility is mine and I must, I take
> a very firm hold on the handles of the baby carriage and I wheel it
> into the traffic.
>
> —Grace Abbott, 1934

The responsibility Grace Abbott assumed for bringing the needs of children to the attention of the federal government reflected a shift in the way we view children and the appropriate role of government in providing for their care. Women had led humanitarian movements before. But where the goal had been to improve the unfortunate circumstances of society's neglected young, the notions

* This analysis is based on the proceedings of the seven White House Conferences: the Conference on the Care of Dependent Children (1909), the Conference on Child Welfare Standards (1919), the White House Conference on Child Health and Protection (1930), the White House Conference on Children in a Democracy (1940), the Midcentury White House Conference on Children and Youth (1950), the Golden Anniversary White House Conference on Children and Youth (1960), and the White House Conference on Children and Youth (1970). They are available from the U.S. Government Printing Office, Washington, D.C.

Harvard Educational Review   Vol. 43   No. 4   November 1973, 653–668

for reform had been largely informal and nongovernmental, specific to local communities and run by people from them, and constrained in scope by the family's grip on children as private property. Twentieth century social reformers had different views. Children, they said, were this country's most precious natural resource—and in this metaphor the discussion of policy governing child welfare was shifted to the public domain. Once it was there, they reasoned, the federal government had to recognize the needs of children along with its other national interests. Formal governmental agencies and procedures were necessary. As Lillian Wald wrote, "The national sense of humor was aroused by the grim fact that whereas the federal government concerns itself with the conservation of hogs and lobsters and has long since established bureaus to supply information concerning them, citizens who desire instruction and guidance for the conservation and protection of children have no responsible governmental body to which to appeal."[1] The reformers prevailed upon President Theodore Roosevelt to hold a national conference to promote the establishment of such a governmental body.

Thus, the first White House Conference on Children was created to discuss and marshal support for governmental planning and protection of the nation's children. But the Conference was more than a political and practical event. It was a symbolic act of government, stating explicitly that certain needs of children would come within its purview. Once every decade since 1909, the federal government has convened such a conference, reaffirming its commitment to monitor and report on children's status in society.

But what, exactly, does that commitment entail? How are those certain needs settled on? Have they shifted over time? Other than providing a symbol, what is the federal responsibility for the welfare of children, and how is it related to the family, the community, the experts, and the other agencies which share the job of childrearing? The Conferences have left behind a rich written record that illuminates these and other questions. The proceedings and recommendations, reverends' prayers and presidential addresses, experts' reports and concerned citizens' testimony provide a tapestry of information, weaving the needs of children with other dominant social, political, and economic themes. The style, tone, and content of the written documents vary greatly, as must have the Conferences themselves. In part, the differences can be explained by major historical events, changes in the characteristics of the participants, or leaps in knowledge or sophistication.

[1] Robert H. Bremner, ed. *Children and Youth in America*, Vol. II. (Cambridge, Mass.: Harvard University Press, 1971), pp. 257-258.

But some of the distinctive features are due to the constantly evolving way in which this society sees and treats children. The proceedings of the White House Conferences on Children provide fascinating material for reflecting on this evolution.

The 1909 White House Conference on the Care of Dependent Children was organized by Jane Addams and Lillian Wald, leaders of the settlement house movement, along with the National Child Labor Committee, a group seeking to limit child labor, and other political and social leaders. These people were humanitarians, outraged by the abuses they saw dependent groups suffer in the growing cities and the depressed rural areas. Not only children, but immigrants, women, and those unable to compete in the fierce marketplace of industrialization were the objects of their concern. But they also were worshippers of industrialization and the precision, efficiency, and objectivity it introduced into the language and thinking of the country. Corporate management experts mapped out the flow of products and manpower to increase efficiency and production; planning and organization seemed to "pay off"; and gathering facts in order to direct the use of material resources was lauded as enlightened public policy. In an effort to apply this policy to human resources, 200 experts from the fields of medicine, education, data collection, and social work were invited to set an agenda for a Children's Bureau. The Bureau would gather statistics; compare rates of growth, mortality, dependency; make information available to states and individuals; and plan and support scientific research needed for the rational planning of programs for the nation's human resources. Jane Addams' address to the 1909 Conference sums up its motivation:

If my topic contemplated the devices for minimizing the labor in harvesting a field of wheat or producing a gross of buttons, if I were asked to name the world's famous inventions for minimizing mechanical friction or for saving human labor, there is no doubt that the inventions would all be American, and that if I were challenged I could quite simply invite you to take a walk through the neighboring patent building. But when we are asked to consider together the newest devices for minimizing dependency, those inventions to keep wage-earning parents alive and able to care for their own children, unfortunately for our pride we are obliged to enumerate the devices found in every other modern nation in greater abundance than they were found in America.[2]

The second Conference, the White House Conference on Standards of Child Welfare, was held in 1919. The mood of this Conference is best represented by

[2] *White House Conference,* 1909, p. 99.

the word "standards," reflecting the focus of the new Children's Bureau which had finally been approved by Congress in 1912. There had been doubt in both Senate and House about the appropriateness of a federal body to oversee child welfare. Some congressmen seriously questioned the constitutionality of federal regulations in an area which was formerly the province of the states. Voluntary groups such as the Society for the Prevention of Cruelty to Children were afraid that a federal agency would constrain their activities, and the Department of Education saw the recordkeeping and information functions of the Bureau as a threat to its sphere of influence. Amid much opposition, the Children's Bureau came into being with modest plans for action and modest funds to carry out those plans. In the 1912 debate one senator noted, "Congress has appropriated $25,000 to conduct the work of the Children's Bureau. This Congress is not wont to be so parsimonious in matters of property. Why become so economical in matters of human life? This body has already appropriated $600,000 for dealing with hog cholera. It has provided $375,000 for the study of the cotton-boll weevil. The most precious asset of the Nation is not its swine nor cotton crop. It is the army of children. With them rests the future of the Republic."[3] Careful not to threaten various interest groups, the Bureau focused its work narrowly on infant and maternal mortality and health. It gathered statistics and launched educational programs for mothers to reduce the incidence of deaths associated with childbirth. In a crash program to register all births and raise the consciousness of mothers regarding child health, May 1, 1918, was designated Child Health Day; it was followed by Baby Week; and the 1919 Conference was the culmination of Children's Year.[4] Thus, the 1919 Conference was dominated by physicians with facts and figures reporting the state of maternal and child health. Emphasis on efficient use of human resources still prevailed, but the Conference delegates were careful not to overstep their perceived mandate, limiting recommendations to revising standards rather than advocating more active programs.

The 1930 Conference was on Child Health and Protection and it was a radical departure from the previous Conferences. Broad in scope, it said something about almost every aspect of childhood and adolescence. Education, mobility, labor, vocational training, the family, and recreation were included as well as concerns about health, the handicapped, and child growth and development. Each of the

[3] Bremner, pp. 776-777.
[4] Dorothy E. Bradbury, *Five Decades of Action for Children: A History of the Children's Bureau* (Washington, D.C.: U.S. Department of Health, Education and Welfare, Social Security Administration, 1962), p. 12.

first two Conferences had 200 participants; the 1930 Conference assembled "3,000 men and women, leaders in the medical, educational, and social fields as they touch on the life of the child."[5] Although representatives of many local groups concerned with children were included, the reports of pediatricians and educators, and a growing number of presentations by child psychologists, dominated the proceedings.

As our mechanism has become more intricate the need for education and training of the expert . . . becomes more and more evident. If we compare the mother of the past who nursed her own child to the one who must now rely on prepared foods, we find that between the mother and the child we have a whole series of persons and forces upon which the safety of the child depends . . . Beyond babyhood we have substituted another whole series of organized services between the mother and her child and have replaced much of the home training of the child with these activities . . . kindergartens, playgrounds and schools under government or private auspices. . . . We face the absolute necessity of making good in all of this through expert service. It is probably true that it is beyond the capacity of the individual parent to train her child to fit into the intricate, interwoven and interdependent social and economic system we have developed. The gospel of instinct is obsolete.[6]

The tension between the role of experts and natural parents in caring for children was manifested in the Conference's ambiguous outlook toward the family as the primary childrearing institution. President Hoover summed it up in 1930 by saying:

. . . such responsibility as was assumed for children outside the home was in the beginning largely based on what we call charity. We have seen what was once charity change its nature under the broader term welfare and now those activities looked upon as welfare are coming to be viewed merely as good community housekeeping. In a word, parental responsibility is moving outward to include community responsibility.[7]

However, he went on, " . . . we must force the problem back to the spot where the child is. This primarily means, and should mean, the home. Our function should be to help parents, not replace them."[8]

President Hoover thus reaffirmed one of the most sacred institutions of America: the family. In 1909, the conferees stated unequivocally that "Home life is

[5] *White House Conference*, 1930, p. vii.
[6] *White House Conference*, 1930, p. 17.
[7] *White House Conference*, 1930, p. 16.
[8] *White House Conference*, 1930, p. 23.

the highest and finest product of civilization," and that a child should not be deprived of it except for urgent and compelling reasons.[9] Each Conference echoed this sentiment. However, there were subtle differences in tone. The 1930 Conference was more casual about the family; it recognized its limitations and called for extra-familial institutions to supplement parental responsibility. In this period there is less gloomy talk about the demise of the traditional family:

Statistics on marriage, divorce, size of families have been interpreted to indicate disintegration of family life. . . . And all the conditions of production and consumption are tending to remove from the home certain functions formerly considered inherent in family life. On the other hand, evidence equally indicates that the family is not undergoing any fundamental changes. . . . The very fact that it has survived to the present time is an indication that it fulfills deep-seated needs of the human race.[10]

Rather than panic about family stability, the 1930 Conference urged family change through parent education. It said,

An interesting feature of all researches on the family is the resistance of the rural family to change. A recent study has shown them to be disinterested in money matters, antagonistic to change, and staunch in the maintenance of older ideals of family life. . . . The apparent discrepancy between the picture of the stable family presented by rural culture and the poorer adjustment of rural children seems to warrant conjecture that there are aspects of the older family pattern which should be changed.[11]

The Depression formed the backdrop for the 1930 Conference and shaped the tone of the recommendations. Individuals were urged to pitch in and work hard to prevent economic privations from permanently damaging the young. Sensitivity to the needs of children—all children rather than only dependents, the whole child rather than the child with particular handicaps—probably was enhanced by Dewey and the Progressives. Throughout the proceedings, caution was urged against the overuse or misuse of standardized intelligence tests or other statistical means to rank order and single out children.

In 1940, the nation knew that despite its reluctance, it would be drawn inexorably into World War II, and the Conference bore the stamp of that international burden. The proceedings of the White House Conference on Children in a Democracy reads like the kind of propaganda statement we later attributed

[9] *White House Conference*, 1909, p. 5.
[10] *White House Conference*, 1930, p. 134.
[11] *White House Conference*, 1930, p. 137.

to the Soviets. The word "democracy" appears so often it seems trite. Every aspect of child development, health, education, welfare, or family life was tied to patriotism, freedom, democracy, and the American way of life. Infant and maternal mortality had to be eradicated so that a free nation would lead the way in scientific progress. Families should remain stable and the number of children increased so there would be more freedom-loving people on the earth to counterbalance the forces of oppression. Mobilization for war, and the resulting disruption of communities as wives and children moved to be near their men in military bases, became the impetus for remarkable strides in maternal health and community cooperation in planning health and education services. The ideal of cooperation, left over from the New Deal era and revitalized by the sacrifices for the war effort, was invoked in support of the welfare of children as well as the democratic way of life. The Conference's statement of purpose expressed these overriding considerations: "Can a free people by conscious effort rear their children so that their capacities will be developed for cooperative citizen action in exercising their responsibilities of citizenship in a democracy?"[12]

This Conference placed major responsibility for meeting children's needs on a centralized public school system. Rhetoric surrounding the functions of the family was strikingly demystified. The committee report entitled "The Family as the Threshold of Democracy" limits parental responsibilities to basics: "Giving the child food, shelter, and material security is the primary task of the family."[13]

Judging from the Midcentury Conference on Children and Youth, 1950 was a tense and threatening year for Americans. Midcentury was a time for pausing and assessing what had been accomplished, and reflecting on how the future might benefit from past experience. Although the Conference formally recognized this, the majority of its speakers, including the President, were preoccupied with the terrible fear of nuclear obliteration. They could not rouse themselves from their pessimism to plan constructively for the needs of children. Conference participants were transfixed by the atomic bomb and the realization that it could be used by others, the tense cold war, the fear which would soon allow McCarthy to exercise his repressiveness, and mobilization for yet another war, this time in Korea.

A surprising number of clergymen addressed the 1950 Conference. Most reports invoked the name of God to guide the wisdom of the recommendations, to enter

[12] *White House Conference on Children in a Democracy,* 1940, p. 4.
[13] Rochelle Kessler. Unpublished working paper of the Carnegie Council on Children, New Haven, May 2, 1972, p. 7.

into the home and preserve the family, to speak to youths and stop their wanderings, and to watch over the fate of the world. It is as if in a time of crisis the nation as a whole had turned to religion for psychological support. President Truman, in one of the most tentative and qualified opening addresses ever given at a White House Conference, said, "We cannot insulate our children from the uncertainties of the world in which we live or from the impact of the problems' which confront us."[14] The threats to healthy growth and development were articulated in the 1950 Conference more clearly than ever before: the damage to individuals from industrialization ("We live in a machine civilization.... The machine may be a Frankenstein monster.... It threatens men's free spirits. It makes them uniform and conditions them to an automatic response—which is just as tyrants wish."[15]); the damage to communities by urbanization ("We live in an urban civilization with ... low standards of competitive success and the mass anonymity that dwarfs personality. Brick chasms echoing to a lonely tattoo of multitudinous feet."[16]); the multiple dangers of war, the bomb, and communism; and the dissolution of home life ("Our mechanistic, urban and worrying world has wreaked its worst havoc on the home. . . ."[17]). A clergyman summed it up by saying, "In such a world it is strange that any child survives. There must be a special providence watching over fools and children."[18]

Whatever doubts paralyzed the thinking of the Conference, it did move ahead in two important areas: broadening participation generally, and increasing the power of professionals. The membership of previous White House Conferences had been drawn predominantly from professional groups with participation by some leading citizens. The 1950 Conference, however, sought to involve citizens' groups from the beginning. Labor union representatives particularly were asked to help design programs resulting from the Conference's recommendations. At the same time, the 1950 Conference document was the most sophisticated yet in language and in recommendations relying on developmental psychology and social work. Although youth were included for the first time in planning and attending the Conference, the major theme was one of professional wisdom. Dr. Spock talked about the overriding importance of mother love, but recommendations overflowed calling for more research and pointing out the need for increased

[14] *White House Conference,* 1950, p. 52.
[15] *White House Conference,* 1950, p. 53.
[16] *White House Conference,* 1950, p. 53.
[17] *White House Conference,* 1950, p. 54.
[18] *White House Conference,* 1950, p. 55.

professional qualifications and expertise in relating to children. As the number of lay people invited to the Conferences increased, so did the impact of the professionals.

The 1960 White House Conference on Children and Youth reflected the growing alienation of youth which was incipient in 1950. Although a number of important advances had been made during the 1950's in health, psychological research, and education (most notably the formal end to racial segregation), the 1960 Conference was disproportionately concerned with adolescents or "teenagers" in trouble. In 1950, a disturbing number of youths had been showing signs of alienation and uprootedness. A list was presented of groups of adolescents found wandering the country. Called "Children on the Move," it estimated numbers of homeless or dislocated youths, including migrant agricultural workers' children, children in families who move to industrial or construction areas, immigrant children, children of military families, runaways, and transient youth.[19] In 1960, the Conference was set on finding ways to turn these youths' isolation and discontent away from destructiveness and delinquency and toward constructive citizenship. Increase in violent crimes committed by adolescents, the growing culture of gangs, lack of obedience or ambition, and social and political apathy were the foci for most of the presentations at the Conference. Some spokesmen argued that international aggression waged by adults was responsible for breeding interpersonal violence among youths. The tone of the Conference was one of desperate handwringing over juvenile delinquency. National emphasis on youth was also attacked as placing too much pressure on that age group.

In contrast to the 1930 Conference, changes in the family were no longer regarded calmly in 1960, but were seen as dangerous signs heralding the future breakdown of society. A large number of recommendations called for parent education beginning in high school to help young people understand the responsibilities of marriage and the privilege of parenthood. The 1950 Conference had pledged to "work to conserve and improve family life," and called for further study of the underlying causes of broken homes and divorce.[20] In a speech entitled "The Key Role of the Family," a 1960 participant said, "The family occupies a place of centrality in American society; its sovereignty is essential to the child's development which is its basic task. In the fulfillment of this goal, the family has been strengthened and protected by American law and tradition. The

[19] *White House Conference,* 1960, p. 270.
[20] *White House Conference,* 1950, p. 30.

96

family should continue to occupy a key place in our planning for education and health." But, he continued, "The current American attitude toward the family is akin to what happens when a man is hit by a truck—no one dares to touch him for fear of hurting him more. Some pray—and all resolve not to get involved."[21] Involvement was what the Conference recommended, however, with specific motions urging uniform state laws to raise the marriage age to eighteen for females and twenty-one for males, "to strengthen divorce and separation laws, including a mandatory 'cooling off' period with counseling."[22]

The 1970 Conference marked another radical departure from the preceding ones. There were major differences in presentation, language, and emphasis. The report is almost slick in format compared with the routine, staid, research-like documents of the six earlier Conferences; it has modern streamlined printing, categorized and separated by three-color drawings of flowers simulating children's art. Children's essays, poetry, and literature were used along with other kinds of evidence to illustrate points or programs. Children's developmental, health, and educational "needs" were transformed into their "rights," the foundations of which were the same inalienable rights of life, liberty, and the pursuit of happiness guaranteed to every adult citizen. "We conceive of 'rights' as the intrinsic entitlements of every human born or residing in the United States. . . . We must recognize [children's] inherent rights which, although not exclusively those established by law and enforced by the courts, are nonetheless closely related to the law."[23]

The 1960 Conference had some 7,600 participants and in its concern with the problems of adolescents it overlooked concerns of young children. The planners of the 1970 Conference remedied this by proposing two separate conferences: one for children (ages 0–13) and one for youth (ages 14–24). Some 450 pages were devoted to the concerns of the former group. Thus, the care taken in presentation, the forcefulness of the language, and the attention paid to young children reflect the importance of providing for the early years of life.

The chairman of the Conference described the mood of the participants. "Many brought to Washington a deep unease . . . a strong sense of urgency—a feeling that we must act *now* if our society is to flourish."[24] Repeated over again in each of the forums and present in a majority of the recommendations is a demand for

[21] *White House Conference*, 1960, p. 99.
[22] *White House Conference*, 1960, p. 160.
[23] *White House Conference*, 1970, p. 347.
[24] *White House Conference*, 1970, p. 12.

the federal government to reorder national priorities. Perhaps indicating the mood of the participants, standards and statistics were replaced by calls for action and advocacy. Several separate forums came up with the idea of a Federal Office of Child Advocacy to connect with advocates in local communities and ensure that the rights of children were being upheld.

In 1970, two different ways of looking at the family emerged. One, foreshadowed in 1960, assumed that women would seek activities outside the home and that this trend could not be legislated away. In 1960, a resolution "that except for the most urgent reasons, mothers refrain from work outside the home which interferes with the primary parental responsibility of childrearing" was defeated.[25] Instead, the group recommended the establishment of day care centers and other services to aid the working mother. This recommendation was extended in 1970 to emphasize universal comprehensive day care and allied services. On the other hand, income maintenance was seen as another alternative for contributing to family support: " . . . since family stability is essential to observance and demonstration of a healthy value system, we recommend a family assistance plan based upon a family income standard that will assure reasonable economic security."[26] With the conviction that programs for children could not circumvent the family, it was urged that developmental, cognitive, health programs have increasing participation of and concern for the whole family.

Several intriguing ironies emerged as one reads through the proceedings of all the Conferences. First, although each Conference was called specifically to gather information, plan programs, and set priorities for the next decade, every Conference turned out to be more a reflection of the preceding decade than a plan for the future. It is fascinating that no one at the Conferences seemed to realize this. Each opening address begins with a brief summation of the past Conferences and then goes on to say that the present one will digest all this information and lay out a map for the coming decade. Yet each Conference then devotes most of its rhetoric and recommendations to solving dilemmas of the decade before, which often are not the major concerns of the next decade.

A second irony is that each Conference is nostalgic for the good old days. Later Conferences bemoan the complexity of their tasks and long for the "simpler" problems of the first few Conferences. Yet the problem of the first Conferences do not seem simple at all. The participants greatly feared that the old

[25] *White House Conference*, 1960, p. 167.
[26] *White House Conference*, 1970, p. 11.

order was breaking down with a rapidity and callousness that threatened the fabric of society. The 1950's and 1960's saw that television and jet travel were shrinking the world and disrupting communities; yet in the 1940's radio and the automobile were reputed to have had the same effects; and even earlier there are chronicles of a time, before the 1890's, when "... neither the radio nor the phonograph brought the outer world into our precincts..." and before "bicycles came in and flocks of young people wheeled past their elders sitting on the porches...."[27] It is true that later conferences perceived better the relationship between general social reform and child welfare and often were overwhelmed by the complexity of the task. They discussed helping children indirectly by eliminating racial discrimination or by improving their family's economic condition. But problems such as infant mortality were just as knotty in 1909 as they are today.

Related to this inflated nostalgia is the disparity between how Conference participants pictured rural life and what in fact it was. The story goes that America began as an agrarian culture, and the family and other institutions were comfortably matched to that lifestyle. Then wrenching demographic changes upset the ecological balance and caused problems for children's emotional, intellectual, and physical development. Yet Conference after Conference shocks itself with statistics that show farm or rural children in worse condition than city children. Despite the hazards of higher rates of divorce, illegitimacy, industrial accidents, and moral depredation of the cities, a 1930 study of 8,000 school children found that "urban children seem to be better adjusted than rural children."[28] As more people migrated to cities, services for them became more economical and the need for them was more clearly perceived. Services required equally urgently by scattered rural residents were overlooked. Rural life was idealized wistfully even as the poverty, illness, and deprivation there extended beyond that of cities.

Another irony is the distance between recommendation and implementation, between rhetoric and reality. The language which is most hopeful as one reads through Conference reports raises children above the materialistic concern with resources, labor, or specific illness and talks about their needs in comprehensive and developmental terms. The 1930 Children's Charter was such a statement, and it looks remarkably like the 1970 Children's Bill of Rights drawn up by Mary Kohler. These documents stress rights such as parental love and respect for children, a society free from discrimination, equality of educational oppor-

---

[27] Kessler, p. 11.
[a] *White House Conference,* 1930, p. 178.

tunity, elimination of abject poverty, and the freedom to pursue different developmental paths based on individual choice or need. It would be reasonable to expect that these kinds of statements, uttered at a White House Conference by the nation's political and professional leaders, would shift the terms of discussion about children, making them people in their own right. If any such movement has occurred, it has been at a glacial pace. Over the sixty years of Conferences, any recommendations which frontally attack these issues have been tabled or defeated at the administrative or legislative level. For example, the 1930 Conference suggested that the federal government provide subsidies for some states to help them meet their educational expenditures in order to equalize educational opportunity among states. In 1940, this discussion was expanded and it is hard to distinguish it in sophistication and logic from *Private Wealth and Public Education*,[29] the book which in 1970 laid the conceptual groundwork for the *Serrano* case. With the Supreme Court's recent verdict in *Rodriguez*, federal aid to equalize school financing may well be an agenda item again at the 1980 Conference. Only the more prosaic recommendations have made a discernible legislative or bureaucratic impact. Myriad standards for affecting numbers of counselors in schools, student-teacher ratios, minimum physical education requirements, vocational education recommendations, and so on have been made and have found their way into many state departments of education and schools.

The Conferences since 1930 have said they were interested in *all* the nation's children, yet in reality only special needs or special groups have been given adequate attention in proposed programs, appropriations, and research. The state has long had some responsibility for society's dependent children: orphans, illegitimates, handicapped, emotionally disturbed, mentally retarded, physically or morally abused or abandoned. Conference participants have told themselves and the nation that "what the best and wisest parent wants for his own child, that must the community want for all its children."[30] But, until the 1970 Conference, heavy emphasis was placed on providing for children "at risk" or children with special needs.

A final irony, which some would find wholly predictable, is that although discrimination against racial, ethnic, or religious groups has been deplored at all the Conferences, this injunction has had little effect on the differential quality of educational, health, and other social welfare services available to minority

[29] John E. Coons, Williams A. Clune III, and Stephen D. Sugarman, *Private Wealth and Public Education* (Cambridge, Mass.: Harvard University Press, 1970).
[30] Bremner, p. 751.

children. Every Conference has offered recommendations to end discrimination. The sociological and psychological studies reported in 1940 and 1950 on the adverse effects of poverty and segregation for the health, emotional well-being, and educational achievement of minority children contributed to the evidence used in the *Brown* decision in 1954. However, again, movement in this area has been painfully slow despite the overwhelming consensus and proclamations of the White House Conferences.

Reading seven transcripts of White House Conferences—each with more participants, more studies, more recommendations and more pages than the preceding one—could leave the impression that these meetings have had more than symbolic importance. The federal government has been exhorted to establish, to maintain, and to embellish its responsibility for the care of children over the years. And in some crude measure, they have been fruitful. Certainly more federal personnel, programs, and dollars are directed to children now than ever before. But the proceedings also give evidence of several significant barriers to federal intervention.

Ever since the first White House Conference, there have been deep-seated fears about the encroachment by government on the fundamental American values of voluntarism, individualism, family autonomy, and localism. Although the trend has been toward more federal responsibility for greater numbers of children, this trend has not been unopposed. After all, there is a strong tradition of voluntarism in America. In colonial times few formal institutions were needed to cope with dependents or persons in need. The community and the church informally provided for these people. In the late nineteenth century and on into the twentieth, many of the humanitarian agencies established (e.g., the Societies for Prevention of Cruelty to Animals and Children, the settlement houses, foundations, etc.) were private, voluntary agencies which maintained staunch independence from local government in order to set their own standards and policies. Even in the 1930's and 1940's when federal intervention took a quantum leap, the Presidents prevailed upon the population voluntarily to sacrifice and cooperate with the policies which were invoked only because of the magnitude of the crises (and which, it was assumed, would disappear once the economy was healthy or the war was over). As the growth of federal responsibility continues, so the reflex toward voluntarism never entirely abates. When a new menace is encountered, the first response is for private rather than public regulation. As an example, the 1950 and 1960 Conferences acknowledged the potentially dangerous influence of the electronic media on children. But their major recommendations were for network maintenance of good taste, producers' thoughtfulness regarding programming, and, as a last resort, regulation by the Federal Communication Commission, not a particularly powerful influence on the content of the media.[31]

American pride of individualism exerts the same kind of countervailing influence. In 1930, President Hoover gave his views: "In democracy our progress is the sum of the progress of the individuals. . . . Their varied personalities and abilities must be brought fully to bloom; they must not be mentally regimented to a single mold."[32] Similarly, in 1940, in order to safeguard against the homogenizing implications of extensive public education, the Conference maintained, "The supreme educational and social importance of individual traits should be recognized throughout the educational system. An educational system that truly serves a democracy will find no place for the philosophy or the methods of mass production."[33] Federal intervention in the lives of children is to some extent equated with mass production methods. Interestingly, however, the federal government has increased its involvement in the lives of children by using this very romanticization of individualism. In the 1950's and 1960's, the slogan for education was "maximizing individual potential"; in the 1970's it is "individualized instruction." In order to implement these objectives, federal involvement and support has grown steadily.

Belief in the inviolacy of the family also has moderated Conference enthusiasm for federal intervention. The 1930 Conference, while urging unprecedented steps by various levels of government to help needy children, sought to soften the impact of these recommendations by warning, "We want a minimum of national legislation in this field. No one should get the idea that Uncle Sam is going to rock the baby to sleep."[34] In 1950, one participant observed that in America " 'Rugged individualism' is in fact 'rugged family-ism.' "[35]

Perhaps the strongest opposition to large federal provision for children comes from the political forces that protect states' rights and local government. When the Children's Bureau was proposed in 1909, senators and congressmen who considered "general welfare" to be reserved to the states, argued it to be unconstitutional. Although subsequent Conferences have often urged far-reaching comprehensive services or coordination of services, the enabling legislation has usually been defeated (e.g., federal aid to education was first advised in 1930 but not

[31] Kessler, p. 3.
[32] White House Conference, 1930, p. 13.
[33] White House Conference, 1940, p. 365.
[34] White House Conference, 1930, p. 24-25.
[35] White House Conference, 1950, p. 270.

legislated until 1965). It is interesting to note that the thrust for direct federal intervention may be diminishing. The failure of much of the social welfare legislation of the 1960's, funded and managed by the federal government and often deliberately avoiding state authorities, seems to have persuaded some social reformers to try a different plan. The 1970 Conference, while the most comprehensive of all in terms of recommending services, federal expenditures, and potential target groups of children, made an overarching recommendation that the federal government should encourage and support the efforts of state groups involved in the White House Conference process. It urged every state to establish an effective and permanent "assessment of the status of children" commission, jointly funded by federal, state, and local resources, whose major functions would be: a) to develop an accountability mechanism which would enable local communities to measure their needs and progress; and b) to implement those programs and policies which would enhance the status of all children. Thus, along with an increase in federal expenditures, would come decentralization of decision-making to smaller units of government, working closely with the family.

It has been said that the voices of some groups are notoriously missing from their own histories. Obvious examples spring to mind such as blacks, working class people, and immigrants. Children are in an even worse position than other oppressed groups because they are disenfranchised—completely silent legally. Thus the documents dealing with children omit their voices almost entirely. The proceedings of the Conferences read like a history of ideas and programs, with problems seen through the eyes of adults, rather than reports dealing with flesh and blood children. Whatever the intentions of the writers (and most were good-hearted, well-meaning social reformers, child psychologists, pediatricians, and educators), and whatever their real contact with children, their prescriptions for programs, their definitions of needs, their causes for concerns somehow lose the child in the process. In the sweep of seven decades, the image conveyed is one of children, smaller than anyone else, lighter in physical weight and political clout, easily picked up and blown wherever the winds of economic, political, and social movements were heading.

Myths and Realities in the Search for Juvenile Justice: A Statement by The Honorable Justine Wise Polier

HON. JUSTINE WISE POLIER

Children's Defense Fund

The Honorable Justine Wise Polier retired from the bench of New York's Family Court in 1973 to head the Children's Defense Fund's program in juvenile justice, emphasizing the right to care and treatment. She has served as a judge since 1935. During those years, her work led her to become deeply involved in the lives of children in trouble. She has served as founder and president of the Wiltwyck School for Boys, member of the New York State Citizen's Committee for Children, the Mayor's Committee on Foster Care, the Advisory Board of the League School for Seriously Disturbed Children, the Board of the New York School for Nursery Years, the Policy Committee of the Office of Children's Services of the Judicial Conference, and the Judicial Advisory Committee on Crime and Delinquency, among others. Juvenile Justice Confounded *was written under her chairwomanship of the Committee on Mental Health Services in the Family Court. Judge Polier is also the author of books and studies on the law and social welfare including* Everyone's Children, Nobody's Child.

The increase in juvenile delinquency, crimes of violence by juveniles, and the number of school drop-outs has moved citizen groups to seek new ways of correcting or helping youth in large and small communities. With impetus from the 1967 Report of the President's Commission on Law Enforcement and the Administra-

Harvard Educational Review Vol. 44 No. 1 February 1974, 112–124

tion of Justice,[1] and the offer of federal funds, there is now a growing movement away from the position that juvenile courts are the remedy to these problems. Instead, new answers are being sought through systems of youth bureaus or youth service centers.

Grant applications to HEW from many states reveal vast differences in the approaches to reform. Some propose new services, including preventive services, provision for shelters, foster homes, open schools, remedial help, and programs that promise community involvement and new approaches for children with special problems. In others, the aim is largely to coordinate present services and to organize a system of referral to existing agencies. Evaluations of new approaches are meager; it is too soon to predict the results of varying efforts to reduce delinquency, violence, and school drop-outs. However, the combination of citizen concern and the availability of new funds should help to remove some of the ugliest forms of neglect that have made a mockery of juvenile justice since the early part of the twentieth century. Despite the lack of national standards, local citizen groups are examining the juvenile courts and are demanding reforms, like an end to the persistent use of jails and prison-like institutions as depositories for children and youth.

The positive commitment to establish legal rights for children and to secure due process for them in the courts is welcome. At the same time, the drive to divert children or youth from the courts should not be used to avoid many of the hard and unresolved issues in the juvenile justice system. Of major concern is the denial of basic and equal services still omnipresent in America's treatment of its children and youth. To prevent a repetition of the failures of the earlier juvenile court movement, it is important to recognize that the unfulfilled goals of this movement went beyond rescuing children from the criminal courts, from prison, and from the stigma of criminal records. The founders also battled against child labor in mines and factories, against racial prejudice, and for educational, vocational, and recreational opportunities for all children. Unfortunately, in later decades, in addition to being plagued by the shortcomings of those who administered them, the juvenile courts were given too few funds because they were preceived as serving only the poor, the mentally disabled, and the minority groups of America. Such inadequate support has not been unique to the juvenile courts. It has haunted public schools, city hospitals, state institutions, welfare and the criminal

[1] President's Commission on Law Enforcement and the Administration of Justice, Task Force on Juvenile Delinquency, "Task Force Report: Juvenile Delinquency and Youth Crime" (Washington, D.C.: U.S. Government Printing Office, 1967).

courts. Therefore new approaches to delinquency will require changing public attitudes toward those who most need services in this as well as other areas.[2]

To lay the groundwork for the changes in attitudes and social action needed to press for children's rights, it is necessary to confront a series of myths about what we have done and are still doing in the field of juvenile justice. These are myths which have prevented delivering services to children in the past and continue to threaten sound planning by those who are rightly critical of the present system of juvenile justice. The first misconception is that specialized juvenile or family courts function throughout all our states. In fact, among the fifty states, there are generally only specialized courts for children in large metropolitan areas, and even these generally have inadequate probation and clinical services. Beyond such areas one finds courts with fragmented jurisdiction where judges sit occasionally on juvenile cases. Many judges who sit in juvenile matters have no legal training and have no skilled personnel to guide them.

The second myth is that juvenile courts deal primarily with juvenile delinquents or ungovernable children now described as status or non-criminal offenders (PINS or CINS, Persons or Children in Need of Supervision). The fact that these courts hear large numbers of cases concerning children brought before them as abused, abandoned, or neglected is ignored. It is these children who present the most difficult problems and perhaps the greatest challenge for preventive services. Since passage of amendments to the Social Security Act, requiring as a condition of federal funding that there be a judicial determination that continuation of a child in his own home is contrary to his welfare, many thousands of cases previously handled by administrative agencies are now brought before the juvenile courts.[3] In addition, an increasing number of cases involving issues of permanent neglect, adoption, and custody are being presented to these same courts. We are thus witnessing two opposing and inconsistent trends. One directs that more and more juvenile delinquents and status offenders be diverted from the destructive and stigmatizing effects of juvenile court experience. The other leads to a steady increase of dependent and neglected children directed to these same courts, which are under attack and receive little or no staffing to meet new responsibilities.

The third myth, widely proclaimed, is that status offenders are little more than truants or disobedient children whose parents are unwilling to accept responsibility for disciplining them. My experience and the findings of recent study of

[2] See J. Lawrence Schultz, "The Cycle of Juvenile Court History," *Crime and Delinquency*, 19 (October 1973), pp. 457-476.
[3] See, 1967 Amendments Soc. Sec. Act. Title 4A; C.R.F. 45; Sec. 2221.0 (8).

such children by the Office of Children's Services in New York State[4] present a far different picture. Many of these children are likely to pose the most serious problems. Behind the formal parental petition alleging truancy or late hours, we have found that drug abuse, hard drug use, stealing from the home, periods of disappearance, promiscuity, excessive drinking, or gang involvement emerge in many cases. One sees parents at the end of their wits, fearful of what may happen next to their child. One also finds a higher proportion of emotionally disturbed children in need of residential treatment among these children and youth than among those children who have committed a criminal act and who are therefore found to be delinquent.

The assumption that mentally disabled children will be identified by the juvenile court and given special services is a fourth myth. Most juvenile courts do not have the clinical help needed to identify such children. Judges are handicapped not only by the lack of such assistance but by the awareness that the identification of special needs will rarely lead to the necessary services. When youth present behavior problems, in addition to mental disabilities, state hospitals and state schools do everything to avoid their acceptance. Children thus rejected are finally sent to custodial institutions where there are few specialized services. Or, in other cases, they may be transferred to criminal courts on the grounds of the severity of their conduct, their past histories, or the absence of appropriate facilities available to the juvenile courts. In a study of jails in four counties in one state, the Children's Defense Fund found that all of those jails had held mentally retarded children during the preceding twelve-month period.[5] Such statutory escape-hatch provisions as waivers to the criminal courts serve only to remove the pressure for securing adequate services. They make it possible for policy makers to freeze present levels of resources, thus denying quality treatment for juveniles.

Reaction to failures of the juvenile courts has led to some mythical hopes. For instance, simply the removal or change of the label attached to a child is too often projected as a correction for old injustices or the denial of services. Happily, in some instances more is sought than a change of label. Thus, for example, when Massachusetts recently replaced the designation of the "stubborn child" with the "child in need of services" (CHINS), the state's new goals included emphasis on preventive services, the creation of new services, and the acceptance of fiscal re-

[4] See Office of Children's Services, *PINS, A Plethora of Problems* (New York: Judicial Conference of the State of New York, December 1973).

[5] Carl Denny Abbott, "Juveniles in Jail in Alabama." Unpublished study of the counties of Calhoun, Cuffman, Walker, and Tuscaloosa conducted under the auspices of the Children's Defense Fund, Juvenile Justice Project, New York City, August, 1973.

sponsibility for the children, as well as diversion from the juvenile court and a change of label.[6] It is reported that in Ontario, both neglected and incorrigible children are placed in the category of children in need of services, without the requirement that the court find fault against either parent or child.[7] Such legislative changes focus on services that are needed rather than on the label assigned. In themselves, however, they are not sufficient to assure the creation of needed and improved services. They will need to be monitored and will require continuing concern.

Finally, there are some who disagree with the basic premises of the juvenile courts and would reverse these premises. For example, one hears that the juvenile courts may have focused too much on the individual offender and his personality problems, and that the focus should now be shifted to the offense. Unfortunately, those who take this position are unaware that despite the original goals of the juvenile court and much continuing rhetoric, neither care nor treatment has been geared, except in very few cases, to meet individual needs. Where treatment has been tailored to meet such needs, it has usually been restricted to the brighter child for whom treatment promised the likelihood of success.

Regardless of the future form in which juvenile justice may be administered, such myths demonstrate the wide discrepancy between conventional beliefs and the harsh realities for children in need of protective or rehabilitative services. These misconceptions are significant because they have served to obscure understanding of what is needed to protect the rights of children. The prevalence of the myths warns also that the rights of children cannot be regarded as separable from society's duty to make such rights meaningful. It is therefore necessary to examine the constitutional right to due process, the right to privacy, and the right to equal protection, because they figure importantly in the implementation of children's rights.

The Right to Due Process

While the *Gault*[8] decision has been hailed as assuring due process for children, the decision was in fact limited to a hearing on the issue of the delinquency of a child who might, at a dispositional hearing, be subject to a subsequent loss of

[6] Commonwealth of Massachusetts, Chapter 1073, 1973.
[7] Dennis R. Young and Janet Fink, "The Organization of Juvenile Correctional Services." Unpublished study prepared for the Institute for Quantitative Analysis of Social and Economic Policy, University of Toronto, 1973.
[8] *In re Gault*, 387 U.S. 1, 61 (1967).

freedom. Despite this ruling, there are still many courts where children and their parents are not informed of their rights. Within one state, for instance, the right to counsel varied in its implementation from 0 percent in one county to 100 percent in another. In a different state, one judge said he appointed a counsel, told him what he wanted, and if the counsel did not conform, he got other counsel. In a third state, if a counsel selected from a panel "makes waves," he finds he is not called again for a long time. In such instances, counsel rightly is seen as an agent of the court rather than as a representative of the child.[9] Unless the counsel is independent, the right to counsel becomes a mockery.

Gault suggests, but does not define, due process safeguards for neglected, abandoned, abused, or dependent children. Nor does it deal with the most difficult problem area before juvenile courts, namely, the rights of a child at the dispositional hearing. It is at this stage that the presence of counsel has often proven to be of greatest significance. Some states provide by statute for such representation, and it is to be hoped that the Supreme Court will ultimately hold that is is constitutionally required. Moreover, the right to counsel needs to be extended to all children brought before a court whether they be labeled neglected, abandoned, abused, dependent, or runaways so long as the court has power to dispose of their future. Due process and its potential meaning for the rights of children only begins with *Gault*. The language of the opinion of Mr. Justice Fortas challenges the failure of juvenile justice to provide the care and treatment appropriate to help or rehabilitate a child. It warns that more may be required in the future. But the decision does not establish the constitutional rights of a child to appropriate care or treatment under the dispositional order of a juvenile court.

There are still other areas in which the content of due process rights should be given substance. Thus, for instance, where children are committed to foster care by courts or public agencies, there should be judicial review at periodic intervals so that children will not continue to be left in limbo year after year, or left without appropriate care. In New York such review has uncovered many situations where children should be freed for adoption or returned home.[10]

Finally, as part of due process, courts must have the power to compel cooperation from other government agencies. Without such power the court is often for-

[9] Oral report from a Legal Aid attorney in a northeastern state made to the Children's Defense Fund in October, 1973, outlining family court practices in the jurisdiction which is serviced by his agency.

[10] Family Court of the State of New York, City of New York, "Statistical Report for the Quarter, January-March, 1973," Table 7.

ced to dispose of a child wherever there is an empty bed. In New York such statutory power has made it possible for the family court to direct a mental hospital to provide treatment for a mentally ill child.[11] In another case the court directed a public school to readmit rather than transfer a child when impartial evidence established this to be in the child's best interest.[12]

The courts will also have to take a more positive judicial stance by not accepting uncritically whatever level of funding is provided by the legislative or executive branches for staff and facilities without regard to whether they enable fulfillment of statutory obligations. There are some indications of judicial movement in this direction. In Missouri, a family court judge compelled the City Council of St. Louis to re-instate provisions for probation staff after the council summarily reduced the appropriation for the positions in the city's budget.[13] In Pennsylvania, the Appellate Court upheld a decision that where officials neglect or refuse to meet reasonable requirements of a court, they may be forced to do so.[14] In July, 1973, the National Council of Juvenile Court Judges passed a resolution stating that a juvenile court "has the power to, and shall, require other agencies of government to provide the court with the staffing and facilities essential to secure care and treatment appropriate to meeting the needs of each child within its jurisdiction."[15]

The Right to Privacy

The intial promise of the juvenile justice system to protect the privacy of children has not been kept. Erosions of that promise have taken many forms. Juvenile records are included in probation reports at the point of adult sentencing. Records have been shared by the juvenile courts with police departments, the armed services, and with private employers. Even if these records are not shared, the proliferation of questionnaires by public and private employers has begun to coerce individuals to reveal their own past juvenile records.[16] These question-

[11] Unreported decision of Judge Thurston, New York State Family Court, New York County, 1973.

[12] *In re John M., New York Law Journal*, October 9, 1973, page 10, column 2-3. This is the opinion of Judge Jacob T. Zuckerman, New York State Family Court, Kings County.

[13] *State ex rel Weinstein v. St. Louis County*, 451 S.W. 2d 99 (1970).

[14] *Commonwealth ex rel Carrol v. Tate*, 442 Pa. 45, 274 A.2d 193 (1971).

[15] This resolution was adopted by the National Council of Juvenile Court Judges at their annual meeting held in Louisville, Kentucky, in July, 1973.

[16] See Richard A. C. Doe, *Highlights of Activities* (San Francisco: Youth Law Center, July 1972-June 1973), p. 2.

naires include questions about whether the applicant has ever been convicted or arrested, accompanied by threats of prosecution or loss of work if they are not correctly answered. In Mississippi, for example, the law requires that a child's name and the names of his parents be published in the newspaper of the county where the child resides when he is adjudged delinquent for a second time or more.[17]

Such violations of privacy are slight compared to those which affect children and youth who become involved in publicly funded programs within or outside the juvenile courts. A flood of computerized procedures now threaten invasions of privacy in many ways.[18] The exclusion of juvenile delinquents from the Computerized Criminal History Index (CCH) gathered by the National Crime Information Center System (NCIC) under the aegis of the F.B.I. is not extended to children or youths waived or bound over to the criminal courts.[19] Moreover, the federal government has demanded the submission of data on youth to the Client Oriented Data Acquisition Process (CODAP) as a condition for funding of pre-trial drug programs for youths. When challenged in Massachusetts, the federal justification was that the required data provided "individuation," not identification. According to computer experts[20] this is a meaningless distinction. It is also rationalized that persons seeking help in the federally funded programs enter them voluntarily. However, the use of the word "voluntary" has been properly described as misleading when the treatment offered is an alternative to court action, and when there is a procedure for retrieving the youth and taking him to court if he fails to continue in treatment. Questions have also been raised about the use of the word "voluntary" in regard to youths who may not know the full implications of consent to enter such programs.[21]

These examples are but instances of what is now becoming an accepted way of

[17] Mississippi Family Court Act. Title 43. Ch. 23. Sec. 43-23-17. See Mississippi Code of 1972.

[18] Alan F. Westin and Michael A. Baker, *Data Banks in a Free Society* (New York: Quadrangle Books, 1972).

[19] Lawyer's Committee for Civil Rights Under Law, *Law and Disorder III* (Washington, D.C.: Author, 1973), p.44.

[20] Massachusetts showed rare concern for the rights of its citizens when its Governor and the Mayor of Boston refused to submit to a federal demand for data collection as the price of funding pretrial narcotic treatment programs. They did so on the finding by the acting Commissioner of the Massachusetts Department of Mental Health that the program should be rejected on scientific, clinical, and civil libertarian grounds. Public officials were supported in their rejection of federal requirements for data collection by the Massachusetts Advocacy Council.

The Justice Department was reported to have dropped a court action to require Massachusetts to grant the federal agencies access to its criminal information records. See *New York Times*, Sept. 27, 1973.

[21] Massachusetts Advocacy Center, *Treatment Alternatives to Street Crime Juveniles* (Boston: Author, 1973).

accumulating and storing data concerning human beings who receive public or publicly funded services. Violations of the right of privacy have been the subject of Congressional hearings, and a resolution has been introduced to create a Select Committee on Privacy.[22] While questions are being raised in Congress, the federal government continues to extend data collection. In response to federal expectations, state agencies in competition for grants proclaim their willingness or competence in the collection of data, even about children and youth who will be the recipients of programs.

Immunity from being listed in a computerized information system seems largely limited to those who can pay for private services, or those designated as "private." For the comparatively affluent who can secure private services, no data is assembled and the confidential physician-patient relationship is protected despite the tax-deduction benefits to which the patient is entitled or the tax-exemption benefits of the institution which renders the services. Information is now computerized about a person, whether adult or child, receiving welfare services or mental health services in a public hospital or clinic. The extent to which such data will subsequently be made available, and to whom, will depend on the development of public policy and its administration. Apart from the political and professional leaders in Massachusetts, however, there appear to be few administrators, agencies, or government officials who have developed standards to protect the privacy of those whom they claim to serve.

The poor and members of minority groups have traditionally been the recipients of inferior services and violations of their self-respect have been the price of aid. Therefore there is additional reason to be concerned about how data on the poor will be used, not only in determining subsequent court sentences, but also in establishing employment disabilities and in developing histories of individuals that may constitute life-long threats to their privacy. Concern for shielding children and youth from the stigma of labeling through the juvenile court system must involve firm resistance to the collection of data that can haunt the future of a child. The widespread denial of the right to privacy for troubled and troubling youth, whether because of courts or diversion programs, must be considered by all concerned with juvenile justice. In the words of Sheldon Messinger:

... current emphasis on 'diversion,' which I expect to continue, points in some part to a contrary trend, one that frees the police and others to channel the lives of persons with-

[22] See Congressional Record-House of Representatives, December 14, 1973. It contains a statement by Congressman Harrington (Mass.) as co-sponsor of Resolution 633 to create a Select Committee on Privacy, and statements of other Congressmen in support of the Resolution (H11471-11480).

out sufficient check on the strength of their grounds for assuming this power. By the year 2000, I expect we shall be very much concerned with this matter having discovered, once again, that in the name of humanity and reformation we have increased the power of the agents of criminal justice over our lives.[23]

The Right to Equal Protection

Unequal and inferior services, and the denial of services to children from minority groups, have shadowed every aspect of child care and juvenile justice. The absence of equal protection has taken many forms and continues to prevail within both governmental and voluntary agencies. The present trend to divert children from public institutions by the purchase of services from voluntary agencies has not corrected discrimination against minority group children. Thus, after studying youth services in one community, the John Howard Association found that "most youth diagnosed are white, most youth committed to training schools are black; most youths in purchase of care services in the community are white and delinquent; most CINS cases are white and the majority of CINS youths are actually delinquent."[24] Unfortunately, these findings could be replicated in one area after another. They reflect the basic denial of appropriate services, not only to black or other minority group children but to poor children and to mentally disabled children as well.

Traditional reliance by the states on voluntary agencies to provide care for dependent or neglected children has permitted exclusion or denial of services to children on the basis of race or religion. Such discrimination, whether practiced by agencies licensed by the state or by agencies from whom services are purchased, is at last being challenged in the federal courts. In Alabama, a current action challenges the exclusion of black dependent and neglected children by sectarian group homes licensed by the state, and also challenges the state's failure to develop alternative public services.[25] In Illinois, cases have been brought to contest the right of the state to transfer dependent children who are wards of the state to state hospitals or state schools without a hearing and counsel.[26] In the Illinois

[23] Sheldon L. Messinger, *The Year 2000 and the Problem of Criminal Justice.* Paper prepared for the Conference on Criminal Justice of The Center for Study of Democratic Institutions and The Center for Studies in Criminal Justice (Santa Barbara, Calif.: June, 1973).
[24] John Howard Association (Chicago), "Comprehensive Long Range Master Plan Department of Juvenile Services State of Maryland, Summary Report." Unpublished report, June 1, 1972.
[25] *Player v. Alabama,* Civ. Act. No. 3835 (DCMD Ala., 1972).
[26] *In re Lee et al.,* Civ. Act. Nos. 68 J (D) 1362; 66 J (D) 6383; 68 J 15805 (Cir. Ct. Cook County, Illinois, 1972).

cases it is alleged that the statutory prohibition against public services, which results in total reliance on the discretion of voluntary agencies, has led to discrimination against black children and children who most need services. In New York, there are statutory prohibitions against developing direct services for children in need of foster care, unless the Commissioners of Public Welfare can demonstrate to the State Board of Social Welfare that needed services are not available through an authorized agency under the control of persons of the same religious faith as the child.[27] A federal action now pending in New York also challenges the constitutionality of state statutes requiring religious matching of children with agencies controlled by persons of the same faith, and the consequent lack of equal opportunity for black Protestant children to enter agencies which provide better treatment services.[28]

Law in this field is slowly being developed, case by case, in the federal courts. Hopefully, it will establish positive standards of equal protection for care and treatment, regardless of whether the services are provided directly or through purchase from private agencies by the government.

New Directions

As previously mentioned, the 1967 Report of the President's Commission on Law Enforcement and the Administration of Justice,[29] together with growing concern about juvenile delinquency and crime, have stimulated greater concern for children and increased governmental support for new efforts. Public law firms have challenged established institutions, including the courts. Significant new concepts of juvenile justice demand services for children in their own homes or in community-based facilities. Criticism of custodial care has been translated into programs to remove children from the destructive effects of cold, hard, punishing, and uncaring institutions. Great emphasis has been placed on "decriminalizing justice procedures and doing away with labels. Efforts are being expanded to secure constitutional protections against cruel and unusual punishment or the denial of equal protection. Among voluntary agencies, governmental agencies, and citizen groups one finds increased interest in correcting old abuses and a greater will-

---

[27] N. Y. Social Welfare Law, Art. 6, Secs. 374 (b), 398.6 (g).
[28] *Wilder v. Sugarman*, 73 Civ. 2644 (DCSDNY, 1973).
[29] See President's Commission on Law Enforcement and the Administration of Justice, "Commission Report: The Challenge of Crime in a Free Society" (Washington, D.C.: U.S. Government Printing Office, 1967), especially Ch. 3.

ingness to meet the recognized needs of children. Yet when the hope born of these factors is measured against what needs to be done, there is no reason for complacency.

If not carefully monitored, new concepts, like old ones, are subject to opposition, abuse, and insufficient support. Thus, we find the concept of the local catchment areas for mental health services misapplied to exclude persons with no alternative services available. We find state hospitals and state schools for the retarded, under the lash of public criticism about their size, remoteness, and lack of services, responding by closing their intake procedures or discharging patients prematurely before providing alternative services. We find the "right to treatment" concept interpreted to exclude children from whatever facilities are available and to justify condemning them by transfer or waiver to the criminal courts on the rationalization that the juvenile court does not have services appropriate to meet their needs. In an effort to avoid placement of neglected children by the courts and to ease the courts' burdens, discharging children to public welfare agencies is approved despite the low community image of welfare and its lack of services. Incorrigibles are also being added to welfare responsibilities in some states.

Unquestioning support is granted for projects describing themselves as community-based or as youth service bureaus without careful examination of the quantity or quality of services rendered in group homes or half-way houses, or examination of whom they accept or exclude. There is a euphoric faith in the purchase of services from voluntary agencies that continues to screen out those most in need and discriminate against children on the basis of race or religion. When the promise of community services results in lost children, and there is a failure to plan adequately for children who are a danger to themselves or others, communities become angry and take repressive measures against the children who have been denied appropriate services. Such measures may include the increased use of secure detention, increased waivers to the criminal courts, a higher percentage of commitments rather than the use of probation, and even a return to the use of remote and prison-like custodial institutions. These may be inevitable difficulties of a transitional period, but they will be surmounted only if those responsible for new programs remain vigilant and honest about what they can and cannot do. This in turn requires persistent fact-finding about unmet needs. New facts must be given a voice if new concepts are to be translated into meaningful change.

Within our society there is one other great threat to the development of meaningful services to children. Our ethos or system of rewards is such that, in the words of Dr. Paul Lemkau, "the farther away a person gets from working directly with the people he is supposed to serve, the higher his salary becomes."[30] We find teachers who do not wish to teach, physicians who do not wish to heal, social workers who do not wish to leave their offices. It is therefore troubling to find reflections of such values in the literature concerning the youth service bureaus. It has been urged that they should plan, coordinate, make referrals, but limit direct services[31] to those given on an experimental or temporary basis. They are even warned "not to get bogged down in service." Hopefully, we will not encourage the further development of a new management class that sees itself as superior because it docs not render or become too involved in rendering services that are desperately needed.

Finally, in choosing to purchase services, whether as supplementary to or in lieu of public direct services, the makers of policy will have to decide how far they can or should delegate public responsibility for the provision of services. To fulfill their final accountability for meeting service needs, they will have to decide what responsibilities should remain in the public sector for planning and monitoring. They will also have to decide to what extent public services must be maintained as primary facilities, as back-ups to private facilities, or as demonstration pace-setters or yardsticks. Policy-makers must understand that neither crisis situations nor the expediency of the moment can warrant abdication of basic public responsibility for the welfare of all children.

[30] Unpublished letter from Dr. Paul V. Lemkau, The Johns Hopkins University School of Hygiene and Public Health, Baltimore, Maryland, December 12, 1973.
[31] See Sherwood Norman, *The Youth Service Bureau* (Hackensack, N. J.: National Council on Crime and Delinquency, 1972), p. 96.

Radical Correctional Reform: A Case Study of the Massachusetts Youth Correctional System*

LLOYD E. OHLIN
ROBERT B. COATES
ALDEN D. MILLER
Harvard University

The authors raise three principal questions. First, what part should traditional training schools play in providing treatment for youthful offenders? Second, what is the relative effectiveness of community based in comparison to institutional treatment services for juvenile delinquents? Third, what problems arise in undertaking a radical change in policy and program from institution to community based services? To answer these questions, the Center for Criminal Justice at the Harvard Law School is evaluating the reforms undertaken by the Massachusetts Department of Youth Services since 1969. This article offers a preliminary report

*Prepared under grants from the National Institute of Law Enforcement and Criminal Justice, Law Enforcement Assistance Administration, Department of Justice, and from the Massachusetts Governor's Committee on Law Enforcement and Administration of Criminal Justice. Points of view or opinions stated in this document are those of the authors and do not necessarily represent the official positions or policies of the funding agencies.

The authors wish to express appreciation to John Albach, Judy Caldwell, Barry Feld, Robert Fitzgerald, David Garwood, Paula Garwood, Alan Johnson, Arlette Klein, Cliff Robinson, Barbara Stolz, Arthur Swann, Christian Teichgraeber, Ann Yates, Alma Young for their work in collecting data for the project on which this article is based.

Harvard Educational Review Vol. 44 No. 1 February 1974, 74–111

and description of the problems and progress of these reforms through three phases: the emergence of a mandate for reform, the reform of institutional treatment, and the move from institutions to community corrections. Interviews with staff and youth so far indicate a positive response of youth to the new programs.

The most fundamental assumptions in the field of youth corrections are under attack. The Massachusetts Department of Youth Services has become the most visible national symbol of a new philosophy of corrections through its repudiation of the public training school approach and its advocacy of therapeutic communities and alternative community-based services.

The radical symbolism of the Massachusetts reforms is heightened by the fact that the first public training school for boys in the United States was established at Westboro, Massachusetts, in 1846, and the first public training school for girls at Lancaster, Massachusetts, in 1854. Since then the public training school has become the last resort for dealing with delinquent youth, though a small number may face adult criminal court and confinement in adult prisons.

A key organizing principle of traditional training schools is punishment. There are efforts at vocational and general education in the training schools, but the institutions are basically custodial and authoritarian. Resocialization efforts are commonly reduced to instruments for creating conformity, deference to adult authority, and obedience to rules. Regimented marching formations, shaved heads and close haircuts, omnipresent officials, and punitive disciplinary measures have been the authoritative marks of the training school, along with the manipulation of privileges, such as cigarette smoking, T.V. watching, home visits, or release to reward compliance.

Criticism of the traditional training school comes from three major sources. For many years the documentation of high rates of recidivism among training school graduates has created pressure for new solutions. For example, the pioneering studies of Sheldon and Eleanor Glueck offered painstakingly assembled evidence of the high rates of arrest and conviction of new offenses among those exposed to training school experiences.[1] The classical studies by Shaw and McKay in the Chicago area project and the Illinois Institute of Juvenile Research documented the role of traditional training schools as agencies for socializing young people into adult criminal careers.[2] They showed how exposure to these institu-

---

[1] Sheldon Glueck and Eleanor Glueck, *Criminal Careers in Retrospect* (New York: Commonwealth Fund, 1943).

[2] Clifford R. Shaw, *The Jack Roller, A Delinquent Boy's Own Story* (Chicago: University of Chi-

tions labeled young people as "delinquent" or "criminal," and how family, school, neighborhood, job market, and criminal justice agencies reinforced the stigma, resulting in high rates of recidivism.[3] These early studies have been supported by more recent work.[4]

A second source of criticism comes from the development of new ideologies of treatment in the human services. These approaches argue that individual and group counseling and therapy will lead to personal insight and better social adjustment. They urge that the problems of youth offenders be considered in the context of family and communal relations where preparation for law-abiding adulthood ordinarily occurs.[5] This search for community based treatment resources has derived support from research studies that document the pervasiveness of delinquent conduct throughout all social classes.[6] These studies have underscored the bias involved in employing public training schools as a principal means of control and treatment for primarily lower class offenders.[7] Practitioners have accordingly begun to stress the efficacy of benign non-intervention, diversion to non-criminal justice treatment programs, or privately purchased services for the poor as more constructive and less stigmatizing solutions to the authority problems of lower class youthful offenders, and more nearly equivalent to solutions employed extensively in the middle class for similar problems.[8]

A third major source of challenge to the traditional training school has come from those concerned with protecting the civil rights of children. The U.S. Su-

---

cago Press, 1930); Clifford R. Shaw et al., Social Factors in Juvenile Delinquency, A Study for the National Commission on Law Observance and Enforcement, Vol. 2, No. 13 (Washington, D. C.: U. S. Government Printing Office, 1931).

[3] Henry D. McKay, "Report on the Criminal Careers of Male Delinquents in Chicago," in President's Commission on Law Enforcement and Administration of Justice, Task Force on Juvenile Delinquency Report: Juvenile Delinquency and Youth Crime (Washington, D.C.: U. S. Government Printing Office, 1967).

[4] Paul Lerman, "Evaluative Studies of Institutions for Delinquents: Implications for Research and Social Policy," Social Work, 13 (July 1968), 55–64.

[5] President's Commission on Law Enforcement and Administration of Justice, Task Force on Juvenile Delinquency, Report, Ch. 2.

[6] James F. Short, Jr., and F. Ivan Nye, "Extent of Unrecorded Delinquency, Tentative Conclusions," Journal of Criminal Law, Criminology and Police Science, 49 (November-December 1958), pp. 296–302; Ronald L. Akers, "Socio-Economic Status and Delinquent Behavior: A Retest," Journal of Research in Crime and Delinquency, 1 (January 1964), pp. 38–46.

[7] President's Commission on Law Enforcement and Administration of Criminal Justice, Task Force on Juvenile Delinquency Report: Juvenile Delinquency and Youth Crime (Washington, D.C.: U.S. Government Printing Office, 1967).

[8] Elizabeth Vorenberg and James Vorenberg, "Early Diversion from the Criminal Justice System: Practice in Search of a Theory," in Lloyd E. Ohlin, ed., Prisoners in America (Englewood Cliffs, N. J.: Prentice-Hall, 1973).

preme Court decision *in re Gault* in 1967 stimulated test cases exploring the constitutionally protected rights of children.[9] These cases are beginning to focus on what due process means for children and to raise issues relating to a "right to treatment" as well as a "right to be let alone."[10] They have called greater attention to whether treatment programs adequately take account of the best interests of the child. Given this new critical exploration of the rights of children, it is understandable that the concepts and practices of the traditional training school have come under increasing attack.

These challenges to training schools have posed problems for Massachusetts and many other states. What new system of services or intervention criteria should replace the existing system? How is it possible to change the system into one which relies primarily on community based treatment? What programs should be created? How should resources be re-allocated, staff developed, and appropriate distributions of private and public responsibilities for service be arranged? Finally, how can we be sure that the new system produces better results than the one it supplants?

The response in Massachusetts to these questions is discussed in the following account. It draws freely on a variety of evaluation studies of the Massachusetts Department of Youth Services conducted by the Center for Criminal Justice at the Harvard Law School over the past three and one half years.[11] It is a preliminary report. A final appraisal must await more complete analysis, but the widespread interest in the Massachusetts experiment justifies at this time a review of the reform effort and some of the problems it encountered.

Phase I: Emergence of a Mandate for Reform

A series of crises in youth correctional services in Massachusetts culminated in March, 1969, with the resignation of the Director of Youth Services and prepared

[9] Sanford J. Fox, *Cases and Materials on Modern Juvenile Justice* (St. Paul, Minn.: West Publishing, 1972).

[10] Ted Rubin, *Law as an Agent of Delinquency Prevention* (Washington, D.C.: U.S. Department of Health, Education and Welfare, Social and Rehabilitation Service, Youth Development and Delinquency Prevention Administration, 1971).

[11] We will not attempt to describe here the nature of these studies or the methodology employed. For those wishing a more complete account of the methodology, copies of a descriptive statement entitled "Evaluation of the Effects of Alternatives to Incarceration of Juvenile Offenders," unpublished document dated August, 1973, are available from the National Institute on Law Enforcement and Administration of Justice, Law Enforcement Assistance Administration U.S. Department of Justice, Washington, D.C.

the way for reform. Prior to 1948 Massachusetts judges committed children directly to individual institutions for the care of delinquent boys and girls. New legislation in 1948 and 1952 created a Youth Service Board and a Division of Youth Services (DYS) nominally within the Department of Education but administratively autonomous. The Youth Service Board, whose chairman was also director of DYS, made decisions concerning the placement of youth within the institutions, their transfer, parole, and discharge.

The Director from 1952 to 1969, Dr. John D. Coughlin, was an articulate and vigorous advocate of the philosophy of youth training schools. Over these years the rhetoric of rehabilitation and conspicuous successes in such programs as the forestry camp and other helpful enterprises obscured the basically custodial and authoritarian grounding of this system. The available results of earlier studies are fragmentary but the rates of recidivism varied from 40 to 70 percent depending upon the age group, length of follow-up, and criteria of recidivism employed.[12] At the time of Coughlin's resignation in 1969 the DYS included a unit for delinquency prevention, an office for the supervision of parole for boys and one for girls, and ten institutions including four detention and reception centers, a forestry camp, a school for pre-adolescent boys at Oakdale, a school for younger male adolescents at Lyman, an industrial school for older boys at Shirley, the Institution for Juvenile Guidance for troublesome and emotionally disturbed boys at Bridgewater, and an industrial school for girls at Lancaster.

From 1965 to 1968 the DYS was the subject of six major critical studies. The initial investigations were stimulated by reports of brutal and punitive treatment of youth at the Institution for Juvenile Guidance at Bridgewater. The publicity attending these charges led Governor John A. Volpe to request a study and recommendations from technical experts in the Children's Bureau of the U.S. Department of Health, Education and Welfare.

The HEW study found many deficiencies in the Massachusetts system.[13] It pointed to the dominance of custodial goals and practices over those of treatment, the lack of effective centralized supervision and direction of child care, the absence of an adequate diagnostic and classification system, the failure to develop flexible and professional personnel practices, and the ineffectiveness of parole supervision. These findings were confirmed by a blue ribbon committee of local

[12] Estimates provided in interviews with DYS officials and former DYS officials.
[13] U.S. Department of Health, Education and Welfare, Welfare Administration, Children's Bureau, "A Study of the Division of Youth Service and Youth Service Board, Commonwealth of Massachusetts" (Washington, D.C.: U.S. Government Printing Office, 1966).

experts appointed by Governor Volpe in 1967 under the sponsorship of Dr. Martha Elliot, Chairman of the Massachusetts Committee on Children and Youth and former Director of the Children's Bureau in HEW. The criticisms developed in these studies and their recommendations were supported by further investigations initiated by the Attorney General and by Senate Committees. These investigations crystalized the formation of a coalition of civic and professional groups in support of major reforms. Periodic crises in the DYS became increasingly the focus of newspaper attention and mobilized a critical audience in the general public.[14]

The liberal coalition led by the Massachusetts Committee on Children and Youth introduced reform legislation in 1968, but passage was deferred until the following year. In the interim a new major crisis developed at the Institute for Juvenile Guidance at Bridgewater. Staff factions developed within the institution around clinical as opposed to punitive treatment of youth behavior problems and this conflict was documented in the public press. A local community group, the Committee for Youth in Trouble, organized to support the clinical services faction. It joined with the Massachusetts Committee on Children and Youth to broaden the attack on the goals and policies of the DYS and the ability of the Director and his staff to administer an effective treatment program.[15]

In January, 1969, Governor Francis Sargent was inaugurated to complete the unexpired term of Governor Volpe. Governor Sargent expressed his strong support for the reform legislation. He secured the resignation of the Director, appointed an interim Director and a blue ribbon committee to undertake a national search for a new commissioner, signed into law new legislation reorganizing the DYS in September, 1969, and appointed Dr. Jerome Miller as Commissioner of the reorganized Department of Youth Services in October, 1969, on the recommendation of the search committee.

Commissioner Miller took charge of the new Department with a mandate from the legislative and executive branches of the state government and the liberal reform groups to initiate more progressive policies and treatment of delinquent youth. Though some specific recommendations for change in the goals of the Department had been proposed in the earlier investigations, primarily

[14] The exploitation of crises for the formation of coalitions of criticism and defense of public agencies in the process of reform is described more fully in Lloyd E. Ohlin, "Organizational Reform in Correctional Agencies" in Daniel Glaser, ed., *A Handbook on Criminology* (New York: Rand McNally, 1974).

[15] For a more detailed statement of these events see Yitzhak Bakal, ed., *Closing Correctional Institutions* (Lexington, Mass.: D. C. Heath, 1973), pp. 151–180.

in the direction of more effective clinical and diagnostic services and community supervision, the mandate was in the main broad and undefined.

Phase II: Reforming Institutional Treatment

Commissioner Miller had earned his doctoral degree in social work while in military service, and subsequently had organized a new institution for the disturbed or delinquent children of American Air Force personnel in England. For a brief period following his service discharge he served as training officer in the Department of Youth Corrections in Maryland. He then taught in the School of Social Work at Ohio State University where he helped develop training and treatment programs in both the juvenile and adult correctional services in Ohio.

The search committee was especially impressed with Miller's deep concern for youth in trouble and his sense of urgency, as well as confidence, that better ways could be developed to help them. He expressed special attraction to a post as commissioner where a commitment to reform had already been made. He thought that the effectiveness of institutional services for youth could be greatly increased by applying the treatment principles developed in therapeutic communities for adults by Maxwell Jones in England and Scotland.[16] These strengths overcame the search committee's two major reservations about Miller's administrative and political competence. First, his professional career had not tested his capacity to administer a human service agency of this size and scope. Second, he had not had experience dealing with the political considerations that deeply penetrate the organization and operation of state bureaus in Massachusetts.

During the first two years of his administration, Miller sought to humanize services for delinquent children, and to build a more therapeutic climate within the institutions. Throughout this period his efforts were severely hampered by financial and personnel constraints. First, it was almost a year before he obtained appropriations to staff the new positions and services authorized by the reform legislation. Appropriations were still allocated within the line budget of the DYS to particular institutions, staff positions, and services. To reallocate funds was a very cumbersome and lengthy process that wound its way through the state Administration and Finance Office and the legislative appropriations committee. Second, the rigidity of the civil service system made it virtually impossible to transfer personnel between institutions and services except on a voluntary basis.

---

[16] Maxwell Jones *et al., The Therapeutic Community* (New York: Basic Books, 1953).

Massachusetts personnel practices mix political patronage with civil service procedures for recruiting and protecting employees in the positions to which they are certified. With few staff vacancies and without new or transferable funds the prospects of effecting major reforms during the first year appeared remote indeed. Even with additional funds during the second year the pervasive wait-and-see attitude of entrenched staff promised little change. The challenge confronting Miller was to mobilize and release energy for change.

Articulation of Goals

Shortly after his appointment the new Commissioner began to define the goals of his administration. He stated to the staff, the press, and civic, professional, and religious groups that he intended to humanize the treatment of offenders and to build therapeutic communities within existing institutional facilities. This model of treatment would require a democratic relationship between staff and youth in small units. A social climate had to be created in which both staff and youth were encouraged to express their feelings and concerns freely and honestly. Decisions relating to housekeeping problems, discipline, privileges, home visits, and release were to be made openly in cottage meetings after full discussion.

This treatment model challenged the basic features of the traditional training school system. Little change could be expected until the differences in philosophy, goals, staff and youth roles, and the processes of decision-making could be dramatized, justified, and enforced.

One of the first directives, issued by the new Commissioner in November, 1969, ordered that henceforth youth in the institutions would be allowed to wear their hair as they chose. The "haircut edict" raised a storm of protest and cries of permissiveness among staff long accustomed to shaving boys' heads on admission, regulating length, and using haircuts as punishment. It is doubtful that Miller fully recognized at first the sensitivity of this issue. In the emerging youth style of the times, thirty-eight-year-old Miller wore his own hair longer than most state officials. Hair style and length were hotly contested in many families, schools, and business establishments as a visible symbol of youth revolt against adult regulations. Miller vigorously defended the edict to dramatize the new administration's desire to accord committed youth greater freedom and shrugged off derogatory staff references to the "hippy commissioner." The resonance of this issue with a large number of moral issues relating to authority, allocation of discretion, responsibility, initiative, and self-expression gave the directive a symbolic value of great importance. It clearly cast Miller as a youth advocate in opposition to traditional expectations and established the basic issues and roles of future dramas.

As the protest simmered down, other directives followed. It was ordered that youth should be allowed to wear their own street clothes rather than institutional garments. The practice of marching in silent formation from one activity to another was discontinued. Staff protested: greater freedom of movement made running away easier and street clothes made committed youth more difficult to identify if they had run away. The edicts signified to staff that custodial concerns would increasingly be subordinated to treatment objectives.

Miller became convinced that he could not successfully establish the therapeutic community model until he had removed the basic supports of the traditional system. He looked especially to the fear of greater punishment, deprivation, or personal degradation that constituted the keystone of the authority system throughout the institutions. He immediately turned, then, to the Institute for Juvenile Guidance at Bridgewater and Cottage #9 at Shirley, reserved for those youngsters seen as most disturbed or rebellious. These institutions represented the final sanctions in a graduated set of possible control measures to induce conformity by restrictions on freedom of movement, denial of privileges, physical abuse, enforced idleness, silence, and gestures of deference toward adult authorities. Miller initiated measures to humanize both sites. A general order forbade any staff member to strike or physically abuse youth. Other directives tried to eliminate the stultifying routines of enforced idleness and silence in the punishment units and the use of strip cells and other measures of extreme isolation. An effort was made to introduce more constructive activities. Greater controls were imposed on screening and assignment to these units and the duration of stay. Frequent, unannounced inspection visits were used to discourage evasions of the new directives. Even these measures did not seem sufficient. By mid-summer of 1970 the Commissioner had paroled or transferred the youth committed to Bridgewater and he then closed the Institution. Cottage #9 at Shirley remained in some measure a symbol of the old system until in the winter of 1971-72 it, too, was closed.

The difficulty the Commissioner encountered in changing procedures in these facilities testified to the tenacity of the principles of punishment and enforced adult authority. Cottage and program staff over the years had come to accept them as indispensable to preserving order and inducing conformity. Other methods of establishing adult authority through superior knowledge, mutual trust and respect, admiration, emulation, and affection were also occasionally evident.

The new administration sought to encourage these more difficult and demanding forms of authority relationships with youth. However, to achieve this, they felt convenient resort to traditional punishment measures had to be removed or made much more difficult.

The new administration took other steps to alter the control system. For example, a new directive authorized youth eligible to smoke to carry their own cigarettes. Previously, youth surrendered their cigarettes to staff members who issued them as a reward for doing chores or withheld them as punishment. Doling out cigarettes or denying access to them constituted for staff a simple but very useful control measure for enforcing authority. Like the "haircut edict," the "cigarette edict" both dramatized a change in goals and altered control alternatives available to staff.

All of these administrative actions led to strong protests by line staff members to institution superintendents and friends in the legislature. For a time resistant staff members or their friends appeared regularly when Miller gave speeches to community groups to raise questions about the loss of control and the threat of mass runaways to local communities. To the extent that staff capacity to control youth relied on these traditional control measures, their complaints were indeed justified. It was not clear when these directives were issued whether the administration could retrain staff in the uses of authority.

New Treatment Programs and Policies

The new administration sought to demonstrate the value and feasibility of new models of treatment. As funds became available staff was recruited and assigned to the newly created bureaus of institutions, education, clinical services, and aftercare. Assistant commissioners were appointed to direct each of the four bureaus. By the end of Miller's first year, his central office staff exercised a more definitive role in the development of programs to implement the new philosophy of treatment. Despite the hostility of conservative staff members, many youth and especially younger professional staff members expressed a desire to experiment with a therapeutic community model. However, no one except Miller seemed to know how such a treatment program should be operated and what it would require of staff and youth.

To help answer some of these questions the Commissioner persuaded Dr. Maxwell Jones, whose methods he had observed in England, to lead a three-day conference of staff and youth at the Shirley Institution. Jones explained the principles of a therapeutic community and directed a series of demonstrations involving youth and staff. The demonstration groups created an open climate for staff and youth to express feelings and concerns and to direct them toward constructive ends. Jones' personal skill and warmth during these demonstrations drew applause from most staff and youth, but it was clear that for many staff members the shift from traditional staff roles would not only be very difficult and slow but in many cases impossible to achieve.

The conference, however, reinforced the new policy of decentralization at Shirley so that not only cottage life experiences but also educational, vocational, and other forms of counseling or therapy would be self-contained within each cottage unit. The pressure from the new Boston Office administrators to adopt the new group treatment policies spread from Shirley to Lyman and Lancaster during the next year and a half, reinforced by dramatic changes in staff assignments, described below. Many cottages continued to operate in the traditional manner, but others experimented, sometimes with remarkable success, in establishing a therapeutic community.

In the summer and fall of 1971 the Center for Criminal Justice at Harvard University conducted studies in cottages at Shirley, Lyman, Lancaster, and Topsfield. These studies compared the attitudes of staff and youth in traditional cottages to those trying the therapeutic model. Table 1 shows differences in youth reactions to the social climate of experimental and traditional cottages just prior to the closing of the major institutions in the late fall of 1971 and early 1972. These, and results of related studies, demonstrate consistently that decentralized cottage treatment and group therapy could lead to remarkably better reactions and experiences even for youth within the same institution. The reactions of the youth reveal significant differences between the therapeutic community and the traditional custodial model. The idea of the therapeutic community is to restructure the authority system of the cottage, with youth taking new responsibilities for decisions affecting themselves and each other, on matters ranging from privileges in the cottage to home visits and ultimately release on parole. It seeks to cultivate a sense of group cohesiveness to offset the usual tendency for the cottage to splinter into "tough," "punk," "good kid" and staff cliques that achieve control by allowing the toughest youth to dominate the others.

Several attempts were made to create programs for girls and boys in the same institution and even the same cottage. The first such program set up a cottage for girls transferred from Lancaster to the Lyman School for Boys. A cottage was also created at Lancaster for young boys from Oakdale for whom home placements were difficult to find. This made it possible to train older girls in the care

TABLE 1
Youth Response to Social Climate Items in Experimental and Traditional Cottages.

Social Climate Item*	Cottage Type	
	Experimental (Percent)	Traditional (Percent)
If the kids really want to, they can share in decisions about how this cottage is run.	94	85
Kids in the cottage will help a new kid get along.	91	65
Kids in this cottage usually tell someone when they think he's done something wrong.	89	77
I feel very much that I fit here.	82	52
The cottage staff deals fairly and squarely with everyone	80	57
If a kid messes up, the staff will punish her/him.	66	81
Most kids here are just interested in doing their time.	65	81
If a kid does well, other kids will tell him so personally.	61	34
Other kids will reward a kid for good behavior.	60	37
Other kids here give you a bad name if you insist on being different.	38	61
The kids in this cottage have their own set of rules on how to behave that are different from those of the staff.	36	57
There are a few kids here who run everything.	35	59
There are too many kids here who push other kids around.	33	62
This cottage is more concerned with keeping kids under control than with helping them with their problems.	30	61
Real friends are hard to find in this cottage.	25	44
This cottage is pretty much split into two different groups, with staff in one and kids in the other.	19	55

*The items in this table differentiate between the Experimental and Traditional cottages more strongly than one would expect to be the case by chance at the .05 level. In the Experimental cottages, the number of youth responding to each question varies from 85–89; and in the Traditional cottages, from 82–86.

and management of younger children. After a serious fire at the girls detention and reception center in Boston, girls were housed in the same building as boys in Boston and later at a new detention and reception cottage for girls at Lyman. Coed cottages were established on the grounds of the Shirley Institution and later at Lancaster and Topsfield. It was expected that if boys and girls shared the same institution or the same cottage, their demeanor, grooming, speech, and conduct would improve. Stereotypic sex role beliefs and attitudes on the part of both boys and girls might be changed. Comparative data on youth reactions in coed and non-coed settings are not yet available but staff reports suggest that many of these expectations were realized and a high level of staff acceptance emerged despite initial fears of sexual promiscuity and lack of discipline.

When Miller came into office the average length of stay for youth in the institutions was eight months. Since he had become convinced that the traditional training school programs ordinarily did more harm than good, he began to encourage a more rapid turnover. By the end of the first year, the more liberal parole policies had begun to create tension with the courts, probation, and police departments in a number of communities, especially urban ones. Many staff members in these agencies felt that confinement for less than nine months was too short to realize the benefits of reeducation or community protection for which commitment had been ordered. To deal with these concerns, while the new treatment programs were being developed, the Commissioner ordered that committed youth be kept in the institutions a minimum of three months before becoming eligible for parole, except in unusual cases. Youth and staff rather quickly interpreted the three month minimum as a maximum, and so the normal institutional confinement dropped to around three months.

The more rapid turnover meant that educational and vocational training programs patterned on an academic year had to be redefined and reorganized. The emphasis shifted to tutorial programs involving community volunteers and paid professionals. The former vocational training programs that continued were used for basic maintenance services within the institution or for the occupation of idle time.

The STEP program illustrates the effect of changing policies on the organization of retraining programs. STEP (Student Tutor Educational Program) used trained tutors for small group programs to create an interest in learning among imprisoned offenders and a desire to pursue higher levels of education. The program had been developed in adult correctional institutions but was introduced for youth at Shirley in 1970. Subject matter included both formal and informal instruction in such subjects as English, arithmetic, social problems, photography, and auto mechanics. Reading and arithmetic skills were taught in the context of auto mechanics, which interested many boys.

As the new administration policies shifted from centralized institutional pro-grams to decentralized cottage programs, the STEP instructors confined their tutorial activities to particular cottages. They began to integrate their work into the counseling and therapy programs of the cottages. The shorter periods of confinements shifted emphasis from the assimilation of organized learning ma-terials to the redirection of attitudes, motivation, and training in social inter-action. The STEP instructors gradually became full-time cottage treatment staff members and STEP as a special institutional program was discontinued.

The new Commissioner urged staff members throughout DYS to suggest and implement ideas for better treatment programs. While some staff members en-joyed the new freedom to try out their ideas, they complained, sometimes bitterly, that their efforts were not sufficiently supported by the administration. For ex-ample, the STEP tutors complained on several occasions about the lack of adequate support for their program and particularly the lack of direction or a "broad master plan."

The Commissioner firmly believed the traditional training school practices would not be tolerated if they were fully exposed to public view. He therefore encouraged community visitors and volunteers to help run the programs in the institutions, advocated a much more active use of local community facilities and programs suitable for young offenders, and used people from universities and civic groups throughout the state in volunteer programs. In addition, youth left institution grounds for various educational and recreational field trips. In general, these efforts to involve the community were not promoted vigorously by institutional staff. Perhaps one of the most successful programs was developed between the Westfield Reception and Detention Center and the School of Edu-ucation at the University of Massachusetts. The Westfield institution was becom-ing severely overcrowded, and the staff saw community programs as a means of relief The use of student and faculty volunteers as teachers and counselors was incorporated into the curriculum of the School of Education with students re-ceiving academic credit for their work at Westfield.

The Problem of Staff Development

The new program ideas could not be realized without the help of staff committed to the new philosophy of treatment and competent to develop programs to im-plement it. Miller's problem of recruiting or retraining staff for this purpose was formidable. The civil service system in Massachusetts was grafted onto a system of political patronage grounded in an ethnically based structure of political power. The legal requirement to give absolute preference to veterans, in addition to the tradition of political sponsorship, had served on the whole to subordinate merit as a qualification for state employment. Once past the probationary period, employees obtained virtually absolute security in their civil service positions. Miller could not bring in many new staff members unless he secured new funds and created new positions or unless voluntary retirement and resignation became widespread.

Miller's options were limited. He could fill job vacancies with new staff members of his own choosing while searching for loyal adherents of the new philosophy within the existing staff; he could reassign authority and responsibility without regard to civil service classification; or, he could retrain and educate older staff members to the new philosophies of treatment. He pursued all three options, tentatively during the first year, and more vigorously during the second year as new funds became available.

A survey of staff members of the Department of Youth Services during the summer of 1970 showed that many of them, especially those in academic, clinical, or Boston Office assignments, wanted to give the new policies and philosophy of treatment a chance. Table 2 shows the percentage among various staff groups and committed youth who strongly approved of new or proposed policies and programs in the Department. The vocational staff was least approving, followed by general staff (i.e., cottage parents or supervisors) and field administrators of the institutions. The parole staff members usually had little contact with the institutions. Predictably, therefore, they favored reorganization in general since it pointed to institutional reforms primarily, but did not approve of cottage groups making decisions, especially about release on parole, furlough, or work in the community which would affect the normal range of the parole officer's responsibilities. Youth responses were most enthusiastic about policies allowing personal discretion about hair style, clothing, smoking, and coeducational programs.

These responses sensitively reflect the new directions of DYS and the resulting internal distributions of power, responsibility, and reward.[17] Later, for example, one institution's barber reminisced about the days he taught his trade to

[17] For the theoretical analysis relating the new goals of the Department and the internal distribution of power responsibility and reward, see Alden D. Miller, Lloyd E. Ohlin, and Robert B.

TABLE 2
Percentage in Each Interest Group "Strongly Approving" Reforms.

Item	General Staff	Academics	Clinicians	Vocational	Parole	Field Administrators	Boston Office	Committed Youth	Other
Reorganization of the Department by the legislature in 1969.	12	16	32	16	33	22	33	–	6
Decision to transfer or parole boys (girls) up to the staff of the institution (instead of Boston Office)	24	48	48	20	0	28	21	17	28
Allowing cottage groups of staff and boys (girls) to make decisions about:									
Discipline	18	33	53	4	19	17	35	20	20
Release	8	22	38	8	5	12	21	22	13
Furlough and home visits	12	33	41	4	5	12	32	28	19
Assignments to work details	15	33	48	4	10	12	27	13	19
Permitting boys (girls) to make individual decisions about:									
Hair styles	11	44	59	4	35	11	38	49	15
Clothes	7	44	56	4	25	11	38	50	13
Smoking	5	26	34	0	14	0	29	45	13
Elimination of severe disciplinary measures such as long confinement in isolation, physical punishment, and hard labor.	35	67	77	28	57	59	67	–	45
Boston Office program developments to create a "therapeutic community"	12	41	41	4	20	12	29	13	19
Expanding the Outward Bound program and forestry camps.	26	41	37	20	40	28	49	16	34
Introducing STEP type of educational programs such as the one at Shirley.	7	22	26	12	43	12	29	8	11
The following three plans suggested for development of Topsfield as:									
A staff training center	18	37	34	16	29	33	53	–	21
A special drug treatment center	32	52	28	20	33	22	38	–	30
An experimental center for group therapy programs	20	48	32	4	24	17	50	–	21
Expansion of use of volunteers in institutional program activities.	26	41	44	8	14	22	44	18	19
Closing Bridgewater and allowing each institution to deal with its own security problems.	20	26	22	8	14	19	47	21	15
Making some institutions coeducational	15	26	55	4	19	12	59	52	13
Number	76	27	31	25	21	18	34	166	53

a few boys well enough so they could obtain certification, because they stayed long enough to learn and short hair styles were mandatory. A printing shop

Coates, "A Theoretical Synthesis for Promoting Change in Social Service Systems." (Unpublished paper, Center for Criminal Justice, Harvard Law School, October, 1973).

instructor felt the same way. The general staff and field administrators also sensed the emerging challenge to their authority by program innovators from the Boston Office and the greater familiarity that academic and clinical staff seemed to have with the new cottage-based treatment programs. Parole staff were reluctant to share decision making with youth—an essential requirement for negotiating successful placements in new community-based programs. Most of the parole staff defined themselves as much like juvenile bureau police officers: their job was to keep paroled youth out of trouble by advice, surveillance, and threats of official sanctions. The new image of the parole officer as a youth advocate and organizer of community services and opportunities for youth represented a radical and threatening change.

The Commissioner relied on members of the existing staff able to relate to the new philosophy of treatment. At the same time he recruited new top aides among youth workers in Ohio and in Massachusetts who had both professional credentials and enthusiasm for the job. As appropriated funds became available in the second year Miller appointed these aides to posts with program and policy development responsibilities.

The Commissioner circumvented civil service constraints by assigning authority and responsibility without regard to formal civil service rank. This caused insecurity and administrative confusion when job titles and pay assignments bore little relationship to effective responsibility. At one point a new administrator functioning in effect as Superintendent of the Industrial School for Boys at Shirley was in fact assigned and paid from the job category of maintenance worker.

The third tactic, retraining and reeducating the staff, met with relatively little success despite considerable staff interest. The three-day conference with Maxwell Jones, which gave staff for the first time a clear inkling of what Miller had in mind, was followed in September, 1970, with a training session run by Dr. Harry Vorrath, Superintendent of the Red Wing Reformatory in Minnesota. At this point some staff members had accepted the inevitability of training and were responsive to the mixture of control and treatment ideology which Dr. Vorrath espoused. An effort to routinize staff retraining at a new training center at Topsfield faltered when community resistance to this new Topsfield facility, acquired by DYS shortly before Miller's appointment, prevented its full use. These difficulties led to a gradual phasing out of this retraining effort. It demonstrated, however, that retraining would be at best a very gradual process. It would be financially costly and divisive since it would involve the articulation and resolution of fundamental differences in attitudes, values, and beliefs about the reeducation of youth in trouble. It would also have to be undertaken within each institution for all staff members to have lasting effect.

The Development of Fiscal Resources

Money was a constant problem. Unless funds could be freed from the support of traditional institutional programs, practices, and facilities, the chance to develop alternative treatment measures would be severely limited. The appropriation process in Massachusetts for all state agencies relies on supplemental and deficiency budgets to pick up and support commitments not adequately covered in the initial appropriation. This process is deeply immersed in political considerations and bargaining; whether a state department or subunit gets the funds it wants rests on its own capacity to influence the legislative process. For a newcomer like Miller, despite public support from the Governor and his staff, acquiring these skills took time.

The Commissioner did not rely exclusively on the state but requested federal support. He secured grants from the Federal Law Enforcement Assistance Administration in the U.S. Department of Justice both directly and through the Massachusetts Governor's Committee on Law Enforcement and Administration of Justice, from Title I of the Federal Education Act, and Title IV of the Office of Manpower Development and Training in the U.S. Department of Labor. This federal funding permitted Miller to bring in top staff committed to his philosophy, without the restrictions of the civil service system and to establish new types of community based treatment services and supportive summertime educational, recreational, and training services in the institution. The new funds underwrote a planning unit directed by a vigorous advocate of community based treatment for youth. This unit grew rapidly as a cadre of sensitive and dedicated people. In the spring of 1971, it worked with the key departmental administrators to produce a seven point plan setting out the direction of reform. It called for a) regionalization; b) community based treatment centers; c) expansion of the forestry program; d) relocation of detention; e) increased placement alternatives; f) grants-in-aid to cities and towns; and g) an intensive care security unit. These became the chief goals of DYS during the third year of the new administration. The planning unit and the top staff dealt with constant crises in the progress toward those goals. They also carried major responsibility for procuring new federal funds. Without this articulate infusion of new thought and ideas, the funds they procured and the crises they helped to solve, the rapid transition from the training school structure to noninstitutional alternatives would have been most difficult to achieve.

The Results of Phase II

The first two years of the new administration was a period of constant crisis, confrontation, and confusion. The Commissioner possessed neither a blueprint, nor the staff and financial resources to impose a new model of treatment services. The only stable guidelines were the broad goals of the new system, i.e., that confinement of children should be as humane as possible and their treatment as therapeutic and responsive as staff could devise. The needs of children rather than administrative orderliness or staff prerogatives and preferments were to be given top priority.

The Commissioner regarded most of the existing administrative rules and staff protections as major obstacles to change and believed the new philosophy of treatment could·not be effectively established until the punitive aspects of the older system had been fully exposed and the system for distributing responsibility, authority, and rewards reconstituted. For twenty years under the previous administration, staff had acquired a set of beliefs about delinquent youth, conceptions of appropriate staff and youth relationships, and career expectations consistent with the traditional training school philosophy. Many felt rejected and threatened by the new philosophy of treatment and responded with hostility, acts of sabotage, passivity, or apathetic compliance. They magnified the confusion resulting from many of the new directives, passively endured or even encouraged runaways, and complained constantly of permissiveness and loss of authority. Although some older staff members were excited by the new philosophy and joined in with the new recruits, the first two years of the new administration were characterized by a progressive intensification of conflict and polarization of views. During the first year the new Commissioner was largely dependent on converts to his philosophy among older staff members to implement his directives. The fiscal and civil service constraints gradually produced a chaotic pattern for the assignment of administrative responsibility and authority. Former administrators placed on leave status were replaced in effective authority by adherents to the new philosophy without much regard for rank or civil service status. A fluid pattern of staff assignment developed. Staff from the Boston Office and from the institutions were reassigned to new positions as crises developed. The frequent shift of staff members to new administrative positions undermined expectations and created insecurity about career advancement based on traditional criteria of promotion.

Deposed and alienated adherents of the older philosophy were not without resources for fighting back. Most of them had long periods of service in the DYS, relatives or friends in the legislature, and influential associations in the small towns in which they resided close to the institutions. They also had long established working relationships with many judges, probation officers, and public officials who shared their views about the function and operation of training schools. Stories about policies and case decisions that documented the permissive and chaotic state of administrative practices were magnified and circulated. Many judges, probation officers, and police officials, even those initially sympathetic to the idea of reform, began to oppose the new administration. And by the fall of 1971, two legislative investigations of DYS were underway.

The results of this phase of the reform movement are difficult to assess apart from a longer range evaluation of the total movement toward community based treatment services. It is clear, however, that the concept of small group therapeutic communities had some success. This experiment showed that traditional training school environments based on a cottage system could be decentralized. One could organize within some cottages a group therapy approach creating for both youth and staff a new set of rules, expectations, and practices. The data revealed reactions from youth and staff that justifies such efforts elsewhere and are consistent with previous studies in other settings.

Whether the favorable responses of youth to the group therapy approach is translated into better adjustment in the home, school, or neighborhood cannot yet be determined. The data on recidivism rates and community adjustment of youth in these different programs are still being assembled.

Phase III: From Institutions to Community Corrections

The new administration found itself unable to change staff attitudes and beliefs or to impose a therapeutic community in all of the cottages. Table 3 provides some evidence of this; it shows a consistent pattern of differences in staff response to the items on custody and treatment as one moves from the most traditional

TABLE 3

Staff Selection of Statements They Feel Best Reflect The Purposes of The Institutions

Tools of Institutions	Custody-Oriented Cottages				Treatment-Oriented Cottages			
	Cottage Nine	Cottage Eight	Elms Cottage	Westview Cottage	Sunset Cottage	Shirley Cottage	Tops-Field	I Belong
Percent of staff choosing three custodial purposes	47	33	32	37	13	21	15	9
		34				16		
Percent of staff choosing three treatment purposes	42	50	58	52	80	67	69	81
		51				72		
N	(27)	(15)	(40)	(29)	(15)	(16)	(15)	(8)

Source: Barry Feld, *Subcultures of Selected Boys' Cottages in Massachusetts Department of Youth Services Institutions in 1971*, Center for Criminal Justice, Harvard Law School, October, 1972. Staff were asked to choose three from a list of eleven statements of possible goals commonly associated with institutions for delinquents.

to the most treatment oriented cottages. Miller was aware of the entrenched resistance thus reflected in many traditional cottages, and was impatient with the slow pace of change. He suggested late in 1970 that, despite the storminess of the preceding year and the feeling of traditional staff that DYS was being turned completely upside down, there had really been little or no fundamental change. He felt the same way a year later, even after some of the therapeutic community oriented cottages began to achieve conspicuous success.

Miller finally concluded that therapeutic communities could be run success-fully in only a few cottages within the institutions. However, he felt they might be much more successful outside the existing institutions. In community settings greater professional resources would be available to provide volunteer and pur-chased services in relation to which traditional expectations about juvenile pri-sons might no longer have force. The successful treatment cottages could then be redefined as staging cottages which would later be moved off the institutional grounds to become community-based facilities.

Closing the institutions raised the problems of building a new structure of services more closely integrated with community life. This would be the challenge of the third phase of reform. It came to involve the decentralization or region-alization of services into seven regions; the development of new court liaison staff working with juvenile judges and probation personnel to coordinate de-tention, diagnostic and referral policies, and individual case decisions; a new

140

network of community services including residential and non-residential place-ments for individuals and small groups; some centralized services for the institu-tional treatment of dangerous and disturbed offenders; ways to monitor the quality of the services increasingly purchased from private agencies; and staff development programs to reassign, retrain, or discharge former staff members in ways minimizing personal hardship and injustice.

Deinstitutionalization

In the winter of 1971-72 DYS closed two major institutions, Shirley and Lyman. Lancaster was converted partly to privately run programs on the institutional grounds later in 1972. Oakdale, originally an institution for very young boys, and then a reception center, was finally closed in late 1972. No strong public reaction immediately appeared in response to the closing of the institutions. The Commissioner had succeeded in exposing these facilities as brutalizing en-vironments for youth and staff alike. When Shirley closed, the press featured stories and pictures of Miller, members of the legislature, staff, and youth for-merly confined at Shirley sledge hammering the bars and locks of the segregation cells of Cottage #9. The Commissioner emerged as an advocate in the public eye of new opportunities for youth, his opponents as advocates of punishment and repression. The staff and supporters of the now "evil" institutions reacted with stunned disbelief and feelings of betrayal for their years of work. The radical shift in correctional philosophy seemed too swift and uncompromising to accord them their due. How could the new approach suddenly be so right and the older one, in which they had staked their careers and future, so wrong?

Closing the institutions involved finding alternative placements for the youth and reassignment for the staff. The University of Massachusetts Conference was organized to transfer a large number of youth out of the institutions into the community quickly enough to avoid excessive disruption and to get the job done before crippling opposition could develop.[18] Ninety-nine boys and girls from Lyman, Lancaster, and two detention centers were taken to the University of Massachusetts for a month in January and February, 1972. College students served as advocates for the DYS youth while placements for them were worked out at the Conference. The college students were selected from three colleges and uni-versities in the area by members of the Juvenile Opportunities Extension, a Uni-

[18] For a fuller discussion of this Conference see, Robert B. Coates, Alden D. Miller, and Lloyd E. Ohlin, "A Strategic Innovation in the Process of Deinstitutionalization: The University of Massa-chusetts Conference," in Bakal, *Closing Correctional Institutions*, pp. 127-148.

versity of Massachusetts student organization that had been participating extensively in the program at the Westfield institution. Arrangements for future placement of youth, e.g., sending the youth home, placing youth in a foster home or in a group home, were worked out in a collaborative manner between the DYS staff, the advocates, and the youth themselves by considering the range of program alternatives and the needs of specific youth.

The move was accomplished with much fanfare involving a caravan of cars from Lyman to the University of Massachusetts at Amherst. The Governor appeared later at the Conference to lend his support. The Conference, through the student advocates, succeeded in placing sixty-five youth in other than institutional settings. Approximately equal proportions of those remaining were placed in other institutions, ran away, or remained unplaced.

The drama of the Conference as a way of quickly closing institutions is suggested by reactions of staff members at the Lyman Institution. Staff there had been told months before that the institution would be closed but simply could not believe it. A cottage which had burned was painstakingly rebuilt by staff who were standing at the door waiting for youth to be assigned the day the motorcade to Amherst virtually emptied the institution in a matter of hours. A few weeks later staff members were exchanging rumors of mass escapes, chaos, and widespread sexual misconduct at the Conference, which would soon result in the youth being brought back to the institution. In contrast, one university official, after the Conference, remarked that the DYS youth had actually been less trouble to the university than a convention of the American Legion.

Recidivism data obtained from the central probation office records after an eleven month follow-up period yielded an overall official court appearance rate after the Conference of 48 percent with most of the appearances (79 percent) occurring during the first four months. While calculations on the rates of reappearance in court on new charges are not yet completed for the various samples of youth in the research study, the recidivism rates reported here for youth in the Conference are probably somewhat lower than court appearance recidivism rates characterizing youth from the traditional training school programs.

The youths relocated and the staff reassigned, the grounds and buildings of the large institutions which have been closed still remain with the haunting possibility that they may be used again as a primary treatment resource. Planners and administrators in DYS are convinced that DYS must divest itself of these institutions to consolidate the new policies. In addition, the Lancaster Training School is still in use although over half of the population there is in programs privately administered. The actual use of this institution probably constitutes a more serious threat to the stability of reform than the mere continuing existence of other facilities.

Regionalization

The shift from a custodial to treatment orientation had already abridged institutional autonomy, lodging greater control in the central office; with the movement toward highly decentralized community based services, control had to be reallocated to the new regional offices.

Each of these regional units consists of a small suite of business offices to serve the administrative need to coordinate and implement services for youth in each region. Unlike an institution, a regional office cannot house youth on the premises. Youth must be referred quickly to appropriate residential or non-residential programs.

With support from the Boston Office, the seven regional offices have developed placement opportunities for youth referred or sentenced to the DYS by the courts. They make contractual arrangements, usually within the region, for these services. They also handle detention, so that a youth's contact with DYS now is always at least nominally through some regional office. DYS is also trying to organize the budget by regions, somewhat as it was organized around the institutions in the past, but with less stringent controls over intradepartmental transfers.

For the youth in the DYS, regionalization has immeasurably improved service since regional offices know more about possible placements in the communities, where the youth are, and how they are doing. This now makes successive trial placements feasible, if necessary, so that ultimately youth can hope to get the best possible placement. For example, a youth might be placed in one or more foster homes before assignment to a group home, perhaps with a program of group therapy better suited to his needs. Sometimes a trial period in a particular program is explicitly agreed on by the youth and the staff with the option of trying something else if it does not work out. In other cases, evidence of poor adjustment such as a recurrent tendency to run away or persistent defiance of authority, signals the need for a change. Most staff members in interviews expressed their belief that regionalization provides new opportunities to work more effectively with youth—ways that simply did not seem available under the old system. For planners and administrators, regionalization has meant a closer fit between programs and the needs and resources of each region. The University of Massachusetts Conference placement staff had felt hampered by having to work on a statewide level.

There are still signs of newness in the work of the regions. Records and current operating information systems are only gradually developing to link the regions with the Boston Office. Perhaps the greatest continuing need, associated with the transition from the institutional structure, is to divert funds from excess staff positions left in the institution budgets to the new regional programs.

Development of New Detention, Court Liaison, and Referral Programs

Before 1972 nearly all youth detained prior to trial were held in high security institutions. DYS regards this as unnecessary for most youth and even destructive for those who are not dangerous.

Alternatives have been developed with the help of private agencies. Foster care has been greatly expanded for detention purposes. Shelter care units have been set up in several regions, each generally housing between twelve and twenty youth. These are group homes with program activities which allow for rapid turnover. Local YMCA's have proved to be the most productive private resource for such facilities. The units are staffed with a combination of YMCA and DYS personnel to involve youth in constructive activities and to discharge DYS's custodial responsibilities to the courts.

DYS created the court liaison role to deal more effectively with needs of youth while they are still under the care of the court. The court liaison officer recommends placement possibilities within the DYS system and sometimes, as well, other alternatives to conventional detention. Thus, if a youth is referred or committed to the Department of Youth Services the time between such action and placement is minimized, and the reception phase in many instances is no longer distinct from detention. In seeking other options to commitment and to reduce labeling effects, DYS has encouraged the courts to *refer* youth on a voluntary basis prior to or after adjudication instead of formally sentencing or *committing* them to DYS. From a legal standpoint *referred* youth are still within the jurisdiction of the court while *committed* youth are released to the jurisdictional authority of the Department. The services available to both groups are much the same. The principal advantage of a referral status is that the youth avoids having a formal commitment on his record. Referrals have increased greatly throughout the system, with, of course, regional variations. It is estimated that between one-fourth and one-third of all youth in both residential and nonresidential programs are now referrals instead of commitments.

The DYS staff regard the detention, court liaison, and referral programs as important components in consolidating regionalization. The regional offices have largely taken over development of these programs while quality control, monitor-

144

ing, and general administrative matters have remained in the Boston Office. The court liaison and referral programs also appear to have created more constructive working relationships with the courts. DYS is providing services which the courts did not previously have readily available and is able to draw on a statewide referral and quality control system difficult for the courts to develop themselves.

Private contracting agencies, especially the YMCA's, find these new programs an opportunity to expand their own services. A number of judges and probation staff have made effective use of the new referral opportunities and the assistance of the court liaison officers in utilizing these alternatives. In other instances they have been critical of the resistance of the DYS staff to high security facilities for a greater number of youth.

While the range of detention alternatives has been greatly increased, the older large security facilities, such as Roslindale, continue to be used. The inability of DYS to find a substitute for Roslindale or to make it a decent, habitable facility has puzzled visitors supportive of the Massachusetts reforms. A detailed history of Miller's efforts to humanize this institution—and their failure—would reveal the whole spectrum of forces (conflicting conceptions of the delinquent and appropriate treatment, the abuses of authority, untrained staff, overcrowding, civil service constraints, court and police demands for security, community resistance to new shelters or secure facilities, boredom, idleness, fear, and violence) that turns large institutions for juvenile delinquents into prisons. Physically secure units are necessary for certain youth, but such units should probably be small in size, administer a diversified program, and provide responsive care.

As in the past, detention services for girls lag somewhat behind the alternatives available for boys. The court liaison program, while providing benefits to some courts and some regions, is still not operating across the entire state.

The new referral system is not without potentially serious policy problems. It is sound to reduce the harmful results of a youth being committed. However, if youth are now being referred who otherwise would not have been committed to DYS, the risk of labeling youth earlier is also enhanced. There is some evidence that referrals to DYS are increasing without compensating statewide reductions in commitments. Whether the additional youth will unnecessarily acquire invidious labels, or whether their presence will lessen the degree to which the youth who had always been in DYS acquire such labels, is a question demanding urgent concern and investigation. There are many issues to be resolved. If the DYS programs become less punitive, more therapeutic, and more readily available they will be used more often. Yet if they provide a treatment of last resort for the most

TABLE 4

Cost of Program Types per Youth per Week

Type of Program	Costs per Youth per Week
Residential:	
Intensive Care	$145 – $290
Group Homes	$145 – $150
Foster Care	$ 30 – $ 40
Non-residential	$50

dangerous and disturbed youth, all of the youth serviced may be perceived in the same way unless clear and possibly harmful distinctions are maintained.

Development of New Residential and Non-Residential Placements

One of the most pressing problems confronting the Department of Youth Services as the institutions were closing was the development of alternatives to institutional confinement.[19] The Boston Office had begun exploring placement alternatives in 1971, and stepped up its activities with the University of Massachusetts Conference in January, 1972. At first this activity focused on the development of group homes, but when it became obvious that many youth might be stranded as the institutions closed, emphasis was shifted to the development of non-residential alternatives, day or night programs in which youth participate while living at home or in some other setting. Since 1972 developing placements has become almost exclusively the responsibility of the regions.

There are roughly 80 non-residential programs across the state, in which DYS places youth, about 120 residential programs, and about 200 foster homes. About 700 youth are placed in residential group homes, and about 250 in foster homes. About 800 youth are in the non-residential programs such as Neighborhood Youth Corps, a recreation program at Massachusetts Maritime Academy, and programs at community colleges. The two most heavily used programs for committed and referred youth are group homes and non-residential services, with foster homes being considerably less used, and the use of traditional parole varying greatly from region to region. The group homes represent an alternative of moderate cost, while the non-residential services are inexpensive (see Table 4).

[19] For a report on problems in overcoming community resistance to the establishment of community based residential facilities see, Robert B. Coates and Alden D. Miller, "Neutralization of Community Resistance to Group Homes," in Bakal, pp. 67–84.

146

If problems of providing prompt payment to vendors are worked out soon, the use of foster care, even less expensive than non-residential services, will probably expand.

One of the serious problems plaguing placement in general is the time lag between provision of services and payment for services. It has sometimes become so great that contracting agencies question whether regional directors really have the authority to contract for the DYS; as a consequence some smaller agencies are threatened with bankruptcy. The problem of long delayed payments is endemic to all the state services and especially in those departments which make substantial use of private vendors. The legislature has been reluctant to appropriate funds for purchased services especially when the somewhat unpredictable costs require deficiency appropriations. Even where funds are available, payments are delayed by a complicated system for setting rates, approving contracts, or authorizing payments in each case. All of these difficulties were aggravated in the case of DYS. Insufficient funds were available from the state, and the federal grants contained program and accounting requirements which DYS had difficulty meeting in time to establish the needed group homes. The rapid closing of the institutions created an immediate demand for alternatives which the cumbersome funding process could not meet.

No phase of Miller's administration has come under stronger criticism than his decision to initiate new programs before the resources to back them up were in hand. He took the calculated risk that the support of reform by federal funding agencies and the state executive and legislative leadership was strong enough to fulfill his promises of reimbursement in the end. In doing so he exposed his administration to a series of investigations and charges of fiscal mismanagement, irresponsibility, and administrative incompetence. In response, he has charged that the system had to be forced to meet the legitimate needs of youth for appropriate services or the development of these services would have been delayed many years.

There is ample justification for the charges on both sides. Miller's driving ambition to create a more flexible and responsive set of services for delinquent youth was reinforced by his impatience with red tape and his ability to tolerate a lot of administrative confusion as long as "helping kids" came first in every decision. His critics acknowledged his concern for youth and his credibility with them, but felt at the same time that the pace of change was harmful to both staff and youth. They argued that many youth committed to DYS needed more prolonged, professional, and intensive care than the hastily contrived new programs could furnish. DYS's readiness to place youth in newly created, untried programs might do more harm than good for many of them. The neglect of the legitimate needs of staff members showed a callous disregard for years of service and acquired skills which could still find fulfillment in the new system of services. In the new programs exploitation of staff idealism and commitment to youth services ought not to preclude provision for their economic survival and career investments.

It is still too soon to judge fairly these claims and countercharges. Short-run assessments may lack fair consideration of the long range goals which these changes were designed to achieve in terms of economic and social adjustment and community protection.

Development of New Special Programs for Dangerous and Disturbed Offenders

There is widespread agreement that most people, both youth and adult, who are now locked up need not be. There is also widespread agreement that some of those now routinely locked up, both youth and adult, really must continue to be confined. It is also widely recognized that it is extremely difficult to separate out with a tolerable margin of error those who need to be locked up from those who do not. However, recent experience in DYS with community placements has shown that with youth this problem is not as difficult as is generally assumed. Many youth clearly and obviously belong in community placements. Some clearly belong in secure settings. A few are problematic. An obvious need that emerged as the institutions closed was the provision of secure settings with intensive treatment for dangerous and disturbed youth, coupled with safeguards that would prevent misuse of these facilities.

DYS distinguishes youth who are behavior problems from youth who need psychiatric care. For both sorts of youth the Department has tried to purchase services and in December, 1973, approximately 125 youth were in intensive care placements. For the youth with behavior problems, a program run by ex-offenders who relate directly to these youth while "taking no nonsense" has had some success. This program stresses use of community resources within a framework of appropriate custodial security. For youth needing psychiatric care, DYS has purchased services from private agencies. It has also tried to coordinate more closely with the Department of Mental Health. For example, in October, 1973, it finally opened a special unit for up to six youths needing intensive psychological services at the Medfield State Hospital. Safeguards for the youth in these dif-

TABLE 5

Number and Percentage of Persons Committed to the State Adult
Correctional System and County Correctional System by Year and Age

	State Correctional System			County Correctional System		
Year	Total Commitments	17 and Younger	Percent	Total Commitments	17 and Younger	Percent
Jan-March						
1973	199	6	3.0%	—*	—*	—*
1972	1,127	50	4.4%	5,499	252	4.6%
1971	1,091	47	4.3%	6,474	240	3.7%
1970	859	38	4.4%	8,119	287	3.5%
1969	875	30	3.4%	8,108	247	3.0%
1968	855	42	4.9%	8,467	283	3.3%
1967	739	32	4.3%	8,550	263	3.1%
1966	826	39	4.7%	8,990	275	3.1%
TOTAL	6,571	284	4.3%	54,207	1,847	3.4%

*Data not available.
Source: Massachusetts Department of Corrections, May 30, 1973.

ferent settings rely on advance agreements about decision making and frequent case review.

One danger is that the courts, lacking what they believe to be secure commitment facilities, will bind over youth considered dangerous or disturbed to adult courts. These might result in confinement in an adult jail or prison. So far (up to April, 1973) this has not happened. The commitment of persons seventeen or younger from 1966 to 1973 remained very stable in the state correctional system (see Table 5). For the county jails there has been a slight rise in the percentage of all commitments represented by youth but lower numbers of youth committed in 1971 and 1972 than in previous years, except for 1969.

DYS has continuing needs in this area. It needs a program for girls, and it may need more funds for psychiatric treatment alternatives. And it needs to work with all juvenile judges to implement better ways of treating these youth than binding them over to adult courts, or relying excessively on maximum security facilities.

Development of New Quality Control Procedures

Quality control of detention, residential, and non-residential placements, and high security programs received little attention in DYS until the development of new programs made the issue inescapable. The basic problem is how to maintain control over the quality of programs contracted to private agencies. Private groups have not been accustomed to account for program quality to a public agency.

Three units have become involved in evaluation of ongoing programs. Two units in the Bureau of Aftercare have monitored some of the non-residential and residential programs. Another evaluation unit more recently organized has been more systematic. Programs are now rated on such dimensions as quality of facilities, administration and staff, controls, program, clinical services, diversion, and budget. Information from all three units has been used by the Boston Office and regional staff for recommending program changes, and in some instances program termination.

The Boston Office staff acknowledges that quality control is not fully operational, but the fact that some programs have been terminated on the basis of evaluations has encouraged staff in their belief that DYS can collect evaluative data and make decisions on the basis of it. Regional directors, a number of whom were at first skeptical of the evaluation and information system, are now calling for more evaluation to improve their own placement decisions.

The development of a fully operational quality control unit is the most essential requirement of a system relying primarily on the purchase of services from private vendors. The latter are free from the rigid constraints of public civil service and line budgets dependent on the political process of legislative approval. However, this freedom does not in itself guarantee quality programs. DYS terminated placement at several group homes. In one case the facility was found to be structurally unsound and the treatment of youth inhumane, i.e. the building had broken windows which were not being replaced and youth were being fed only once a day to cut costs. In a second instance a project was terminated because the promised services, counseling, education, and work experiences, were not being provided. In yet another case the project was stopped because the program was administered in an overly regimented, institutional manner.

The experience of other states also justifies vigorous and powerful quality control procedures. The professional or sectarian orthodoxies of private agencies may prove as inflexible and ultimately as harmful to youth as the regimen of the traditional training school. Furthermore, their tendency to admit only those youth most amenable and acceptable for treatment leaves the public agency responsible ultimately for the care of the most difficult and most economically and socially disadvantaged youth. Great care must be taken in drawing up contract requirements for the purchase of private services to guarantee access for the quality control unit. DYS seems cognizant of these problems and has demonstrated its ability to evaluate programs and eliminate those that do not perform adequately. However, it has not allocated enough resources to build a quality control system capable of monitoring all programs regularly.

The Problem of Personnel Development

Early state-wide attempts at staff retraining programs were not very successful. With regionalization and deinstitutionalization, staff training programs also changed and are now handled regionally. Deinstitutionalization and the new practice of purchasing service has put old staff members in positions where they have had to learn new skills on the job. The Boston Office has attempted to provide displaced staff with opportunities to transfer to different work, including new casework and other alternatives under the regional offices, or to join private non-profit treatment agencies that contract services to DYS. The problem nonetheless remains serious; half or more of the staff of DYS could be transferred out of the Department without impairing its functioning since most of the services provided by staff in the past are now purchased from the private sector. DYS records for 1969 show that 531 employees were assigned to the major institutions that have since been closed or converted partly to private programs. The number currently assigned to these institutions is 120; of these, 61 provide maintenance services and care for 25 youth in two cottages at Lancaster, while 59 simply maintain the facilities of two other institutions. Forty-four of the 59 will be transferred to other departments in state government destined to take over those institutions in the near future. Many of the original institutional staff not thus accounted for are associated with regional offices, which did not exist in 1969, and now employ 269 persons. The central administration in Boston has dropped from 160 to 94 employees.

Many staff members who have involved themselves in the new system have been satisfied with it. Others who have been unable or unwilling to break with past traditions have found the experience distressing. Still, the staff union leadership, with increased understanding of what is being done and why, has not opposed the changes as it did in earlier years.

The staff development problem has also been hindered by the organization of the budget. The majority of the staff that actually operates programs for youth are now in private agencies contracting services to the state; this should be reflected in the budget if staff development is to continue successfully.

The Results of Phase III

Data on youth adjustment to the new community settings are being collected through cross-sectional surveys of youth in programs and by longitudinal cohort analysis involving periodic interviews with a sample of youth as they pass through programs of the DYS. Preliminary data from the cross-sectional survey of youth in representative residential settings in two regions compared with data obtained from youth in traditional and experimental cottages before the institutions were closed suggests progress in creating better environments.

Probably one of the more salient concerns in socialization, whether in the context of the family, the school, or a program designed to aid youth in trouble, is the distribution of rewards and punishments. The development of a reward-based system is documented in Table 6. Youth in the three types of cottage environments agreed that they would be rewarded by staff for good behavior. The initial cohort data show specifically *how* they think they will be rewarded in the community based programs. The most frequently mentioned response was "staff will make me feel good about what I am doing." The second most frequently mentioned response was "staff will give me additional privileges."

The role of youth themselves in the distribution of rewards provides some of the most striking contrasts across the three cottage environments. Only 37 percent of the youth in the traditional cottages believed that other youth would reward them for good behavior. In the experimental cottages the figure was 60 percent. This is a dramatic change which suggests that youth in community based programs are learning how to support others in a positive manner, and are in turn being supported by their peers. If this contrast between the cottage types is supported by data we are still collecting, it will be a strong indication that the new programs are producing some important, positive, and immediate effects.

While reward patterns are important in any context of socialization, punishment patterns are equally important. Again, there are contrasts across cottage environments, here in the perceived frequency of staff punishing kids who "mess up."In the traditional cottages, 81 percent of the youth believed that staff would punish. Sixty-six percent of youth in the experimental cottages indicated that staff would punish. And 44 percent of the youth in the community based programs reported that staff would punish. Punishment seems less salient in the community based programs than in the other cottage environments; discipline relies more on reward. It is also possible that punishment in the newer programs is

152

TABLE 6
Youth Perception of Reward and Punishment by Type of Program

Question	Traditional Institutional Cottage (%)	Experimental Cottage in Institution (%)	Community Based Program (%)
The staff will reward a kid for good behavior			
Agree	77	78	76**
Disagree or DK	23	22	24
Total	100	100	100
N	85	89	34
If you do well, will the staff reward you?			
No			33*
Include me in things			7
Additional privileges			26
Make me look good in front of others			7
Make me feel good about what I am doing			28
Total			100
N			43
Other kids will reward a kid for good behavior			
Agree	37	60	80**
Disagree or DK	63	40	20
Total	100	100	100
N	82	87	35
If a kid messes up, the staff will punish him/her			
Agree	81	66	44**
Disagree or DK	19	34	56
Total	100	100	100
N	83	86	39
If you screw up, will staff here punish you?			
No			21*
Separate from group			13
Take away privileges			45
Hit			16
Embarrass in front of others			3
Make me feel guilty			3
Total			100
N			38

**Source: Cross-sectional survey of youth in programs
*Source: Cohort Analysis

more sophisticated and less likely to be perceived as punishment *per se* by the youth. This may often be the case in more "caring" situations. On the basis of the preliminary cohort data the type of punishment most often perceived by youth in the community based programs is the taking away of privileges.

Youth in the experimental and traditional cottages and in the community based programs saw different purposes in their respective programs. Sixty-one percent of the youth in traditional cottages believed that the cottage staff were more concerned with keeping kids under control than with helping them with their problems. Only 30 percent of the youth in the experimental cottages reported that that was the case, and only 14 percent of the youth in the community based programs believe that control is a greater concern of the staff than helping to solve problems.

Youth in the cohort study have been asked how staff in the community based programs try to help them stay out of trouble. The majority of respondents indicate that the staff encourage them by telling them that they can make it. Over twenty percent of the youth reported that staff helped them to get jobs, to join youth groups, to obtain placement in new school programs and things like that.

TABLE 7
Youth Perception of Staff Control and Support by Type of Program

Question	Traditional Institutional Cottage (%)	Experimental Cottage in Institution (%)	Community Based Program (%)
This cottage is more concerned with keeping kids under control than with helping them with their problems			
Agree	61	30	14**
Disagree or DK	39	70	86
Total	100	100	100
N	85	87	35
Do the staff here help you stay out of trouble?			
No			23*
Encourage			53
Help get jobs, into school, groups, etc.			23
Total			100
N			43

**Source: Cross-sectional survey of youth in programs
 *Source: Cohort Analysis

We will be able to say more about the relative impact of moral support or en-couragement and concrete support such as finding jobs as the cohort analysis proceeds.

In order to know how youth in the cohort analysis perceive relationships with others after they have been through a program, we have tabulated responses from the semantic differential test on two items, good-bad and fair-unfair, with respect to the youth's perceptions of each of nine categories of persons. The two items, good-bad and fair-unfair, are strongly related and are reliable indi-cators of a generally positive evaluation of a category. We have ordered the objects of evaluation in Table 8 by the ratings given them by our cohort youth on the good-bad item, and presented the average scale response to the good-bad item and the fair-unfair item. The scale range possible on each item was one to seven. Higher scores mean ratings indicating better or fairer.

"Mother" and "Program Staff" received the highest evaluations, while the "Department of Youth Services" and the "Police" receive the lowest, both on goodness and fairness. "Me" and "My Friends" are in the middle, along with "School Teacher." "My Friends" would rank higher in the ordering if the order-ing were based on fairness instead of goodness.

Particularly noteworthy is the difference in evaluation given Program Staff and the DYS. Program Staff are, of course, the direct personal contact between DYS and the youth, so the concept of DYS which is rated so negatively must signify something to the youth other than their immediate experiences in programs. The similarity of DYS and police evaluations suggests that youth see the DYS in general, as opposed to program staff, as linked with the police and the courts as agents of the youth's loss of freedom. It is also possible that the youth simply associate DYS with the old, unreformed system. The youths' ranking of categories of persons corresponds loosely to what we might expect a ranking of closeness and personalness of relationships to look like. In this context it is significant that Program Staff in the community-based programs are ranked second from the top, after Mother, on both goodness and fairness.

Conclusion

The traditional training school system that existed in Massachusetts prior to the recent reforms is still the dominant pattern for youth corrections throughout the country. In fact, preliminary results of a national survey of juvenile corrrec-tional practices reveal that there are as many states increasing the number of

TABLE 8

Mean Response Scores on Two Semantic Differential Items

Category of Persons Being Described	"Goodness"	"Fairness"
Mother	6.0	5.7
Program Staff	5.2	5.3
Father	5.1	4.9
Me	4.9	4.9
My Friends	4.7	5.1
Schoolteacher	4.7	4.6
Other Kids Here	4.6	4.4
DYS	3.6	3.6
Police	3.0	2.4

N=39.

delinquent youth confined in institutions as there are showing decreases.[20] For many of these states the Massachusetts experience will provide useful guidance to the problems major reforms must confront.

The Massachusetts reforms have closed the traditional training schools and developed a variety of alternative residential and non-residential services based in the new state regions. Our research on these reforms, however, is not yet complete. There has not yet been sufficient exposure time in the community for those in the new programs to provide a valid, follow-up comparison with those treated in institutions. In addition, the collection of recidivism information has been delayed pending the development of approved regulations for access by research personnel to criminal history information of juvenile and adult offenders. These arrangements have just been completed.

Additional issues need further analysis and study. One is whether the same broad changes could have been pursued as successfully more gradually. Miller and his aides have expressed the view that gradual implementation of such major changes would permit the mobilization of conservative groups inside and outside the agency to block changes. This view is not easily discounted, given other states' experiences in reform efforts.

Another issue concerns administrative confusion and neglect of staff development in the transitional period. The rapid changes in staff assignments and

[20] Wolfgang I. Grichting, *Sampling Plans and Results, The University of Michigan National Assessment of Juvenile Corrections Project* (Ann Arbor: University of Michigan, Institute of Continuing Legal Education, School of Social Work, 1973).

responsibilities created a highly fluid administrative situation. It provided greater freedom to experiment with new treatment methods, stimulated staff members
to considerable creativity and initiative, and enabled the administration to avoid
premature commitment and consolidation of insufficiently tested programs. However, it has been charged that this approach unnecessarily alienated both old
and new staff members.

Commissioner Miller has also been criticized for leaving Massachusetts in
January, 1973, to become the new Director of Family and Children's Services
in Illinois. He left before financial and personnel problems had been resolved
and before a new alternative system of residential and non-residential services
had fully replaced the old. He believed that reform commissioners are inevitably expendable since the hostility aroused by major changes becomes too great
a barrier to further progress. He thinks that the consolidation of the Massachusetts community based services will now proceed faster with his successor, Commissioner Joseph Leavy, in charge.[21] It is too soon yet to know if he is right.
The 1974 Departmental budget, with additional support from federal funds,
enables the Department to catch up with its financial commitments on purchased services. The budget also provides more time for staff transfers and retraining. This should greatly aid in consolidating a new consensus.

The Massachusetts Department of Youth Services has undertaken a major
pioneering step in correctional reform. It has demonstrated that radical changes
in the official ideology, policies, and programs of treatment for delinquent youth
can be achieved in a short period of time. Evidence thus far indicates that youth
perceive the new system as more helpful and staff more responsive. There is
widespread agreement that it encourages more humane treatment of youth and
offers staff more resources for reintegrating youth into their home communities.
Whether in the long run these new policies and programs will result in better
protection for the community and more effective help for troubled youth is
still to be determined.

[21] Interview with Jerome Miller by research staff, February, 1973.

Foster Care—In Whose Best Interest?*

ROBERT H. MNOOKIN

University of California at Berkeley

Under existing law, judges have wide discretionary authority to remove "neglected" children from their natural parents and place them in state-controlled foster care. The children are for the most part from poor families. The author describes the process by which the state can coercively remove children from their parents, and he analyzes the best interests of the child test, the legal standard courts usually employ to decide whether a neglected child should be removed from parental custody. He suggests that this standard requires predictions that cannot be made on a case by case basis and necessarily gives individual judges too much discretion to impose their own values in deciding what is best for a child. While critical of the procedural informality of the current juvenile court process, he believes additional procedural safeguards for children and their parents are in themselves unlikely to remedy the

* Research for this article was supported by grants to the Childhood and Government Project, University of California, Berkeley, from the Ford Foundation and the Carnegie Corporation of New York. For a later development of some of the ideas in this article, with greater emphasis on law and legal theory, see Robert H. Mnookin's "Child Custody Adjudication Judicial Functions in the Face of Indeterminacy," *Law and Contemporary Problems,* 39 (1975).

I wish gratefully to acknowledge the research assistance of Susan Waisbren, graduate student, Department of Psychology, University of California, and Kate Bartlett, a second year student at the School of Law, University of California, Berkeley. Many of my colleagues at Berkeley made helpful comments on an earlier draft. In particular, I wish to thank Jessica Pers, Raymond Marks, Randall McCathren, Arlene Skolnick, Louis Freedberg of the Childhood and Government Project, and Professors Jerome Skolnick, Paul Mishkin, Herma Hill Kay, Caleb Foote, John Coons, Stephen Sugarman, David Kirp, and Kermit Wiltse. Finally, I have benefited considerably from conversations with Robert Walker, Esq., of the Youth Law Center, San Francisco.

Harvard Educational Review Vol. 43 No. 4 November 1973, 599–638

*situation. He goes on to propose a new standard to limit removal to cases where
there is an immediate and substantial danger to the child's health and where there
are no reasonable means of protecting the child at home. In addition, a standard is
proposed to ensure that prompt steps are taken to provide children who must be removed with a stable environment.*

Most American parents raise their children free of intrusive legal constraints or
major governmental intervention. Although compulsory education and child labor laws indicate there are some conspicuous legal limitations on parents, it is the
family, not the state, which has primary responsibility for child rearing.[1] Despite
this predominant pattern, there are about 285,000 children under eighteen[2] among
the nation's nearly 70 million[3] for whom the state has assumed primary responsibility. These children live in state sponsored foster care, a term used in this paper
to include foster family homes, group homes, and child welfare institutions.
For a number of the children in foster care, the state has assumed responsibility
because no one else is available. Some children are orphans; others have been voluntarily given up by a family no longer willing or able to care for them. A significant number of children, however, are placed in foster care because the state has
intervened and coercively removed the child from parental custody.

No national statistics are available to indicate what proportion of the children in
foster care have been removed because of state coercion. When parents oppose

[1] Language in several Supreme Court opinions can be read to suggest that these are constitutional underpinnings for the primary of the parental role. See, e.g., *Pierce v. Society of Sisters*,
268 U.S. 510, 534-35 (1925) where the court struck down an Oregon statute that required parents
to send their children to public schools, stating that the statute "unreasonably interferes with the
liberty of parents and guardians to direct the upbringing and education of children under their
control." See also *Meyer v. Nebraska*, 262 U.S. 390 (1923). Compare *Prince v. Massachusetts*, 321 U.S.
158 (1944) where the court affirmed the child labor law conviction of an aunt who had a nine-
year-old niece in her custody sell Jehovah's Witness literature at night on the street in her presence. The Court emphasized that "the state has a wide range of power for limiting parental freedom and authority in things affecting the child's welfare; and that this includes, to some extent,
matters of conscience and religious conviction," *id.* at 167.

[2] HEW estimates that on March 31, 1970, there were 326,700 children under eighteen in foster
care, approximately 284,500 of whom were under the complete or partial auspices of a public welfare agency. Of the 284,500, 243,600 were in foster family homes; 3,600 were in group homes; and
37,300 were in child welfare institutions. An additional 42,200 children were in foster care under
the auspices of voluntary child welfare agencies. See U.S. Dept. of Health, Education and Welfare,
*Children Served by Public Welfare Agencies and Voluntary Child Welfare Agencies and Institu-
tions March 1970*, Publication No. [SRS] 72-03258, March 10, 1972, Table 6.

[3] U.S. Bureau of the Census, *Census of Population: 1970 General Social and Economic Characteristics, United States Summary*, PC(1)-C1, (Washington, D. C.: U.S. Government Printing Office,
1972), Table 85, p. 1-380.

foster care placement, a court can nevertheless order removal after a judicial proceeding if the state can demonstrate parental abuse or neglect. But if parents consent to foster care placement, no judicial action is necessary. Many foster care placements, perhaps one-half or more, are arranged by state social welfare departments
without any court involvement. In California, for example, the State Social Welfare Board estimated recently that one-half of the children in state-sponsored foster
care were "voluntary" placements where the parent(s) consented to relinquish custody without a formal court proceeding.[4] A study in New York City found that 58
percent of the natural parents of foster children had agreed to foster care placement.[5]

A substantial degree of state coercion may be involved in many so-called voluntary placements, making the distinction between voluntary and coercive placement illusory. Many social welfare departments routinely ask parents to agree to
give up their children before initiating neglect proceedings in court. Some parents who would have been willing to keep their children may consent to placement to avoid a court proceeding against them. If one were to use the legal standards of voluntariness and informed consent applied in the criminal law to con-
fessions[6] and to the waiver of important legal rights,[7] many cases of relinquish-
ment after state intervention might not be considered voluntary. On the other
hand, not all court-ordered foster care placements involve coercion of the parents.
Some take place with their full concurrence. In some cases State welfare agencies
require even parents who desire to place their children in foster care to go through
a court proceeding. There is a financial incentive for the State to do this because
under the Social Security Act, a state can be partially reimbursed by the federal
government only if a court orders placement.[8]

Although it is unrealistic to make precise estimates given the complexities just
outlined, I would judge that at least 100,000 children around the country are now
in foster care because of coercive state intervention. Whatever their exact number,
the state's role in placing them in foster care suggests a significant social responsibility. Even though state coercion can occur outside of court, judges usually have
been responsible for deciding whether or not to remove children over parental ob-

---

[4] California State Social Welfare Board, *Report on Foster Care, Children Waiting* (Sacramento,
Calif.: Department of Social Welfare, 1972). p. 7.

[5] See Shirley Jenkins and Mignon Sauber, *Paths to Child Placement, Family Situations Prior to
Foster Care* (New York: Community Council of Greater New York, 1966), p. 74.

[6] See, e.g., *Escobedo v. Illinois,* 378 U.S. 478 (1964).

[7] *Johnson v. Zerbst,* 304 U.S. 458 (1938).

[8] See 42 U.S.C. §608(a).

jection. Law provides the principal framework to inform and constrain judicial action. This paper therefore addresses two basic questions. First, what legal standards should govern the judicial decision to remove a child over parental objections and place the child in foster care? And second, how can the law ensure developmental continuity and stability for children who must be so removed?

As background, the present legal standards for removing children, the process of intervention, and what is known about foster children and the foster care system are briefly described. I think three principles, currently violated, should govern its operation:

1. Removal should be a last resort, used only when the child cannot be protected within the home.

2. The decision to require foster care placement should be based on legal standards that can be applied in a consistent and even-handed way, and not be profoundly influenced by the values of the particular deciding judge.

3. If removal is necessary, the state should actively seek, when possible, to help the child's parents overcome the problems that led to removal so that the child can be returned home as soon as possible. In cases where the child cannot be returned home in a reasonable time, despite efforts by the state, the state should find a stable alternative arrangement such as adoption for the child. A child should not be left in foster care for an indefinite period of time.

Current legal standards for removal, under which courts increasingly purport to make individualized determinations of what is in the best interests of the child, contribute significantly to the failings of the present foster care system. My criticism is not that present standards fail to give adequate weight to parental interests, as compared to the child's interests; indeed, the focus of social concern probably should be on the child. Nor do I believe that it is always inappropriate to remove a child from parental custody for placement in foster care; in some circumstances nothing less drastic will protect a child from abusing or neglectful parents. Instead, what is wrong with the existing legal standards is that they call for individualized determinations based on discretionary assessments of the best interests of the child, and these determinations cannot be made consistently and fairly. They result in the unnecessary placement of children in foster care and do little to protect children against remaining in foster care for too long. Accordingly, substantial changes in the legal standards are needed, designed to make it more difficult to remove children initially and to provide more continuity and stability for children if removal is necessary. These changes will entail more than added procedural safeguards.

How the State Removes Children from their Parents

Source of the Power

The power of government to protect children by removing them from parental custody has roots deep in American history. And in colonial times just as today, the children of the poor were the most affected. Seventeenth century laws of Massachusetts, Connecticut, and Virginia, for example, specifically authorized magistrates to "bind out" or indenture children *of the poor* over parental objections.[9] Although it is unclear how frequently this power was exercised, the records of Watertown, Massachusetts, for instance, show that in 1671 Edward Sanderson's two oldest children were bound out as apprentices "where they may be educated and brought up in the knowledge of God and some honest calling." The reason given: poverty.[10]

By the early nineteenth century, the *parens patriae* power of the state, i.e., the sovereign's ultimate responsibility to guard the interests of children and others who lacked legal capacity, was thought sufficient to empower courts to remove a child from parental custody. Significantly, the reinforcement of public morality, and not simply the protection of children from cruelty, was seen as sufficient justification for the exercise of this power. Joseph Story, the renowned Massachusetts legal scholar who sat on the Supreme Court from 1811 to 1845, stated in his treatise on equity courts:

Although, in general, parents are intrusted with the custody of the persons, and the education of their children, yet this is done upon the natural presumption, that the children will be properly taken care of, and will be brought up with a due education in literature, and morals, and religion; and that they will be treated with kindness and affection. But, whenever this presumption is removed; whenever (for example,) it is found, that a father is guilty of gross ill-treatment or cruelty towards his infant children; or that he is in constant habits of drunkenness and blasphemy, or low and gross debauchery; or that he professes atheistical or irreligious principles; or that his domestic associations are such as tend to the corruption and contamination of his children; or that he otherwise acts in a manner injurious to the morals and interests of his children; in every such case, the Court of Chancery will interfere, and deprive him of the custody of his children, and appoint a suitable person to act as guardian, and to take care of them, and to superintend their education.[11]

[9] See Robert Bremner, ed. *Children and Youth in America* (Cambridge, Mass.: Harvard University Press, 1970), I, pp. 64-70.
[10] Bremner, p. 68.
[11] Story, 2 *Equity Jurisprudence* Sec. 1341 (1857) (footnotes omitted from quote). For a dis-

Today, every state has a statute allowing a court to intervene into the family to protect a child; this authority is usually conferred on the juvenile or family court.[12] Apart from situations where the child has engaged in wrongful behavior of some sort, the statutes in most states allow the court to intrude into the child's life if, for whatever reason, he or she lacks a parent or guardian (dependent or abandoned children), if the parent has neglected properly to care for or to support him or her (neglected children), or if the parent has willfully injured the child (abused children). Frequently the terms "dependent" and "neglected" are used to describe all children subject to a juvenile court's jurisdiction who have not engaged in any wrongful behavior. In this paper, the term "neglected" is so used, and is meant to include dependent and abused children as well.

In several respects present-day legislative standards defining the circumstances where a court may intervene into the family bear a remarkable similarity to Story's nineteenth century characterization. They are vague and open-ended, they require highly subjective determinations, and they permit intervention not only when the child has been demonstrably harmed or is physically endangered but also when parental habits or attitudes are adverse to the inculcation of proper moral values. Typical statutory provisions allow court intrusion to protect a child who is not receiving "proper parental care,"[13] "proper attention,"[14] "whose home is an unfit place for him by reason of neglect, cruelty, depravity, or physical abuse,"[15] or whose parents neglect to provide the "care necessary for his health, morals or well being."[16] The Minnesota statute explicitly specifies that emotional neglect of the child is relevant to intervention.[17]

The Process of Removal

While the legal standards for court intervention are scarcely more precise today than 100 years ago, far more complex administrative processes are involved.[18] In

---

cussion of the history of child neglect laws, see Mason P. Thomas, "Child Abuse and Neglect, Part I: Historical Overview, Legal Matrix, and Social Perspectives," *North Carolina Law Review*, 50 (1972), p. 293.

[12] A recent collection of the citations to these provisions can be found in Sandford N. Katz, *When Parents Fail, The Law's Response to Family Breakdown* (Boston: Beacon Press, 1971), pp. 83-85.

[13] See, e.g., Colo. Rev. Stat. Ann. Sec. 22-1-1 (1963).

[14] See, e.g., Mass. Ann. Laws ch. 119, Sec. 24 (1965).

[15] See, e.g., Cal. Welfare and Institutions Code Sec. 600 (d) (West 1972).

[16] See, e.g., Ohio Rev. Code Ann. Sec. 2151.03(c) (1969).

[17] See, e.g., Minn. Stat. Ann. 260.015 (b) (d) (1969).

[18] For a historical description of how neglected children were cared for, see generally, Homer Folks, *The Care of Destitute, Neglected, and Delinquent Children* (New York: Macmillan, 1902). Various documents can be found in Robert Bremner, ed., *Children and Youth in America*, Vols. I, II(A) and II(B) (Cambridge, Mass.: Harvard University Press, 1970).

Story's time, social workers and probation departments did not exist. Today a case usually reaches court after weaving through a complicated social welfare bureaucracy where numerous officials including social workers, probation officers, and court personnel, may have had contact with the family.

Unfortunately, very little is known about how the discretion of these various administrative officers is exercised before a case reaches court. The process is usually initiated by a report from a social worker or the police, or less frequently from a neighbor, medical professional, or school staff member.[19] Although practices vary, a member of a special unit of the social welfare or probation department is usually responsible for an initial investigation of the report. Customarily this investigation is not extensive; often it will only involve a visit to the home and a telephone conversation with the person who turned in the report. The investigator, sometimes together with a supervisor, then must decide whether to close the case, to suggest that the welfare agency informally (and non-coercively) provide services or supervision, or to file a petition in court.

Filing a petition initiates a judicial inquiry that usually has two stages. First, the court must determine whether it has jurisdiction over the child. This involves deciding on the basis of exceedingly broad and ill-defined statutory provisions whether the parents have failed to live up to acceptable social standards for child rearing. If it is determined that they have, then such jurisdiction empowers the court to intervene into the family. In the words of one juvenile court judge, "It is the ultimate finding of neglect which releases the court's wide discretionary powers of disposition, a discretion beholden to and circumscribed by the law's most challenging aphorism, 'the best interests of the child.' "[20] The second stage involves a dispositional hearing, where the judge decides the manner of intervention. Re-

[19] The child is sometimes taken into custody by the state at the time of this initial report—before any court hearing. The laws of many states authorize "emergency" removal from parental custody without prior court authorization by police, and sometimes social workers and doctors. In California, for example, a policeman with "reasonable cause for believing" the child is neglected or abused can take a child into custody without prior judicial authorization (Cal. Welfare & Institutions Code Sec. 625). The child must be released to the parents within forty-eight hours, however, unless a petition is filed to institute a juvenile court proceeding (Cal. Welfare & Institutions Code Sec. 631). Moreover, even if a petition is filed, the statute requires the court to hold a detention hearing within twenty-four hours to determine whether the child should remain in state custody during the pendency of the judicial proceedings (see Cal. Welfare & Institutions Code Sec. 632), which can often take several weeks. Because there are situations in which swift removal is of crucial importance to a child's safety, the power to remove for short periods of time without prior court approval seems plainly desirable. The important questions relating to what the standard for emergency removals should be, and how prompt judicial review of such interim actions can be insured are beyond the scope of this paper.

[20] Thomas Gill, "The Legal Nature of Neglect," *National Probation and Parole Association Journal*, 6 (1960), p. 14.

moval from the home is by no means mandatory. The court can instead require supervision within the child's own home, psychological counseling for the parents and/or the child, or periodic home visits by a social worker, probation officer, or homemaker.

No national data is available, but it appears that children are removed from parental custody in a significant percentage of the cases when the juvenile court assumes jurisdiction. In 1972, for example, the Los Angeles juvenile courts ordered removal in 1,028 out of 1,656 of the cases where jurisdiction was assumed—62 percent.[21] For San Francisco in the same year, 65 percent were ordered removed (262 out of 402).[22] Although some of these children were placed with relatives, over 80 percent of those removed were placed in foster care. Likewise, a study of dispositions in New York State during the years 1957-60 showed that the probability of removal from the home was as great as that of supervision by the probation department—each occurred in slightly over 30 percent of the neglect petitions adjudicated by the court.[23] More recently, Professor Peter Straus has estimated that in New York the child is taken from its home "in about half" of the cases of abuse or neglect.[24]

Children in Foster Care:

The Characteristics of Foster Children—The Reasons for Removal

The social welfare literature provides some information about the age and eco-

[21] Letter dated September 25, 1973, from Los Angeles County Department of Public Social Services. Calculations based on this same source suggest that in 1972, the 3,518 juvenile court petitions filed by the Los Angeles Department of Public Social Services were disposed of as follows:

Total Petitions		3,518
Dismissed by Department of Public Social Services before final court determination		1,480
Transfer to other jurisdictions		75
Decided by Juvenile Court		1,963
Dismissed by Court		307
Jurisdiction Assumed by Court		1,656
Supervised within home		628
Removal Ordered		1,028
Placed with relatives	149	
Placed in foster care	879	

[22] Unpublished yearly statistical compilation for the San Francisco Juvenile Court Annual Report for 1972. This data shows that in 1972, there were hearings in cases involving 544 children; the court transferred 22 to other counties and dismissed 119 more without assuming jurisdiction. Of the 402 children for whom the court took jurisdiction, 141 were supervised within their own home, 59 were ordered placed with relatives, and 203 were placed in foster care.

[23] See N. Y. Joint Legislative Committee on Court Reorganization: Report No. 2—The Family Court Act, McKinney's Session Laws of New York 3428, 3443 (1962).

[24] "The Relationship Between Promise and Performance in State Intervention in Family Life,"

nomic circumstances of the children placed in foster care. Most of the children are quite young at the time of removal; a majority are probably six years of age or younger.[25] Their families are usually very poor, often on welfare.[26] A disproportionate number are from single parent families.[27]

Unfortunately there is very little systematic information about the circumstances that result in foster care placement over parental objections. Although some social welfare research attempts to analyze why children are placed in foster care, these studies are based on samples where many parents agreed to placement or sought it. There is no reason to assume that the circumstances leading a family to wish to give up a child are the same as those leading professionals to decide the state should compel removal. The most extensive work on reasons for foster placement has been done by Shirley Jenkins and her associates at Columbia University, published in 1966. Jenkins and Sauber analyzed 425 families whose children were placed in foster care in New York City. Using five major categories, they describe the "main reason for placement" as follows:

(1) physical illness or incapacity of child-caring person, including confinement, 29 percent; (2) mental illness of the mother, 11 percent; (3) child personality or emotional problems, 17 per cent; (4) severe neglect or abuse, 10 per cent; (5) 'family problems,' 33 percent. The last group includes cases of unwillingness or inability to continue care on the part of an adult other than a parent, children left or deserted, parental incompetence, and conflicts or arrests.[28]

A later study published in 1972 by Jenkins and Norman found the following distribution of families according to reason for placement.[29] (See Table 1.)

Columbia Journal of Law and Social Problems, 9 (1972) p. 30, citing Note, "An Appraisal of New York's Statutory Response to the Problem of Child Abuse," *Columbia Journal of Law and Social Problems*, 7 (1971), p. 72.

[25] See, N. Y. Jt. Legislative Committee on Court Reorganization; p. 3442. (In neglect proceedings, fifty percent are children under age six, ninety percent under twelve.)

[26] See, e.g., Shirley Jenkins and Elaine Norman, *Filial Deprivation and Foster Care* (New York: Columbia University Press, 1972), pp. 2, 25-30; Martin Rein, Thomas E. Nutt, and Heather Weiss, "Foster Care: Myth and Reality," in Alvin Schorr (ed.), *Children and Decent People* (New York: Basic Books, forthcoming). For a careful analysis of how the judicial system treats custody decisions for the poor, see Herma Hill Kay and Irving Phillips, "Poverty and the Law of Child Custody," *California Law Review*, 54 (1966), p. 717. See also Jacobus ten Broek, "California's Dual System of Family Law: Its Origin, Development, and Present Status," *Stanford Law Review*, 16 (1964), p. 257 (Part I); p. 900 (Part II); *Stanford Law Review*, 17 (1965), p. 614 (Part III).

[27] See e.g., Jenkins and Norman, *Filial Deprivation*, p. 35, indicating that only eleven per cent of the foster children in their sample of 533 foster children in New York City were living with both parents at the time of placement.

[28] Jenkins & Sauber, *Paths to Child Placement*, p. 80.

[29] See Jenkins & Norman, *Filial Deprivation*, p. 55.

TABLE 1
Distribution of Families According to Reason for Placement

Reason for Placement	Number of Families	Percent Distribution
Mental illness	86	22
Child behavior	63	16
Neglect or abuse	54	14
Physical illness	44	11
Unwillingness or inability to continue care	41	11
Family dysfunction	36	9
Unwillingness or inability to assume care	30	8
Abandonment or desertion	30	8
Other problems	6	1
Total	390	100

Neither study is particularly helpful for analyzing antecedents of the legal decision to place children in foster homes. In the first study, parents were known to have objected to placement in only ten percent of the sample cases, and the percentage distribution of reasons for placement among this subgroup is not given. While it is suggested that the "severe abuse or neglect" category included most of the objecting parents, that category, as its label shows, is no more helpful in describing the reason for the decision than the underlying statute. The later study is also based on samples that include voluntary and non-voluntary placements. It too uses descriptive categories lacking definitional clarity and combining situations where parents no longer want child care responsibility with those where a professional has decided the parent is not competent. Finally, as these researchers realized, more than one reason frequently can be identified for foster care placement, making the selection of a single reason difficult or inappropriate. Other social welfare research has sought to analyze the factors influencing a social worker's preference for placement outside the home as opposed to provision of services in the child's own home.[30] None, however, focuses primarily on judicial determinations.

Nor do judicial opinions or legal scholarship provide a solid basis for generalizations about the circumstances leading courts to remove children over parental

[30] See Michael H. Phillips, Ann W. Shyne, Edmund A. Sherman, and Barbara L. Haring, *Factors Associated with Placement Decisions in Child Welfare* (New York: Child Welfare League of America, 1971); Bernice Boehm, "An Assessment of Family Adequacy in Protective Cases," *Child Welfare*, 41 (January 1962), pp. 10-16; Eugene Shinn, "Is Placement Necessary? An Experimental Study of Agreement Among Caseworkers in Making Foster Care Decisions," Diss., Columbia University School of Social Work, 1968.

objections. Legal scholarship usually is based on reported cases. It cannot be assumed these are reliable guides to the circumstances leading to removal for two reasons. First, juvenile and family court judges rarely dispose of cases with written opinions at all, much less reported ones. Second, although appealed cases often result in reported opinions very few neglect cases are appealed. I estimate during the past six years that only about one in every thousand cases where a California court has ordered foster care placement has resulted in a reported appellate opinion.[31] There is no basis for assuming these cases are representative.

Despite the paucity of data, it appears that removal over parental objections takes place most often where the court determines the parents' supervision and guidance of the child are inadequate, where the mother is thought to be emotionally ill, or where the child has behavior problems.[32] Although highly publicized, cases involving child battery, where a parent has intentionally abused or injured a child, are in a distinct minority.[33]

Where the Children Go

After a court decides to remove a child from home, a public agency, often the social welfare or probation department, is assigned responsibility for placing the

[31] In California, for example, for the period from January 1, 1967, through August 30, 1973, there are a total of fourteen reported appellate opinions for neglect cases—not one by the California Supreme Court. At the present time there are about 15,000 children in foster care for whom a court ordered removal. Most of these were first placed during that period. It seems reasonable to assume that at least as many children both entered and exited foster care during that period as were initially placed before 1967.

[32] This conclusion, based on observations of juvenile court and interviews with social workers and probation officers is consistent with the findings of Phillips, *Factors Associated with Placement,* p. 72-79, 88, based on a simulation study of the behavior of three juvenile court judges.

[33] For 1968, David Gil estimated that a total of 10,931 reports of child abuse were made under state reporting laws. *Violence Against Children, Physical Child Abuse in the United States* (Cambridge, Mass.: Harvard University Press, 1970), p. 92. At that time every state had a law requiring that child abuse be reported. For that same year HEW estimated that Juvenile Courts in the United States handled approximately 141,000 dependency and neglect cases. See United States Children's Bureau, *Juvenile Court Statistics 1968* (Statistical Series No. 95, 1970), p. 15. Although many cases of child abuse go unreported, it is reasonable to assume that most abuse cases that go to court are reported. Moreover, some reported cases of abuse do not result in juvenile court petitions. Therefore, one could reasonably estimate for that year that less than nine per cent of the dependency and neglect petitions handled by juvenile courts involved child abuse. There has apparently been an increase in reported abuse cases since 1968, however, while the number of neglect cases handled by courts declined to 130,900 for 1971. See *Juvenile Court Statistics 1971.* Moreover, abuse cases are perhaps more likely to lead to removal than other cases. Based on preliminary work here in California, I would estimate that probably fifteen to twenty per cent, and certainly no more than a quarter of the cases where removal is ordered involve intentional physical abuse by a parent.

child. In 1933 about half of the nation's neglected children were in large institutions, and a large proportion were supervised by some religiously sponsored voluntary agency.[34] In 1970 only 42,200 children lived in foster care under the auspices of voluntary agencies, while over 284,000 were under the supervision of state social service agencies. Of the state-supervised children, 243,600 lived in foster family homes, 3,600 in group homes, and only 37,300 in child welfare institutions.[35]

Foster family homes are usually licensed by the state, with regulations regarding aspects such as the size of the home, number of children, and age of foster parents. Under a contract, foster parents are paid a monthly fee for each child in their care.[36] Most foster parents, it appears, are middle- or lower-middle-class and are forty years old or older.[37] Although foster parents are responsible for the day-to-day care of the children, the contract between the agency and the foster parents usually requires the foster parents to acknowledge that "the legal responsibility for the foster child remains with the Agency," and to "accept and comply with any plans the Agency makes for the child," including "the right to determine when and how the child leaves" the foster home.[38]

How Long Do Children Remain in Foster Care?

In theory, "the distinguishing aspect of foster care is that it is designed to be a temporary arrangement. The family is broken up only so that it can be put to-

[34] See Alfred Kadushin, "Child Welfare: Adoption and Foster Care," in *Encyclopedia of Social Work*, Ed. R. Morris, 16th ed. (New York: National Association of Social Workers), 1971, Vol. 1, p. 104.

[35] See *Children Served by Public Welfare Agencies*, at Table 6. Part of the reason for the preference for foster family care over institutional care is cost. In California, as of June, 1973, for example, the average monthly payment for residential care per child in a foster family home was $124.96; the average monthly payment for children in the institutions was $487.87. California State Department of Social Welfare, *Aid to Families with Dependent Children—Boarding Homes and Institutions Case Load Movement and Expenditure Report* (Department of Social Welfare, Sacramento, June, 1973)

[36] In California the monthly rates per foster child paid to foster families are set by the county and vary widely among counties—from $72 to $160 in 1972. California State Department of Social Welfare, Aid to Families with Dependent Children. Differences in the cost of living do not justify these differentials, and one suspects that—as is true for school spending—the differences are in part related to the local wealth. Compare *Serrano v. Priest*, 5 Cal. 3d 584, 487 P.2d 1241, (1971). The financing of foster care is extremely complex, with funds coming from both state and federal government. The federal government, as part of the Social Security Act, reimburses states for a portion of cost of foster care for children meeting financial eligibility. See 42 U.S.C. Sec. 608(a). For a complete description of the complexities of the financing of foster care in California, see Childhood and Government Project, Earl Warren Legal Institute, University of California, Berkeley, "The Finance of Foster Care," (Staff Working Paper), 1973.

[37] See, e.g., Martin Wolins, *Selecting Foster Parents* (New York: Columbia University Press, 1963), p. 201; Alfred Kadushin, *Child Welfare Services* (New York: Macmillan, 1967), p. 371.

[38] Joseph Goldstein and Jay Katz, *The Family and the Law, Problems in Decision in the Family Law Process* (New York: Free Press, 1965), pp. 1021-22.

gether again in a way that will be less problematic for the child."[39] It would be reassuring to know that children who enter foster care remain there only a short time, then either return to their parents or are adopted by some other family. Some children indeed do remain in foster care only a short period, but the evidence suggests that this pattern is the exception rather than the rule. Foster care is not typically short-term. On the basis of their analysis, Maas and Engler predicted that "better than half" of the more than 4,000 children they studied would be "living a major part of their childhood in foster families and institutions."[40] Similarly, in a study of 624 children under twelve who entered foster care during 1966 and were there at least 90 days, Fanshel found that 46 percent were still in foster care three and one-half years later.[41] Wiltse and Gambrill recently examined a sample composed of 772 San Francisco foster children, about one-half of that city's entire caseload. They found that 62 percent of these children were expected to remain in foster care until maturity; the average length of time in care for all the children in their sample was nearly five years.[42] One juvenile judge has written about his surprise at the beginning of his term when he found that many of the neglected children under his jurisdiction had been in "temporary" foster care for five to six years.[43]

One way the state might minimize the length of time children remain in foster care is to work intensively with the natural parents to correct the deficiency which led to coercive removal. However, natural parents are rarely offered rehabilitative services after the children are removed. In examining foster care in nine communities, Maas and Engler found that:

More than 70 percent of the fathers and mothers of the children in this study either had no relationship with the agencies responsible for the care of their children or their relationship was erratic or untrusting. In many instances the agencies' resources were such that their staff's time was entirely consumed with the day-to-day job of caring for the children. They had no time for the kind of continuous work with the parents of the children which could effect the rehabilitation of the home. Frequently agencies fail to appreciate the dynamics of intrafamily relationships as a whole and work only with the child.[44]

[39] Kadushin, *Child Welfare Services,* p. 411.

[40] Henry S. Maas and Richard E. Engler, Jr., *Children in Need of Parents* (New York: Columbia University Press, 1959), p. 356.

[41] David Fanshel, "The Exit of Children from Foster Care: An Interim Research Report," *Child Welfare,* 50 (February 1971), pp. 65-81.

[42] Kermit Wiltse and Eileen Gambrill, "Decision-Making Processes in Foster Care," unpublished paper, School of Social Welfare, University of California, Berkeley, Calif., 1973.

[43] See Ralph W. Crary, "Neglect, Red Tape and Adoption," *National Probation and Parole Association Journal,* 6 (1960), p. 34.

[44] Maas and Engler, *Children in Need,* pp. 390-91.

Interviews during the last six months with a number of social workers in Northern California suggest that after removal, caseworkers focus attention almost exclusively on the child and the foster parents, spending little if any time with the natural parents. This may reflect lack of clarity about the parental default which must be corrected, or absence of available techniques or resources to correct the deficiencies, or both.

Whether or not rehabilitative services would help, the present reality is such that for "only a fraction of children now in foster care is there a possibility of return to their own homes."[45] Wiltse and Gambrell found in their San Francisco study that return to home was expected in only fifteen percent of the cases[46]; Maas and Engler concluded on the basis of their study of 4,281 children in nine communities that for "no more than twenty-five percent" was it probable that the foster child would return home.[47]

Although many foster children never return to their natural parents, long-term plans that would provide these children with a sense of security and stability are seldom made and rarely implemented. One study concluded that "for nearly two-thirds (sixty-four percent) of the children in foster care the public agencies reported that the only plan was continuation in foster care."[48] Moreover, because neither the foster parents nor the agency is under an obligation to keep the child where originally placed, children are often moved from one foster home to another.[49] Adoption probably provides the best chance for stability and continuity. It creates the same legal relationship between child and adult in terms of custody, support, discipline, and inheritance as exists between a parent and a biologically-related, legitimate child. But very few foster children are ever adopted. In one study of foster children supervised by public agencies, only thirteen percent of the children were considered likely to be adopted.[50] Social welfare agencies are frequently reluctant to place foster children for adoption because this requires final termination of the natural parents' legal rights, an act that necessitates a separate legal proceeding often involving more stringent standards then those

[45] Maas and Engler, p. 383.
[46] Wiltse and Gambrill.
[47] Maas and Engler, p. 379.
[48] Helen Jeter, *Children, Problems and Services in Child Welfare Programs* (Washington, D.C.: U.S. Government Printing Office, 1963), p. 87.
[49] Jeter, p. 5; fifty-eight per cent had more than one placement; Wiltse and Gambrill state that the foster children in their sample typically had two placements.
[50] Jeter, p. 87. This same study anticipated only twelve per cent would return home. See also Mary Lewis, "Foster-Family Care: Has It Fulfilled Its Promise?" *The Annals*, 355 (1964), pp. 31, 36.

used for the initial removal. Wishing to avoid anything drastic, and uncertain of their legal ability to act, these agencies do nothing, and, as more time goes by, adoption becomes less possible.[51] Indeed, it appears that after a child has been in foster care for more than eighteen months, the chance of either returning home or being adopted is remote.[52]

In summary, children removed by the state from the home of their parents are often destined to remain in limbo until adulthood, the wards of a largely indifferent state. On the one hand, they frequently are unable to return to their natural parents, who are offered little rehabilitative help. On the other hand, they are usually placed with a foster family and cautioned not to become too attached. These children thus grow up without a permanent and secure home.

What is Wrong with the Best Interests Standard?

We now turn to a close examination of the "best interests of the child" test, the legal standard usually employed by courts to decide whether a child should be removed from parental custody in the dispositional stage of neglect proceedings. This standard has long been used to decide matters of child custody, particularly in disputes between parents. In an opinion written nearly fifty years ago, Benjamin Cardozo described as follows the role of the judge in any child custody proceeding brought before a court of equity:

He acts as *parens patriae* to do what is best for the interest of the child. He is to put himself in the position of a 'wise, affectionate, and careful parent' . . . and make provision for the child accordingly. He may act at the intervention of a kinsman, if so the petition comes before him, but equally he may act at the instance or on the motion of any one else. He is not adjudicating a controversy between adversary parties, to compare their private differences. He is not determining rights 'as between a parent and a child'; or as between one parent and another. . . . He 'interferes for the protection of infants, *qua* infants, by virtue of the prerogative which belongs to the Crown as *parens patriae*.'[53]

Cardozo's description appears in a decision involving a dispute between estranged parents over who should have custody of the children. Today some version of the best interests standard is incorporated in the divorce legislation of nearly

[51] See Crary, p. 39.
[52] Maas and Engler, p. 390. "In community after community it is clear from the data in the study that unless children move out of care within the first year to year and a half of their stay in care, the likelihood of their ever moving out sharply decreases."
[53] *Finlay v. Finlay*, 240 N. Y. 429, 433-34, 148 N.E. 624, 626 (1925).

every state.[54] But Cardozo's expansive language makes it easy to understand how the test could be applied not only in disputes between parents, but also in neglect proceedings. Presently, the best interests test is widely used to decide what should be done for a child over whom a juvenile court has assumed jurisdiction[55]; indeed it is sometimes used to decide whether jurisdiction should be assumed.[56]

For the dispositional decision in neglect cases, the best interests test would appear to have much to commend it. It focuses principally on the child rather than on arbitrary legal rights of parents. It implicitly recognizes that each child is unique, and that parental conduct and home environments may have substantially different effects on different children. It also seems to require that the judge find out as much as possible about the child, the child's circumstances, the parents, and the available alternative arrangements. In fact, the best interests standard embodies what David Matza has described as a basic precept of juvenile court philosophy: the principle of "individualized justice." This principle requires each dispositional decision, in Matza's words, "to be guided by a *full understanding* of the client's personal and social characteristics and by his 'individual needs.' "[57]

Nonetheless, a careful analysis reveals serious deficiencies in the best interests test when it is used to decide whether the state should remove a child from parental custody and place the child in foster care. I will discuss some of the test's shortcomings as it is applied in foster care cases.

Conceptual Problems with the Test

One obvious objection to the best interests of the child test is that by its very terms it ignores completely the interests of the parents. Obviously a child's par-

---

[54] Zuchman & Fox, "The Ferment in Divorce Legislation," *Journal of Family Law* 12 (1972), pp. 515, 571-576.

[55] See e.g., In Re Rocher, 187 N.W.2d 730, 732 (Iowa, 1971): "Neither the trial court nor this one has—or claims—omniscience. It is never a pleasant task to separate parent and child. We can only take the record as we find it and reach a conclusion which appears to be for the best interest of the children. Both the statute and our previous decisions demand that we do so." *In re East,* 32 Ohio Misc. 65, 288 N.E.2d 343 (C.P. Juv. Div. Highland County 1972); *In re Kindis,* 162 Conn. 239, 294 A.2d 316 (1972); *In re Johnson,* 210 Kan. 828, 504 P.2d 217 (1972); *In re One Minor Child,* 254 A.2d 443 (Del. Sup. Ct. 1969); *In re B.G. & V.G.,* 32 C.A. 3d 365, 108 Cal. Rptr. 121 (1973); *Hammond v. Department of Public Assistance,* 142 W.Va. 208, 95 S.E. 2d 345 (1956).

[56] See *In Re Cager,* 251 Md. 473, 479, 248 A.2d 384, 388 (Md. Ct. App. 1968): "It is clear that the ultimate consideration in finding neglect which will serve as a basis for removing a child from its mother's custody is the best interest of the child."; *Todd v. Superior Court,* 68 Wash. 2d 587, 414 P.2d 605 (1966); *State v. Pogue,* 282 S.W. 2d 582 (Springfield Mo. Ct. App. 1955).

[57] David Matza, *Delinquency and Drift* (New York: John Wiley & Sons, 1964), pp. 114-15.

ents have important interests at stake when the state seeks to intervene; a parent can derive important satisfactions and pleasures from a relationship with a child, and the destruction of this relationship can have an enormous effect on the parent quite apart from benefits or losses to the child. I doubt whether courts ignore the effects of judicial action on parents, but the best interests of the child test disallows explicit consideration of parental interests, making the process more high-sounding, perhaps, but less honest.

But even if we assume that it is appropriate to focus attention exclusively on the child's interests, there remain conceptual difficulties with the best interests test. Its application assumes the judge will compare the probable consequences for the child of remaining in the home with the probable consequences of removal. How might a judge make this comparison? He or she would need considerable information and predictive ability. The information would include knowledge of how the parents had behaved in the past, the effect of this parental behavior on the child, and the child's present condition. Then the judge would need to predict the probable future behavior of the parents if the child were to remain in the home and to gauge the probable effects of his behavior on the child. Obviously, more than one outcome is possible, so the judge would have to assess the probability of various outcomes and evaluate the seriousness of possible benefits and harms associated with each. Next, the judge would have to compare this set of possible consequences with those if the child were placed in a foster home. This would require predicting the effect of removing the child from home, school, friends, and familiar surroundings, as well as predicting the child's experience while in the foster care system. Such predictions involve estimates of the child's future relationship with the foster parents, the child's future contact with natural parents and siblings, the number of foster homes in which the child ultimately will have to be placed, the length of time spent in foster care, the potential for acquiring a stable home, and myriad other factors.

Obviously one can question whether a judge has the necessary information. In many instances he or she lacks adequate information even about a child's life with his or her parents. Moreover, at the time of the dispositional hearing, the judge typically has *no* information about where the child will be placed if removal is ordered; he or she usually knows nothing about the characteristics of the foster family, or how long that family will want or be able to keep the child. In deciding who should raise a particular child, the court in a neglect proceeding is comparing an existing family with a largely unknown alternative. In this regard, the dispositional phase of a neglect proceeding stands in sharp contrast with a divorce

174

custody dispute, where the best interest test is also widely employed. In a divorce custody contest, the judge is settling a dispute between two adults, usually both before the court, each of whom had a prior relationship with the child and each of whom wishes to assume full parental authority.[58] In a neglect case, the judge is deciding in a state-initiated proceeding whether to remove a child from parental custody and have the state assume responsibility by placing the child in a state-sponsored home about which the judge knows few, if any, particulars.

Even if the judge had substantial information about both the child's existing home life and the foster care alternatives, our knowledge about human behavior provides no basis for the predictions called for by the best interest standard. No consensus exists about a theory of human behavior, and no theory is widely considered capable of generating reliable predictions about the psychological and behavioral consequences of alternative dispositions. This does not imply a criticism of the behavioral sciences. Indeed, Anna Freud, who has devoted her life to the study of the child and who plainly believes that theory can be a useful guide to treatment, has warned that theory alone does not provide a reliable guide for prediction: "In spite of . . . advances," she suggests, "there remain factors which make clinical foresight, i.e., prediction, difficult and hazardous," not the least of which is that "the environmental happenings in a child's life will always remain unpredictable since they are not governed by any known laws. . . ."[59]

[58] The best interest test has been criticized in the divorce context. For a thorough review of the behavioral science research as it relates to the effects of divorce custody determinations, and an excellent argument for specific statutory presumptions for divorce custody disputes, see **Phoebe C. Ellsworth and Robert J. Levy**, "Legislative Reform of Child Custody Adjudication," *Law & Society Review*, 4 (1969), p. 167.

[59] Anna Freud, "Child Observation and Prediction of Development—A Memorial Lecture in Honor of Ernst Kris," *The Psychoanalytic Study of the Child* (New York: International University Press, 1958), XIII, pp. 92, 97-98. After this article was submitted for publication, I discovered two fascinating essays, one by Anna Freud entitled, "The Child is a Person in His Own Right" and one by Joseph Goldstein, "The Least Detrimental Alternative to the Problem for the Law of Child Placement." Both are found in *The Psychoanalytic Study of the Child* for 1972 (New York: Quadrangle Books, 1973), and are parts of a soon-to-be published book co-authored by Freud, Goldstein, and Albert Solnit entitled *Beyond the Best Interests of the Child*. Goldstein's essay, which takes the form of a judicial opinion, suggests that courts should seek out the "least detrimental available alternative" rather than ask what is in a child's best interests in custody cases. Goldstein's analysis is consistent with my own in that it emphasizes the importance of stability and consistency in parent-child relationships; it criticizes the best interests standard for misleading judges into thinking "they have more power for 'good' than for 'bad'" in what they decide; and it suggests that courts should focus on available alternatives, Although I wonder whether in terms of information, predictions and values Goldstein's alternative standard (if applied to removing children from parental custody for initial placement in foster care) might not be subject to many of the same criticisms as the best interest standard, I do not wish to base my judgment on the two essays alone for they are obviously part of a more elaborate analysis presented in the forthcoming book. In my expansion of this article

The limitations of psychological theory in generating verifiable predictions is suggested by the numerous studies which have attempted to trace effects of various child-rearing techniques and parental attitudes on adult personality traits. Under Sigmund Freud's influence, many psychologists have assumed the importance of a child's early years, searching for the importance of timing and techniques of nursing, weaning, toilet training, and the like. But in Sibylle Escalona's words:

The net result of a great many studies can be compressed into a single sentence: When child-rearing techniques of this order are treated as the independent variable, no significant relationship can be shown to exist between child-rearing techniques and later personality characteristics. Some parental attitudes do relate to child characteristics at school age and in adolescence, but no significant relationships have been demonstrated between parental attitudes towards a child during the first three or four years of life and the child's later characteristics.[60]

Studies that have attempted to trace personality development to specific antecedent variables have assumed that a particular practice would have the same effect on different children. This assumption is now widely questioned by experimental psychologists such as H. R. Schaffer. Schaffer and others think that infants experience in individual ways.[61] The implication of this for prediction is described very well by Arlene Skolnick: ". . . if the child selectively interprets situations and events, we cannot confidently predict behavior from knowledge of the situation alone."[62]

The difficulty of making accurate predictions is shown clearly by a study undertaken by Joan Macfarlane and her associates in Berkeley, California.[63] Using various tests and interviews, the Berkeley group studied during a thirty-year period a group of 166 infants born in 1929. Their objective was to observe the growth—emotional, mental, and physical—of normal people. As Skolnick observed:

Over the years this study has generated several significant research findings, but the most surprising of all was the difficulty of predicting what thirty-year-old adults would be like

that will be published this coming May in the *California Law Review*, I hope to analyze in some detail the Freud, Goldstein, Solnit book, which should soon be available.

[60] Sibylle Escalona, *The Roots of Individuality: Normal Patterns of Development in Infancy* (Chicago: Aldine, 1968), p. 13.

[61] H. R. Schaffer, *The Growth of Sociability* (Baltimore: Penguin, 1971), p. 16.

[62] Arlene Skolnick, *The Intimate Environment, Exploring Marriage and the Family* (Boston: Little Brown, 1973), p. 372.

[63] Joan W. Macfarlane, "Perspectives on Personality Consistency and Change from the Guidance Study," *Vita Humana*, 7 (1964), pp. 115-126.

even after the most sophisticated data had been gathered on them as children. . . . the researchers experienced shock after shock as they saw the people they had last seen at age eighteen. It turned out that the predictions they had made about the subjects were wrong in about two-thirds of the cases! How could a group of competent psychologists have been so mistaken?

Foremost, the researchers had tended to overestimate the damaging effects of early troubles of various kinds. Most personality theory had been derived from observations of troubled people in therapy. The pathology of adult neurotics and psychotics was traced back to disturbances early in childhood—poor parent-child relations, chronic school difficulties, and so forth. Consequently, theories of personality based on clinical observation tended to define adult psychological problems as socialization failures. But the psychiatrist sees only disturbed people; he does not encounter 'normal' individuals who may experience childhood difficulties but who do not grow into troubled adults. The Berkeley method, however, called for studying such people. Data on the experience of these subjects demonstrated the error of assuming that similar childhood conditions affect every child the same way. Indeed, many instances of what looked like severe pathology to the researchers were put to constructive use by the subjects. . . .[64]

Even if accurate predictions were possible, a fundamental problem would remain. What set of values is a judge to use to determine what is in the child's best interests? Should the judge be concerned with happiness? Or should he or she worry about the child's spiritual goodness or economic productivity? Is stability and security for a child more desirable than intellectual stimulation?[65] Should the best interests of the child be viewed from a short-term or a long-term perspective? The conditions that make a person happy at age ten or fifteen may have adverse consequences at age thirty.

The neglect statutes themselves are of little help in providing guidance about the values that should inform the decision. And, our pluralistic society lacks consensus about child-rearing strategies and values. By necessity, a judge is forced to rely upon personal values to determine a child's best interests.

The Problem of Fairness

What is wrong, one may ask, with reliance on individual values and judgments? For one thing, it offends a most basic precept of law. As John Rawls wrote: the rule of law "implies the precept that similar cases be treated similarly."[66] This aspiration is not always met, but any legal test that requires impossible predictions and

[64] Skolnick, pp. 378-79.
[65] See *Painter v. Bannister*, 258 Iowa 1390, 140 N.W. 2d 152 (1966).
[66] John Rawls, *A Theory of Justice* (Cambridge, Mass.: Harvard University Press, 1971), pp. 237.

reliance on the decision-makers own values invites injustice.

As long as the best interests standard or some equally broad standard is used, it seems inevitable that petitions will be filed and neglect cases will be decided without any clear articulation or consistent application of the behavioral or moral premises on which the decision is based. This conclusion is supported by a simulation study which analyzed the factors influencing a judge's decision whether to provide a child with services within the child's own home or to remove the child.[67] Three judges, each with at least five years experience, were independently given the actual files for 94 children from 50 families. Each judge was asked to decide whether the child should be removed or services should be provided. The three agreed in less than one-half of the cases (45 out of 94). Even more significantly, when the judges were asked to indicate the factors influencing their decisions, the study concluded, "Even in cases in which they agreed on the decision, the judges did not identify the same factors as determinants, each seeming to operate to some extent within his own unique value system."[68]

A judge's reliance on personal values is especially risky when class differences confound the problem. The foster care system is frequently accused of being class biased, one "in which middle-class professionals provide and control a service used mostly by poor people, with upper-lower and lower-middle class foster parents serving as intermediaries."[69] The fact that most foster children come from poor families does not, of course, prove that there is an inherent class bias in the system. There are other plausible explanations for the high proportion of poor children. The condition of poverty may lead to family breakdown and a greater likelihood that children are endangered in times of crisis. Alternatively, since poor families are more subject to scrutiny by social workers who administer welfare programs, their faults, even if no more common, may be more conspicuous. Finally, since poor families have access to few resources in the event of family crisis, their children may be forced into the foster care system because other forms of substitute care, such as babysitters, relatives, and day care centers, are not available.[70]

Although these other explanations are plausible, the fact remains that the best interests standard allows the judge to import his personal values into the process, and leaves considerable scope for class bias. An examination of available reported cases dramatically illustrates how a judge's attitude toward child rearing, sexual mores, religion, or cleanliness can affect the result of court proceedings. These

[67] Phillips *et al.,* pp. 69-84.
[68] Phillips *et al.,* p. 84.
[69] Rein *et al.* See also Katz, *When Parents Fail,* p. 91.
[70] See Rein, *et al.*

178

cases, while not typical, clearly reveal the risks of "individualized" decisions under vague judicial standards. There are a number of reported cases, for example, where a judge has decided parental behavior was immoral and, without any systematic inquiry into how the parental conduct damaged or was likely to harm the children, the judge then determined the children to be neglected and removed them from their home.[71] A New York judge declared five small children neglected, and ordered custody to be transferred to the father on the ground that the mother "frequently entertained male companions in the apartment . . . and, on at least one occasion, one of them spent the night with the [mother] and, in fact, slept with her, to the knowledge of the children." The court openly acknowledged:

The statutory definition of neglect, therefore, being in general terms, has resulted in a dearth of cases reported; and the tendency has been to leave it to the judge in a particular case to make his own decision as to whether or not there is neglect, based upon the particular and unique set of facts in the case at bar. It therefore has developed upon the courts to establish the moral standards to be followed by persons to whom is entrusted the care and custody of children. And never has there been a greater need for the courts to maintain a high level of moral conduct than exists today. This court intends to give more than lip service to the principle that the fabric of our society is composed of the family unit and when the family unit is damaged, the fabric of society suffers. Our courts will continue to insist upon a high level of moral conduct on the part of custodians of children, and will never succumb to the 'Hollywood' type of morality so popular today, which seems to condone and encourage the dropping of our moral guard. We have not yet reached the point where, when parents who have tired of each other's company, may be free to seek other companionship with complete disregard of the moral examples they are setting for their children. This is the crux of the case at bar.[72]

In deciding whether to remove a child from parental custody, various other judges have thought it relevant that a mother had extramarital sexual relations,[73] was a lesbian,[74] or had several illegitimate children.[75] Religion, like sex, has also triggered strong responses from judges. Religious fanaticism and unconventional beliefs of parents[76] have been considered relevant factors in neglect proceedings.

[71] See generally, Michael F. Sullivan, "Child Neglect: The Environmental Aspects," *Ohio State Law Journal,* 29 (1968), p. 85.
[72] In re Anonymous, 37 Misc. 2d 411, 238 N.Y.S. 2d 422, 423 (Fam. Ct. Rensselaer County, 1962).
[73] See *In re Booth,* 253 Minn 395, 91 N.W. 2d 921 (1958).
[74] *In re Tammy F.,* Cal. Dist. Ct. App., 1st Dist. Div. 2, No. 32643 (1973).
[75] *In re Three Minors,* 50 Wash. 2d 653, 314 P.2d 423 (1957). See *In re Fish,* 288 Minn. 512, 179 N.W. 2d. 175 (1970).
[76] See *In Re Watson,* 95 N.Y.S. 2d 798 (Dom. Rel. Ct. 1950): three children were declared ne-

Finally, there are cases where a child is removed from his parental home because the court determines the *physical conditions* in the home are unsuitable for the child. In a recent California case, an appellate court affirmed a juvenile court decision removing children from a dirty home. The parents claimed there was no evidence showing that the children had been harmed, but the appeals court maintained that the state " was not required, as appellants assert, to prove that the conditions of the above cause 'sickness and disease of mind or body' in order to establish 'neglect' . . . the welfare of the child is of paramount concern, and a purpose of the juvenile court law is to secure for each minor such care and guidance as will serve the spiritual, emotional, mental, and physical welfare of the minor and the best interests of the state."[77] Some "dirty homes" may seriously endanger a child's growth and well-being, but most may merely offend middle-class sensibilities. One suspects courts may sometimes be enforcing middle-class norms of cleanliness where both economic and cultural circumstances make it both unfair and inappropriate.[78]

During the past ten years there have been several appellate court decisions[79] rejecting extreme attempts by trial court judges to use neglect laws "to impose middle-class mores upon families and to punish a parent's undesirable conduct unless that conduct can be shown to result in damage to the child."[80] For two reasons, however, these cases do not significantly limit the discretion of the judge who hears the case. First, the appellate decisions suggesting that specific factors are not appropriate for consideration also emphasize the continuing need for individualized determinations and wide latitude for trial judges.[81] Second, juvenile court judges

---

glected because their mother was "incapable by reason of her emotional status, her mental condition and her allegedly deeply religious feeling amounting to fanaticism to properly care, provide and look after the children."; *Hunter v. Powers*, 206 Misc. 784, 135 N.Y.S.2d 371 (Dom, Rel. Ct. 1954): mother, an ardent Jehovah Witness, who left the child alone while she attended Bible discussion, compelled the child to distribute religious literature on the streets during parts of the day and night; *In Re Black*, 3 Utah 2d 315, 283 P.2d 887 (1955): children removed from their parents' home because their parents believed in and practiced plural marriage which they thought to be the law of God.

[77] In the Matter of Deborah Gibson, decided June 29, 1973, Cal. Court of Appeal, 2nd App. Dist., Div. 1 (2d Civil No. 40391). See *In Re Q*, 32 Cal. App. 3d 288, 107 Cal. Rptr. 646 (1973).

[78] See Monrad G. Paulsen, "Juvenile Courts, Family Courts, and the Poor Man," *California Law Review* 54 (1966) p. 694.

[79] See, e.g., *In Re Raya*, 255 Cal. App. 2d 260, 63 Cal. Rptr. 252 (1967): reversing neglect determination premised only on the fact that the parents were living unmarried, with new partners, because they were unable to afford divorce; *State v. Greer*, 311 S.W.2d 49, 52 (Ct. App. Mo.) (1958): reversing a juvenile court decision to remove a baby girl who was "concededly adequately housed, fed, clothed and attended, personally and medically" simply on the ground that mother had on occasion visited taverns, had been arrested for reckless driving, and had a child out of wedlock.

[80] Katz, *When Parents Fail*, p. 69.

[81] See *In re A.J.*, 274 Cal. App. 2d 199, 78 Cal. Rptr, 880 (1969).

can often disguise a decision based on an "improper" factor by vague recitation of general language. The real reasons may be very different than the stated ones.

David Matza thought individual treatment in juvenile court dispositions was a "mystification" and his observations have relevance to the best interests standard:

> To the extent that it prevails, its function is to obscure the process of decision and disposition rather than enlighten it. The principle of individualized justice results in a frame of relevance that is so large, so all-inclusive, that any relation between the criteria of judgment and the disposition remains obscure.[82]

The Risks of Foster Care Placement

The best interests test also makes it too easy for a judge to ignore the possible detrimental effects of removing a child from parental custody. The dangers of leaving a child at home often seem compelling, and because the judge is often unaware of or unable to evaluate the psychological risks of foster care, an individualized determination under a best interest standard may be biased in favor of removal. An assessment of the risks involved in separating children from their parents requires explicit knowledge of the foster care system. What happens to foster children? Are they happy while in foster care? What harm, both short-term and long-term, can result from being put into this system? How many children "fail" in foster homes?

Since predictions of how an individual child will fare in foster care have not proved reliable,[83] there is no reason to believe a judge can accurately assess the risks of placement. For the social scientist, analysis of the differential effects of foster placement on a child's development raises severe methodological problems; these include defining a control group, establishing a standard of "successful development," and isolating the factors responsible for any noticeable effects. No studies prove either that foster care benefits or harms children. The most famous longitudinal study, published in 1924, traces what happened to 910 former foster children who had spent one year or more in a foster home. The research question was, "Has the subject shown himself capable (or incapable) of managing himself and his affairs with ordinary prudence?"[84] The results of the study showed 615 subjects (67.5 percent) as "capable," 182 subjects (20.0 percent) as "incapable," and 113 subjects (12.5 percent) as of "unknown capability." Needless to say, criteria for success were defined in only the most vague and arbitrary terms. Moreover, one cannot judge whether these results were good or bad without a control group, and

---

[82] David Matza, *Delinquency & Drift*, p. 115.

[83] Compare Roy Parker, *Decision in Child Care* (London: Allen & Unwin, 1966) with Harry Napier, "Success and Failure in Foster Care," *British Journal of Social Work*, 2 (Summer, 1972), pp. 187-204.

definition of such a group presents overwhelming problems. More recent studies have not been able to overcome the methodological difficulties nor provide definitive answers about the long-range effects of foster care.[85]

Empirical studies *do* exist, however, to illustrate the conditions of children while in foster care. These suggest there is "rather persuasive, if still incomplete, evidence that throughout the United States children in foster care are experiencing high rates of psychiatric disturbance."[86] Maas and Engler, for example, in their study, found that "forty to fifty percent or more of the children in foster care in every one of our nine communities showed symptoms of maladjustment."[87] Other studies concur with this finding.[88]

The factors responsible for the emotional problems observed in foster care are difficult to isolate. For years, the effects of "separation trauma" were studied,[89] with the argument that the "act of placement in itself creates what is known as a separation trauma" and therefore may be harmful.[90] Many psychologists would agree.

[84] Sophie Theis, *How Foster Children Turn Out* (New York: State Charitable Aid Association, 1924), p. 19.

[85] Joan McCord, William McCord, and Emily Thurber, "The Effects of Foster-Home Placement in the Prevention of Adult Antisocial Behavior," *Social Service Review* 34, (1960), pp. 415-420. This study matched a group of nineteen potentially delinquent boys living at home with nineteen boys placed as a last resort in foster care. Contrary to their hypothesis, the results showed that "a significantly higher proportion of those who had been placed in foster homes had criminal records in adulthood. See also Elizabeth Meier, "Current Circumstances of Former Foster Children," *Child Welfare* 44 (1965), pp. 196-206. A group of eighty-two persons who had been in foster care five years or more were interviewed and their "adjustment" was evaluated. A higher than normal incidence of marital breakdown and a higher proportion of illegitimate births were found. On the other hand, one-half owned or were buying their own homes, few needed social services, and nearly all were self-supporting. See also Elizabeth Meier, "Adults who were Foster Children," *Children*, 13 (1966), pp. 16-22; Anne Roe, "The Adult Adjustment of Children of Alcoholic Parents Raised in Foster Homes," *Quarterly Journal of Studies on Alcohol*, 5 (1944), pp. 378-393. Since 1964, a research group at Columbia University has been engaged in longitudinal research relating to foster care. The volume on what happens to the children in the long-run has not yet been published.

[86] Leon Eisenberg, "The Sins of the Fathers: Urban Decay and Social Pathology," *American Journal of Orthopsychiatry*, 32 (1962), p. 14.

[87] Henry Maas, "Highlights of the Foster Care Project: Introduction," *Child Welfare*, 38 (July 1959), p. 5.

[88] Gordon Trasler, *In Place of Parents: A Study of Foster Care* (London: Routledge & Kegan Paul, 1960); Eugene Weinstein, *The Self-Image of the Foster Child* (New York: Russell Sage Foundation, 1960); Jessie Parfit, ed., *The Community's Children: Long-term Substitute Care: A Guide for the Intelligent Layman* (New York: Humanities Press, 1967).

[89] Ester Glickman, "Treatment of the Child and Family after Placement," *Social Service Review*, 28 (September 1954), p. 279. See also John Bowlby, *Maternal Care and Mental Health*, Monograph No. 2 (Geneva: World Health Organization, 1952). Ner Littner, *Some Traumatic Effects of Separation and Placement* (New York: Child Welfare League of America, 1956).

[90] Glickman, p. 279.

Any child who is compelled for whatever reason to leave his own home and family and to live in foster placement lives through an experience pregnant with pain and terror for him and potentially damaging to his personality and normal growth. It is abnormal in our society for a child to be separated for any continuing length of time from his own parents and no one knows this so well as the child himself. For him placement is a shocking and bewildering calamity, the reasons for which he usually does not understand.[91]

Later, some psychologists modified this position arguing that children who remained in their own homes with neglectful or indifferent mothers experienced greater psychological harm than children in foster homes.[92] However, when researchers observed the effects of separation on older children, concern was again expressed about the risks of removing a child for placement in foster care.[93] Although the debate is far from over, it is generally assumed that separation carries substantial risks for the child, risks that are related to the age of the child at the time of separation. Concern has been expressed particularly about children separated between six months and three years of age, at about six years of age, and at puberty.[94]

Another way the foster care system itself may cause psychological harm involves the anomalous position of a child within a foster home. "Family life can be complex indeed for the foster child."[95] The child often experiences conflict over which set of parents, natural or foster, to trust and rely on when in trouble. Moreover, the child may observe power struggles among the natural and foster parents, the social workers, and the judge, each of whom has a reason to be concerned about the child's care and future. A foster home is supposed to provide, insofar as possible, a normal family environment. But agencies often become concerned if the foster parents grow too attached to a child. In one case, the highest

[91] Leontine Young, "Placement from the Child's Viewpoint," *Social Casework*, 31 (1950), p. 250.
[92] See, e.g., *Deprivation of Maternal Care; A Reassessment of its Effects* (Geneva: World Health Organization, 1962); Lawrence Casler, *Maternal Deprivation: A Critical Review of the Literature*, Monograph No. 26 (Chicago: University of Chicago Press for the Society for Research in Child Development, 1961); Anna Freud and Dorothy Burlingham, *Infants Without Families; The Case for and Against Residential Nurseries* (New York: International University Press, 1944). Much of the early "separation" literature was addressed to the question of institutionalizing children—especially infants. The maternal deprivation literature began focusing on the need for a continuous relationship with the child-caring person—whether at home, in an institution, or in a foster home.
[93] Martin Wolins and Irving Piliavin, *Institution or Foster Family: A Century of Debate* (New York: Child Welfare League of America, 1964). Rosemary Dinnage and M. L. Kellmer Pringle, *Foster Home Care, Facts and Fallacies: A Review of Research in the United States, Western Europe, Israel and Great Britain between 1848 and 1966* (London: Longmans, Green, 1967).
[94] See Bowlby, Freud, and Napier.
[95] Weinstein, p. 47.

state court in New York approved the transfer of a child from a foster home to an unknown alternative because the foster parents "had become too emotionally involved with the child."[96] The court upheld an agency determination "that the child's best interests necessitated her placement in another environment where she would not be torn between her loyalty to her mother and her boarding parents."[97] Although the effects of ambiguous relationships are impossible to measure, there is a good theoretical argument and some suggestive evidence that a child's basic security and ability to form other relationships are shaken when he or she is torn by conflicting expectations and loyalties.[98] Lack of a solid identity, which most children acquire largely in their relationship with their parents, perhaps causes the most harm.[99] "Without an adequate conception of who he is, where he is, and why he is there, it is difficult to see how the foster child could develop well in a situation that is as complex and problematic as placement."[100]

A third psychologically detrimental factor in foster care is the instability of the system itself. As noted earlier, children are often moved from home to home,[101] and there is rapid turnover of social workers[102] and judges[103] involved in the case. Studies strongly indicate that personality problems are more frequent among children who have been moved often[104]; Maas and Engler, for example, concluded that "instability in relationships fosters personality disturbances."[105] On the other hand, the frequency of moves may depend on the child's adjustment before he or she even enters foster care: a "disturbed child who enters foster care is more likely to experience more numerous replacements, and his symptoms increase

[96] *In re Jewish Child Care Ass'n,* 5 N. Y. 2d 222, 226, 156 N.E. 2d 700, 702 (1959).

[97] Id. For some intriguing materials on the *Jewish Child Care Association* case see Goldstein and Katz, pp. 1027-34.

[98] See Weinstein, pp. 47-57, 66-70.

[99] J. Bowlb,, *Forty-four Juvenile Thieves: Their Characters and Home-life* (London: Bailliere, Tindall & Cov, 1946). Bowlby concludes that children separated from their parents often develop "affection-less characters," incapable of forming lasting attachments and of adhering to society's rules. Elsewhere Bowlby states "The impairment of the capacity for successful parenthood is perhaps the most damaging of all the effects of deprivation," in *Maternal Care and Mental Health,* p. 327.

[100] Weinstein, *Self-Image,* p. 66.

[101] See footnote 49, and Lewis, p. 37.

[102] See Lela Costin, *Child Welfare: Policies and Practice* (New York: McGraw Hill, 1972); Alfred Kadushin, *Child Welfare Services,* p. 420.

[103] In many states, such as California, judges are typically rotated through the juvenile court on a yearly basis.

[104] Maas and Engler, p. 389. See Elizabeth Meier, "Adults Who Were Foster Children," *Children,* 13 (1966), pp. 16-22.

[105] Maas and Engler, p. 422.

accordingly."[106] Whatever the reason, both former foster children and experienced social workers agree that moving a child from foster home to foster home is a painful and at times damaging experience.[107]

Present Legal Standards Fail to Make Removal a Last Resort

It would seem that foster care entails substantial risks of psychological harm. This does not imply that a legal standard should be adopted to make it impossible to take children from their parents and place them in foster care. But it does suggest a child's life may not be improved by removal unless the dangers of remaining at home are immediate and substantial and there are no means of protecting the child within the home.

Placing a child away from home is often referred to as a "last resort," but in fact most communuities offer few preventive or protective services for children within the home while a family is helped through a crisis. Day care or baby sitting services, along with parental counseling, might make removal unnecessary in a wide variety of circumstances; such services typically are unavailable. A national survey conducted by the American Humane Association in 1967 concluded that *"no state* and *no community* has developed a child protective service program adequate in size to meet the service needs of all *reported* cases of child neglect, abuse, and exploitation."[108] Even when such services are available, neglect statutes and the best interest standard do not require that before ordering removal a court conduct an inquiry into whether the child can be protected if left in parental custody.[109] Anecdotal evidence strongly suggests that children are often placed in foster care without a carefuly analysis of whether less drastic forms of intervention might be preferable. Thus, for instance, children have been placed in foster care because their parents' home is filthy even though a homemaker's services might have remedied the situation and done so at far less cost to the state.[110] Also, an undernourished child may

[106] Wiltse and Gambrill.

[107] See Young, p. 251. "One child in the process of replacement expressed his bitterness well, 'The social workers are the bat and I'm just the ball they sock from one place to another.' "

[108] American Humane Association, *Child Protective Services, A National Survey* (Denver, Colo.: American Humane Association, 1967), p. 20. See Monrad G. Paulsen, "Juvenile Courts, Family Courts, and the Poor Man," *California Law Review,* 54 (1966), p. 694.

[109] Minnesota is an exception for its statute provides that a child may be removed from the parents "only when his welfare or safety and protection of the public cannot be adequately safeguarded without removal." Minn. Stat. Ann. Sec. 260.011.

[110] See Children's Aid Society of New York, "Nine-to-Twenty-four hour Homemaker Service Project," *Child Welfare,* Part 1, 41 (March 1962), p. 99, and Part II, 41 (April 1962), p. 103; Sue Minton, "Homemaker Classes: An Alternative to Foster Care," *Child Welfare,* 52 (March 1973), pp. 188-91.

be taken from the home without any prior effort to educate the parents about nutritional needs.[111] Even in child abuse cases, where removal from the home is very likely, many experts believe that the child can often be left safely at home if the parents receive appropriate treatment and support.[112]

Removal would seem appropriate only when there are no means to protect the child within the home. Given the size and quality of present institutional arrangements for children who are removed, and given the widely shared view that parents, not the state, should ordinarily be responsible for child rearing, any legal standard should incorporate a substantial presumption favoring a parent who has expressly indicated that he or she wishes to retain custody. Because of the importance of the parent-child relationship and because of the risks of removal, I believe the state should not be allowed to remove children unless less drastic means of intervention cannot protect the child.

Is Judicial Application of the Best Interests Standard the Issue?

My analysis has been couched largely in terms of how *judges* behave in the *dispositional* phase of neglect proceedings. Despite problems with the best interests standard, it might be thought that the statutory standards determining when a juvenile court should assume *jurisdiction* are sufficiently stringent to exclude all but the most extreme cases from the dispositional phase of any juvenile court proceeding. But the jurisdictional phase of the court's proceeding provides no such safeguard. As already noted, some courts now appear to use the best interests standard for determining jurisdiction.[113] As indicated earlier, the statutory standards for jurisdiction are extremely vague and broad, and require findings of parental unfitness or neglect.[114] These standards provide no more guidance to a court than does best interests and do little to limit judicial discretion. Indeed, the jurisdictional provisions have been subject to a steady barrage of criticism in the legal literature for the last two decades.[115]

Finally, and I think this is the nub of the problem, the jurisdictional decision is the same whether a court is going to supervise the child within the home or remove the child. Consequently, to assume jurisdiction need not in itself be seen as a particularly important decision. My own strong impression based on inter-

[111] See *In Re Q*, 32 Cal. App. 3d 288, 107 Cal. Rptr. 646 (1973).
[112] See Ray Helfer and C. Henry Kempe, *Helping the Battered Child and His Family* (Philadelphia: Lippincott, 1972).
[113] See Footnote 56.
[114] See pp. 601, 604-605 above.
[115] See, e.g., Sullivan.

views and courtroom observation is that the judge and social worker consider the dispositional decision of whether to remove the child from the home as the key issue and that courts are not at all reluctant to assume jurisdiction. The fact that the juvenile courts assume jurisdiction in a very high percentage of cases suggests the same conclusion.[116]

It might be argued that social workers, probation officers, psychologists, and psychiatrists involved in the foster care system actually are the ones who decide when children should be removed, and that standards governing the judicial process therefore are of secondary importance. It may be true that judges rely on the advice of these other professionals. But deciding the direction of the causal link is no easy matter, since social workers are known to sometimes shape their recommendations according to what they think a particular judge will want to decide. In all events, the same problems that plague a judge plague these professionals too, lack of information, lack of predictive models, and the need to rely on individual values.

The Agenda for Law Reform

Is there something better than the "best interests of the child" standard? Can an adequate legal standard be developed, given our limited knowledge of human behavior, our pluralistic value system, and the realities of present foster care arrangements? Any standard devised will necessarily involve values—values that can be questioned and attacked. But it is essential that the new standard expose for analysis what is now hidden behind the "best interests" shield. I believe any new standard must be premised on three basic principles, implicit in much of the previous discussion.

1. Removal should be only when the child cannot be protected within the home.

2. To the extent possible, the decision to require foster care placement should be based on legal standards that can be applied in a consistent and even-handed way.

---

[116] I think the jurisdiction/disposition division of the judicial process in neglect cases is not a useful one. Substantive standards should be established for each type of coercive intervention, with more stringent standards for more intrusive forms of intervention. In other words, there might be one standard for a court to be able to compel protective services; a different standard for a court to allow a child to be removed from his home during the pendency of the case; and yet another standard (such as that suggested in the last section of this article) for the court to remove the child for indefinite period.

3. The state should make every effort to provide children who must be removed with as much continuity and stability as possible.

Two Unlikely Solutions

Against the backdrop of these principles, it is useful to analyze why two plausible methods of legal reform hold no great promise. These are, first, stricter enforcement of criminal child neglect statutes and, second, additional procedural safeguards in neglect proceedings. Every state now has criminal child neglect, abuse, or cruelty statutes. Better articulation or enforcement of these standards of minimum parental conduct, and greater use of criminal sanctions, will not improve the foster care system and will do little or nothing to correct the causes of child neglect, and does not serve two goals of criminal law, deterrence and rehabilitation. Insofar as poverty and emotional problems are at the root of many child neglect cases, increased reliance on the criminal sanction would probably be counter-productive,[117] and would have little deterrent effect. "A command impossible to fulfill does not alter the incentives of the person subject to it."[118] A jail sentence provides no rehabilitation for the parent and at the same time forces a separation between the parent and child. Retribution against the parent is achieved, but at what cost to the child?

There also have been frequent proposals in dependency and neglect cases for procedural reform.[119] Presently, neglect proceedings are highly informal. Few parents, and far fewer children, are represented by counsel; typically hearsay evidence of all sorts is admissible. The trial court often decides neglect cases without insisting on specific findings to reveal the basis for its determinations. Appellate

[117] See Monrad G. Paulsen, "The Law and Abused Children," in *The Battered Child*, ed. Ray Helfer and C. Henry Kempe (Chicago: University of Chicago Press, 1968).

[118] Richard Posner, *An Economic Analysis of the Law* (Boston: Little, Brown, 1973).

[119] Since *In Re Gault*, 387 U.S. 1 (1967), held that some safeguards available in criminal trials had to be applied in juvenile court delinquency proceedings, there have been numerous articles that have advocated more stringent requirements in dependency proceedings as well. An especially thoughtful analysis of the procedural requirements appropriate in child protective cases is Robert A. Burt, "Forcing Protection on Children and their Parents: The Impact of *Wyman v. James*," *Michigan Law Review*, 69 (1971), p. 1259. Other articles on the subject include Thomas T. Becker, "Due Process and Child Protective Proceedings: State Intervention in Family Relations on Behalf of Neglected Children," *Cumberland-Sanford Law Review*, 2 (1971), p. 247; Dianne M. Faber, "Dependent-Neglect Proceedings: A Case for Procedural Due Process," *Duquesne Law Review*, 9 (1971), p. 651; Joseph J. Mogilner, "Admissibility of Evidence in Juvenile Court: A Double Standard or No Standard," *Journal of the State Bar Association of Colorado*, 46 (1971), p. 310; Note, "Child Neglect: Due Process for the Parent," *Colorado Law Review*, 70 (1970), p. 465; Note, "Representation in Child-Neglect Cases: Are Parents Neglected?" *Columbia Journal of Law and Social Problems*, 4 (1968), p. 230.

review, infrequently sought, usually results in a rubber stamp affirmation of the trial court's decisions, particularly with regard to dispositional determinations. This procedural picture is not a happy one. Convincing arguments can be advanced that due process requires something more.[120] I believe that certain procedural reforms might have beneficial effects. If lawyers were introduced into the process, for instance, they might play a significant role in finding witnesses, presenting evidence, and suggesting alternative dispositions not considered by the state's social workers. If judges in turn were required to make factual findings, the involvement of lawyers in the process might make judges more self-conscious about how their values affect their decisions. Also, procedural reforms would impose higher transaction costs on an agency seeking to remove a child, perhaps reducing the number of petitions filed or limiting them to the most egregious cases.

But procedural reform alone cannot correct the fundamental fault in the system: the court's wide discretion.[121] Imagine a procedural reform guaranteeing parent and child separate legal representation in all neglect cases. How would the child's advocate determine what to advocate under a best interests standard? Ordinarily, a lawyer can look to the client for direction, and if the child is fourteen years old or even seven years old, the child is an appropriate source for information, even guidance. But a majority of children involved in neglect proceedings are younger. A lawyer with a very young client is placed in a position not dissimilar to that of the judge. He must make his own set of predictions and use his own set of values to ascertain what is in the child's best interests, and then advocate that position. The judge might agree with the lawyer's recommendation, but why should we assume the lawyer's recommendation is any more appropriate than the judge's would be? In all events, if the judge reaches some other conclusion, the chances of reversing this decision in an appellate court are slight. If the best interests standard is applied, even with additional procedural safeguards at the hearing, appellate courts will continue to give wide latitude to the trial court's individualized decision.

[120] Two cases have held recently that due process requires state assigned counsel for parents when the state is seeking permanently to remove their children. See *Nebraska v. Caha*, decided June 8, 1973 (Neb. Sup. Ct.); *Danforth v. Maine Dept. of Health*, decided April 17, 1973 (Me. Sup. Ct.).

[121] Lon Fuller develops a distinction between "person-oriented" and "act-oriented" legal rules which usefully explains why procedural reform is not likely to eliminate discretion if the legal standard is the best interest of a child "which by its nature cannot be rule-bound." Lon L. Fuller, "Interaction Between Law and Its Social Context," *Sociology of Law*, Summer 1971, University of California, Berkeley (bound class materials), Item 3.

The Direction of Legal Change

First priority for legal reform must involve changing the underlying legal standard for removal. Although I will not attempt here to formulate a definitive legal standard, the direction of change is clear: judicial discretion to remove children should be more limited, and if possible the standard should be made more objective. One example of such a standard would be the following:

A state may remove a child from parental custody without parental consent only if the state first proves: a) there is an immediate and substantial danger to the child's health; and b) there are no reasonable means by which the state can protect the child's health without removing the child from parental custody.

Before removing the child, I would further require the court to specify in writing the basis for the conclusion that the child was immediately and substantially in danger, with an explanation of which less drastic means of intervention had been contemplated, and why these were inadequate for the child's protection. Unlike the best interests test, the proposed standard is very explicit in its value premises: children are to be left at home except when there is real danger to them. It would take courts away from evaluating parental morality or sexual conduct, except in those rare cases when the child's health was endangered by it. The test would also focus judicial inquiry on whether the child could be protected within the home. A dirty-home case would no longer justify removal, because the state could usually protect the child by sending in a homemaker or housekeeper. Similarly, a child who was malnourished because a mother did not know anything about nutritional needs could be protected either by having a social worker teach the mother about nutrition, or by having someone sent into the home to prepare the child's meals.

Within the context of these new standards, additional procedural safeguards, such as separate counsel for the parents and the child, are desirable. When removal is sought, the attorney for the state would have the burden of demonstrating why the child's health is endangered and why the child cannot be protected within the home. Counsel for the parents would attempt to show why the child is not in danger, and would propose alternative methods that might allow the family to remain intact. Counsel for the child might sometimes side with the parents, other times advocate alternative services, or other times urge removal. The child's lawyer would be responsible for evaluating the case after consulting with the child and making an independent investigation.

In addition, requiring the trial judge to make findings on these issues could make appellate review of the initial determination more meaningful. Although appellate courts would not often second guess a judge's conclusions about a witness's credibility, appellate review could serve an important role in defining how much danger was sufficient to justify intervention, and how far the state would have to go in providing alternatives. Indeed, standards of general applicability could evolve by a process not unlike that of common law.

The trial judge's role under the proposed standard would still not be easy. Judges would face the problem of predicting when the risks to the child were so great that the stricter standard for removal would be met. The terms "immediate" and "substantial" are not self-defining and would require interpretation. Nevertheless, the proposed standard is much more restrictive than existing standards. The justification for a more restrictive standard was best put by Ernst Freund, who observed: "in the absence of scientific certainty it must be borne in mind that the farther back from the point of imminent danger the law draws the safety line of police regulation, so much the greater is the possibility that legislative interference is unwarranted."[122]

The term "health" poses particularly difficult policy issues. When there is an immediate and substantial danger to a child's *physical* health and the child cannot be protected at home, it is reasonable to predict that his or her lot will be improved by placement in foster care. Foster care does a reasonable job of protecting a child's physical health. But there is, of course, good reason to be concerned about a child's emotional health as well. Regarding the mental health of the child, it strikes me as extraordinarily difficult to predict when a child is emotionally endangered. Moreover, there is no evidence whatsoever that foster care is psychologically therapeutic. I am therefore very concerned that individualized determinations concerning emotional health could, on balance, do more harm than good by introducing a highly speculative element into the process. On balance I think "health" should be limited to "physical health", although this is a very difficult issue and requires more thought.

Another policy problem associated with the new standard relates to the question of how far a state must go in order to demonstrate that alternatives to removal will not work. The economic questions posed here are not trivial. For example, what if the means of protecting the child in the home are extraordinarily expen-

[122] Ernst Freund. *Standards of American Legislation* (Chicago: University of Chicago Press, 1917), p. 83.

sive? In a dirty-home case, what if a child could be protected only if a full-time maid were available in the house? The word "reasonable" allows the court to take into account the costs of alternatives, and to consider the economic question in the context of a specific case. Two general observations should be made, however. Because the costs of foster care are substantial, always several thousand dollars per year,[123] any method of protecting the child within the home which costs less than foster care would certainly be reasonable. I do not think it would be reasonable for a state to allow the level of resources available for home-based services to vary substantially among local jurisdictions merely because their capacity to raise revenue differs.

One clear goal of the new standard is to require states to devote more resources to the protection of children within the home. It is important that certain types of services such as homemakers, housekeepers, and public health nurses be available. But one unintended consequence of the proposed standard might be that the state would neither provide services to protect children within their homes, nor remove them when they are in danger. If this were the state's response the situation might well end up worse than it is today. Children who need protection would be left in danger. Fortunately, I think this response is unlikely, both because of public concern about children and because of the vested political interest of the existing social welfare bureaucracy.

Standard for Stability

A principal objective of law reform should be to establish a legal process ensuring a greater degree of stability for the child. For children who must be removed, there should be a statutory requirement fixing the maximum length of time they can remain in "temporary" foster care. The most direct way of doing this would be to require the judge at the end of a *fixed* period (perhaps twelve or eighteen months after placement) to choose between returning the child to the parents and placing the child either in an adoptive home or some other stable long-term environment. To allow this, I would change existing laws to provide for final termination of parental rights at the end of the required period if the child could not be safely returned to the home, and if the state had made reasonable efforts to rehabilitate the parents while the child was living away from the home.

At the time of removal, I would require the state to outline to the court the ser-

---

[123] See David Fanshel and Eugene B. Shinn, *Dollars and Sense in the Foster Care of Children: A Look at Cost Factors* (New York: Child Welfare League of America, 1972).

vices it would make available to the parents. A court hearing might be required every three months during the interim period to ensure that the social welfare agency reported on its efforts and results. I would also put the burden on the state at these interim hearings to show that the child could not be safely returned to the home.[124] If the child could not safely be returned home at the end of the statutory period, adoption would be the favored alternative. Some foster children would be difficult to place for adoption because of age, health, or behavior. Subsidized adoption would be an appropriate way to expand adoption possibilities. Short of adoption, certain other alternatives exist which are rarely employed today. Several years ago it was suggested, for instance, that social welfare agencies should encourage the grant of legal guardianship to foster parents who had a long-term interest in a child.[125] Guardians do not have a legal duty to support a child from their own funds, but unlike foster parents they do have the legal right to custody of the child and do have powers much like normal parents with regard to the everyday guidance and control over the child's life. Guardianship thus would promote a degree of continuity often lacking in foster care.

I am not prepared to state categorically what the fixed time unit should be when the court must make a permanent decision. Although no recent national data is available, Maas and Engler found that most children who are in foster care for more than eighteen months never return home. This suggests the necessity of research for the development of such criteria. It might be possible to develop different time limits for different kinds of cases. But in all events, the fixed time limit should be established at the time of removal on the basis of criteria that could be consistently and fairly applied. For example, a shorter period might be appropriate for very young children.[126] Future research might show that rehabilitative prognosis of the family in certain identifiable types of cases is sufficiently poor to allow a quick decision. The great advantage of a fixed time period rather than an open-ended one is that it eventually requires courts and social welfare agencies to make permanent plans. In the past, periodic review procedures have not been sufficient to

[124] Despite these procedural safeguards, an occasional case might arise where the state failed to make reasonable efforts to rehabilitate the parents. Termination of parental rights after the fixed time period might nevertheless be appropriate for the child's sake. Alternatively, because of the unfairness to the parent, perhaps the judge should be allowed to do everything short of termination to provide a stable environment for the child, give the parents a damage action against the state for the failure to provide past services, and compel the provision of such services for an additional period of time.

[125] Hasseltine B. Taylor, "Guardianship or 'Permanent Placement' of Children," *California Law Review*, 54 (1966), p. 741.

[126] Professor Michael Wald of Stanford University Law School suggested to me the possibility of a shorter time limit for younger children.

break bureaucratic inertia. Instead, routine extensions have been the rule. Any fixed time period is necessarily arbitrary; a slightly longer or shorter period might be better for a particular case, and inevitably some parents' rights will be finally terminated even though with more time they might have been able to pull themselves and their families together. Nevertheless, I think this method is more desirable on balance than a system based on individualized determinations giving a judge the discretion to leave children in the limbo of foster care, granting extension after extension even though it is highly improbable that the child will return home.

The proposed standard also does much more than the present law to require the state to work with the natural parents in the home situation after removal. By working with parents, social welfare agencies could acquire information to assess what should be done for the child at the end of the statutory period. This raises difficult questions of confidentiality; if the state has access to information from the parents' therapy, for example, this may in itself inhibit the therapy. On the other hand, the state has a very substantial interest in making permanent plans for the child with the best information possible.

How Reform Can Occur

Litigation has been used to challenge existing neglect statutes, on the ground that they are unconstitutionally vague[127] and on the ground that the state has ordered removal without first assessing whether the child could be protected within the home.[128] To my knowledge no court has upheld either kind of claim. But the legal arguments available for such challenges are substantial, and a victory would move the operation of the system in the right direction. Alternatively, a state court might interpret existing neglect statutes to allow removal only under the circumstances described in the new standard. Although litigation is a possible avenue for improvement, reforms along the lines outlined here can be best achieved through new legislation. The American Bar Association has spurred legislative reform recently by establishing a Juvenile Justice Standards Project. This project will make a comprehensive reassessment of laws relating to minors, reexamining among other things all the legal standards concerning dependent and neglected children.[129]

[127] See, e.g., Minor Children of F. B. v. Caruthers, 323 S.W. 2d 397 (Mo. Ct. App. St. Louis 1959); *In re Black* 3 Utah 2d 315, 283 P.2d 887 (1955); *In re Cager*, 251 Md. 473, 248 A.2d 384 (Md. Ct. App. 1968).
[128] See, *In re Jeannie Q.*, 32 Cal. App. 3d 288, 107 Cal. Rptr. 646.
[129] Through conversations with Professors Michael Wald and Robert Burt of the University of

Conclusions

The standards proposed in this article are intended to limit the wide discretion presently given to the professionals involved in the foster care system. There are costs associated with limiting this discretion. Some children who would substantially benefit from placement in foster care might be excluded from the system under the new standard. Similarly, there would undoubtedly be parents whose rights would be terminated under the proposed standard who might, given more time, have been able to work things out. The underlying issue, however, is whether we would have a fairer system, and one that on balance was more helpful to children.

Although this article has been directed primarily at the problems of children who are coercively removed from their parents, the analysis has broader implications, particularly for children who are "voluntarily" placed in state-sponsored foster care with the consent of the natural parents. Usually there is no court supervision of these children, even though from the *child's* perspective, placement is no less coercive simply because the state and parents agree. While state provision of foster care for children whose parents seek it may often be desirable, it must be remembered many children voluntarily placed remain in the limbo of foster care for years. In San Francisco, for example, the average stay for these children appears to be slightly *longer* on average than for court-ordered placements.[130] Moreover, social workers have suggested in interviews that many parents who voluntarily place their children are ambivalent about wanting to raise them, but also feel guilty about waiving parental responsibility. Consequently, they often are unwilling either to keep their children at home or to allow a stable alternative to develop. Their children, like ping pong balls, are paddled back and forth between parents and the social welfare system.

In voluntary placements, consideration should be given to imposing standards similar to those suggested for court-ordered placement. Before a child is voluntarily placed, the state might offer, but not compel, alternative services to enable the parent to keep the child at home. If placement were nevertheless desired by the parent, the parent might be told that the child can remain in such care for no

Michigan, the Reporter's for the relevant portion of the ABA Project, after I was well into writing this paper, I know that they were independently giving consideration to standards that would narrow the grounds that should justify removal and that would establish time limits for foster placement after removal.

[130] I am grateful to Professor Kermit Wiltse, School of Social Welfare, University of California, Berkeley, for this finding.

more than a fixed period of time. At the end of that period, if the parent were unwilling or unable to have the child return home, the state would make another permanent arrangement for the child. While not without problems requiring further analysis, such a standard might have two benefits. First, some parents might decide to keep their children at home in the first place rather than placing them unnecessarily in the foster care system. Second, both parents and the social welfare bureaucracy would be required to make a permanent decision after a reasonable period of time.

The new standard also might have implications for dispositions in juvenile court cases where jurisdiction rests not on neglect, but on the wrongful behavior of the minor—i.e., in delinquency and "pre-delinquency" cases. In a delinquency case, for example, the critical question is often what the juvenile court judge does in the dispositional hearing. Although jurisdiction turns on the issue of whether the state has proved beyond a reasonable doubt that the minor has committed an act which for an adult would be a crime, the judge's analysis in that hearing very often focuses on neglect-type considerations: the quality of the child's home life, his relationship with his parents, etc. Many of the criticisms I have leveled against the use of an individualized "best interests" standard in the dispositional phase of neglect proceedings can be made with regard to dispositions in delinquency cases.[131]

Finally, the questions examined in this article are closely related to those involved in a number of other areas of the law where officials are given the power to make coercive individualized determinations even though they lack information, theoretical tools to make predictions, proven methods of therapy, and a consensus with regard to values. The use of the best interest standard poses issues analogous to those raised by discretionary sentencing in the criminal law, where the therapeutic ideal has been used to justify giving judges, probation officers, and parole boards enormous discretion.[132] Indeterminate sentences are justified on the grounds that experts should shape the length of a prison term to the time required to bring about rehabilitation, a period which may be short or extend over many years. Similar problems are raised by the involuntary "civil" commitment of those thought to be mentally ill. In all these areas, I think it would be useful to analyze closely whether

---

[131] See Matza; Edwin M. Schur, *Radical Non-Intervention: Rethinking the Delinquency Problem* (Englewood Cliffs, N.J.: Prentice-Hall, 1973).

[132] See American Friends Service Committee, *Struggle for Justice, A Report on Crime and Punishment in America* (New York: Hill and Wang, 1971).

additional procedural safeguards alone can ever be enough, and whether less individualized standards might not be the more important legal reform. "Ignorance, of itself, is disgraceful only so far as it is avoidable. But when, in our eagerness to find 'better ways' of handling old problems, we rush to measures affecting human liberty and human personality on the assumption that we have knowledge which, in fact, we do not possess, then the problem of ignorance takes on a more sinister hue."[133]

In closing it is wise to acknowledge that changing the legal standard for removing children is by no means the only strategy for bringing about needed reforms in the foster care system. It is arguable, in fact, that political efforts for reform should be devoted not so much toward changing the law as toward improving the foster care system by securing additional resources and devising "better ways" of providing useful services. Certainly facilities should be improved; more public support also would be useful. Dramatic improvements in the operation of the foster care system of new information about its present effects might influence my conclusions. But in analyzing the present foster care system, I am impressed by the relevance of an observation made in another context by Francis Allen:

We shall be told that progress is obstructed by the lack of public interest and support and by the absence of adequate funds. That these factors are real and their consequences devastating few would care to deny. Yet, these familiar scapegoats do not provide the most fundamental explanations. We should not overlook the fact that, in many areas, our basic difficulties still lie in our ignorance of human behavior and its infinite complexities.[134]

---

[133] Francis A. Allen, *The Borderland of Criminal Justice* (Chicago: University of Chicago Press, 1964), p. 13.
[134] Allen, p. 12.

Abused and Neglected Children in America: A Study of Alternative Policies*

RICHARD J. LIGHT

Harvard University

*Both the print and electronic media recently have highlighted the problems faced
by severely abused and neglected children in America. Many suggestions have
been offered for ameliorating the conditions leading to child abuse and neglect,
but few hard data exist to tell us which social policies can be most effective in
combatting these conditions. In this article, several sources of data are examined
to estimate the incidence of abuse, its social and demographic features, and the
nature of available child abuse case reports. Three potential social policies are
analyzed in detail: national health screening, education in child rearing, and the
development of profiles of abusing families with the hope of offering them preventive help. Each analysis has two underlying themes. First, even with incomplete data it is often possible to evaluate the probable effectiveness of a social
policy before it is implemented. Second, data initially collected in a non-experi-*

* This essay reports on work being done in my capacity as research associate in the Faculty
Studies Program, Institute of Politics, John F. Kennedy School of Government. The assistance of
the Institute of Politics in facilitating this effort is gratefully acknowledged. Many individuals
were helpful in this research, and I wish particularly to thank David G. Gil for making available
his collection of data and papers. Many useful suggestions were also given by Joan S. Bissell,
Anthony S. Bryk, Thomas R. Cerva, William B. Fairley, Gregory A. Jackson, Mary Beth James,
Bonnie H. Lamar, Thomas J. Marx, Eli H. Newberger, Jean S. Savage, Marshall S. Smith, Paul V.
Smith, Herbert I. Weisberg, and Richard J. Zeckhauser.

Harvard Educational Review Vol. 43 No. 4 November 1973, 556–598

198

mental setting can still be used to suggest improvements in policy. The author concludes with a series of recommendations urging more systematic and carefully designed investigations of reporting systems and ameliorative efforts. Such investigations are necessary to enable firm inferences about the comparative effectiveness of different programs to reduce the incidence of child abuse and neglect.

> It is likely that the battered child syndrome will be found to be a more frequent cause of death than such well recognized and thoroughly studied diseases as leukemia, cystic fibrosis, and muscular dystrophy, and it may well rank with automobile accidents and the toxic and infectious encephalides as causes of acquired disturbances of the central nervous system.
>
> Editorial, *Journal of the American Medical Association*, 1962

Governmental agencies are charged with the task of developing coherent social policies toward children, yet this task is confounded by the substantial disagreement in many segments of society about what constitutes the ideal family, school, or play environment for children. Whereas the majority of families in one town might prefer rigid discipline in schools, the majority in another might want just the opposite. Working women in one area might support allocation of tax dollars toward group day care centers and in another area angrily oppose such action. Public agencies faced with so many conflicting goals are often hesitant or simply unable to initiate worthwhile programs.

In this context of different views, one issue is almost unique in mobilizing widespread agreement that "something be done": the existence of a large number of abused, battered, and severely neglected children. Over the last few years, as the news media have publicized the extent and severity of child abuse and neglect cases, public awareness and support for ameliorating this problem has grown.[1]

[1] In 1973, especially, because of consideration of Bill S. 1191 in the Committee on Labor and Public Welfare of the United States Senate, the "Child Abuse Prevention and Treatment Act" has received extensive press coverage. The North Central Wisconsin chapter of the National Association of Social Work reported from a survey in 1968 that eighty-six per cent of responding parents indicated knowledge of a Child Abuse Reporting Law. This high level of awareness was found to be independent of sex and age group of respondent. Seventy-nine per cent of respondents knew of an agency to contact if they thought a child was being abused. Even allowing for some exaggeration in such reports of awareness, these findings suggest an adult public that is surprisingly well aware of the existence of the problem of abuse, and also which social agencies can offer help. For more details, see A Study in Child Abuse Reporting, Chapter of the National Association of Social Work (Wausau, Wis.: N.C.W., 1969).

But public support for programs to deal with child abuse is just a first step. The next step, developing programs that are truly effective, is up to researchers and policy makers. It is here that much remains to be done. Many suggestions have been offered, but few have been carefully tested and proven effective.

In this article I discuss data on child abuse and neglect and analyze several policy suggestions for alleviating the problem. Three themes are emphasized. First, substantially more data on child abuse exist than have been carefully studied. Second, policy suggestions that have been offered have rarely been developed from existing data. Third, it is often possible, well in advance of implementation, to predict whether a social policy is likely to work. These themes are illustrated by using specific examples from existing data on child abuse, and by examining the probable implications of several recent policy suggestions.

I begin with a brief historical review, and next consider some difficulties in estimating the incidence of abuse. A model is presented for revising existing estimates. The importance of knowing current incidence is illustrated with an example of how the probable success of one social policy, national health screening, depends critically upon how many children are abused. Two other social policies, educational curricula on child development and identification of high risk families, are then analyzed. The primary data source for these analyses is David Gil's extensive collection of child abuse reports in 1967 and 1968.[2] Although these reports are subject to substantial biases, I present a strategy for seeking relationships in the data which are generalizable to the complete population of abusing families. Finally, after evaluating how two causal models of abuse can be empirically tested. I conclude with several specific suggestions for data collection and controlled field studies to improve our understanding of different programs' effectiveness.

A Brief Overview

Child abuse can be defined formally as a situation "in which a child is suffering from serious physical injury inflicted upon him by other than accidental means;

[2] The Gil data are currently the most comprehensive and in-depth set of reports available on individual cases, collected in a systematic manner across different states. With a grant from the Children's Bureau of the U.S. Department of Health, Education and Welfare, Gil collected basic data on every case of physical child abuse reported throughout legal channels in the entire United States in 1967 and 1968. He then took a well designed sample of these reports from the 1967 cases, and collected more detailed information. The complete study is reported in David G. Gil, *Violence Against Children: Physical Child Abuse in the United States* (Cambridge, Mass.: Harvard University Press, 1970).

is suffering harm by reason of neglect, malnutrition, or sexual abuse; is going without necessary and basic physical care; or is growing up under conditions which threaten his physical and emotional survival."[3]

The problem is not new, largely because of an historical tradition of viewing children as chattel. Aristotle wrote, "The justice of a master or a father is a different thing from that of a citizen, for a son or slave is property, and there can be no injustice to one's own property."[4] In a similar spirit, the Old Testament tells us "spare the rod and spoil the child." The 1633 *Bibliotheca Scholastica* repeats this admonition. The *Patria Potestas* gave to a Roman father the legal right to sell, abandon, kill, or offer in sacrifice all of his children. Colonial America gave a father the statutory right to put his child to death, and, if necessary, to call upon the assistance of the colony officers to do so.[5] The child's legal status has changed considerably during the past hundred years. A child is now viewed as belonging to himself, in care of his parents, although social enforcement of his rights has lagged. The development of state social service agencies has increased public awareness of the maltreatment suffered by many children. Still, in 1970 the Society for Prevention of Cruelty to Animals in New York City had more contributors than the Society for Prevention of Cruelty to Children.

It is primarily in the last decade that governmental programs have begun to take form. All fifty states have passed laws either encouraging or requiring citizens to report incidents of child abuse. Hospitals, police, and social service agencies are also required to report. The U.S. Department of Health, Education, and Welfare has assumed responsibility for providing national leadership in formu-

[3] C. Henry Kempe *et al.*, "The Battered-Child Syndrome," *Journal of the American Medical Association*, 181 (July, 1962), pp. 17-24. This definition is consistent with terminology that has been written into formal statutes in most states. It is essentially the definition suggested by C. Henry Kempe, Director of the National Center for Prevention of Child Abuse and Neglect, in papers presented to the Hearings of the Subcommittee of Children and Youth of the Committee of Labor and Public Welfare, United States Senate, March 31, 1973, and the Harvard Inter-Faculty Seminar on Child Rearing in Urban America, May 1, 1973. It was Dr. Kempe and his colleagues who published the first formal statement on cases of physical abuse.

[4] Commenting on Aristotle's view, Bertrand Russell, in *The History of Western Philosophy* (London: George Allen and Unwin Ltd., 1969), p. 186, tells us, "Aristotle's opinions on moral questions are always such as were conventional in his day. On some points they differ from those of our time, chiefly where some form of aristocracy comes in. We think that human beings, at least in ethical theory, all have equal rights, and that justice involves equality; Aristotle thinks that justice involves, not equality, but right proportion, which is only sometimes equality."

[5] For an extensive discussion of children's rights, or the lack of them, in the early Roman empire, see E. Gibbon, *The Decline and Fall of the Roman Empire* (New York: Peter Fenelon Collier, 1899), pp. 352-353. An excellent and detailed discussion of the early history of children's rights appears in Mary Van Stolk, *The Battered Child in Canada* (Toronto: McClelland and Stewart Ltd., 1972), Chapter 16.

lating policy to counter child abuse and neglect through administration of particular sections of Title IV-A (AFDC), Title IV-B (Child Welfare Services), and Title V (Maternal and Child Health Programs) of the Social Security Act. Total funding for these programs has increased from four million dollars in 1960, to ten million in 1965, forty-nine million in 1970, and seventy-six million in 1972.[6] Research reports have begun to appear in the pediatric, child welfare, and social service literature.

Despite this recent growth of concern, effort, and funding, surprisingly little is yet known about many aspects of child abuse. Although a number of causal theories have been put forth to explain the occurrences of abuse, substantial guesswork is still involved. Perhaps most serious is the lack of firm evidence about what forms of service programs are most effective in dealing with families who maltreat children. Carefully designed field studies to examine different policies are yet to be undertaken. The limited available data, however, can provide useful preliminary insights about several policy suggestions.

Incidence of Abuse and Neglect

The incidence of child abuse can be defined as the proportion of all children under 18 who are abused or seriously neglected. The existing data on national incidence are not good. Like studies of venereal disease and drug addiction, research on child abuse is handicapped because many cases are simply not reported. This is not for lack of legislation requiring such reports. A recent study by The National Center for Prevention and Treatment of Child Abuse and Neglect found that:

1. In forty-nine out of fifty states reporting of suspected abuse is mandatory. (New Mexico, the one exception, simply has a child abuse reporting statute.)

2. The upper limit on age of children covered by these statutes ranges from twelve (Georgia) to eighteen, to any person who is mentally retarded regardless of age (Washington state). In most states the upper limit is eighteen.

---

[6] From documents provided by the Department of Health, Education, and Welfare to the United States Senate Committee on Labor and Public Welfare, March, 1973. The dollar figures given in the text are for total funding of Titles IV-A, IV-B, and V. What proportion of these dollars was spent on child abuse activities, narrowly defined, is not available. The Office of Child Development estimated in early 1973 that only a small fraction of these dollars for children's protective services were focused specifically on child abuse efforts. In October, 1973, new program efforts totalling four million dollars were announced by the Office of Child Development and the National Institute of Child Health and Human Development.

3. Every state in the union grants immunity to persons required to report. However, some states grant immunity only in situations regarding civil liability (Connecticut).

4. Thirty-nine states have removed the evidentiary problem of privileged communications in cases of child abuse. The great majority have removed the privileged status of communication between husband and wife and doctor and patient.

5. Twenty-eight states have established some form of central registry for keeping track of suspected cases of child abuse. At least one state's statutes make provision for cooperation with other states in exchanging information in this area and establishing a federal registry (Washington).

6. Twenty-nine states provide criminal sanctions for failure to report.[7]

Despite these state laws, reporting remains scanty and erratic. Therefore, estimates of how many children are abused in America vary widely. In 1968, reports of child abuse filed in all state registries amounted to approximately 11,000. By 1972, although no precise data are available, the number of reports had more than doubled. Henry Kempe, a major contributor to the development of both public and professional awareness of child abuse, estimates that approximately

[7] This testimony was given by Brian Fraser, staff attorney for the National Center for the Prevention and Treatment of Child Abuse and Neglect, to the Senate Subcommittee of Children and Youth, March 31, 1973. It should be noted that state laws vary widely in terms of the type of report that is required, who receives waivers, who is required to report, and to whom or what social agency reports must be made. A detailed summary of state by state requirements is given in a report developed by Vincent De Francis, "Child Abuse Legislation in the 1970's" which appears in *Rights of Children, 1972*, Hearing before the Subcommittee on Children and Youth of the Committee on Labor and Public Welfare, United States Senate; Part 2 (Washington: U.S. Government Printing Office, 1972). In Canada, the history of legislation is based upon the Ontario Act of 1893 which includes "An Act for the Prevention of Cruelty to and Better Protection of Children." This is summarized in Mary Van Stolk, *The Battered Child*, a brief submitted to the Canadian Bar Association in Quebec, February, 1971. See also P. Harrison, *Never Enough—75 Years with the Children's Aid Society of Ottawa* (Ottawa: Children's Aid Society, 1968). For related papers on legislative and reporting issues, see Allan H. McCoid, "The Battered Child and Other Assaults upon the Family," *Minnesota Law Review*, 50 (1965), pp. 1-58; B. Simon sand E. F. Downs, "Medical Reporting of Child Abuse: Patterns, Problems, and Accomplishments," *New York State Journal of Medicine*, 68 (1968), pp. 2324-2330; Monrad G. Paulsen, "Legal Protection Against Child Abuse," *Children*, 13 (April, 1966), pp. 43-48; Monrad G. Paulsen, "The Legal Framework for Child Protection," *Columbia Law Review*, 66 (April, 1966), pp. 679-717; Monrad G. Paulsen, "Child Abuse Reporting Laws: The Shape of the Legislation," *Columbia Law Review*, 67 (January, 1967), pp. 1-49; Monrad G. Paulsen, "The Law and Abused Children," in *The Battered Child*, ed. R. E. Helfer and C. H. Kempe (Chicago: University of Chicago Press, 1968); Vincent De Francis, *Child Abuse Legislation in the 1970s* (Denver, Col.: American Humane Association, 1970); Colin Low, "The Battering Parent, the Community, and the Law," *Applied Social Studies* (Oxford), Vol. 3, section 2, pp. 65-80 (1971); National Council of Juvenile Court Judges, "Handbook for New Juvenile Court Judges," *Juvenile Court Journal*, 23 (January, 1972), pp. 1-31.

60,000 children were seriously abused in 1972.[8] A 1970 survey of physicians, hospitals, institutions, and police departments in Massachusetts produced a statewide rate of occurrence which on the national level would amount to approximately 200,000 cases annually.[9] Going even further, Vincent J. Fontana, chairman of the New York City Task Force on Child Abuse and Neglect, estimated in June, 1973, at an American Medical Association meeting, that there will be approximately 1.5 million cases of child abuse in America in 1973.

Because of the severe underreporting, David Gil employed a quite different strategy to estimate the national incidence of child abuse and neglect. In October, 1965, he commissioned the National Opinion Research Center (NORC) to question its standard survey of 1520 respondents about whether "they personally knew families involved in incidents of child abuse resulting in physical injury during the twelve months preceding the interview."[10] Since 45 respondents, or 3 percent of the people, reported such familiarity, Gil suggested an upper bound of between 2.5 and just over 4 million cases of child abuse. He stressed that this was indeed an upper bound and that the actual number of cases was probably substantially fewer.[11]

There are several reasons for the great disparity in estimates of national incidence. First, the reported instances of abuse vary enormously from state to state. For example, in 1968 in New York 9.6 cases of abuse per 100,000 children under age eighteen were reported, while in neighboring New Jersey only 1.5 cases per 100,000, or one-sixth as many, were reported.[12]

Second, the annual rate of increases in cases reported diverges widely among

[8] Testimony given to the Senate Subcommittee on Children and Youth and paper presented to the Harvard Inter-Faculty Seminar on Child Rearing in Urban America.

[9] *Report of the Governor's Committee on Child Abuse,* to Francis W. Sargent, Governor, Boston, Massachusetts, October, 1971.

[10] These data were collected by N. O. R. C. in study SRS-868, October, 1965, Amalgam survey. The questionnaire defined child abuse as "when an adult physically injures a child, not by accident, but in anger or deliberately. Sometimes the person injuring the child is a parent, older brother or sister, or other relative. It could be a baby sitter, a teacher, or someone else who is not related to the child—but it would always be someone who is at least temporarily taking care of the child."

[11] Gil developed his estimated upper bound as follows, "At the time of the survey there were about 110 million adults, twenty-one years of age and over in the United States, who constituted the universe sampled by the survey. Sample proportions obtained in the survey may be extrapolated to this universe within a known margin of error, which in the case of 3 per cent, at the 95 per cent level of confidence, is less than 0.7 per cent. Accordingly, it is possible to state that 2.3 per cent to 3.7 per cent of 110 million adults, or 2.53 to 4.07 million adults throughout the United States, knew personally families involved in incidents of child abuse during the year preceding the survey." See Gil, *Violence Against Children,* p. 59.

[12] Gil, p. 95.

204

states, depending largely upon how concerted an effort is made by state agencies to enforce reporting of abuse and neglect. For example, Wisconsin reported 402 cases in 1970, 409 in 1971, and a sudden jump to 600 in 1972.[13] Colorado followed a similar pattern with corresponding yearly reports of 125, 176, and 373.[14] Unless we hypothesize that 1972 was a particularly bad year for children, these large increases indicate that we do not have good data on incidence.

A third factor contributing to the unreliability of data is the unwillingness of physicians to report cases of abuse or neglect. Of 3,000 reported cases of child abuse collected from New York City's Central Registry, only eight were reported by physicians.[15] Similar proportions have been evidenced in data from other cities. Vincent Fontana is one of many who argue that this particular bias leads to the far greater likelihood of reports on low-income families than on their middle-class counterparts.

Thus, the use of actual reported cases is bound to lead to a severe underestimate of the true national incidence of child abuse. It appears somewhat more promising to use the NORC 1965 survey results to develop an estimate. Gil's calculated upper bound of 2.5 to 4.1 million cases is based on the assumption that each of the 1520 NORC respondents knew only a single family.[16] An adjusted estimate can be developed from these data by making several assumptions. First, let us assume

[13] Wisconsin Department of Health and Social Services, *Child Abuse in Wisconsin* (Milwaukee, 1970, 1971, 1972).

[14] Data compiled by the Children's Division, American Humane Association, Denver, Colorado, July, 1973.

[15] Report by Thomas T. Becker, executive director of the New York Society for the Prevention of Cruelty to Children, to the American Medical Association, New York City, June 25, 1973.

[16] The Gil estimate involves two assumptions. Gil (p. 59) notes that in generalizing to a large population of adults there is likely to be some overlap in the cases of abuse known to different respondents. It is this caution that Gil cites when calling his estimate an upper bound. But Gil's estimation procedure, referenced in footnote 12, also implicitly assumes that each respondent to the NORC survey, and also each adult in the U.S. population, knows only one family with one or more children under eighteen. This leads to a substantial overestimate of the actual number of abusing families in the population. To use more precise sampling terminology, the error occurs in choosing the appropriate weight inverse of the sampling fraction. The problem is to estimate what proportion of families abuse. The sampling procedure used can be thought of as a cluster sample where the primary sampling unit is the respondent and the second stage sampling units are families with children under eighteen known by the respondent. Thus, to estimate the true proportion of abusing families in the population, we need to know the total number of families with children under eighteen known by the 1520 primary sampling units. These data were not collected in the N.O.R.C. survey, and Gil's estimate assumes that each of the primary sampling units knew a total of only one family with children under eighteen. Since no estimate of the average number of families with children under eighteen known per respondent was given by Gil, a small Task Force at the Harvard Graduate School of Education attempted to estimate these numbers. The data are reported in Figure 2. While these new data must be viewed as approximate, they lead to substantial modifications of Gil's estimated incidence rate.

that each respondent knew more than one family with at least one child under eighteen. Second, let us assume that we can divide up the families known by each respondent into three groups: those families the respondent knew well, those the respondent knew moderately, and those the respondent knew just a bit. Two further assumptions lead to an estimate of the number of abused children nationally: a) a respondent was more likely to know of a case of actual abuse if it occurred in a family he knew well than if it occurred in a family he knew moderately or just a bit; b) the more families with children under eighteen any respondent knew, the less likely he was to know about an actual occurrence of child abuse, and this relationship is a slowly decreasing linear function.

Using the general form of these assumptions, the model given in detail in Figure 1 enables us to develop a revised estimate of the incidence of abuse. Figure 2 presents two sample calculations from this model. We begin by assigning values of 5, 5, and 20, respectively, for the number of families with children under eighteen

FIGURE 1
A Rough Model to Estimate National Incidence of Abuse

Select sample of n respondents.

Let:

a_i = number of abusing families known by ith respondent.

k_{1i} = number of families ith respondent knows "well."

k_{2i} = number of families ith respondent knows "moderately."

k_{3i} = number of families ith respondent knows "a bit."

p_{1i} = probability that if a family ith respondent "knows well" abused, ith respondent would know it.

p_{2i} = probability that if a family ith respondent "knows moderately" abused, ith respondent would know it.

p_{3i} = probability that if a family ith respondent knows "a bit" abused, ith respondent would know it.

$f(k_{ji})$ = $1.00 - 0.01\ k_{ji}$ for all i, $0 \leqslant k_{ji} \leqslant 99$

$f(k_{ji})$ = 0.01 for all i, $k_{ji} > 99$

where:

1. n, a_i, and k_{ji} are available from survey data.
2. p_{ji}'s are estimated by researcher.
3. $f(k_{ji})$ is a decreasing linear function of k_{ji}, arbitrarily specified by researcher.

Then, using above survey data and researcher estimates, the estimated proportion of abusing families is:

$$P_A = \frac{1}{n} \sum_{i=1}^{n} a_i \frac{1}{\sum_{j=1}^{3} k_{ji}\ p_{ji}\ f(k_{ji})}$$

FIGURE 2
Estimating National Incidence of Abuse, Using Gil's 1965 NORC Survey Data

1. A best estimate. Use the model in Figure 1.

   $n = 1520$

   $\sum_{i=1}^{n} a_i = 45$

   Assume that for all i:

$k_{1i} = 5$	$p_{1i} = 0.8$	Then, $f(k_1) = 0.95$
$k_{2i} = 5$	$p_{2i} = 0.5$	$f(k_2) = 0.95$
$k_{3i} = 20$	$p_{3i} = 0.1$	$f(k_3) = 0.80$

   $P_A = \dfrac{45}{(7.80)\,(1520)} = 0.004$

2. A revised upper bound.

   $n = 1520$

   $\sum_{i=1}^{n} a_i = 45$

   Assume that for all i:

$k_{1i} = 3$	$p_{1i} = 0.7$	Then, $f(k_1) = 0.97$
$k_{2i} = 3$	$p_{2i} = 0.2$	$f(k_2) = 0.97$
$k_{3i} = 10$	$p_{3i} = 0.05$	$f(k_3) = 0.90$

   $P_A = \dfrac{45}{(3.07)\,(1520)} = 0.010$

known well, moderately, and just a bit by the average respondent. These values appeared reasonable after an informal survey.

Further, in the case of families an average respondent knew well, we assume an 80 percent probability of the respondent's knowing of abuse if it in fact existed; for families known moderately well, 50 percent; and for those known just a bit, 10 percent. Given these values, the model in Figure 1 yields the revised estimate that *0.004 of all American families physically abuse a child.* This value is our "most reasonable" estimate. It is just over ten per cent of Gil's upper bound of 0.03 abusing families in America.

Although this estimate is our best guess, it seems appropriate to work through one additional estimate. We can reestimate an upper bound on the proportion of abusing families. Let us use values for the number of American families with children under eighteen that the average respondent knew well, moderately, or just a bit, together with probabilities that a respondent would know about abuse if it existed, which would lead to a maximum estimate of the proportion of abusing families. This requires assuming fewer families known by the average respondent at each of the three levels of familiarity as well as a lower probability that, if abuse occurred at any level, the respondent would know about it. Using the values 3, 3, and 10 for the number of families known at the three levels, and probabilities of 0.7, 0.2, and 0.05 of knowing about abuse at the corresponding level, we come to *an upper bound estimate that approximately 0.01 of all American families physically abuse a child.* This is our best guess at the maximum; it is one-third as large as Gil's maximum.

The reader may be willing to accept the general strategy laid out in Figure 1 for estimating the number of abused children, but may disagree with the values used for number of families with children under eighteen known well, moderately, or just a bit. Or the reader may disagree with the assigned probabilities of a respondent's knowledge of abuse at each level of family familiarity. In this event, a revised estimate can be obtained by substituting in Figure 1 other values that seem more reasonable.

To convert the percentages in Figure 2 into an estimated number of cases, we will assume that the 45 cases of abuse reported among the 1520 respondents were different cases; that no two respondents reported the same case. This seems a reasonable assumption in a national survey. We can now estimate the number of physically abused children. The 1970 U.S. Census reports that approximately 31 million families have at least one child under eighteen. Thus the number of physically abusing families can be estimated as approximately (0.004) $(31,000,000) = 124,000$. If each abusing family abused only one child, this would be a point estimate of the number of abused children. But several case studies indicate that the average number of abused children per family is close to 1.6.[17] Using this value increases the estimated number of physical abuse cases to approximately 200,000. Similarly, we estimate that a reasonable upper bound to the number of physical abuse cases is (0.010) $(31,000,000)$ $(1.6) = 500,000$.

Gil's survey dealt specifically with cases of physical abuse, and not with severe neglect or sexual molestation. No comparable large scale survey data exist on incidence of child neglect or molestation. Several small scale in-depth studies, carried out in New York State and particularly New York City, show that serious

---

[17] See, for example, the data reported in Angela E. Skinner and Raymond L. Castle, *Seventy-eight Battered Children: A Retrospective Study* (London: National Society for the Prevention of Cruelty to Children, September, 1969); also, see *Child Abuse in Wisconsin*. Data for Australia is given in "Committee of Investigation into Allegations of Neglect and Maltreatment of Young Children: Report to the Honorable the Chief Secretary And The Honorable The Minister of Health," (Melbourne, Australia: Chelsea House, December, 1967).

cases of neglect and maltreatment, including sexual abuse, occur more than twice as frequently as physical abuse.

Specifically, the New York State Department of Social Services estimates that seventy per cent of all child maltreatment cases are attributable to severe neglect or sexual abuse. These estimates, if reasonably accurate, indicate an additional expected number of 465,000 neglect and other maltreatment incidents. A corresponding upper bound for these additional incidents is 1,175,000.

To convert these data into the proportions of children who are abused, we note there are approximately 67 million persons under eighteen in America in 1973. The following table summarizes both the estimated number of cases, and the proportions of all children, in different abuse categories (Figure 3). We conclude, therefore, that approximately one child in every hundred in America is physically abused, sexually molested, or severely neglected. Throughout the rest of this report, we use the term "abuse" as a general one, which includes as subcategories physical abuse, sexual molestation, and severe neglect.

FIGURE 3
Adjusted Estimates of Incidences of Physical Abuse, Neglect, and Sexual Molestation

		Estimated Yearly Number of Cases	Estimated Proportion of All Children Under 18 Subject to Maltreatment	Upper Bound on Estimated Yearly Number of Cases	Upper Bound on Proportion of All Children Under 18 Subject to Maltreatment
	Physical Abuse	200,000	0.003	500,000	0.008
Type of Maltreatment	Severe Neglect or Sexual Abuse	465,000	0.007	1,175,000	0.018
	Totals	665,000	0.010	1,675,000	0.026

Using Incidence Data to Evaluate a Policy of National Health Screening

Is knowing the approximate incidence of child abuse important for policy, or is it simply intellectually interesting? After all, one might argue that the actual number of abused children really doesn't matter—one abused child is one too many.

But knowing incidence is extremely important, since it aids the evaluation of public policy suggestions.

In testimony before the U.S. Senate and elsewhere, one policy proposal would identify abuse through a national health screening. Henry Kempe has noted that while children over six years old are usually seen regularly by health personnel in school, infants under six may never be seen, and there is thus little chance of detecting abuse or severe neglect at this age.[18] To remedy this situation, he has proposed that the nation adopt a public policy of national health visitors.

We suggest that a health visitor call at intervals during the first months of life upon *each* young family and that she become, as it were, the guardian who would see to it that each infant is receiving his basic health rights. . . . It is my view that the concept of the utilization of health visitors would be widely accepted in this country. Health visitors need not have nursing training, and intelligent, successful mothers and fathers could be readily prepared for this task at little cost. . . . In those areas where it is not practical to have health visitors, health stations could be established in neighborhood fire houses.[19]

Why is it necessary to know the incidence of abuse in order to evaluate this suggested policy of national health inspection? One reason concerns the technique of detecting abuse. A child with broken bones or fractures that have healed but had never been treated medically is at first screening a possible abuse candidate. An extensive radiologic literature attests to the value of X-ray diagnosis in ascertaining actual abuse in such cases.[20] Suppose that an X-ray for every child were to become a standard diagnostic procedure. If one child in a hundred is really abused, then even if this case were detected via X-ray, ninety-nine would be needlessly exposed to X-ray diagnosis. Assuming that the cumulative effects of X-rays are even minimally harmful, it is not clear that the benefit of detecting the one

[18] Kempe, testimony for hearings of the Senate Subcommittee of Children and Youth.

[19] Kempe, paper presented to Harvard Inter-Faculty Seminar on Child Rearing in Modern Urban America.

[20] D. H. Baker *et al.,* "Special Trauma Problems in Children," *Radiologic Clinics of North America,* 4 (August, 1966), pp. 289-305; John Caffey, "Multiple Fractures in the Long Bones of Infants Suffering from Chronic Subdural Hematoma," *American Journal of Roentgenology,* 56 (August, 1946), pp. 163-173; John L. Gwinn, Kenneth W. Lewin, and Herbert G. Peterson, Jr., "Roentgenographic Manifestations of Unsuspected Trauma in Infancy," *Journal of the American Medical Association,* 176 (June, 1961), pp. 926-929; Hannibal Hamlin, "Subgaleal Hematoma Caused by Hair Pull," *Journal of the American Medical Association,* 204 (April, 1968), p. 339; C. Douglas Hawkes, "Craniocerebral Trauma in Infancy and Childhood," *Clinical Neurosurgery,* 11 (1964), pp. 66-75; J. McCort *et al.,* "Visceral Injuries in Battered Children," *Radiology,* 82 (1964), pp. 424-428; Ching Tseug Teng, Edward B. Singleton, and C. W. Daeschner, Jr., "Skeletal Injuries of the Battered Child," *American Journal of Orthopedics,* 6 (1964), pp. 202-207; A. Tardieu and Fredric N. Silverman, "Unrecognized Trauma in Infants, the Battered Child Syndrome, and the Syndrome of Ambroise Tardieu," Rigler Lecture, *Radiology,* 104 (August, 1972), pp. 337-353.

case outweighs the cost of cumulative exposure of the other ninety-nine children.

Suppose, on the other hand, that forty children in a hundred are abused. Then the benefit of mass screening might outweigh the cost. It is extremely difficult to quantify the human costs of needless exposure to X-rays and to trade them off against the human benefits of detecting an abused child. Yet the trade-off depends heavily upon the incidence of abuse.

A second reason for the importance of abuse incidence figures lies in the assessment of the costs and benefits of alternative treatments. If a national health exam for all children were instituted, how much time and effort should be spent searching for abuse? That would seem to depend upon the incidence of abuse relative to the incidence of other health problems. For example, suppose one per cent of children are abused, while twenty percent suffer from poor nutrition. It may then be much more valuable to focus a health exam on a child's nutrition and to spend time with a parent counseling him or her on how to provide better nutrition. Although in principle it would be desirable for a health examiner to search for both abuse and poor nutrition, in the real world scarce resources force us to trade off many competing possibilities. Focus must be placed on the kind of examination most likely to yield the greatest overall benefit to the children who need help.

The foregoing reasons for knowledge about incidence are essentially conceptual. The third reason can be illustrated much more specifically (see Figure 4). With the institution of a national health examination for child abuse the desired outcomes would be to examine an abused child and conclude that he or she is abused, or to examine a non-abused child and conclude that he or she is not abused. Two kinds of errors are possible. One (a false negative) lies in examining a child who is in fact abused but not detecting the abuse. The second error (a false positive) is concluding that a child has been abused when he or she really has not been.

In a national health examination program, both types of errors would have to be minimized. If the examination produced too many false negatives, there would be little point in conducting it. Too many false positives, on the other hand, would invite the intolerable situation of falsely accusing large numbers of parents of abuse. What in fact could be expected should a national health examination program be instituted?

The answer depends on three factors. First, how good are health examiners at detecting abuse if it has occurred? In Figure 4 this is denoted as $P(A)$. Second, how good are health examiners at determining that abuse has *not* occurred? Call this $P(N)$. Third, what is the national incidence of abused children? Call this $P(I)$.

FIGURE 4

Table Giving Proportion of Children Diagnosed as Abused at First Screening Who Were Really Abused.

P(A) = proportion of abused children who are correctly diagnosed at first screening.
P(N) = proportion of non-abused children who are correctly diagnosed at first screening.
P(I) = proportion of children in America who are abused.

		P(I)						
		.001	.004	.007	.010	.020	.026	.030
	P(N)							
	.80	.003	.014	.024	.034	.067	.084	.098
P(A)=.70	.90	.007	.027	.047	.066	.125	.153	.178
	.95	.014	.053	.090	.124	.222	.270	.304
	.99	.065	.219	.330	.414	.588	.641	.684
	.80	.004	.016	.027	.039	.075	.095	.110
P(A)=.80	.90	.008	.031	.053	.075	.140	.174	.198
	.95	.016	.060	.100	.140	.246	.291	.331
	.99	.074	.243	.361	.447	.620	.672	.712
	.80	.004	.018	.031	.043	.084	.106	.122
P(A)=.90	.90	.009	.035	.060	.083	.155	.189	.217
	.95	.018	.067	.113	.154	.268	.320	.358
	.99	.083	.265	.388	.476	.647	.697	.736
	.80	.005	.019	.032	.046	.088	.110	.128
P(A)=.95	.90	.009	.037	.063	.088	.162	.199	.227
	.95	.019	.071	.118	.161	.279	.332	.370
	.99	.087	.276	.401	.490	.660	.710	.746

Although we have no good data on the quality of diagnosis, we might ask how different rates of correct diagnosis affect the success of the screening policy. We might also ask how incidence rates affect it. The data in Figure 4 answer the specific question, "If every child in America were examined, then for the given values of P (A), P (N), and P (I), *what proportion of children diagnosed as being abused were really abused?*" The values in the body of the table have been computed using Bayes' theorem.

A study of Figure 4 can lead to important implications for evaluation of a program of national health examinations. Let us assume, optimistically, that when a child has been abused, it is correctly detected 90 percent of the time. Further, assume that non-abuse is correctly detected 95 percent of the time. Finally, use the most reasonable estimate of abuse incidence rate, 0.010, that was developed earlier. The number in Figure 4 corresponding to P (A) = .90, P (N) = .95, and P (I) = 0.010 is 0.154. This reveals that, of the children diagnosed by the health examiners as having been abused, only 15.4 per cent were *really* abused. Clearly this presents an unacceptable basis for social policy. Approximately 85 percent of the parents accused of abusing their children would have been falsely accused.

The value of 15.4 per cent emerges when the incidence rate of 0.010 is used. If we increase the actual incidence rate to our estimated upper bound, .026, Figure 4 shows that, of all children diagnosed as being abused, only 32.0 per cent would really have been abused. Approximately 68 percent of parents or guardians would be falsely accused. Again, this seems unacceptable.

The results in Figure 4 may appear highly counter-intuitive. How can correct diagnosis rates of 90 percent and 95 percent yield 85 percent false positives? The answer is that in using the incidence rate of one child in each hundred, even a small error rate on the other 99 would lead to relatively many false positives. In our example, the error rate on the other 99 would be 5 percent: 1.0 minus .95. A 5 percent error rate in diagnosing 99 non-abused children would result on the average in nearly five incorrect diagnoses of abuse. One of the hundred children was really abused, and he would be correctly diagnosed with .90 probability. Thus, if many groups of a hundred children were examined by health personnel, just under six children per group on the average would be diagnosed as abused, when of these six only one was really abused. This roughly one out of six correct positive diagnoses gives the .154 in Figure 4, and the corresponding .846 of false positive diagnoses.

If the assigned diagnosis rates of P (A) = .90 and P (N) = .95 do not seem reasonable, Figure 4 gives the proportion of false positives for many other diagnostic rates.

Finally, it should be stressed here that the value of this kind of analysis is not only to help policy makers choose a successful policy; it may also suggest modifications of an idea under study. For example, the results in Figure 4 should not foreclose consideration of any kind of national health examination for children. But they underline the importance of remembering that if such a policy were designed, two features would be particularly important. First, diagnostic personnel would need excellent training, as the data in Figure 4 indicate that the quality of diagnostic skills would play a major role in determining the success of a national examination. Second, a multiple stage checking procedure should be instituted. At the first stage, where large numbers of children are examined, the primary focus should be on avoiding false negatives, missing real cases of abuse. But subsequent stages should steadily work towards winnowing out questionable cases, leaving the focus at the final stage on avoiding false positives, and the resulting false accusations of parents.

Educational Curricula on Child Rearing

A national health examination involves detection of abuse after it occurs. Another policy has been advanced by educators which aims to reduce the incidence of abuse through a preventive strategy. They argue that one reason parents may abuse is simple lack of knowledge about what to expect from a child at different stages of development.[21] Pediatricians studying abusing parents frequently report that parents "didn't know what they were in for" when they had a child. Some people are unprepared for the sustained effort and attention-giving that parenthood requires.

These observations suggest the possibility of dealing with child abuse through education. Perhaps teenagers should be exposed to very young children in day care settings and taught some basic principles of child development in order to be better prepared for family planning and successful parenthood.

Evaluation of the probable success or failure of such educational efforts presents a difficult problem. A rigorous solution would be to design a serious controlled field study.[22] First, a curriculum would have to be developed. Then large groups of teenagers would have to be randomly assigned to a curriculum treatment and a control group. Extremely large samples would be necessary, since child abuse is relatively infrequent in the population. Finally, the treatment and con-

---

[21] Brandt F. Steele and Carl B. Pollock, "A Psychiatric Study of Parents Who Abuse Infants and Small Children," in *The Battered Child*, ed. Ray E. Helfer and C. Henry Kempe (Chicago: University of Chicago Press, 1968), pp. 103-147; Katherine Bain, "Commentary: The Physically Abused Child," *Pediatrics*, 31 (June, 1963), pp. 895-898; Ray E. Helfer and Carl B. Pollock, "The Battered Child Syndrome," *Advances in Pediatrics*, 15, pp. 9-27; Barbara Marie Korsch, Jewell B. Christian, Ethel Kontz Gozzi, and Paul V. Carlson, "Infant Care and Punishment: A Pilot Study," *American Journal of Public Health*, 55 (December, 1965), pp. 1880-1888; R. B. Hiller, "The Battered Child: A Health Visitor's Point of View," *Nursing Times*, 65 (1969), pp. 1265-1266; Grace S. Gregg, "Physicians, Child Abuse Reporting Laws, and the Injured Child: Psychosocial Anatomy of Childhood Trauma," *Clinical Pediatrics* 7 (December, 1968), pp. 720-725.

In an excellent review of the psychology of abusing parents, John J. Spinetta and David Rigler ("The Child Abusing Parent: A Psychological Review," *Psychological Bulletin*, 79 (April, 1972), pp. 296-304) conclude that "abusing parents lack appropriate knowledge of child rearing, and that their attitudes, expectations, and child rearing techniques set them apart from non-abusive parents. The abusing parents implement culturally accepted norms for raising children with an exaggerated intensity at an inappropriately early age." In accord with this idea, Ray E. Helfer argued in testimony before the Subcommittee of Children and Youth, *op. cit.*, March 31, 1973, in favor of family rearing and development courses for parents

[22] The word controlled field study in this context means essentially a well designed field experiment. Some of the methodological and political issues confronting the implementation of controlled field studies are presented in Richard J. Light, Frederick Mosteller, and Herbert S. Winokur, Jr., "Using Controlled Field Studies to Improve Public Policy," *Report of the President's Commission on Federal Statistics*, II (Washington, D.C.: U.S. Government Printing Office, 1971).

trol groups would have to be followed over a period of years, to determine whether the treatment group showed lower abuse rates.

Such an experiment could provide valuable inferences about the effectiveness of education for the prevention of abuse. But these curricula, like any others, also must be checked in opportunity and cost terms. Given the finite number of instructional hours, how many hours could be devoted to a program whose primary goal is the prevention of a rare event? Perhaps the suitability of such an educational program for teenagers should be argued not on the grounds of preventing child abuse, but rather on the broader grounds of the overall value of the study of child development.

Since an experiment in prevention would take several years to evaluate, what can be done in its absence to study the preventive value of childhood education? Data on families that abuse would be needed, especially the answers to two specific questions about family characteristics. How many children are in the family of each abused child? What is the birth order of the abused child in his family? Studying these data would lead to the following procedure. Focus first on all families with two or more children. The more frequently the oldest child is abused, the more support is given to the hypothesis that lack of preparation for childrearing accounts for the abuse. When it is a younger child who is abused, some other explanation would have to be found. If the abused child were the youngest of four, it would be difficult to argue that lack of preparation was the explanation for abuse. A more tenable explanation in this case has been suggested by Gil and others: large numbers of children create extreme stress under certain circumstances.[23]

A second and related analysis might focus on the question: what proportion of all abuse occurs in single-child families? If this proportion were much higher than the proportion of single-child families in the general population, the hypothesis that education is potentially valuable would seem more valid.

Data on birth order are surprisingly rare. The only extensive report was pre-

[23] Studies indicating this finding, as well as offering some explanations and speculation as to why stress leads to abuse, include: Kempe *et al.,* "The Battered Child Syndrome"; Shirley M. Nurse. "Familial Patterns of Parents Who Abuse their Children," *Smith College Studies in Social Work,* 35 (October, 1964), pp. 11-25; Patricia T. Schloesser, "The Abused Child," *Bulletin of the Menninger Clinic,* 28 (September, 1964), pp. 260-268; Skinner and Castle, "Seventy-eight Battered Children"; Grace S. Gregg and Elizabeth Elmer, "Infant Injuries: Accident or Abuse?" *Pediatrics,* 44 (September, 1969), pp. 434-439; Allan J. Ebbin, Michael H. Gollub, Arthur M. Stein, and Miriam G. Wilson, "Battered Child Syndrome at the Los Angeles County General Hospital," *American Journal of the Diseases of Children,* 118 (October, 1969), pp. 660-667.

FIGURE 5
Data on Family Size and Birth Order in Three Countries

U.S.A. Number of Children	Abusing Families; Percent in Gil Survey	U.S. Census Family Size Distribution Families with Children under 18
1	18.0	31.8
2	22.3	29.7
3	20.2	18.9
4 or more	39.5	19.6
	100.0	100.0

New Zealand Number of Children	Abusing Families; Percent in DSW Survey	New Zealand Family Size Distribution Families with Children under 18
1	13.5	33.2
2	19.2	30.8
3	20.8	21.9
4 or more	46.5	14.1
	100.0	100.0

England Number of Children	Abusing Families; Percent in NSPCC Survey	England Family Size Distribution Families with Children under 18
1	23.1	34.4
2	44.8	33.2
3	19.2	20.5
4 or more	12.9	11.9
	100.0	100.0

pared by the National Society for the Prevention of Cruelty to Children in England.[24] Data on family size of abused children are more extensive. A summary of several major studies appears in Figure 5, which reveals that in the United States, England, and New Zealand, the average family size for abusing families substantially exceeds the national average. In particular, in each country, approximately

[24] Skinner and Castle.

216

33 percent of all families with any children under eighteen have just one child.[25] Yet among the abusing families in each country, the percentage with one child is sharply lower; 18 percent in the United States, 23 percent in England, and only 13 percent in New Zealand. These data yield little evidence that the explanation for abusing parents can be found in the lack of proper education for parenthood. Two stronger possibilities are that some parents have trouble coping with the demands made by large families or that a family crisis situation (such as severe financial problems) will have a more serious effect on larger families than on smaller families. Education for teenagers in various aspects of childrearing and child development can be advocated because of its general importance for an educated citizenry. But there appears to be little agrument for it on the specific grounds of preventing child abuse.

Developing Profiles of Abusing Families

Some pediatricians and psychologists have suggested that parents who abuse children might have certain profiles. It would then follow that if reliable profiles could be developed, certain families could be viewed as high risk families and cared for preventively. For example, at the June, 1973, American Medical Association meeting, Arthur H. Green made the case that doctors should try to identify high risk parents in the course of providing routine prenatal care or other medical treatment of family members.[26] Ray Helfer, a pioneer in developing case management strategies, has reported a first effort toward developing a predictive profile.[27]

[24] Skinner and Castle.

[25] For United States, see U. S. Bureau of the Census, "Current Population Reports, March, 1972. Household and Family Characteristics," #246 (Washington, D.C.: U.S. Government Printing Office, 1973); for England, see General Register Office, *Sample Census 1966, England and Wales, Household Composition Tables* (London: Her Majesty's Statistical Office, 1968), pp. 214-215; for New Zealand, see the *New Zealand Census, 1966* (Wellington, New Zealand: New Zealand Government Printer, 1966).

[26] Report to panel on child abuse at the *American Medical Association* meetings in New York City, June 25, 1973.

[27] See the Appendix on developing a profile in C. H. Kempe and R. E. Helfer, *Helping the Battered Child and His Family* (Chicago: University of Chicago Press, 1971). Gil developed a "typology of child abuse" and based on a factor analytic study reported seven factors which appear to underlie most cases of abuse (pp. 125-132). Finally, in a less empirical study, interactions of mental, physical, and emotional stress were found to be associated with cases of abuse by Betty Simons, Elinor F. Downs, Madeline M. Hurster, and Morton Archer, "Child Abuse: Epidemiologic Study of Medically Reported Cases," *New York State Journal of Medicine*, 66 (November, 1966), pp. 2783-2788.

This predictive approach raises an interesting methodological problem.[28] To develop a useful profile of abusing families, features must be isolated that effectively set abusing families apart from other families. This would require ideally either a good random sample from both populations (abusers and non-abusers) or complete population data. Fortunately, the U.S. Census supplies excellent social and demographic data on "all U.S. families with children under eighteen." Given the earlier estimate that ninety-nine per cent of all American families are not abusers, the census data can provide good estimates of the features of non-abusing families.

Unfortunately, no parallel set of good data exists for abusing families. By far the best information available is the extensive survey reported by Gil in his book *Violence Against Children*.[29] Gil's data concern approximately 6,000 cases each in 1967 and 1968 that were reported to state agencies. The data are divided into two sets. One set consists of a few variables on every reported case of abuse in America for 1967 and 1968. The variables in these data include age and sex of child, circumstances and type of abuse, and information on perpetrator such as age, sex, and relationship to child. The second set of data consists of a sample of 1380 cases taken in 1967, for which much more extensive information was collected. Over fifty variables were included on the abused child, including school status, family status, family demographic characteristics, and personal characteristics. Over twenty-five variables were included for the perpetrator, including employment history, education, housing accommodations, income, criminal convictions, and prior involvement in an abuse case. Finally, seventeen variables describe the circumstances of the abuse incident. This second set of data, called the "comprehensive" data, is the focus of our study. This is not a random sample of all cases. The crucial question, then, becomes how to analyze a set of data from a non-random sample that is non-random in ways we do not understand well and is based on a population whose size and features we also do not understand very well. A strategy for analyzing such data follows, with a summary of results.

[28] The predictive approach also raises ethical questions when it is tied into possible policy suggestions. Suppose a set of new parents are found by a profile analysis to be ten times more likely than random parents to abuse their child. What does this imply about intervention? The answer is not clear; probably a reasonable suggestion is that an offer of *voluntary* social services could be proffered. Clearly this is an extremely difficult issue, both morally and legally. There is no facile answer, and we do not deal with this issue here.

[29] David Gil was particularly helpful in not only supplying all of his data on computer cards and tapes, but also in clarifying questions of definition and coding. It is difficult to imagine a comparable set of data so helpfully documented.

Strategy for Analysis

The key to the analysis of the abuse data lies in the differences between marginal totals and interactions among variables. First, consider the marginal totals: for example, the income of abusing families. Define a "rich" family as having an annual income greater than $8,000 and a poor family as having income less than $8,000. Gil's data show that 31 percent of abusing families are rich and 69 percent are poor. Using census data we find that the proportions of non-abusing families in the rich and poor categories are close to .50 and .50. If we than assume that a "finding" has emerged—that abusing families are in general poorer than non-abusing families—a serious error might be made. Such a finding depends entirely upon the marginal totals of both the census income data and the abusers' income data. But although the census data are excellent, the accuracy of the abusers' marginal totals is unknown. Thus, to the extent that systematic reporting errors influence the marginal totals of any variable, a comparison of marginal totals between the census and Gil's abuser survey will be little more than a reflection of those unknown biases. Generating serious policy inferences from such data is unlikely to prove a fruitful enterprise.

The analysis of interactions between variables would therefore seem a better focus. But under what circumstances will a relationship discovered in the abuser survey represent a real relationship in the population of abused children? The displays in Figure 6 illustrate several circumstances.

In Panel A there are four 2 x 2 tables: the two tables in the left column describe data from the abuser survey; the two tables in the right column describe data from the U.S. Census on non-abusing families. Consider, for instance, studying the relationship between residence (urban, rural) and family size (large, small) to see if the structure of this relationship is different for families that abuse and families that do not abuse. We can distribute all high-income abusers among the four cells of the upper left-hand table. If the data fall primarily into the upper left and lower right hand cells (indicated by x's in these cells), it would appear that rich abusing families tend to be primarily large rural families and small urban families.

Next the low-income abusing families are distributed among the four cells in the lower left-hand table. If these data, similarly, clump into the upper left and lower right cells, a first inference becomes possible. Since both rich and poor abusing families tend to be primarily large rural and small urban families, the fact that the data for income marginal totals may be biased will not affect the estimate of the size of abusing families by area relationship. In other words, that the proportion of rich abusers may be underestimated in the survey data does not influence the inference as to the relationship between family size and area of residence for *all*

FIGURE 6

Searching for Two-Variable Relationships That Discriminate Between Abusing and Non-abusing Families

PANEL A

Shows discrimination between abusers and non-abusers.

Area		Abuser Family Size			Area		Non-abuser Family Size		
		large	small				large	small	
	rural	x				rural		x	
	urban		x			urban	x		
		High income .31					High income .50		

Area		Abuser Family Size			Area		Non-abuser Family Size		
		large	small				large	small	
	rural	x				rural		x	
	urban		x			urban	x		
		Low income .69					Low income .50		

PANEL B

Shows no discrimination between abusers and non-abusers.

Area		Abuser Family Size			Area		Non-abuser Family Size		
		large	small				large	small	
	rural	x				rural	x		
	urban		x			urban		x	
		High income .31					High income .50		

Area		Abuser Family Size			Area		Non-abuser Family Size		
		large	small				large	small	
	rural	x				rural	x		
	urban		x			urban		x	
		Low income .69					Low income .50		

PANEL C

Shows a three-variable interaction.

	Abuser Family Size				Non-abuser Family Size	
	large	small			large	small

FIGURE 6 *(continued)*

		large	small
Area	rural	x	
	urban		x

High income .31

		large	small
Area	rural	x	
	urban		x

High income .50

Abuser
Family Size

Non-abuser
Family Size

		large	small
Area	rural	x	
	urban		x

Low income .69

		large	small
Area	rural		x
	urban	x	

Low income .50

PANEL D
No inference permissible because of unknown effects of reporting bias.

Abuser
Family Size

Non-abuser

		large	small
Area	rural	x	
	urban		x

High income .31

High income .50

Abuser
Family Size

Non-abuser

		large	small
Area	rural		x
	urban	x	

Low income .69

Low income .50

abusing families,[30] because the relationship is the same in both high and low income groups.

[30] What we are looking for in this analysis are various kinds of interactions in a four dimensional contingency table. The four dimensions are income, abuse/non-abuse, area of residence, and family size. We focus in our analysis on a search for two-variable interactions nested within categories of a third variable, as described in Figure 6. The analysis we present is essentially equivalent to estimating effects from a log linear model fit to multivariate contingency tables. For a particularly lucid exposition of this idea, see James A. Davis, "The Goodman Log Linear System for Assessing Effects in Multivariate Contingency Tables," National Opinion Research Center Lithograph, June, 1972. Discussions of how to view interactions in multivariate tables are given in Leo A. Goodman,

On the right side of Panel A, the rich non-abusers according to the census data are divided among the four cells in the upper table. Suppose the data fall primarily in the upper right and lower left, indicating that among rich families in America rural families are generally small while urban families are generally large. If low-income families from the census display the same pattern, a useful profile of abusing families begins to emerge. The analysis in Panel A indicates that *abusing families differ from non-abusing families* in that abusing families are large rural and small urban, while non-abusing families are large urban and small rural. Further, this inference is tenable even though substantial bias may exist in the income levels of reported abusers. Whenever a display of data takes the general form given in Panel A, the existence of a two-variable relationship that discriminates abusing families from non-abusing families is strongly indicated.[31]

Suppose, however, that when the data analysis is carried out, the series of 2 x 2 tables assumes the pattern given in Panel B. This panel indicates that abusing families tend to be large rural and small urban regardless of income, and that exactly the same is true for non-abusing families. In this event, the inference is that the family-size-by-residence relationship does *not* discriminate abusers from non-abusers.

What if the data appear as in Panel C? In this event, a three-variable interaction is indicated. For example, the data in Panel C suggest that rich abusers and non-abusers have the same family-size-by-residence relationship, but that poor abusers and non-abusers have a different relationship.

Finally, if the data on abusing families appear as in Panel D, where rich abusers have a different family-size-by-residence relation than poor abusers, no inference is possible. Since rich abusers differ from poor abusers, making an inference for *all*

"The Multivariate Analysis of Qualitative Data: Interactions Among Multiple Classification," *Journal of the American Statistical Association*, 65 (March, 1970), pp. 226-256; also, Leo A. Goodman, "The Analysis of Multidimensional Contingency Tables: Stepwise Procedures and Direct Estimation Methods for Building Models for Multiple Classification," *Technometrics*, 13 (February, 1971) pp. 33-61; Leo A. Goodman, "A Modified Multiple Regression Approach to the Analysis of Dichotomous Variables," *American Sociological Review*, 37 (March, 1972), pp. 28-46. For other examples of fitting models to multidimensional tables, see Yvonne M. M. Bishop, Stephen E. Fienberg, Paul Holland, Frederick Mosteller, and Richard J. Light, *Discrete Multivariate Analysis: Theory and Practice* (Cambridge, Mass.: M. I. T. Press, in press).

[31] It should be noted here that while we are searching for two-variable relationships that discriminate abusing from non-abusing families, the general procedure permits us to next search for three variable relationships that discriminate, then four variable relationships, and so on up. As this is a "first look" at fitting the Gil data to a multivariate model, we restrict ourselves here to two-variable discriminators.

FIGURE 7
Illustration of Iterative Proportional Fitting

Suppose data for abusers had the following form in a 2 x 2 table:

TABLE 1   Quarters Shared

		no	yes	
Income	high	108	88	196
	low	976	251	1227
		1084	339	1423

Then a measure of association between income and sharing quarters is given by the crossproduct ratio, α,

$$\alpha = \frac{(108)\ (251)}{(\ 88)\ (976)} = 0.32.$$

One may find this table a bit difficult to interpret because of the unbalanced marginals. There are many more low-income abusers than high-income abusers. Also, there are many more families who do not share quarters than who do share. The question may then be asked, what would the table look like if the marginal totals are all identical, if all the cell entries in the table sum to 1.0, and if the crossproduct ratio, or level of association, remains unchanged? To answer this question, we set required row and column totals to 0.5, and proceed through the following steps.

A. Multiply each cell in each row of table 1 by the ratio of the required row total to the actual row total in table 1. The required row totals are 0.5 for both rows. This gives:

TABLE 2

		Quarters Shared		Actual	Required
		no	yes	totals	totals
Income	high	0.310	0.190	0.500	0.500
	low	0.418	0.082	0.500	0.500
Actual totals		0.728	0.272		
Required totals		0.500	0.500		

B. Repeat the procedure on the columns, multiplying column one in table 2 by $\frac{0.500}{0.728}$ and column 2 in table 2 by $\frac{0.500}{0.272}$. This gives:

TABLE 3

		Quarters Shared		Actual	Required
		no	yes	totals	totals
Income	high	0.213	0.350	0.563	0.500
	low	0.287	0.150	0.437	0.500
Actual totals		0.500	0.500		
Required totals		0.500	0.500		

C. Repeating the iterative procedure for 4 cycles, the adjusted table converges to:

FIGURE 7 *(continued)*

TABLE 4

		Quarters Shared		
		no	yes	
Income	high	0.181	0.319	0.500
	low	0.319	0.181	0.500
		0.500	0.500	1.000

Thus we see that low-income abusers are relatively much less likely than are high-income abusers to share their quarters. Table 4 has the same cross-product ratio as table 1; $\alpha = 0.32$. But the adjustment helps to clarify the kernel of the income-quarters shared relation, and also facilitates comparison of this 2 x 2 table with other 2 x 2 tables with different marginals.

abusers in the population would require knowledge of the true proportions of rich and poor abusers in the population, and this is precisely the data that may be systematically biased. Thus, no matter what the census data on non-abusers may show, we can not make an inference.

In applying this analysis strategy, it is often difficult to compare sets of 2 x 2 tables with different sample sizes. To facilitate such comparison, we adjust the raw cell counts in each table using a procedure called iterative proportional fitting.[32] This is a method by which the cell entries in each table are adjusted so that each row and column total can be set by the data analyst. The cell entries then add up to these totals while the cross-product ratio, a measure of association between the two variables, remains constant.[33] Not only does this fitting procedure allow the

[32] The iterative proportional fitting method was developed for adjusting small sample observations to agree with a set of marginal totals obtained from census data by William Edwards Deming and E. Frederick Stephan. "On a Least Squares Adjustment of a Sampled Frequency Table When the Expected Marginal Totals are Known," *Annals of Mathematical Statistics*, 11 (September, 1940), pp. 427-444. Further discussion of these procedures are given by Yvonne M. M. Bishop, "Multidimensional Contingency Tables: Cell Estimates," Diss. Harvard University Department of Statistics, 1967; Stephen E. Fienberg, "The Analysis of Multidimensional Contingency Tables," *Ecology*, 51 (September, 1970), pp. 419-433; Stephen E. Fienberg, "An Iterative Procedure for Estimation in Contingency Tables," *Annals of Mathematical Statistics*, 41 (December, 1970), pp. 907-917; Frederick Mosteller, "Association and Estimation in Contingency Tables," *Journal of the American Statistical Association*, 63 (March, 1968), pp. 1-28. The main attractive feature of iterative proportional fitting in a 2 × 2 table is that the cross-product ratio $n_{11}n_{22}/n_{12}n_{21}$, which provides a measure of the interaction structure of the table, is preserved. While we only consider 2 × 2 tables in this discussion, extensions to larger tables are given in Bishop.

[33] Consider the cross-product ratio for a 2 × 2 table, $n_{11}n_{22}/n_{12}n_{21}$. Multiply the entries in row one of this table by the number r_1, multiply the entries in row two by r_2, multiply the entries in column one by c_1, and multiply the entries in column two by c_2. Then, the cross-product ratio for

study of several tables with substantially different marginal totals, but it also focuses on association independently of these marginal totals, which for the abuser's sample may be biased. It thus puts the tables into a "comparable form," while preserving the integrity of the association between the two variables in each table. An illustration of the procedure appears in Figure 7.[34] All results of the reanalysis of Gil's data are presented below using iterative fits.

Results of Reanalysis

A summary of the reanalysis appears in Figures 8a and 8b. Figure 8a lists the twenty-one variables that were studied in detail. Notice that this represents only a subset of all of Gil's variables. These were selected because they paralleled variables in the U.S. Census, thus permitting a comparison between abusers and non-abusers of the kind described in Figure 6.[35] Notice further the division of the twenty-one variables into two groups: "table" variables and "splitter" variables. Splitter variables are described in Figure 6 as providing the marginal total comparisons. They are the variables most likely to be subject to reporting biases and other non-sampling er-

---

this "adjusted" table becomes $(r_1 c_1 n_{11})(r_2 c_2 n_{22})/(r_1 c_2 n_{12})(r_2 c_1 n_{22})$, where r_1, r_2, c_1, c_2 are all greater than zero. This "adjusted" cross-product ratio reduces precisely to the original one. That this procedure provides the maximum likelihood estimates for cell entries has been proved by Bishop. That this iterative scheme converges, providing the desired marginal values, has been proved by C. Terry Ireland and Solomon Kullback, "Contingency Tables with Given Marginals," *Biometrika*, 55 (February, 1968), pp. 179-188.

[34] Notice that using iterative proportional fitting to examine the "kernel" of association between two table variables also has the advantage of giving protection against reporting bias in the row variable, the column variable, or biases in both independently. Take, for example, the row variable in Figure 7; urban versus rural place of residence. Suppose that an abuser in an urban area were r_2 times more likely to be reported, or "caught," than an abuser in a rural area. Then, using the strategy outlined above for searching out pairs of variables that discriminate abusers from non-abusers, and examining the relationships using iterative proportional fitting, the r_2 rate of relative over-reporting of urban abusers would *not affect the cross-product ratio*. The same is true if either category of the column variable in a table is over-reported relative to the other column category. The one kind of reporting bias that we have no protection whatever against is *interactive reporting bias*. Thus, if there exists a non-additive over-reporting of, say, small rural families, there is no way that we can "adjust for this." The results of the reanalysis of Gil's data must thus be tempered with the caution that we have presently little idea of what pairs of "table" variables are subject to interactive reporting bias. As data is collected much more carefully in the future, special attention must be paid to this problem of what kinds of interactive reporting biases are possible, or even likely.

[35] The census cases were acquired from a Public Use Sample of cases from the 1970 U.S. Census (1970 State, one in 10,000). From this sample we generated a stratified sample of children aged zero to fourteen living in families, including data on the children, their parents if present, and their household. It must be kept in mind when interpreting the results from these analyses that all children living in any kind of institution are excluded from the census data.

FIGURE 8a

List of Variables from Gil Survey That Were Compared With Identical U.S. Census Variables.

TABLE VARIABLES	SPLITTER VARIABLES
Child's age	Child's ethnic group
Child's sex	Mother's ethnic group
Father's employment status	Father's ethnic group
Father's duration of employment	Child's school status
Mother's education	Family income per month
Father's education	Income per person per month
Family structure	
Number of persons under 18 in house	
Number of persons over 18 in house	
House or apartment	
Number of rooms	
How long in present quarters	
Does family share quarters	
Perpetrator-child age gap	

rors.[36] Table variables make up the series of 2 x 2 or 2 x 3 tables that are "nested" within levels of the splitter variables.[37] In the example given earlier, income was a splitter variable, and family size and residence were table variables. The analysis here involves examining pairs of table variables at different levels of the splitter variables, and doing a comparative analysis for both the abuser data and the census data. When a pattern of the general form given in Panel A of Figure 6 emerges, a relationship between two table variables which discriminates abusing from non-abusing families is hypothesized. These promising table variables can then be studied as to their discriminating effect on *every* splitter variable. If the

[36] The variables chosen to be "splitters" were chosen arbitrarily, but based upon our best judgment of what variables were most likely to have reporting biases. In principle, each pair of variables could be studied defining all other available variables as splitter variables, while requiring that a pair of variables discriminate abusers from non-abusers on each and every splitter variable, and discriminate between them in the same way, before that pair were concluded to be good discriminators.

[37] To permit the multidimensional contingency table analysis, the several variables with a continuous metric were divided into two or occasionally three discrete categories. Thus, for example, the variable "income" was broken into the simple categories high and low. In this process there is some loss of information. But we feel the loss of information is tolerable on two grounds: first, very few variables were continuous in nature, and second, this slight loss in information should not stop us from detecting strong effects if such effects exist. We were searching here for substantial relationships between variables, so that we can see what relationships discriminate abusers from non-abusers. We are thus interested in focussing only on substantial effects, and such effects should survive the loss of information involved in categorizing continuous data.

226

FIGURE 8b

Results of Exploratory Data Analysis: Searching for Two-Variable Relationships That Discriminate Between Abusers and Non-Abusers. (Only the discriminators are presented; cell values are after iterative proportional fitting).

ABUSERS				NON-ABUSERS			
		Dwelling				Dwelling	
		apart-ment	house			apart-ment	house
Father's Employment Status	unemployed	.36	.14	Father's Employment Status	unemployed	.23	.27
	employed	.14	.36		employed	.27	.23
		Family Share Quarters				Family Share Quarters	
		no	yes			no	yes
Father's Employment Status	unemployed	.26	.24	Father's Employment Status	unemployed	.21	.29
	employed	.24	.26		employed	.29	.21
		Father's Education				Father's Education	
		less than 9 yrs.	9 yrs. or over			less than 9 yrs.	9 yrs. or more
No. Persons Under 18	one	.18	.32	No. Persons Under 18	one	.24	.26
	more than one	.32	.18		more than one	.26	.24
		Mother's Education				Mother's Education	
		less than 9 yrs.	9 yrs. or More			less than 9 yrs.	9 yrs. or more
No. Persons Under 18	one	.20	.30	No. Persons Under 18	one	.24	.26
	more than one	.30	.20		more than one	.26	.24
		Father Duration Employment				Father Duration Employment	
		fully	not fully			fully	not fully
Dwelling	apartment	.19	.31	Dwelling	apartment	.23	.27
	house	.31	.19		house	.27	.23

FIGURE 8B *(continued)*

		Father's Education				Father's Education	
		less than 9 yrs.	9 yrs. or more			less than 9 yrs.	9 yrs. or more
Family Share	no	.28	.22	Family Share	no	.24	.26
Quarters	yes	.22	.28	Quarters	yes	.26	.24

		Father's Employment				Father's Employment	
		unemp.	emp.			unemp.	emp.
No. Persons	one	.17	.33	No. Persons	one	.25	.25
Under 18	more than one	.33	.17	Under 18	more than one	.25	.25

		Child's Age					Child's Age		
		0–2	3–6	over 6			0–2	3–6	over 6
Father's	unemployed	.20	.18	.12	Father's	unemployed	.16	.17	.17
Employment Status	employed	.13	.15	.22	Employment Status	employed	.17	.17	.16

discrimination holds up for all splitter variables, a relationship that discriminates abusers from non-abusers has been isolated.

The actual tables of variables that differentiate abusers from non-abusers are displayed in Figure 8b. The results are reported with the iterative proportional fit value for each cell. The common feature of all tables is that the pattern of adjusted cell counts for abuse cases differs substantially from the pattern for census cases. From the several hundred sets of relationships among variables initially examined, only eight paired variables discriminated reasonably well between abusing versus non-abusing families. No tests of significance of these tables are presented because the analysis is exploratory in nature.[38] So many sets of tables were studied and sequentially eliminated as not being discriminators that the reported results must be viewed as descriptive. Although we have reasonably high confidence that these findings will hold up in further studies, the nature of exploratory analysis requires us to view them as preliminary.

[38] For a careful discussion of why significance testing may be inappropriate in doing exploratory work with data, see John W. Tukey, *Exploratory Data Analysis*, 1, Preliminary Edition (Reading. Mass.: Addison Wesley, 1970).

The results of these analyses are given in Figure 8b:

1. Abusing families where the father is unemployed are much more likely to live in an apartment than in a house, relative to comparable non-abusing families where the father is unemployed.

2. Abusing families where the father is unemployed are less likely to "share their quarters" with other persons or families than are comparable non-abusing families where the father is unemployed.

3. Abusing families with less educated fathers tend to have more children than comparable non-abusing families with less educated fathers. Note that this is true even after controlling for family income and ethnic group.

4. Abusing families with less educated mothers tend to have more children than comparable non-abusing families with less educated mothers. This finding is not surprising in view of result (3) above, given the well known high correlation between mother's and father's years of educational attainment.

5. Abusing families where the father has not been fully employed in the past twelve months are more likely to live in an apartment than a house, relative to comparable non-abusing families where the father has not been fully employed. This finding is congruent with result (1).

6. Abusing families with less educated fathers are less likely to share living quarters with other persons or families than are comparable non-abusing families with less educated fathers.

7. Abusing families where the father is unemployed tend strongly to have more children than comparable non-abusing families where the father is unemployed.

8. Among abusing families, if the father is unemployed, abuse is more likely to be directed against a very young child. If the father is employed, abuse is more likely to be directed against an older child.

What do these results imply? Three observations seem reasonable. First, it is striking how few relationships discriminate between abusing and non-abusing families. On the one hand this implies that in many ways abusing families are "just like everyone else." On the other hand the scarcity of results makes development of social policies more difficult.[39]

[39] It is important to recall here that the lack of major social and demographic profiles that discriminate abusers from non-abusers in no way rules out the possibility of a psychological discriminating profile. Several authors have suggested that psychological profiles in fact offer the best hope of identifying potentially abusing families. For details, see Richard Galdston, "Observations on Children Who Have Been Physically Abused and their Parents," *American Journal of Psychiatry,*

Second, despite the general scarcity of discriminators, the variable that shows up most frequently as somehow related to child abuse is father's unemployment. This finding confims a widely held theory that family stress, both emotional and financial, related to unemployment, ties in to incidence of abuse.

A third observation is that overall, few surprises turned up. Examining the relationships that discriminate abusing from non-abusing families, we find that abusing families tend to be characterized by clusters of unemployment, large families, and social isolation. Once again, these are precisely the findings predicted by Gil, Kempe, Brandt, Steele, Vincent De Francis, and other clinicians who have studied abusing families. In terms of developing initial explanations for the phenomenon of child abuse, it is comforting to find that our empirical results accord reasonably well with the clinical insights of these investigators.

Policy Inferences from Descriptive Data

Our studies thus far have revealed both difficulties and possibilities in analyzing data on child abuse and neglect. Different kinds of reporting errors and unknown biases create the difficulties. While reporting biases may create problems for ideal statistical inference, they may simultaneously throw light on current social policies that are also reflected in the data. Consider the following four examples, each illustrating a social process reflected in the gathering of the data.

Abuse Reporting by Ethnicity

Gil's data can be partitioned into state-by-state reports, containing three ethnic categories: white, black, and Spanish-speaking. The ethnic breakdown of reported abuse cases in four northern, urban, industrialized states (New York, California, Michigan, Pennsylvania) was compared to the breakdown in four southern states (Kentucky, Tennessee, Georgia, Texas). In the four northern states, the proportion of reported abuse cases involving a white child was 27.3 per cent. In the four southern states, the proportion of white cases was 72.9 per cent.[40] Two possible

---

122 (October, 1965), pp. 440-443; Michael I. Cohen, David L. Raphling, and Phillip E. Green, "Psychologic Aspects of the Maltreatment Syndrome of Childhood," *Journal of Pediatrics*, 69 (August, 1966), pp. 279-284; R. Komisaruk, "Clinical Evaluation of Child Abuse: Scarred Families, A Preliminary Report," *Juvenile Court Judges Journal*, 17 (Section 2, 1966), pp. 66-70; Vincent J. Fontana, *The Maltreated Child: The Maltreatment Syndrome in Children* (Springfield, Ill.: Charles C Thomas, 1964); Larry B. Silver, "Child Abuse Syndrome: A Review," *Medical Times*, 96 (August, 1968), pp. 803-820.

[40] This gap is not explained by differential proportions of blacks and whites in the two sets of

inferences emerge from this substantial disparity. Either the northern states have drastically different ethnic abuse patterns from the four southern states or the two sets of reporting patterns differ.

The latter seems far more likely.[41] In some southern states, although schools and other public accommodations had been substantially desegregated, agencies providing care for children in serious trouble had not yet been substantially desegregated at the time of the survey in 1967. Few services such as foster care placements were available for black children in the South. Thus, cases of abuse of black children were usually handled in "informal ways," depending upon local authorities, and frequently remained unreported. In the North, on the other hand, the majority of abuse reports were filed by welfare and other social agencies, which have as their primary constituency poor and minority clients. Awareness of this disparity in reporting bias does not enable an estimate of the "correct" ethnic breakdown of national abuse cases.[42] It does encourage caution, however, toward existing national estimates of ethnic breakdowns in child abuse cases, and suggests the need to gather better data on the reporting process.

Reporting characteristics by parent

One of Gil's survey categories for type of abuse was malnourishment of a child. Fifteen cases of severe malnourishment were reported, and in each one both father and mother were living at home. Another variable in the survey was information about the perpetrator, including both mother and father as categories. Even though the fifteen cases were distributed among several states, all characterized the mother as perpetrator. This clearly implies that hospitals, social case workers, and the police define nutrition as a primarily maternal responsibility. This is not the place for a philosophical debate on the allocation of roles to par-

---

states. The proportion of children under seventeen who are white in the four northern states is 88.5 per cent; the proportion of children under seventeen who are white in the four southern states is 83.6 per cent. See "U.S. Summary PC (1)-B1, from the 1970 U.S. Census," in the *Statistical Abstract of the United States,* Bureau of the Census, U.S. Department of Commerce, Tables 36 and 38 (Washington, D.C.: U.S. Government Printing Office, September 1972).

[41] Only the availability of more accurate reports will enable us to understand better these disparities.

[42] It is important to point out that the possible existence of ethnic reporting biases does not affect the reanalysis of the Gil data searching for relationships that discriminate between abusing and non-abusing families. This is because ethnicity was used as a "splitter" variable rather than as a "table" variable, which means that all potential pairs of discriminating variables had to show similar patterns over all three ethnic groups before such pairs were in fact accepted as useful discriminators.

ents. Nonetheless, the data serve to point out that to the extent reporting agencies assign not only the nutritional but also other childrearing responsibilities primarily to the mother, a substantial upward bias may be present in the proportion of abuse cases attributed to mothers.

Natural parents versus "other" parents as abusers:

Several researchers have suggested that child abuse is frequently attributable to parents other than biological parents (especially males). The reanalysis of Gil's data turns up no support for such a speculation. On the contrary, "other" parents (step-parents, adoptive parents, foster parents) are generally slightly *less likely* to abuse, when the perpetrator's sex is controlled as a third variable. The data show that the overwhelming majority (89 percent) of abusing step-parents are male, but this simply reflects the census statistic that few children in 1967 lived with step-mothers; many lived with step-fathers. In divorce proceedings, the custody of children is given to the mother in approximately 90 percent of cases, which accounts for the low proportion of step-mothers in the abuser survey. When controlled for sex of perpetrator, the data show that other parents do not differ from natural parents in such important variables as type of injury, seriousness of injury, and likelihood of repeated injury. In certain other variables, like previous experience in institutions, being themselves abused as children, or being recently hospitalized in a mental institution, other parents have lower incidence rates than natural parents. Available evidence lends no support to the hypothesis that adoptive, foster, or step-parents perpetrate an inordinately high proportion of abuse cases.

Differentiating among types of abuse

Many state reporting forms, as well as individual research efforts, lump together various kinds of abuse cases. Yet the recent work of James Kent makes the point that substantial differences in background variables will emerge if cases of non-accidental injury (NAI) are separated from sexual molestation (SM) and extreme neglect (NEG). Kent studied these three groups in over 500 cases reported in Los Angeles County.[43] Variables differentiating the three groups to a substantial degree included the age of the mother at birth of first child (NEG cases had far younger mothers than the other groups), the number of children in family

---

[43] James T. Kent, "Followup Study of Abused Children," mimeo (Los Angeles, Cal.: Department of Public Social Services-Children's Hospital Los Angeles, Division of Psychiatry, Spring, 1973).

(NEG cases had much larger families), the state of repair of residence (NEG cases were in far worse repair), the dollars per person available in residence (NEG cases were much poorer), and the possession of a telephone (overwhelming majority of SM cases did, majority of NEG cases did not).[44] Measurable child characteristics also differed among the three groups. For example, nearly 50 percent of the NEG cases were below the third percentile nationally in weight; for the NAI group the proportion was 17 percent; and for the SM group it was exactly the expected 3 percent.

Despite these differences in the features of family and child characteristics among the three groups, the original court dispositions of these cases were almost identical. The "current placement" distributions are also similar. The Kent data implies, at least for those cases that reach the courts, that different kinds of child maltreatment do not result in different kinds of case assignment policies.

A policy implication arises here. An earlier analysis sought to isolate a profile of abusing families. We see now that no single profile is likely to be adequate. Just as there is no single profile of an unemployed person, different kinds of abusers have different profiles. An unemployed Ph.D. engineer has a different problem in finding work than an unemployed coal miner. They both need jobs, but for policy purposes few would argue that the identical job training or placement policy would be ideal for both. In the same way, if there were several different profiles describing different kinds of child maltreatment, the policy of case dispositions should vary, depending upon the type of maltreatment. At present this is apparently not the case in Los Angeles. Unfortunately, we do not have similar data for other cities. But if a similar pattern should emerge in other places, further thought would have to be given to the question of how public policy toward child abuse can or should depend upon different family profiles.

Choosing Among Different Explanations for Abuse

The available data not only improve understanding of current public policy, they also permit comparison of how alternative structural models of abuse accord with empirical findings. As an example, we consider two extreme cases in examining the basic question, "How often does abuse occur with respect to child-parent encounters?"

---

[44] In addition, we see in Part 5, Table 1, of the Kent data that records on the parent of the neglect cases corroborates the findings discussed earlier that reporting agencies clearly assign to the mother rather than to the father the role of ultimate responsibility for a child's welfare.

FIGURE 9a
Developing the Random and Stress Models of Abuse

Under the random model, the probability of abuse in a family is independent of the size of that family. Let that probability be p. Denote the number of all families as N, the sampling fraction for abusing families as r, and the sample size (number of abusing families in the sample) as n. Then, using U.S. Census data on distribution of family size (from Figure 5), the following table can be developed. It helps to describe how the random model of abuse can be viewed empirically.

(1) Number of Children in Family: "Family Size."	(2) Number of Abusing Families in America	(3) Expected Number of Abusing Families in an Unbiased Sample	(4) Expected Percentage Breakdown of Abusing Families in Sample	(5) Observed Percentage of Abusing Families from Gil	(6) Percentage of All Children in U.S. by Family Size
One child	.318pN	.318prN	31.8	18.0	12.9
Two	.297pN	.297prN	29.7	22.3	24.2
Three	.189pN	.189prN	18.9	20.1	23.0
Four or more	.196pN	.196prN	19.6	39.5	39.9
	pN	prN=n	100%	100%	100%

Assuming an unbiased sampling procedure, the expected per cent distribution of abusing families by family size in the sample (column 4) is identical to the actual per cent distribution of all abusing families by family size (column 2). Under the random model, the probability of abuse is assumed to be a constant, p, equal for all *families*. If only one child in each sample family were abused, the observed proportions of abusing *families* by size (column 5) would be identical to the proportions of abused *children* by size of family. Thus, under the random model, the ratio of the proportion of abused children by family size in the sample (column 5) to the proportions of all children (column 6) should decline as family size increases.

Under the stress model, the probability of abuse is assumed to be a constant, p, equal for all *children* rather than for all families. If the stress model were correct, then if only one child in each sample family were abused, we would expect that the ratio of observed abusing families by family size (column 5) to per cent of *all* children by family size (column 6) should be the same for all family sizes. On the other hand, the ratio of observed abusing families by family size (column 5) to all families by family size (column 2) should increase with increasing family size.

In the first case, abuse of the child depends wholly upon parent behavior and has no immediate connection to the parent-child relationship. Adults abuse randomly; when the urge strikes, an adult abuses the nearest child, and the random shock instance is over. The nature of the urge and its cause do not have to be specified. The main feature of this first case is that whatever the cause of abuse, it operates entirely through the adult. Call this the "random" model.

In the second case, suppose abuse is occasioned by some feature of parent-child encounters. Then the probability of occurrence increases with the frequency of

FIGURE 9b

Choosing Between the Random and Stress Models of Abuse

Based on the analysis of Figure 9a, we construct a summary table to guide a choice between the random and stress models. The "columns" all refer to Figure 9a.

Ratio of column (5) to:

	column (2)	column (6)
Random abuse model	constant for all family sizes.	decreasing in proportion to the number of children per family.
Stress abuse model	increasing in proportion to the number of children per family.	constant for all family sizes.

We now use this summary table to discriminate between the two competing models.

For one child families,

$$\frac{\text{column (5)}}{\text{column (6)}} = \frac{.180}{.129} = 1.39$$

For families with four or more children,

$$\frac{\text{column (5)}}{\text{column (6)}} = \frac{.395}{.399} = 0.99$$

The results of this test show that neither model is clearly in accord with the empirical analysis, although the stress model appears to offer a substantially better fit than the random model. Under the random model, the ratio for one child families would exceed the ratio for families with four or more children by a factor of five (if we assume that families with four or more children have on average five children). Under the stress model, the ratios would be identical. The observed "ratio of ratios" is 1.39/0.99 = 1.40, which falls between 5.0 (random abuse) and 1.0 (stress abuse), although closer to 1.0.

such encounters. If an adult and child are together for a longer period of time, or if an adult is together with more than one child, abuse is more likely. Again, the actual cause of abuse is unknown. This case simply specifies the locus in which the cause operates. Call this the "stress" model.

Even though these two alternatives are simple, extreme, and incomplete in and of themselves, they are worth considering because they predict different patterns of abuse. In the random model, child abuse would occur just as often in single child families as in multi-child families. The adult always abuses the only child in a one-child family and abuses one random child in a multi-child family. In this extreme case the size of family bears no relationship to the frequency of abuse per family. But it does relate to frequency of abuse per child. A child in a five-child family would be only one fifth as likely to be abused as would an only child.

In the stress model, the probability of abuse is proportional to parent-child exposure. An adult exposed to five children is five times as likely to abuse one of them as an adult exposed to only one child. Thus, an instance of child abuse is five times as likely in a five-child family as in a one-child family. From the standpoint of an individual child, however, this second case implies that all children are equally likely to be abused, regardless of their family size.

Figure 9a gives a discussion of how each model would appear as reflected in data on abuse. Figure 9b formalizes this and then carries out a test that focuses on choosing between the two competing models. The conclusion from Figure 9b is that neither theory is substantiated by empirical analysis. This leads to two inferences: a) a causal model that postulates abuse to operate without regard to parent-child encounters conflicts with the data; but b) a model that postulates the cause of abuse to be wholly within the parent-child encounter is also in conflict with the data. These findings are no surprise to people who have worked with abusing families. Yet this example illustrates how data on abusers can in principle provide a means for emipirically testing intuitive findings.[45]

Certain alternative models of abuse such as the two simple examples below might be more consistent with empirical data.

1. A model which postulates that exposure to children increases the chance of abuse, but that the number of children an adult is exposed to at one time is not important. Thus, as family size grows, the amount of time a parent is exposed to at least one child grows, but not proportionately to the number of children. This alternative is a modification of the stress model.

2. A model which postulates that the adult urge to abuse occurs at random for any family size, but that the probability of the urge's developing increases with family size. For example, the urge might be related to economic or financial pressure, which in turn depends upon number of children. This is a modification of the "random" model.

We cannot resolve the conflict between these two alternatives here. It is the strategy that is important. Using data on family size, in two extreme cases, the class of explanatory models has been narrowed to a range in between them. As this process is continued in future work, this kind of conceptual development, narrowing down the range of admissible models that explain abuse and are reasonably consistent with empirical data, will gradually bring better understanding of the phenomenon of abuse and ultimately improved policies for dealing with it.

[45] Note that we have carried out the analysis without actually knowing the correct values for p, n, N, or r. The suggested test, requiring the computation of a ratio of ratios, is independent of these four parameters.

Summary

What broad conclusions emerge from the various studies presented in this report? Perhaps the most general finding is that few easy answers exist for reducing the maltreatment of children. Ideas that at first seemed attractive appear to need substantial modifications before they hold out genuine promise of resulting in good public policy.

For one, a program of national health exams might well yield too many false reports of abuse unless a several stage checking system is used. But the more layers imbedded in such a national program, the higher its cost. Using local firemen or any other group without serious in-depth training at the diagnostic stage of such a policy would be dangerous. While using existing personnel for diagnosis would be cheaper than many alternatives, cost savings might not compensate for the loss of diagnostic power, a critical factor in determining the number of false reports of abuse.

Second, education in child development, an excellent idea in its own right, has not been shown to decisively affect the specific problems of abuse or neglect. Rather, family size data suggest that widespread family planning education might be more effective in preventing child maltreatment.

Third, the effort to develop a social profile of abusing families, to see how they differ from non-abusing families, simply has not yet produced many combinations of variables that discriminate adequately between the two groups. This area holds promise, however, if the quality of future data on abusing families continues to improve. Here is where careful attention to survey design is particularly important.

Fourth, solutions based on marginal total comparisons ("since rich people abuse less than poor people, reducing poverty will reduce abuse") ignore entirely the reporting bias in the available abuse data. Clearly, eliminating absolute poverty for all families is a desirable social goal. But available data tell us essentially nothing about how or why child abuse should then be expected to decline. This, then, is the important point: policy inferences cannot be based on biased marginal totals, especially when the inference rests entirely on such totals. To illustrate, suppose that every poor family in America were to receive an income supplement of $10,000 per year. Suppose further that the frequency of abuse remained unchanged in any income group. Assume finally that the formerly poor families used their income supplement in part to buy better health care by patronizing a private pediatrician rather than a public clinic. What might happen? If no changes in current reporting patterns come about, a sharp decline in the reported number of cases of child abuse should occur. Yet in fact no such real decline will have occurred. From the point of view of report data, the income supplement will simply have purchased the private pediatrician's lower reporting rates. Once again, a study of marginal totals subject to reporting bias will have led to an incorrect inference.

What directions are promising for future work? Although the studies for this report focused largely on data analysis, acceptance of the general results does not imply a need for more analysis of similar data. Rather, studies should focus on the far more difficult job of conceptual thinking. What programs might work and how can we test them? What kinds of new data are necessary to provide better information about such subcategories of abuse or neglect as malnourishment? How can the quality of the data on abusing families be improved so that future analyses will be more powerful?

The passage of the Child Abuse Prevention and Treatment Act by the United States Senate is a very promising current development. The purpose of this bill is "to provide financial assistance for demonstration programs for the prevention, identification, and treatment of child abuse and neglect, and to establish a National Center on Child Abuse and Neglect. . . ."[46] This Center, and related efforts focussing on the maltreatment of children, should consider both organizational and experimental questions. We conclude by suggesting the following specific lines of investigation.

Organizational efforts

1. Better estimates of incidence are needed. Although this problem is widely recognized, it is difficult to resolve, since many physicians fail to report maltreatment cases seen in private practice. Current estimates could be somewhat improved if careful records of repeat cases were kept on a national basis. Data on repeaters would open up several methods that permit estimating the size of a population.[47]

2. Definitions of different kinds of abuse must be formalized. In addition, information should be developed as to the reliability among different observers in detecting and classifying different kinds of abuse. If reliability is low, doubt is cast on the value of social policies that prescribe different ameliorative treatments for different kinds of abuse cases.

[46] *The Child Abuse Prevention and Treatment Act.* Report to accompany S. 1191. Calendar No. 290, Report No. 93-308. July 10 1973—Ordered to be printed.
[47] When several different institutions keep records over time, it is possible by making certain assumptions to estimate the size of a population. For a discussion of how to develop such estimates,

3. Researchers should deepen their study of the circumstances of life in abusing families. Few good causal theories of abuse exist, and more detailed data would greatly enrich exploratory analysis. For example, it is generally accepted that a high proportion of abusing parents were themselves abused as children. But it is known simultaneously that a large proportion of abused children do not grow up to become abusing parents. Understanding why some such children become abusers while others do not would provide enormous insight into the etiology of abuse.

4. In future analyses of data, efforts should be made to discover the commonalities of cases originally classified as suspected abuse, and later understood to be non-abuse. Because a potential danger of large-scale screening is false accusation of parents, such profiles of initial false positive diagnoses would serve to reduce future diagnostic error rates.

5. A comparative study of different reporting systems should be undertaken. Reporting of abuse cases is legally required in every state, yet reporting mechanisms vary widely. Three issues arise here. First, how effective are different reporting systems in discovering real abuse? Second, how effective are different systems in assigning the various treatments to different kinds of abusers? Third, which systems allow the most effective follow-up, thereby ensuring that a child or family receives the recommended treatment?

Field Study Efforts

1. A pilot study should be devised to probe the value of voluntary preventive detection. It would involve examining the different strategies used in hospitals. clinics, or offices of private obstetricians and pediatricians to explore a family's possible need for assistance during prenatal and neonatal periods. These services should be on a voluntary basis. An extensive literature suggests that a large proportion of families likely to maltreat children will accept such help.

2. Plans for crisis centers should be developed where families can leave children under safe care temporarily and voluntarily. Various formats and structures for such centers should be evaluated to find those that best serve families' needs.

3. A controlled field study should compare the effectiveness of different strategies for dealing with parents already identified as abusive or neglectful. It is likely that interactions will be found, that different kinds of ameliorative strategies will

---

together with the assumptions that they require, see Bishop, Fienberg, Holland, Mosteller, and Light, chapter on "Estimating the Size of Closed Populations."

be seen to be best matched with specific kinds of child maltreatment. A controlled field study will be more difficult to implement than a series of disconnected innovations.[48] But a well designed study offers the most hope for learning what services will be most beneficial for families who maltreat children, and since the services being compared are vital, they should inspire rigorous attention to study design.

[48] See Light, Mosteller, and Winokur, Jr.; also, Alice Rivlin, *Systematic Thinking for Social Action* (Washington, D.C.: Brookings Institution, 1971).

Amphetamines in the Treatment of Hyperkinetic Children

LESTER GRINSPOON and SUSAN B. SINGER

Harvard University and
Massachusetts Mental Health Centre

The authors review research on the effects of amphetamines on children, particularly hyperactive children in the classroom. They point out that there is no clear evidence these drugs should be prescribed as often as they are. The "hyperkinetic syndrome" remains vague both in its diagnosis and its etiology, and the mechanism of amphetamine action is unclear. The assumption that amphetamines have a paradoxical, calming effect on hyperactive children, unlike the stimulating effect they exert on adults, may accurately describe the apparent effects of the drugs on attention and other aspects of socially accepted classroom behavior, but it does not justify the interpretation that amphetamine effects are qualitatively different for children than for adults, without the same potential for harm. The authors conclude that the possible adverse effects of these drugs and their unknown long-term risks require that we reconsider the present policy of amphetamine administration in the schools.

This article is a literature review, but a literature review with definite policy implications. It concerns the widespread use of amphetamines in the nation's schools to control a syndrome which doctors and medical researchers call "hyperkinetic behavior disorder," or "minimal brain dysfunction," and which teachers and parents know as "hyperactivity." We have come to believe that enthusiasm in the administration of amphetamines has outstripped serious discussion about the

Harvard Educational Review   Vol. 43   No. 4   November 1973, 515–555

efficacy of these drugs for treating children's behavioral disorders, and we fear that serious attempts to precisely define and diagnose the hyperkinetic impulse disorder have been supplanted by acceptance of drug therapy for large numbers of American school children who may not benefit from it. Amphetamines have become established as the preferred treatment in many school situations even though doctors themselves remain unsure of the nature, etiology, and cure of hyperkinesis.

The attention of the public was brought to bear on the issue when on June 29, 1970, a sensational article appeared in the *Washington Post* claiming that from five to ten percent of the 62,000 grammar school children in Omaha, Nebraska were being treated with "behavior modification drugs to improve classroom deportment and increase learning potential" (Omaha pupils given "behavior" drugs, 1970). Although reported numbers were subsequently found to be greatly exaggerated—the five to ten percent figure represented the estimated prevalence of learning disabilities among school children in Omaha (*Federal involvement*, p. 53—Treatment for fidgety kids?, 1970) rather than the prevalence of amphetamine use—nevertheless the article did excite public interest and concern about the increasingly widespread and largely unexamined practice of prescribing behavior control drugs. A number of hyperactive, easily distractible children in the Omaha school system were being treated with drugs, purportedly to help them learn better by slowing them down and allowing them to concentrate on their work. A rash of publicity following the appearance of the *Post* article disclosed that this practice was not limited to Nebraska, but was also taking place in a number of other states throughout the nation.

A Congressional Hearing was convened on September 29, 1970, to investigate the extent of government involvement in this practice and the testimonies of various respected government officials disclosed some disquieting facts. According to the testimony of Dr. Ronald Lipman of the FDA, some 150,000 to 200,000 children were then being treated with stimulant drugs and the trend was expected to increase in the future (*Federal involvement*, p. 16). An article in the *Christian Science Monitor* of October 31, 1970, reported an NIMH estimate that "there are up to four million 'hyperactive' children in the United States who could benefit from these drugs ..." (Hunsinger, 1970, p. 1). Interest in the use of drugs for hyperactive children was gaining momentum despite the lack of follow-up studies on the long-term effects of the drugs. Until that time only one systematic follow-up study had been undertaken, directed by Dr. Keith Conners, involving 67 children out of 100 who at one time had been treated by Drs. C. Bradley, E. Denhoff, and M.

W. Laufer. Preliminary results were reassuring; most of the children in the study who had been diagnosed as hyperkinetic and had received amphetamines showed a low incidence of psychiatric disorders in adolescence (*Federal involvement,* p. 10; Laufer, 1971, pp. 521-522). But Congressman Cornelius E. Gallagher, who chaired the Hearing, was justifiably appalled that after 35 years of experience with drugs in the treatment of hyperkinesis, only one study involving 67 cases could be adduced to demonstrate the absence of harmful effects. Clearly this was too small a sample on which to base such a widespread practice.

Since 1970 the drug industry has continued to promote the use of amphetamines for disturbed children and is largely responsible for extending the practice. Nat Hentoff (1972) reported on some remarkable items from a 1971 CIBA territorial sales report, in which a sales executive was urging his salesmen to become "more effective pushers": "Your ingenuity," the report says, "in the promotion of RITALIN FBP (Functional Behavior Problems) is becoming more apparent."

Item: Mr. X, CIBA representative in Paducah, Kentucky, reports having a community of approximately 10,000 that has established a screening program of pre-school children to identify as early as possible those children who would most likely have learning disabilities. This is the only city known where an entire school system will be engaged in such an endeavor. . . .

Mr. Y of South Bend, Indiana, reports that at an inservice meeting of special education personnel . . . a physician brought two hyperactive children to use in a demonstration of the basic symptoms of Functional Behavior Problems. That's getting involvement, folks.

From the same territorial sales report, Hentoff quotes a CIBA man from Kansas City reminding his colleagues

. . . [there are] a few people whom we frequently overlook when making presentations and contacts on functional behavior problems in children. Two in particular are the juvenile court officers and probation officers. The juvenile court system comes in contact with children of all ages but their primary value in this situation would be to discuss Functional Behavior Problems with teachers and school officials with whom they are in contact. [Our man in Kansas City] points out that juvenile bureaus connected with local police are prime targets; even though they are in contact with older children they can spread the word. (Hentoff, p. 21)

Educators have become impressed with the possibilities offered by amphetamines and in many cases have been strong proponents of stimulant treatment for their problem students. In New York, the mother of a child labeled hyperactive by his elementary school teacher received an ultimatum from the teacher—"put the child on drugs or we will not be able to keep him in school" (Hentoff, p. 20). The *Christian Science Monitor* reported a southern California mother as saying, "We've been harassed and pressured by the school for four years now to put our nine-year-old on medication—for hyperactivity—and we've refused for four years. Two family doctors have backed up our decision" (Hunsinger, 1970, p. 6). A Colorado mother told of how she had reluctantly "caved in to the combined requests of the school nurse, the school psychologist, principal, and teachers" that she put her six-year-old son on medication to treat his "learning disability." Another California mother complained that the school would not accept a "no" from a family physician. "Most every parent who has an overactive child in the school is told to go see the same pediatrician," she reported, "because that doctor knows what the school wants." Even in cases where parents have not resisted and perhaps have even supported teachers' pressures to place their children on stimulants, a question still arises about whether educators should have any authority in making such recommendations. In Baltimore, the use of amphetamines to treat unmanageable children in the city school system had reached such alarming proportions by 1970 that Dr. H. M. Selznick, then school system superintendent of special education, was forced to acknowledge that guidelines and controls about who should be responsible for the administration of the drugs were sorely lacking. And his apology continued, "We do not want teachers administering the drugs since they are not medically trained. But, it is our suspicion that some teachers who have had 'wall climbers' do assume this responsibility" (Miller, 1970).

Eric Denhoff, a long-time researcher in the use of amphetamines for children, recognized this abuse as recently as 1971 in an editorial published in a special issue of the *Journal of Learning Disabilities*. He wrote, "In the 1950's, educators learned about [the] . . . psychopharmacological aspect of behavior modification, and began to encourage parents to seek such help from the child's physician. Soon it became evident that these drugs were being used indiscriminately—prescription would depend mostly upon a description of behavior by a teacher or parent" (p. 469).

With the politically inspired, emotionally charged publicity surrounding and following the Gallagher Hearings, the public was alerted to the extensive abuse without being given any solid scientific facts to temper their reaction. Yet the transcript of the Hearings demonstrates that such reassuring facts were generally not available even from those respected government officials whose job it is to regulate the use of drugs. Instead it became clear that amphetamines have been abused in the name of therapy for children. While psychiatrists' estimates of the prevalence of hyperkinesis among elementary school children range from 4 to 10 percent at a maximum (Eisenberg, 1972; Stewart *et al.,* 1966; Stewart, 1970; Prechtl & Stemmer, 1962; Huessey, 1967), educators estimate the incidence to be as high as 15 to 20 percent (Yanow, 1970, p. 2).

By 1973, not much has changed. The issues remain emotionally charged and information is still lacking about the hyperkinetic syndrome as it is diagnosed technically by medical doctors and as it is identified in the schools. The need for clear policy recommendations persists. How should parents, teachers, doctors, and concerned policy-makers respond? What steps can citizens take beyond mere acceptance or indignation? What might be an enlightened policy regarding treatment of hyperkinesis? In this article we will try to lay some of the groundwork for informed public decisions about amphetamine use in the schools, by describing for a lay readership what the medical community knows about the effects of stimulants in the treatment of hyperkinesis. A serious reevaluation of current practices is needed before the country proceeds in dispensing psychoactive drugs to its children.

Early Research on the Use of Amphetamines in Children

The therapeutic use of amphetamines in the treatment of hyperkinetic children dates back to 1937, when Charles Bradley (1937) observed that Benzedrine produced "spectacular" effects on a number of children suffering from behavioral disorders resulting in disturbed school behavior. The disorders ranged from specific learning disabilities, to aggressiveness associated with epilepsy, to withdrawn schizoid behavior. Thirty children were observed within a residential treatment setting. With drug therapy, 14 showed a marked improvement in school performance, indicated by an increase in drive, interest, accuracy, and speed of comprehension (Bradley, 1937, p. 578). On another dimension of change, 15 of the 30 became ". . . distinctly subdued in their emotional responses. . . ." manifesting an increased sense of well-being approaching mild euphoria, diminished mood swings, a more easy-going attitude, and an increased awareness of and interest in their surroundings. Seven children were common to both groups. The remaining children in the sample showed lesser responses of varying degrees. Only one child of the 30 became more hyperactive, although three seemed to cry more readily as if their emotions were more easily aroused. All effects of amphetamine disappeared on the first day that the medication was discontinued.

"It appears paradoxical," Bradley commented, "that a drug known to be a stimulant should produce subdued behavior in half of the children. It should be borne in mind, however, that portions of the higher levels of the central nervous system have inhibition as their function, and that stimulation of these portions might indeed produce the clinical picture of reduced activity through increased voluntary control" (Bradley, 1937, p. 582). It should be borne in mind, too, that the subdued behavior appeared paradoxical because judging from observed effects of amphetamines on adults one would expect amphetamines to energize and hence raise the activity level of a subject. The subdued behavior might very well be an "artifact of observation," however, as C. K. Conners (1966) later pointed out, reflecting not gross body movement and activity level but rather the way activity is organized in relation to the social demands of a situation. The amphetamine-treated subjects might have been expending the same amount of energy as before they were given the medication—and perhaps even more—but if they were channeling it into more socially acceptable activities their behavior would *appear* subdued. Bradley (1950), after twelve years of observing the effects of racemic amphetamine and dextroamphetamine on a total of 388 children, suggested that the effects of amphetamines on these children might not be as paradoxical as they appear. Yet despite this disclaimer research proceeded largely on the assumption that amphetamines did indeed produce a paradoxical calming effect on children, and subsequent developments in the use of amphetamines for children have been very much influenced by this assumption.

In the same year that Bradley reported his original results of treating disturbed children with Benzedrine, M. Molitch and J. P. Sullivan (1937) reported some independent findings which suggested that Benzedrine had a positive effect on test scores. Using 96 boys between the ages of ten and seventeen who were considered behavior problems and had previously been judged delinquents by the juvenile courts, Molitch and Sullivan devised a double-blind experiment to determine the relative efficacy of placebo and Benzedrine on the New Stanford Achievement Test scores of these boys. Basal test scores were determined for each boy, after which the subjects were given either placebo (46 subjects) or 10 mg Benzedrine (50 subjects). They then were retested. The average differences between initial scores and treatment scores definitely favored the amphetamine group but since no statistical analyses were done the precise significance of the results is not clear. The authors themselves recognized the preliminary nature of their findings and suggested the need for more research.

Despite his report of the paradoxical calming effect of amphetamine, Bradley

too found evidence of a stimulating effect on achievement and school performance in almost 50 percent of the children. Among those children who showed a
marked improvement in school performance, the improvement was observed in
all areas of achievement (Bradley, 1937, p. 578), although particularly in arithmetic. Molitch and Sullivan (p. 521) made similar observations.

Thus even in the very first experimentation with amphetamines on disturbed
children, two avenues of research were already suggested: the calming effect on
observed behavior and activity, and the stimulating effect on performance.

By 1950, when Bradley published his summary of studies on 388 disturbed children treated with Dexedrine and Benzedrine representing over a decade of observation and thought, a number of other studies had already supported or amplified
his original findings. These studies were done within a variety of diagnostic categories, and not yet specifically with hyperkinetic behavior disorders. M. Cutler *et
al.* (1940) employed a double-blind experimental technique to determine the
effects of small daily doses of racemic amphetamine (Benzedrine) on mentally
retarded children. They found that neither behavior nor academic performance
was affected by daily doses of 5 to 7½ mg over a period of six months. However,
when a subsample was given 10 mg Benzedrine "as sudden stimulation" (Cutler *et
al.*, p. 64), their performance on tests involving psychomotor functioning was favorably affected and there was a tendency toward improvement on the New Standard
Achievement Test. This suggested a dose-related effect, but findings were inconclusive and awaited further investigation.

In the same year, Bradley and his associate M. Bowen (1941) conducted another
study on the effects of Benzedrine on 100 children who were being treated for a
variety of behavior disorders. Clinical diagnoses included behavior disorders of
psychogenic origin, which were the most numerous, but there were also cases of
convulsive disorders, schizoid personality, structural neurological defect, deficiency
in intellectual functioning, specific reading disability, and post-encephalic behavior
disorders. Although their observations were mostly in accord with Bradley's earlier
findings, they noted this time that a significant minority (19 of the 100 children)
responded not by becoming subdued but by becoming more stimulated in their
affect and energy level, exhibiting increased alertness, initiative, interest in their
surroundings, and aggressiveness in competitive activities. In almost 65 percent of
these stimulated children, the response was considered an improvement from a
clinical standpoint inasmuch as they had originally been shy, withdrawn, and
underactive.

Further insight into the effects of stimulant drugs on disturbed children was

247

provided when L. Bender and F. Cottington (1942) published the results of a study of 28 boys and 12 girls ranging in age from five to thirteen years, treated with Benzedrine in the Psychiatric Division of Bellevue Hospital. Diagnoses included neurotic behavior disorders, psychoneuroses, psychopathic personality, schizophrenia, and organic brain disease. The first two categories were the most numerous, comprising 75 percent of the sample. Both seemed favorably affected by Benzedrine treatment with a maximum of 20 mg daily. In general, the least neurotic children responded with an increased sense of well-being which enabled them to make a less fearful, more positive social adaptation to the therapeutic environment. Later they were able to come to terms with their feelings and express them more freely in both the individual and group therapeutic situations. Many of the more severely neurotic children manifested a decrease in hyperactivity and an increase in attention span, associated with greater integration and constructive activity. These children's therapeutic relationships suffered, however, since they became more evasive and resistant in dealing with their deeper conflicts. It was as if their new sense of well-being mitigated any felt need to deal with underlying emotional problems. Those children with organic brain disease and schizophrenia showed no response whatever to the drug. Very unfavorable effects were observed in the children with psychopathic personalities, who were receiving only 10 mg Benzedrine. They became more tense, depressed, disorganized, and withdrawn, and their medication had to be discontinued.

The authors attempted to explain these individual differences in response to the drug as reflections of the differing personality dynamics of individual children. Whereas the disturbed behavior of the neurotic children may simply have been a manifestation of conflict within basically integrated personality structures, the disturbed behavior of the psychopathic children may actually have been part of an ego structure developed to mask a basic inner lack of emotional integration. In the case of the neurotics, then, the drugs may have facilitated a pre-existing integration, while in the case of the psychopathic personalities, the same drugs may have facilitated a pre-existing lack of integration.

Further investigation of the effect of amphetamine on children's behavior was conducted by B. Pasamanick (1951), specifically to determine the effect of the drug on children with EEG abnormalities. Of the ten children studied, four were found to respond quite favorably to the administration of 20 to 25 mg daily of Benzedrine, whereas anticonvulsant drugs had never produced any improvement in their behavior. Of the remaining six children, however, three showed no change and three actually became worse. These results suggested that EEG abnormality is not an essential predictor of response to amphetamine.

Defining the Hyperkinetic Impulse Disorder

While early investigations on the effects of amphetamine in the treatment of children's behavior disorders were being conducted, other events were leading to the development of the notion of the "hyperkinetic impulse disorder" (Laufer, Denhoff & Solomons, 1957, p. 38). In 1934 E. Kahn and L. H. Cohen published an article noting that a deviant behavioral syndrome which often occurred as a sequel to encephalitis could also be observed in people with no known brain damage. This syndrome was marked by hyperkinesis, an inability to maintain attention and quiet attitudes, a lack of coordination, and an impulsivity. In all subjects observed, these symptoms were associated with neurological signs of central nervous system (CNS) dysfunction. On the basis of this association, and because the behavior itself appeared driven and involuntary, the authors labeled the syndrome "organic drivenness," concluding that it was organically determined by a dysfunction of the brain stem.

Subsequently it was noticed that children who had been brain-injured from causes such as anoxia or head injury during the perinatal period showed a similar syndrome. A Strauss and L. Lehtinen (1947) reported that brain-injured children exhibited hyperactivity as an important part of their distinctive behavior. The long-standing association of hyperkinesis with brain dysfunction ultimately led M. W. Laufer and his colleagues to delineate a new diagnostic category:

It has long been recognized and accepted that a persistent disturbance of behavior of a characteristic kind may be noted after severe head injury, epidemic encephalitis, and communicable disease encephalopathics, such as measles, in children. It has often been observed that a behavior pattern of a similar nature may be found in children who present no clear-cut history of any of the classical causes mentioned.

This pattern will henceforth be referred to as *hyperkinetic impulse disorder*. In brief summary, hyperactivity is the most striking item. . . . There are also a short attention span and poor powers of concentration, which are particularly noticeable under school conditions. Variability is also frequent. . . . The child is impulsive . . . irritable and explosive, . . . [and manifests] low frustration tolerance.

Poor school work is frequently quite prominent. The previously described behavioral items in themselves create a pattern which makes it very difficult for the child to participate in the work of a school room. In addition there is often visual-motor difficulty which, combined with the other difficulties described above, makes for poor work in arithmetic and reading. In writing and reading, 'reversals' are frequent and the handwriting is often crabbed and irregular. (Laufer, Denhoff, & Solomons, 1957, p. 38)

Laufer performed an experiment which led him to postulate an organic determinant for the new diagnostic syndrome. Even without conclusive evidence, this organic determinant became part of its definition. In his experiment he established two groups of subjects from among the patients at a home for emotionally disturbed children, the same one Bradley had used for his studies. The two groups were chosen solely on the basis of presence or absence of the clinically defined hyperkinetic impulse disorder. A history of factors considered capable of producing brain damage was not included in the criteria for selection. In fact, of those subjects identified as hyperkinetic, only 34 percent had such histories. Metrazol, a drug used to test the presence of brain dysfunction, was administered to each subject. For each child the amount necessary to evoke an EEG spikewave burst and a myoclonic jerk of the forearms in response to a stroboscope was determined. Analysis of the mean photo-Metrazol threshold for the two groups of children revealed that the threshold for the hyperkinetic children was significantly lower than the threshold for the non-hyperkinetic children. This was true regardless of whether the histories of the hyperkinetic children showed clear evidence of brain damage. Previously H. Gastaut (1950), who developed the photo-Metrazol test for adults, had presented evidence for the theory that a photo-Metrazol threshold below a certain norm indicates damage to or dysfunction of the diencephalon. Thus, Laufer concluded that the hyperkinetic impulse disorder has an organic determinant, specifically a dysfunction of the diencephalon. Further support for the postulated organic basis of this clinical syndrome was derived from administering amphetamine to the hyperkinetic children and redetermining photo-Metrazol thresholds. Analysis showed the amphetamines increased the threshold of these children to a level characteristic of the non-hyperkinetic group (Laufer, Denhoff, & Solomons, p. 43).

Unfortunately, in Laufer's experiment the effect of amphetamines on the photo-Metrazol thresholds of the *non*-hyperkinetic children was not determined. Nor was any effort made to correlate changes in photo-Metrazol thresholds with changes in behavior, even for the hyperkinetic children. Thus the findings must remain inconclusive, although they are impressive in that they suggest a possible relationship between brain dysfunction and this behavioral syndrome. They also offer a possible way of predicting response to amphetamine. It is perplexing that no one has attempted to replicate the results, since this avenue of research might provide a means for distinguishing amphetamine-responsive syndromes from those which are not responsive to the drugs.

Some Conflicting Findings

In the 1960's a number of disciplines converged on the issue of hyperkinesis. From educational psychologists came the realization that many disturbed children were not amenable to psychotherapy. From educators came a new interest in learning disabilities and their relationship to behavioral disturbances. From medical science came a new diagnostic category—the hyperkinetic syndrome—which seemed to fit many of these problem children, and evidence for its responsiveness to amphetamine treatment. This resulted in great interest in the controlled and systematic study of the effects of stimulants on the hyperkinetic syndrome. But findings have been preliminary and inconclusive despite the number of systematic investigations that have been carried out since the 1960's. In general these studies have raised more questions than they have answered. First, although experimental drug administration has been well controlled, many variables have been uncontrolled. Second, the subject populations in many of the studies have been heterogeneous in their clinical diagnoses, reasons for referral for treatment, and types of learning difficulties. In fact many of the studies do not deal specifically with hyperkinetic children, and even among those studies that do there is no general agreement on essential criteria for selection. Third, the studies are not comparable on rating instruments and measurements used. Thus, although statistically significant findings abound it is difficult to assess their meaning.

Significant improvement in symptoms as rated by parents, teachers, and caretakers is the most consistently reported result. G. Weiss *et al.* (1968) reported significant symptomatic improvement as a major outcome in an uncrossed double-blind study of 38 public school children (32 boys, 6 girls) between the ages of six and twelve. The pupils were selected on the basis of chronic, severe, and sustained hyperactivity or motor restlessness at home and at school. All had an IQ of 80 or above and were free of overt physical or neurological disease. None were psychotic or epileptic. For a small "though not inconsequential number" (p.. 148) of these children (not precisely reported), hyperactivity was associated with psychopathology other than the hyperkinetic syndrome. Dextroamphetamine and placebo were randomly assigned the children in a two to one ratio, 26 receiving the active drug and 12 the placebo. The results indicated that dextroamphetamine administered for three to five weeks up to a maximum dosage of 20 mg daily, depending upon individual tolerance for the drug, was significantly more effective than placebo in producing an "overall" improvement in the children as perceived by their mothers. The rating instrument was designed to assess four behavioral dimensions: hyperactivity, excitability, distractability, and aggressiveness. In contrast to mothers ratings alone, when ratings of mothers, psychiatrists, psychologists, and teachers were pooled, only hyperactivity and distractability showed significantly greater reduction in the drug group over the placebo group. The possibility of rater bias on the basis of expectancy cannot be ruled out, particularly since 35 percent of the dextroamphetamine treated children experienced loss of appetite at the beginning of treatment, which might have signalled to the raters the presence of drugs. Moreover, as the authors themselves point out, the reliability of these findings are uncertain, especially because of the difficulty of assessing such distractibility with a questionnaire. But the findings are in accord with Bradley's early clinical descriptions of children receiving dextroamphetamine, and with several more recent, methodologically sound studies.

Other recent experiments also yield results which suggest symptomatic improvement with drug treatment. In a double-blind study by L. Eisenberg, C. K. Conners, and L. Sharpe (1965) selection criteria were essentially the same as in the Weiss *et al.* (1968) study, with the added qualification that children with psychopathic personalities and children requiring immediate institutional care were specifically excluded. Eighty to ninety subjects were divided into two approximately equal groups (numbers were not specifically indicated). One received either dextroamphetamine, 5 mg BID, or methylphenidate (Ritalin), 15 mg BID. For purposes of analyzing the results these treatments were considered identical since no statistical differences were found between them in this study. The other group was given placebo. This treatment was administered for a period of eight weeks. Clinicians' judgment of improvement at the end of this period, based on school reports, mothers' reports, and psychiatrists' estimates of the children's behavior in the clinic, showed a statistically significant difference favoring the stimulant-treated groups over the placebo group. Teacher ratings significantly favored the stimulant-treated group in five categories of behavior—academic performance, classroom behavior, attitude to authority, attitude to peers, and overall behavior.

But the significance of such results lies more in their potential for misinterpretation than in any suggestion that amphetamines have a beneficial effect on the behavior of hyperkinetic children. Although experimental results superficially appear to be in accord with one another, many contradictions and confusions can

252

be found. L. C. Epstein *et al.* (1968) performed a study with ten subjects selected on the basis of hyperactivity, short attention span, poor concentration, and associated poor school performance. Of the ten, five presented evidence of injury to the central nervous system, while none of the other five presented clear evidence of organic damage. The subjects were used as their own controls and each received dextroamphetamine and placebo for two weeks in doses ranging from 10 to 20 mg daily. Subjective reports given independently by parents and psychiatrists suggested a marked improvement in the organic group in response to the drug, while the inorganic group was judged as virtually unchanged. Superficially, these findings seem to lend support to the speculations of Kahn and Cohen (1934), and Laufer, Denhoff, & Solomons (1957), that "real" hyperkinesis is not just a symptom complex but is organically based. Yet it should be remembered that in the study by Laufer and his colleagues organicity was defined not on the basis of a history of possible damage to the CNS but on the basis of a photo-Metrazol threshold below the norm. Many of his subjects exhibiting the symptom complex had a lower threshold despite the absence in their histories of clear evidence of brain damage. Thus it is not possible to compare the two studies.

The findings of Epstein *et al.* (1968) are perplexing, because amphetamines have often been reported to improve gross symptomatology in diagnostic categories apparently unrelated to brain damage. Bradley reported improvement in children with behavior disorders of psychogenic origin and with schizoid personalities as well as in children suffering from what might have been organically based behavioral difficulties (Bradley & Bowen, 1941, pp. 98-99; Bradley, 1950, pp. 30-31). Bender and Cottington (1942) reported symptom improvement in neurotic children. More recently, a number of investigators have found that amphetamines improve symptomatology of juvenile delinquents (Eisenberg *et al.*, 1963), "disturbed children" in a residential psychiatric setting and in a group foster care institution (diagnoses undelineated) (Conners & Eisenberg, 1963; see also Conners, Eisenberg, & Sharpe, 1964), and children with undifferentiated learning difficulties with associated behavior problems (Conners *et al.*, 1969; Conners, Eisenberg, & Barcai, 1967; Conners, 1969). In a well-controlled double-blind study of "most difficult" (Eisenberg *et al.*, p. 432) institutionalized delinquent boys, both house parents and school teachers noted a significant decrease of disturbing, anti-social, aggressive, and hyperactive behavior in the dextroamphetamine-treated group over placebo and control groups, particularly when the dosage reached 30 to 40 mg daily. When caretakers' ratings of disturbed children in a residential psychiatric treatment setting and in a group foster home were analyzed in combination (Conners & Eisenberg, 1963), a significant improvement in "outwardly-directed symptoms which would be disturbing to caretakers" (Conners & Eisenberg, p. 459) was noted in the group treated with 20 to 60 mg daily of methylphenidate over the placebo group, although large individual differences in responsiveness to the drug were reported (and left undiscussed). In a double-blind study of school children referred to an outpatient clinic with primary complaints of undifferentiated learning disability with or without associated behavior problems (Conners *et al.*, 1969, p. 183), parent symptom ratings showed a significantly greater reduction in "hyperkinetic symptoms" for the group treated with 10 to 25 mg dextroamphetamine than for the placebo group. "Hyperkinetic symptoms" included poor attention span, restlessness, impulsiveness, and temper outbursts (Conners *et al.*, 1969, p. 188). Findings also demand clarification and interpretation lest their appeal lead to abuse of these drugs under the guise of treating a specific disorder.

Amphetamine Effects on the Components of Behavior

What components of behavior are objectively altered by the drugs and account for the global impression of improvement so often reported? Because hyperactivity is one of the more noticeable dimensions of the deviant behavioral pattern showing a positive response to stimulants, one might expect to find objective demonstration of a decrease in activity level. However, interestingly enough, there are no consistent findings on this dimension, despite the "paradoxical" calming effect which the drugs are reported to produce.

R. L. Sprague, K. R. Barnes, and J. S. Werry (1970), in a study of 12 boys who were attending special classes for antisocial, distractible, hyperactive behavior, found that methylphenidate without regard to dosage level significantly reduced activity level as measured by a stabilimetric cushion. Placebo was found to have virtually no effect. Yet J. G. Millichap *et al.* (1968), in a well-controlled study of 30 hyperactive underachievers, found that methylphenidate tended to reduce motor activity, as measured by an actometer (an activity-watch worn on the wrist, which measures locomotion on a horizontal plane). In this study, placebo appeared to have a similar effect and diminished the significance of the findings. In another study by Millichap and E. E. Boldrey (1967), actometer-measured motor activity was actually *increased* when subjects were treated with methylphenidate for one day under controlled conditions, even though subjects were rated by parents and teachers as exhibiting improved motor coordination and reduced impulsivity. T. R. McConnell and R. L. Cromwell (1964) reported similar findings in a group of 57 retarded children diagnosed as "chronic brain syndrome" cases, a loose term implying some degree of unspecified organic etiology. The activity level of each child, as measured by a ballistograph and a rating scale, was determined for each of three treatment conditions: placebo, $7\frac{1}{2}$ mg dextroamphetamine, and 15 mg dextroamphetamine. No significant treatment differences were found on either of the two measures, although drug effects on activity level as measured by the rating scale were in the predicted direction. The subjects were retarded and perhaps essentially different in drug responsiveness from hyperkinetic children of average intelligence.

The contradictory evidence might be explained by the fact that it is likely that the various scales and objective instruments are measuring very different aspects of activity, and that hyperkinesis involves much more than gross body movement. In fact, as already pointed out, the "paradoxical" calming effect of stimulants on hyperkinetic children may be an artifact of observation, reflecting not activity level itself but the organization of activity relative to social demands (Conners, 1966, p. 432).

A noteworthy finding in this regard was reported in a well-controlled double-blind crossover study carried out by Conners and his associates (Conners, Eisenberg, & Barcai, 1967) involving a group of fifth and sixth grade learning and behaviorally disabled black children. These children were "not specifically selected because of psychiatric or neurologic impairment" (Conners, Eisenberg, & Barcai, p. 478). Over a one month period 10 mg of dextroamphetamine was administered daily to each subject. A factor analysis of objective personality and performance tests revealed that dextroamphetamine had no significant effect on a factor representing ability and performance, but did produce a highly significant improvement on a factor representing assertiveness, drive for achievement, and vigor of response. This factor has been reported to correlate with competence, efficiency, and determination (Conners, Eisenberg, & Barcai, p. 484; Hundleby, Pawlik, & Cattell, 1965, p. 139). Despite these mixed findings on objective tests, teachers' symptom ratings as well as their general global ratings indicated improvement for the drug-treated subjects in symptoms and performance in all three rated categories: classroom behavior, attitude toward authority, and attitude toward peers. The teachers had been instrumental in the original referral of these children to the study, and their positive expectations of improvement might well have biased their subjective ratings; nevertheless, the ratings did "sensitively reflect the presence of the active medication" (Conners, Eisenberg, & Barcai, p. 483) in accordance with the unannounced drug crossover. Perhaps what the teachers observed as an improvement in performance was actually a change in the children's attitude and approach to the classroom situation. Such an attitude change would be supported by the positive findings on the assertiveness factor.

As the authors note, the effect seems motivational. Through its CNS stimulating properties the drug may energize the children into making use of previously dormant abilities available to them (Conners, Eisenberg, & Barcai, p. 484). This would parallel Bradley's earlier clinical descriptions of increase in children's drive and interest in their surroundings. Conners concludes, "Despite the finding of rated improvement in three areas of classroom behavior, attitude toward authority, and group participation, it seems doubtful that the medication specifically affects these areas. Rather, it would seem more plausible to assume that teachers observe the calmer, [because] more determined behavior of the pupils, and tend to generalize the benefits to all three areas of rated performance" (Conners, Eisenberg, & Barcai, p. 484).

The perceived symptomatic improvement reported in many studies might simply reflect more organized goal-directed behavior and closer approximation of social norms. As Sprague et al. have suggested (Sprague, Barnes, & Werry, 1970, p. 626), it may be that activity level is only indirectly affected by these drugs, the specific effect depending upon the situation in which the subject is engaged. In a situation requiring great mental effort, for example, increased vigor of response might result in greater concentration and a concomitant decrease in motor activity. In a freer "play" situation, increased vigor of response might result in an actual increase in motor activity, "due to the child's engaging his social environment." But in such a case activity level would not continue to be seen in a negative light, since energy would be channeled into more organized, socially acceptable behaviors. In fact, "Cromwell et al. (1963) have suggested that the 'overactivity' of 'hyperactive' children may be a reflection of the short attention span and rapidly changing goal directions of such children. Thus, these investigators argue that hyperactive children may be thought of as children whose behaviour is fragmented or disorganized and continually changing direction such that an impression of high level activity is created" (Sykes et al., 1971, p. 129). A. A. Strauss and N. C. Kephart (1955) have gone so far as to say that short attention span, distractability, and hyperactivity all refer to the same thing.

Independent findings in other areas support this interpretation. It has been reported that attention, as measured by a variety of objective tests, is enhanced by the administration of amphetamines. D. H. Sykes et al. (1971) demonstrated this with the use of H. E. Rosvold's (Rosvold et al., 1956) Continuous Performance Task

(CPT).[1] Forty chronically hyperactive children (34 boys, 6 girls) between the ages of five and twelve who attended normal classes were subjects for a double-blind study. Specifically excluded were psychotic, epileptic, or grossly brain-damaged, or children whose behavior problems were clearly emotionally based. IQ's were all 80 or above. Methylphenidate was administered to half the subjects with dosage adjusted to individual tolerance. Most children received 30 to 40 mg daily for five to seven weeks. The investigators found that the drug-treated subjects did significantly better than the placebo subjects on this task, making not only more correct responses, but also fewer errors (responses to insignificant stimuli).

Stimulant-related increase in attention also is supported by results on other objective measures, notably the Porteus Maze Test. The Porteus Maze Test is a pencil and paper test in which the child is asked to trace an unbroken line through a maze. The mazes are similar to the puzzles children often find in comic books. The test is entirely nonverbal. The Porteus Maze has been employed in several investigations as an objective measure of planned, organized, and impulse-inhibited behavior (Conners & Eisenberg, 1963; Conners, Eisenberg, & Sharpe, 1964; Eisenberg, Conners, & Sharpe, 1965; Epstein *et al.*, 1968; Conners *et al.*, 1969; Greenberg, Deem, & McMahon, 1972). Stimulant-related improvement on the Porteus Maze in several studies has been cited as evidence that stimulants potentiate the inhibition of impulsive responses. Impulsivity is one of the most notable and disturbing symptoms of the hyperkinetic syndrome, and great import has been accorded this finding.

But "impulsivity" is a global term and can be interpreted in at least two different ways. On the one hand, it could be an inclination to respond in a seemingly disorganized fashion to one thing after another, and to exhibit the "rapidly changing goal directions" Sykes (*et al.*, 1971, p. 129) refers to as characteristic of the hyperactive child. In this sense impulsivity would be an attentional dysfunction related to distractibility. On the other hand, impulsivity could be an inclination to respond without thinking, such that even if active attention to a task were being maintained, actual responses in the performance of the task would be impetuous, hasty, or unreasoned. In this sense impulsivity would be a cognitive and/or motor dysfunction. The latter is probably the more common interpretation and seems to

---

[1] Many tests which purport to measure attention are constructed so as to allow a subject to make up for lapses in attention by working harder in between lapses. However, the CPT designed by Rosvold *et al.* (1956) requires the use of information given unpredictably and thus measures attention more accurately.

be intended when Porteus Maze improvement is cited as evidence of decreased impulsivity. But this interpretation is inaccurate. The Porteus Maze Test can be scored quantitatively as well as qualitatively. The quantitative score is primarily a measure of ability "to sustain attention in the face of the difficulty involved in resolving moderately complex spatial relations" (Docter, 1972, p. 756). As such, if it measures impulsivity at all, it does so in the attentional sense. The qualitative score reflects impulsivity in the cognitive and/or motor sense. The two also do not have the same construct validity. The correlation between them is −.40 (Docter, 1972, p. 753). It is the quantitative scores that are reported in the literature on hyperkinetic children. Any improvement reported can only be interpreted as increased ability to sustain attention under special conditions.

Quantitative improvement on the Porteus Maze Test was demonstrated in the study by Eisenberg, Conners, & Sharp (1965), already described. A highly significant improvement in Porteus Maze performance was reported for the stimulant-treated subjects, whereas only minimal improvement, perhaps resulting from practice effects, occurred for the placebo-treated children. In another study by Conners & Eisenberg (1963), also discussed in Conners, Eisenberg, & Sharpe (1964), disturbed children from two institutions, a residential psychiatric treatment center and a group foster home, were divided into a methylphenidate (20 to 60 mg daily) group and a placebo group. Mean age, initial symptom scores, and IQ were essentially the same for both treatment groups. An improvement score could not be obtained because the Maze tests were not administered before treatment began. Maze tests administered under treatment conditions showed a significant difference between those drug- and placebo-treated subjects in the two lowest IQ groups (65-79 and 80-91 IQ). It is of interest, however, that the high IQ (94-135) subjects showed virtually no differences between treatment groups. This suggests a possible relationship between drug effect and intelligence, although these findings must, as the authors note, be interpreted cautiously in this regard since the analysis of variance showed no significant IQ by treatment interaction (Conners, Eisenberg, & Sharpe, p. 19).

There are two possible explanations for the lack of significant differences between high IQ treatment groups. One is based on the observation that many of the subjects referred to the medication as "smart pills" (Conners, Eisenberg, & Sharpe, p. 16) and had high expectations of becoming smarter, happier, and calmer. These expectations might have provided the more intelligent and insightful placebo subjects with motivation enough to balance the benefit the stimulants provided for the drug subjects. Hence it might have resulted in the absence of significant differences. A second posssible explanation is that the Porteus Maze is not sensitive enough to make fine distinctions for people well above the average in general intelligence, since it was developed originally as a tool for classifying mentally retarded children (Docter, 1972, pp. 751-752, 756).

In another study (Conners *et al.*, 1969) children with primary complaints of learning failure (with or without associated behavior problems) were given dextroamphetamine and placebo. Both groups showed similar improvement on the Porteus Maze Test after two weeks of the study. Only after the last two weeks was the improvement of the two groups significantly different in favor of the group treated with dextroamphetamine. This could have been related to the increased dosage in the last two weeks from 15 mg dextroamphetamine daily to 20-25 mg daily, or it could have been due to a cumulative effect of treatment. It is difficult to evaluate which was the more important variable, since no systematic investigation has been done in this area, and positive effects of stimulants have been reported for differing dosages and over differing time periods.

It will be recalled that in a number of the earlier studies on the effects of amphetamines on learning and behavior disorders in general, some of the preliminary results suggested that cognitive and intellectual functioning was enhanced by administration of these drugs (Molitch & Sullivan, 1937; Cutler, Little, & Strauss, 1940; Bradley, 1937; Bradley & Bowen, 1941). However a number of more recent methodologically sound studies done in this area since that time have resulted in contradictory findings (Greenberg, Deem, & McMahon, 1972; Weiss *et al.*, 1968; Conners *et al.*, 1969; Sprague, Barnes, & Werry, 1970; Conners, Eisenberg, & Sharpe, 1964; Millichap *et al.*, 1968). Conners (1972) has shed some light on this issue. Questioning inconsistencies in a series of studies conducted by himself and his associates on children specifically diagnosed as suffering from minimal brain dysfunction (MBD, the most recently formulated term used to describe the hyperkinetic impulse disorder, discussed further below), he selected the studies which had employed common pre- and post-drug measuring instruments and developed a profile analysis in order to achieve diagnostic homogeneity. One hundred and seventy- eight previously treated subjects (78 on placebo and 100 on drugs) were accepted for this study. Through sound statistical manipulations, Conners found that these subjects could be distinguished in terms of seven different patterns of baseline performance on psychological tests. Specific response to stimulant drugs differed widely among the subjects and was dependent upon their initial profile of abilities as represented by the seven distinct patterns of baseline performance. The sample, though all diagnosed MBD, was heterogeneous in profiles of abilities and deficiencies, and the patterns of changes which could be ascribed to drug therapy differed accordingly.

These studies were preliminary and are not yet useful as diagnostic tools, but they did indicate that some of the apparent inconsistencies in the literature concerning effects of stimulants on intellectual and cognitive functioning in hyperactive children can be understood if initial profiles of abilities and deficiencies are taken into account. As Conners suggests, there is "No single syndrome of hyperkinesis [which] is uniquely responsive to [drug] therapy, . . . and several [discernible] patterns of change of perceptual and cognitive abilities may result from drug therapy" (Conners, 1972, p. 708). It is interesting to consider the mechanism which causes these differing patterns of change. Changes in higher cognitive and intellectual functions may not be a direct effect of the drugs but may be rather a result of "more limited [drug-induced] changes in specific aspects of the information-processing sequence" (Eisenberg & Conners, 1971, p. 414). As has been detailed earlier, and as Eisenberg and Conners have specifically pointed out, "there is good reason to suppose that stimulants alter the child's ability to attend to the task at hand; and given such alterations, almost any task will show enhanced performance . . . ," particularly in areas where the child has been deficient to begin with.

The Mechanism of Amphetamine Action

It has long been believed that the amphetamines must have an entirely different mechanism of action in children than they do in adults since the overall effect appears to be a calming one on hyperkinetic children and a stimulating one on adults. The work of Laufer and his associates (Laufer, Denhoff, & Solomons, 1957) still stands as the best documented pharmacological study of the action of amphetamines in hyperkinetic children. As noted earlier, their work suggested that hyperkinesis results from a diencephalic dysfunction. Normally the diencephalon, which is thought to be the rostral component of the reticular activating system, acts to sort, route, and pattern impulses coming from sensory receptors before they become amplified at higher levels of the brain. In this capacity it functions as an inhibitor of irrelevant stimuli, keeping them from "flooding" the cortex. If the diencephalon is not functioning properly, the cortex can become overwhelmed by more stimuli than it can adequately deal with. Two possibilities were suggested regarding the nature of the presumed diencephalic dysfunction. On the one hand, it could be due to a structural impairment of the brain stem or diencephalon such that the cortex is not properly shielded from stimuli which are irrelevant. On the other hand, it could be due to a maturational imbalance between the diencephalon and the cortex such that a relatively underdeveloped cortex cannot keep up with the demands of a normally functioning diencephalon. In either case, it was thought that amphetamines stimulated the inhibitory functioning of the diencephlon in such a way as not to overwhelm the cortex (Laufer, Denhoff & Solomons, 1957, pp. 45, 47).

Laufer's study did not conclusively demonstrate the specific action of amphetamines in hyperkinetic children. It was merely suggestive since its conclusions relied heavily on evidence from studies of animals and adult humans and not on studies of children. One such study to which he gave particular attention in formulating his theory of amphetamine action was P. B. Bradley's work with cats (P. B. Bradley, 1953), which suggested that "the site of action of amphetamine may be related to the brain stem reticular activating system of Magoun" (Laufer, Denhoff, & Solomons, 1957, p. 47; see also Magoun, 1952). But P. B. Bradley's work could also be interpreted as supporting the theory that amphetamines act by stimulating the reticular activating system in the brain stem and thus serve to increase general alertness in hyperkinetic children. The action of amphetamine is thought to be related to the action of norepinephrine, which is concentrated in the brain stem (Weiss *et al.*, 1968; McLean & McCartney, 1961; Moore, 1963; Sanan & Vogt, 1962; Vogt, 1954). It is generally held that influences of the brain stem reticular formation on the cerebral cortex are largely responsible for the maintenance of alertness (Snyder, 1972). P. B. Bradley and J. Elkes (1957) have shown that amphetamines increase alertness by mediating the reticular formation's influence on the cortical arousal mechanisms. Furthermore, P. B. Bradley and B. J. Key (1958) reported evidence that amphetamines decrease the threshold for arousal responses produced by direct stimulation of the reticular formation.

If amphetamines stimulate the reticular activating system and increase general alertness in hyperkinetic children, this explains the "paradoxical" behavioral findings as the normal effect of amphetamines. Increase in general alertness could result in a concomitant increase in focused attention and a resulting decrease in response to interfering stimuli (Kornetsky, 1970, p. 128, commenting on Conners & Rothschild, 1968). Even if Laufer's hypothesis is correct—that amphetamines stimulate the inhibitory function of the diencephalon—a non-paradoxical interpretation of the amphetamines' action in hyperkinetic children is still suggested. The brain stem reticular formation functions both to maintain the cortex in a state of alertness and to regulate incoming stimuli reaching the cortex (Hilgard &

Bower, 1966). Thus, if an important site of action of amphetamine *is* the brain stem, the drug's stimulating effects would both increase alertness and inhibit interfering stimuli from reaching the cortex. This would mitigate the need to attend to diverse stimuli and enhance the possibility of sustained attention to one thing at a time. It would also agree with the behavioral findings reported.

There is some scant and contradictory evidence available suggesting the cortex as a possible site of amphetamine action. None of this evidence comes from studies on children; in fact, the bulk of it is based upon animal studies. Although prefrontal lesions in monkeys have been shown to release hyperkinetic behavior which is significantly reduced by stimulants (Davis, 1957, p. 619), on the other hand cortical lesions have lowered convulsive thresholds to amphetamine (Blum, Baum, & Chow, 1950, p. 685), and in the rat, cortical lesions have sensitized the animals to drug-induced hyperkinesis (Adler, 1961). Interestingly, what evidence there is of direct cortical response to amphetamine relates primarily to motor activity. This makes sense since motor activity is mediated by the cortex. Yet the motoric dimension of the hyperkinetic syndrome has been shown to be one of the less important dimensions, reflecting attentional difficulties mediated primarily by the reticular activating system. Thus, although there may be a form of hyperactivity mediated by cortical dysfunction, there is no consistent evidence that such hyperactivity is responsive to amphetamines. In addition, other specifically cortical functions, particularly perceptual and cognitive, have not been consistently responsive to the drugs. It is more likely that where the hyperkinetic syndrome is responsive to amphetamine treatment, this responsiveness is mediated by the more direct effect of these drugs on the brain stem reticular formation. In the absence of any evidence to the contrary, it is more parsimonious, as Conners points out, to assume at the present state of knowledge that amphetamines do not have paradoxical pharmacological effects on hyperkinetic children, but that they may, through the mediation of the reticular activating system, ". . . produce more organized perceptual response . . . for a variety of children [as well as adults], with effects being more dramatically noticeable in children with diencephalic lesions, or other forms of imbalance between cortical and subcortical mechanisms" (Conners, 1966, p. 432).

Adverse Effects

Not all hyperkinetic children improve on amphetamines. In some, symptoms have actually been exacerbated. C. Bradley (1950, p. 32) reported that of 275 children treated with Benzedrine almost 11 percent showed an exaggeration of all the hyperkinetic symptoms which had originally attracted the attention of clinicians, and also showed evidence of increased agitation, tension, and anxiety. Of the 113 children treated with Dexedrine, almost 16 percent exhibited comparable exaggerated symptoms. S. Levy (1966) has reported similar findings. A few dramatically adverse reactions have occurred as a result of amphetamine administration in children. R. H. Mattson and J. R. Calverley (1968) have reported amphetamine-induced dyskinesia in three young children, and H. H. Eveloff (1968) reported a similar finding in an eighteen-year-old girl. P. G. Ney (1967) has also presented a case of amphetamine-induced psychosis in an eight-year-old hyperkinetic boy. Although these cases have been very rare, they merit attention.

Even in those children who are behaviorally benefited by amphetamines, toxic effects usually also occur. These effects may include anorexia, insomnia, gastrointestinal distress, dizziness, fine tremor and coldness of the extremities, and pallor of the skin. They are generally reported as mild enough not to necessitate discontinuance of treatment. Most occur within the first week or so of treatment and gradually diminish or disappear as treatment is continued (Bakwin, 1948; Molitch & Sullivan, 1937; C. Bradley & Bowen, 1941; C. Bradley, 1950; Levy, 1966). In cases where they persist in more disturbing form, they are usually minimized or eliminated by adjusting the dosage or time of administration (Weiss *et al.*, 1968, p. 152; Greenberg, Deem, & McMahon, 1972; Conners *et al.*, 1969; Epstein *et al.*, 1968). But significant weight loss has occasionally been reported to occur with continued use of amphetamines, despite the adjustment of dosage (Greenberg, Deem, & McMahon, 1972, pp. 533, 536; McConnell *et al.*, 1964). In general methylphenidate has less toxic effects than racemic amphetamine or dextroamphetamine. The principal toxic effect of this drug is a mild and usually transient insomnia (DiMascio, Soltys, & Shader, 1970, p. 255).

When undesired effects continue to be a problem even with adjusted doses of stimulants, discontinuing medication has been thought to eliminate such undesirable effects completely and almost immediately. But the results of a very recent study by D. Safer, R. Allen, & E. Barr (1972), published in 1972 and since replicated, have called these rather superficial observations into doubt. Nine children who had been on stimulants for two years or more were compared in changes of height and weight with seven children who, although referred for stimulant treatment, had never been treated with the drug due to parental objection. Eight of the nine in the stimulant group showed less annual weight gain than would be expected in relation to their baseline weight recorded before medication was given.

In seven of the nine, percentile weight continued to decrease for the second and third years on medication. Five of the nine showed a similar decrease in percentile height over the period of long-term medication, which correlated highly with the weight suppression. Although the decrease in percentile height did not reach significance when compared with baseline percentiles, it was highly significant when compared with the height changes in the control group of seven unmedicated children, for whom percentile height actually increased. A comparable significant difference was found in weight changes for the two groups.

Another set of data reported in this publication amplified these findings. Twenty hyperactive children were studied who had been on 10 to 15 mg dextroamphetamine daily or 20 to 40 mg methylphenidate daily for the nine months of the school year. They were all white middle class children, 80 per cent of whom were receiving special educational instruction for learning disabilities. Seven of these children continued to receive stimulants for the three summer months, while 13 did not. Although the children gained weight over the nine month period of medication, the amount of gain was less than would be expected under normal circumstances. In fact, for the children taking dextroamphetamine and higher doses of methylphenidate (20 mg and above) weight gain was significantly suppressed in relation to the norm. Lower doses of methylphenidate (under 20 mg) appeared to have less effect on suppression of weight gain, although some effect was noted. Those children taken off stimulants for the three summer months gained more weight than would normally be expected for children of their age, while those who remained on stimulants continued to gain less than the norm. The large weight gain for those taken off medication did not quite compensate for the suppression of weight gain during the previous nine months.

This is one of the very few follow-up studies that have been done on the long-term effects of stimulant use in hyperkinetic children, and it certainly signals caution. Toxic effects have previously been thought to be minimal or insignificant. In fairness, however, Safer's data cannot be taken as evidence that complete compensation would not have been achieved had these children remained off medication for more than the three months. In an unpublished study by Kenneth Zike, cited in a recent editorial by Eisenberg (1972), a group of 83 drug-treated hyperkinetic children who were followed for a period of one to eleven years showed no evidence of suppression of growth. In particular, a subgroup of 31 methamphetamine-treated subjects (average dose, 20 mg per square meter of body surface area) showed a growth curve above the fiftieth percentile on the Iowa grids.

Some Persisting Confusions

There is still no consensus among experts about the nature of the hyperkinetic syndrome or the means for diagnosing it. Although the medical community is increasingly aware of the complexities of defining the syndrome and tracing its etiology, hyperkinesis is no better understood than it was when Laufer and his associates defined it and postulated an organic basis for its existence. Before scientists have had a chance to systematically study and refine the issues, the field has become the domain of educators and the drug industry. As the issue has become more political there has been increasing pressure to recognize the existence of a medically diagnosable entity to justify the use of psychoactive drugs for children's behavior and learning problems.

The assumption that brain dysfunction is associated with the syndrome has now been subtly mitigated by adding the qualifier "minimal." S. D. Clements has officially renamed the syndrome "minimal brain dysfunction syndrome" and has defined it as follows:

The term 'minimal brain dysfunction syndrome' refers ... to children of near average, average, or above average general intelligence with certain learning or behavioral disabilities ranging from mild to severe, which are associated with deviations of function of the central nervous system. These deviations may manifest themselves by various combinations of impairment in perception, conceptualization, language, memory, and control of attention, impulse, or motor function.

Similar symptoms may or may not complicate the problems of children with cerebral palsy, epilepsy, mental retardation, blindness, or deafness.

These aberrations may arise from genetic variations, biochemical irregularities, perinatal brain insults or other illness or injuries sustained during the years which are critical for the development and maturation of the central nervous system, *or from unknown causes*. [Italics added.] (Clements, 1966, pp. 9-10)

This definition is merely a sophisticated statement of ignorance about a certain symptom complex, described within broad boundaries but perhaps arising from any cause at all.

In an excellent article entitled "Hyperactivity and the CNS: An Etiological and Diagnostic Dilemma," C. J. Weithorn (1973) discusses with refreshing logic and clarity the difficulties of characterizing the disorder and of diagnosing it within the framework of the presently limited state of knowledge. Discussing several different, still unproven theories which have been proposed over the years to account

265

for the etiology of the disorder, she suggests that perhaps there are even two distinct forms of the disorder, ". . . one a motor hyperactivity (due to defective inhibitory mechanisms in the cortical motor system), and the other, a generalized hyperreactivity (due to defective inhibitory mechanisms in the sensory sphere)." "Application of this formulation to the behavior of hyperactive children," she continued, "would indicate that there is a distinction to be made between a motorically restless child and one whose movements are in response to a multiplicity of stimuli" (Weithorn, 1973, p. 49). Because attentional measures have been shown more consistently than measures of motor restlessness to be responsive to amphetamine therapy, it is possible that there are distinct forms of the hyperkinetic disorder which are differentially responsive to drugs.

The blurring and confusion of various diagnostic categories meant to differentiate hyperkinetic, perceptually handicapped, or emotionally disturbed children is clearly illustrated by B. Fish (1971) in a well-reasoned article entitled "The 'One Child, One Drug' Myth of Stimulants in Hyperkinesis." She insists that it is lack of agreement about the use of terms such as minimal brain dysfunction and hyperkinesis which has "created the misinterpretations of the literature on stimulants in children that still plague us" (Fish, 1971, p. 193). Fish points out that it is logically incorrect to conclude that behavior disorders with organic components are more responsive to amphetamines than behavior disorders of psychogenic origin, since many children categorized as (organically) hyperkinetic also are diagnosed as having behavior disorders of psychogenic origin. Laufer & Denhoff (1957, p. 470), for instance, have reported that dextroamphetamine is more effective in treating children with behavior disorders of organic etiology, whereas Bender & Cottington (1942) and Fish (1960) have reported that *neurotic* children are more responsive to the drug. Yet Laufer's population were a heterogeneous mixture of personality disorders found in psychiatric treatment settings, and it was only on top of these diagnoses that the label "hyperkinetic syndrome" was superimposed. It already had been postulated that the syndrome had an organic basis, specifically a diencephalic dysfunction. Moreover, of those categorized as hyperkinetic, only 20 per cent had been diagnosed as having chronic brain syndrome and/or convulsive disorders. Among those categorized as non-hyperkinetic the same diagnoses applied, although there were proportionally fewer cases of organic brain syndrome and convulsions, and proportionally more cases of anxiety reaction (Fish, 1971, pp. 194, 195; Laufer, Denhoff, & Solomons, 1957, pp.

40-41). It is clear that "organically" based hyperkinesis and psychogenic disorders are not mutually exclusive, particularly in their response to amphetamines.[2]

More recent studies have shed no further light on the variables which best predict stimulant response in children. As Fish (1971, p. 198) notes, although the study by Conners *et al.* (1969) demonstrated no change in neurotic symptoms with the use of stimulants, no analysis was done to determine whether hyperactive symptoms in children with a diagnosis of "neurotic" were stimulant responsive. Furthermore, heterogeneous samples have been used in so many of the later studies, as we have seen earlier, and individual variability has been so common within significantly improved drug-treated groups, that it is impossible to determine which variables are responsive to amphetamine treatment. This impossibility was well documented by Conners and his colleagues (Conners, Eisenberg, & Barcai, 1967), who pointed out that students who were *not* labeled hyperkinetic nonetheless "improved" markedly while on amphetamines. If the investigators had not taken extreme care to emphasize that there was no reason to suppose the existence of any organic damage or even deep-rooted psychiatric problems, this study quite possibly would be cited as further "evidence" for the effectiveness of amphetamines in improving the school work and general behavior of hyperkinetic children.

A recent study by J. H. Satterfield *et al.* (1973) on EEG and neurological correlates of stimulant response in MBD children is open to a similar misinterpretation. Fifty-seven children diagnosed specifically as MBD by two independent psychiatrists on the basis of history and observation were selected for the study. Each was given an extensive neurological work-up, EEG's were performed, and several psychometric tests were administered. Methylphenidate and placebo were given

[2] Another error which Fish (1971) points out (and which has already been noted above) is that Laufer never gave amphetamines to the non-hyperkinetic children in his sample, and hence it was incorrect to conclude that amphetamines raise the photo-Metrazol level only in hyperkinetic children. Moreover, as already mentioned, no attempt was made to correlate changes in photo-Metrazol threshold with changes in behavior. A further error noted in this article is that although C. Bradley has been considered the first researcher to demonstrate the efficacy of amphetamines for ameliorating the symptoms of hyperkinesis, he never actually made the distinction in his sample between hyperkinetic and non-hyperkinetic children, and his results were inconclusive regarding this distinction. The drugs were useful for ameliorating symptoms in both categories (C. Bradley and Bowen, 1941; C. Bradley, 1950) and as Fish notes, if hyperactive drug responders were more numerous than non-hyperactive drug responders, it was simply because there was a preponderance of hyperactive youngsters in the sample to begin with (Fish, 1971; C. Bradley and Bowen, 1941; C. Bradley, 1950).

in a double-blind experiment for a period of three weeks, in dosages adjusted for good clinical response subject to individual tolerance. When teacher rating scales obtained before and immediately after drug treatment were analyzed, it was found that those MBD children with both an abnormal neurological examination and an abnormal EEG responded significantly better to methylphenidate than did the group of MBD children with normal neurological examination and normal EEG. Ninety percent of the former group showed 30 percent or more improvement as a result of drug treatment, suggesting that a combination of abnormal EEG and neurological examination predicts good response to stimulants. But a full 60 percent of the MBD group with normal EEG and neurological examination also showed 30 percent or more improvement as a result of drug treatment, despite the significant difference between the two groups. Had the author not carefully pointed out the gain among this latter group of subjects, this study too could be cited as further "evidence" for the theory that clinically diagnosed hyperkinetic children respond favorably to stimulants because they suffer from some underlying organic dysfunction. Such examples cast doubt on the validity of some studies in this area, which have uncritically assumed that any improvement following the use of amphetamines is an indication that the child has benefited from amphetamines because he was hyperkinetic in an organic sense.

Amphetamines and School Policy

Because relevant variables for the prediction of response to amphetamine treatment are still unknown and the nature of the hyperkinetic syndrome is still an enigma, there is a need for basic reconsideration of the syndrome. There is supposedly a higher incidence of brain abnormality among children diagnosed clinically as MBD hyperactives than among "normal" controls, although the evidence to date is contradictory. Satterfield *et al.* (1973) have found evidence to support this contention, but Werry and Sprague (1970, p. 398) have pointed out that when the criterion for the selection of subjects has been brain damage as established by intensive neurological examination rather than observation of behavior, hyperkinesis does not occur any more frequently in an "organic" group than in a "normal" (non-brain damaged as measured by neurological testing) control group. Fish (1971, p. 198) insists upon the necessity of a logical system of diagnosis, carefully distinguishing "between diagnoses of mental disorders which define the level and type of total personality disorder and terms which define major developmental symptoms." She concludes from her own clinical experience as well as her observations of the work of other investigators that "the usefulness of amphetamines in children with behavior disorders is [not] limited ... by the presence or absence of overt anxiety or hyperactivity, nor by the presence or absence of minimal brain dysfunctions, ... but the critical controlled study ... has yet to be done" (Fish, 1971, p. 197).

Once one appreciates the confusion within the medical community surrounding hyperkinesis, it is frightening to see the self-assurance with which educators and the drug industry have promoted the use of drugs in the schools. An interesting treatment of the situation appeared in the *Saturday Review* (Ladd, 1970) of November 21, 1970. The reader was confronted with two articles, apparently in opposition to each other. First, there was a thoughtful and well organized article by E. T. Ladd entitled "Pills for Classroom Peace?," in which the author pointed out major dangers involved in the administration of amphetamines to school children diagnosed as hyperkinetic and discussed them one by one. Second, there was a brief insert (taking up less than a page of the Ladd article) written by C. Ellingson entitled, "The Children with No Alternative." According to Ellingson the children who in fact need some kind of "replacement chemotherapy" are not the "normal, active, ebullient youngsters who are chafing under the restraints of classroom discipline," but rather young students whose central nervous systems are not functioning normally, with the result that they are the "victim of forces they cannot control." Ellingson maintains that although these unfortunate children exhibit various types of distractible, disruptive, or disinterested behavior, modification of their behavior is not the primary aim of drug administration. Instead it is merely one of the anticipated results of a correction of some specific but still undefined (hypothetical) chemical imbalance.

Ladd's article is reasonably balanced, avoiding such obvious excesses. He points out that forcing young children to take any kind of medication may constitute an infringement of their civil rights, no matter how expedient such measures appear to school personnel attempting to cope with day-to-day disruptive behavior. He emphasizes that the only objectionable behavior that a school has any legal right to control or modify is that which it *must* police in order to "accomplish its job and protect persons and the institution" (Ladd, 1970, p. 81). When the aims of education are as ill-defined or as poorly articulated as they seem to be in most of our schools today, it becomes frighteningly easy for school administrators, teachers, and even teachers' aides to effectually punish children who "misbehave" under the guise of giving them "medicine."

Even Ladd's article presents a number of problems. He stresses that there is a high risk of producing adverse or toxic physiological damage, including addiction or long-term and even permanent organic changes. But then he dismisses this danger, claiming that amphetamines are not physiologically addictive for children, that pediatricians and other physicians prescribing these drugs for elementary students are being especially cautious, and that in any event the entire situation is being "policed" by the FDA. These arguments are questionable. It is not at all clear that some children do not suffer subtle adverse physiological alterations that may become evident only after many years. In fact, as has been discussed above, more recent evidence from the Safer study (Safer, Allen, & Barr, 1972) suggests that growth may indeed be adversely affected over a period of time. Nor has it been conclusively shown that amphetamines will not produce addiction in the "physical" sense even among young people. Ladd himself entertains the possibility that administering amphetamines to children whose behavior is considered abnormal may subtly condition or dispose them to eventually joining the ranks of the drug culture.

Ladd's faith in the judgment of physicians is not consistent with his knowledge that many physicians do not rely on their own clinical tests, or even firsthand observations, but instead prescribe amphetamines to students solely on the basis of teachers' and school administrators' reports of student "deviancy." These reports often amount to nothing more than a commentary on a healthy but active curiosity or a justified lack of interest in what an insensitive instructor is teaching. And of course the FDA has done little to improve this situation, proving itself again as a notoriously ineffective watchdog.

Using drugs to "modify" classroom behavior constitutes a covert subversion of what *should* be our educational ideals. If an important aim of our educational institutions were really to help young people deal with and learn to regulate their "self-destructive" or even "anti-social" tendencies, it would make little sense to give them drugs as soon as they exhibited restless or unruly behavior. Students, and perhaps especially those at the elementary level, need and deserve educational environments designed to help them "come to grips with their natural dispositions and learn to use in a certain way what Philip Jackson at the University of Chicago has nicely called their own 'executive powers.' Any form of intervention that relieves a restless or unruly child of the need, or deprives him of the opportunity, to use his executive powers deprives him to that extent of the chance to develop insight and skill in self-control" (Ladd, 1970, p. 68).

Plainly such a divergence of intelligent and informed opinion as the one reflected in the Ladd and Ellingson articles is crying out for federal clarification. On

January 11 and 12, 1971, the U.S. Department of HEW called a conference on the use of stimulant drugs in the treatment of behaviorally disturbed school children, in which fifteen specialists from the sciences and social sciences were summoned to discuss the controversial matter and arrive at conclusions concerning the current status of knowledge about the use of these drugs and at a set of conditions under which the drugs should be given to children. Unfortunately, any adequate outcome of the first task precluded a clear resolution of the second. When the Report of the Conference (1971) was published it was a disappointment. A statesmanlike document, written cautiously and in a persuasive style, it managed to arrive at two fundamentally opposite sets of findings, neither of which contained anything that was not already known. The Report stressed the already well-documented difficulties in diagnosing hyperkinesis and the lack of adequate research into the long-term effects of stimulants administered to young children. Then it reversed itself and endorsed the use of these drugs in the medical treatment of what was now officially defined as "minimal brain dysfunction," even though no research had been able to establish the nature of this presumed organic malfunctioning or deficiency. The HEW Report took a moralistic and naively optimistic stand, urging all parties who were "benefiting" from drug treatment to act ethically and show appropriate restraint and good judgment. The drug companies were requested not to send any more representatives to schools to "seek endorsement of their products by school personnel" (Report of the Conference, 1971, p. 529). The media were urged not to continue to treat the matter in a sensational way. Teachers and parents were asked to try affection, psychotherapy, and simple patience before resorting to a medical "solution." Doctors were reminded that they should be certain that their diagnoses were accurate.

The most disturbing aspect of this report was not what it said or did not say, but how it was subsequently used as a basis for justifying the existence of hyperkinesis as an established disease and the over-prescription of stimulants to treat the alleged disease. The Report was mailed to various persons who were described in a flattering cover letter as being "in a position to be concerned, and to influence others concerning the management of hyperkinesis in the schools" (Rapoport & Repo, 1971, p. 96). The document was cited in the press and by other media as an endorsement by "leading experts in medicine, welfare, and education" (Rapoport & Repo, p. 97) for the use of stimulants in treating MBD. In direct disregard of its content, the Report was also cited in advertisements from a number of drug companies as a specific recommendation for the use of their stimulant products.

One critic of the Report has correctly remarked: "The diagnostic tools cited, such as patient histories, psychometric tests and various mechanical devices measuring just how much a child fidgets, do no more than restate what has already been observed: that the child is restless, inattentive, etc. They do not in themselves confirm the hypothesis that these kids are 'brain damaged.' A comparable situation, from a medical point of view, would be if a doctor told you that you were suffering from a kidney disease that could only be detected by the fact that you beat up your wife, cut yourself when you shaved and felt tense and angry at work, and who then proceeded to confirm his diagnosis by finding out how long you had beaten your wife and measuring just how hard you hit her!" (Rapoport & Repo, p. 99). The diagnostic dilemma has been highlighted by a study by T. J. Kenny and R. L. Clemmens (1971) who found that in a sample of 100 children suffering from learning disabilities and/or behavioral difficulties, extensive medical evaluations were "relatively unrewarding" (p. 273). This observation has been supported by other work as well (Freeman, 1971, p. 93).

Looking for Alternatives

The behavior taken as a sign of hyperkinesis is real enough. Restless, angry, disturbed, and inattentive students constitute a major problem for many parents and teachers. It also may be true that some elementary school children exhibit this kind of behavior because of organic brain damage or neurohormonal insufficiencies. But it is impossible to believe that the 200,000 or more school children who are now being routinely administered stimulants are *all* suffering from organic brain damage or deficiencies in crucial CNS chemicals. In other words, there is no justification for the increasingly popular leap from the observation of disruptive or inattentive behavior to the supposition that this is the result of a specific disorder of the central nervous system. Nor does the observation that amphetamines sometimes reduce disruptiveness and increase attention provide any grounds for supposing that even these are true cases of organically-based hyperkinesis. As we have seen, amphetamines can affect behavior and learning problems of psychogenic and environmental etiology in much the same way as they affect problems presumed to have an organic basis.

Our society has been undergoing a critical upheaval in values. Children growing up in the past decade have seen claims to authority and existing institutions questioned as an everyday occurrence, and the classroom has become a major stage on which this value upheaval is played out. Teachers no longer have the unquestioned authority they once had in the classroom, nor do they have at their disposal

272

many well-defined ways of relating to children not based on their presumed authority. The child, on the other side, is no longer so intimidated by whatever authority the teacher has, and demands, often through his behavior, to be acknowledged as an individual and treated with concern. "Hyperkinesis," whatever organic condition it may legitimately refer to, has become a convenient label with which to dismiss this phenomenon as a physical "disease" rather than treating it as the social problem it is. The use of drugs, particularly amphetamines, in the name of therapy often does little more than provide a relatively easy and economical way of making the classroom situation more tolerable and manageable for the teacher.

Even in those instances that may be considered true cases of minimal brain dysfunction, stimulants are not always the drugs of choice. R. D. Freeman (1966, 1970) has reviewed the literature to 1969 on the efficacy of amphetamines in reducing hyperactivity, distractibility, alleged hyperkinesis, or MBD, and has concluded that the lack of controlled, scientific studies, together with the strong possibility of a placebo effect resulting from eagerness on the part of children to please and teachers or physicians or drug companies to be pleased, has made it nearly impossible to determine with any real accuracy whether amphetamines are the preferred drug even for alleviating the specific symptoms of presumed hyperkinesis. He has warned that we should be especially careful in judging the efficacy of a drug with such varied and powerful effects on a set of disorders as ambiguous as learning disabilities. The phenothiazines have proven more useful than stimulants in several instances (Freedman, Effron, & Bender, 1955; Alderton & Hoddinott, 1964; Werry *et al.*, 1966), and lately some very positive results have been demonstrated with imipramine (Graded imipramine regimen, 1969), although the safety of the latter has been called into question by some recent reports of seizures concomitant with the administration of this drug to children (Brown *et al.*, 1973).

There is evidence that even for those children who initially seem to profit from medication, long-term benefits may be insignificant. The only two published follow-up studies on the long-term effects of amphetamines on hyperkinetic symptoms in children, besides the preliminary study reported by Laufer (1971), are not reassuring in their conclusions. One of these studies was conducted by Weiss *et al.* (1971) on a group of 64 children who, on initial interview five years earlier, had been diagnosed as severely hyperactive. The children had all been treated with chlorpromazine (Thorazine) for one to two years, and then had been switched to dextroamphetamine, methylphenidate, or thioridazine (Mellaril) if the original medication had proven ineffective. At the time of follow-up, when most of the

273

children were adolescents, it was found that although the more pronounced manifestations of restlessness were diminished, attentional handicaps persisted. Underachievement in school and general difficulty in academic functions, perhaps related to the attentional problem, were characteristic of the group, evident in 80 percent of the children. This was true even though the children were of at least average intelligence. In addition, 70 percent of the children were emotionally immature and a significant number had no sense of future goals and suffered from low self-esteem and feelings of hopelessness. This study did not employ amphetamines systematically, and it is not possible to draw sound conclusions about the relative efficacy of the drugs. But the results at least indicate that in one case amphetamines and other drugs were not particularly beneficial.

The other study of "hyperactive children as teenagers" analyzed the effects of dextroamphetamine more systematically, and its results were equally unencouraging (Mendelson, Johnson, & Stewart, 1971). Ninety-two percent of the 83 children studied had initially been treated with dextroamphetamine or methylphenidate, and of these, 60 percent had shown improvement for at least six months. At the time of follow-up, although about 50 percent of the total sample were rated as showing some *overall* improvement, over 75 percent of the children still manifested poor concentration, impulsivity, and defiance, although to a reduced degree. A significant minority, approaching 25 percent, were involved in anti-social activities suggesting that they might develop serious pathology as adults. The vast majority continued to have serious difficulties with school work and to suffer from feelings of low self-esteem, probably resulting from a continuing cycle of low motivation, failure, and discouragement. It thus appears that for all the excitement among teachers and the drug industry over the great potential of amphetamines for treating hyperkinetic children, these drugs are not going to perform miracles.

Alternatives to drug therapy are now emerging which are safer and may be more effective in the long run. In 1971, Alvin Toffler reported to the American Psychological Association on the results of a series of experiments using easily learned classroom behavior modification techniques on groups of hyperactive children with either normal or abnormal EEG tracings (Novack, 1971, p. 508). After 24 hyperactive elementary school children with normal IQ's had been administered complete EEG's, they were given simple reinforcement for attentiveness to an academic workbook task in an experimental classroom environment. Their rates of attentiveness, cooperation, and accuracy were measured before, during, and after the application of simple positive reinforcement techniques of praise and reward. These disturbed children consistently showed significant decreases in hyperactivity after behavior modification therapy, and the improvements carried over into their regular school environments. One of the more interesting findings was that the abnormal EEG students showed considerable and highly significant decreases in hyperactivity and increases in overall classroom performance as compared with the students who had been judged hyperactive but showed normal EEG's, even though these latter students also showed marked improvement. No such improvement was noted in a non-treated control group of similarly "disturbed" or hyperactive children (with or without normal EEG's). Toffler concluded that before initiating amphetamine or other drug therapy, and before attempting any depth psychotherapy or even "special class" placement, simple behavior modification techniques should be attempted for even the most severely agitated hyperkinetics since it is their *behavior* which is almost always the criterion by which they are judged psychologically or organically "sick," "deviant," or "deficient." Werry and Sprague (1970) support this conclusion in their recommendation that drugs ". . . should not be used as the only or even the primary treatment, except where circumstances preclude behavior modification techniques" (p. 408).

Behavior modification techniques, while they are no panacea and possess their own significant potential for abuse, do have this virtue: their proper application requires on the part of those who employ them a sensitivity to the needs, talents, and preferences of the individual child. Rather than simply making a child more manageable, as drugs often do, such techniques may bring out his best qualities. Moreover, these techniques allow the child to discover his impulses and to make use of his own powers of self-control in dealing with them. They do not just abolish temporarily the more disturbing impulses, thereby rendering control unnecessary. Behaviors learned through the use of such techniques potentially can be generalized to many situations beyond the specific situation in which the behaviors were originally conditioned (Doubros & Daniels, 1966; Patterson *et al.*, 1965). In contrast, drug-facilitated learning is not only not generalized to a broad spectrum of situations, but evidence suggests it is actually forgotten quite readily (Overton, 1966; Miller, 1966; Turner & Young, 1966).

None of this is to deny the possibility that there is a true, organically based hyperkinesis which may benefit from drug treatment. But it is time that we take an honest look at the evidence to date and admit that where there is such a disorder, it is difficult to distinguish it from other syndromes or disturbances which are expressed by similar behavioral patterns. Symptoms, not causes, have become the focus of treatment, creating a significant potential for abuse.

References

Adler, M. W. Changes in sensitivity to amphetamine in rats with chronic brain lesions. *Journal of Pharmacology and Experimental Therapeutics*, 134 (November 1961), 214-221.

Alderton, H. R., & Hoddinott, B. A. A controlled study of the use of thioridazine in the treatment of hyperactive and aggressive children in a children's psychiatric hospital. *Canadian Psychiatric Association Journal*, 9 (June 1964), 239-247.

Bakwin, H. Benzedrine in behavior disorders of children. *Journal of Pediatrics*, 32 (February 1948), 215-216.

Bender, L., & Cottington, F. The use of amphetamine sulfate (Benzedrine) in child psychiatry. *American Journal of Psychiatry*, 99 (July 1942), 116-121.

Blum, R. A., Blum, J. S., & Chow, K. L. Production of convulsions by administration of Benzedrine following brain operations in monkeys. *Archives of Neurology and Psychiatry*, 64 (November 1950), 685-691.

Bradley, C. Benzedrine and Dexedrine in the treatment of children's behavior disorders. *Pediatrics*, 5 (January 1950), 24-37.

Bradley, C. The behavior of children receiving Benzedrine. *American Journal of Psychiatry*, 94 (November 1937), 577-585.

Bradley, C., & Bowen, M. Amphetamine (Benzedrine) therapy of children's behavior disorders. *American Journal of Orthopsychiatry*, 11 (January 1941), 92-103.

Bradley, P. B. The effect of some drugs on the electrical activity of the brain of the conscious cat, *Electroencephalography and Clinical Neurophysiology*, (August 1953), 21.

Bradley, P. B., & Elkes, J. The effects of some drugs on the electrical activity of the brain. *Brain*, 80 (March 1957), 77-117.

Bradley, P. B., & Key, B. J. The effect of drugs on arousal responses produced by electrical stimulation of the reticular formation of the brain. *Electroencephalography and Clinical Neurophysiology*, 10 (February 1958), 97-110.

Brown, D., Winsberg, B. G., Bialer, I., & Press, M. Imipramine therapy and seizures: Three children treated for hyperactive behavior disorders. *American Journal of Psychiatry*, 130 (February 1973), 210-212.

Clements, S. D. *Task force I: Minimal brain disfunction in children*. National Institute of Neurological Diseases and Blindness, Monograph No. 3, U.S. Department of Health, Education and Welfare (1966).

Conners, C. K. The effect of Dexedrine on rapid discrimination and motor control of hyperkinetic children under mild stress. *Journal of Nervous and Mental Disease*, 142 (May 1966), 429-433.

Conners, C. K. Symposium: Behavior modification by drugs—II: Psychological effects of stimulant drugs in children with minimal brain dysfunction. *Pediatrics*, 49 (May 1972), 702-708.

Conners, C. K., A teacher rating scale for use in drug studies with children. *American Journal of Psychiatry*, 126 (December 1969), 884-888.

Conners, C. K., & Eisenberg, L. The effects of methylphenidate on symptomatology and learning in disturbed children. *American Journal of Psychiatry,* 120 (November 1963), 458-463.

Conners, C. K., Eisenberg, L., & Barcai, A. Effect of dextroamphetamine on children: Studies on subjects with learning disabilities and school behavior problems. *Archives of General Psychiatry,* 17 (October 1967), 478-485.

Conners, C. K., Eisenberg, L., & Sharpe, L. Effects of methylphenidate (Ritalin) on paired-associate learning and Porteus Maze performance in emotionally disturbed children. *Journal of Consulting Psychology,* 28 (February 1964), 14-22.

Conners, C. K., & Rothschild, G. Drugs and learning in children. *Learning Disorders,* 3 (Spring 1968), 195-223.

Conners, C. K., Rothschild, G., Eisenberg, L., Schwartz, L. S., & Robinson, E. Dextroamphetamine sulphate in children with learning disorders: Effects on perception, learning, and achievement. *Archives of General Psychiatry,* 21 (August 1969), 182-190.

Cromwell, R. L., Baumeister, A., & Hawkins, W. F. Research in activity level. In N. R. Ellis (Ed.) *Handbook of mental deficiency.* New York: McGraw-Hill, 1963.

Cutler, M. A., Little, J. W., & Strauss, A. A. The effect of Benzedrine on mentally deficient children. *American Journal of Mental Deficiency,* 45 (July 1940), 59-65.

Davis, G. D. Effects of central excitant and depressant drugs on locomotor activity in the monkey. *American Journal of Physiology,* 188 (February 1957), 619-623.

Denhoff, E. To medicate—to debate—or to validate. *Journal of Learning Disabilities,* 4 (November 1971), 467-469.

DiMascio, A., Soltys, J. J., & Shader, R. I. Psychotropic drug side effects in children, in R. I. Shader and A. DiMascio (Eds.), *Psychotropic Drug Side Effects.* Baltimore: Williams & Wilkins, 1970, pp. 235-260.

Docter, R. F. The Porteus Maze Test. In O.K. Buros (Ed.), *The seventh mental measurements yearbook,* 7th ed. Highland Park, N.Y.: Gryphon, 1972, 751-756.

Doubros, S. G., & Daniels, G. J. An experimental approach to the reduction of overactive behavior. *Behavioral Research and Therapy,* 4 (November 1966), 251-258.

Eisenberg, L. The hyperkinetic child and stimulant drugs. *New England Journal of Medicine,* 287 (August 1972), 249-250.

Eisenberg, L. Symposium: Behavior modification by drugs—III: The clinical use of stimulant drugs in children. *Pediatrics,* 49 (May 1972), 709-715.

Eisenberg, L., & Conners, C. K. Psychopharmacology in childhood. In N. Talbot, J. Kagan, & L. Eisenberg (Ed.), *Behavioral science in pediatric medicine.* Philadelphia: B. Saunders, 1971, 397-423.

Eisenberg, L., Conners, C. K., & Sharpe, L. A controlled study of the differential application of outpatient psychiatric treatment for children. *Japanese Journal of Child Psychiatry,* 6 (Fall 1965), 125-132.

Eisenberg, L., Lachman, R., Molling, P. A., Lockner, A., Mizelle, J. D., & Conners, C. K. A psychopharmacologic experiment in a training school for delinquent boys. *American Journal of Orthopsychiatry,* 33 (March 1963) 431-447.

Ellingson, C. The children with no alternative. *Saturday Review,* 53 (November 21, 1970), 67.

Epstein, L. C., Lasagna, L., Conners, C. K., & Rodriguez, A. Correlation of dextroamphetamine excretion and drug response in hyperkinetic children. *Journal of Nervous and Mental Disease*, 146 (February 1968), 136-146.

Eveloff, H. H. A case of amphetamine-induced dyskinesia. *Journal of the American Medical Association*, 204 (June 1968), 933.

Federal involvement in the use of behavior modification drugs on grammar school children of the right to privacy inquiry: Hearing before a subcommittee of the Committee on Government Operations, House of Representatives, 91st Congress, 2nd Session, September 29, 1970. Washington, D.C.: U.S. Government Printing Office, 1970.

Fish, B. Drug therapy in child psychiatry: Pharmacological aspects. *Comprehensive Psychiatry*, 1 (August 1960), 212-227.

Fish, B. The "one child, one drug" myth of stimulants in hyperkinesis. *Archives of General Psychiatry*, 25 (September 1971), 193-203.

Freedman, A. M., Effron, A. S., & Bender, L. Pharmacology in children with psychiatric illness. *Journal of Nervous and Mental Disease*, 122 (November 1955), 479-486.

Freeman, R. D. Drug effects on learning in children: A selective review of the last thirty years. *Journal of Special Education*, 1 (Fall 1966), 17-44.

Freeman, R. D. Review of medicine in special education: Another look at drugs and behavior. *Journal of Special Education*, 4 (Fall 1970), 377-384.

Freeman, R. D. Review of medicine in special education: Medical-behavioral pseudorelationships. *Journal of Special Education*, 5 (Winter-Spring 1971), 93-99.

Gastaut, H. Combined photic and Metrazol activation of the brain. *Electroencephalography and Clinical Neurophysiology*, 2 (August 1950), 249-261.

Graded imipramine regimen favored in hyperkinetic children. Journal of the American Medical Association, 208 (June 1969), 1613-1614.

Greenberg, L. M., Deem, M. A., & McMahon, S. Effects of dextroamphetamine, chlorpromazine and hydroxyzine on behavior and performance in hyperactive children. *American Journal of Psychiatry*, 129 (November 1972), 532-539.

Hentoff, N. Drug-pushing in the schools: The professionals (I). *The Village Voice*, May 25, 1972, 20-22.

Hilgard, E. R., & Bower, G. H. *Theories of learning*. New York: Appleton-Century-Crofts, 1966.

Huessey, H. R. Study of the prevalence and therapy of the hyperkinetic syndrome in public school children in rural Vermont. *Acta Paedopsychiatrica*, 34 (April-May 1967), 130-135.

Hundleby, J. D., Pawlik, K., & Cattell, R. B. *Personality factors in objective test devices*. San Diego, Calif.: R. R. Knapp, 1965.

Hunsinger, S. School storm: Drugs for children. *Christian Science Monitor*, October 31, 1970, 1, 6.

Kahn, E., & Cohen, L. Organic drivenness: A brain-stem syndrome and an experience. *New England Journal of Medicine*, 210 (April 1934), 748-756.

Kenny, T. J., & Clemmens, R. L. Medical and psychological correlates in children with learning disabilities. *Journal of Pediatrics,* 78 (February 1971), 273-277.

Kornetsky, C. Psychoactive drugs in the immature organism. *Psychopharmacologia (Berlin)* 17 (April 1970), 105-136.

Ladd, E. T. Pills for classroom peace. *Saturday Review,* 53 (November 21, 1970), 66-68, 81-83.

Laufer, M. W. Long-term management and some follow-up findings on the use of drugs with minimal cerebral syndromes. *Journal of Learning Disabilities,* 4 (November 1971), 518-522.

Laufer, M. W., & Denhoff, E. Hyperkinetic behavior syndrome in children. *Journal of Pediatrics,* 50 (April 1957), 463-474.

Laufer, M. W., Denhoff, E., & Solomons, G. Hyperkinetic impulse disorder in children's behavior problems. *Psychosomatic Medicine,* 19 (February 1957), 38-49.

Levy, S. The hyperkinetic child: A forgotten entity, its diagnosis and treatment. *International Journal of Neuropsychiatry,* 2 (August 1966), 330-336.

Magoun, H. W. An ascending reticular activating system in the brain stem. *Archives of Neurology and Psychiatry,* 67 (February 1952), 145-154.

Mattson, R. H., & Calverley, J. R. Dextroamphetamine-sulfate-induced dyskinesias. *Journal of the American Medical Association,* 204 (April 1968), 400-402.

McConnell, T. R., Jr., Cromwell, R. L., Bialer, I., & Son, C. D. Studies in activity level: VII effects of amphetamine drug administration on the activity level of retarded children. *American Journal of Mental Deficiency,* 68 (March 1964), 647-651.

McLean, J. R., & McCartney, M. Effect of d-amphetamine on rat brain noradrenalin and serotonin (26540). *Proceedings of the Society for Experimental Biology and Medicine,* 107 (May 1961), 77-79.

Mendelson, W., Johnson, N., & Stewart, M. A. Hyperactive children as teenagers: A follow-up study. *Journal of Nervous and Mental Disease,* 153 (October 1971), 273-279.

Miller, N. E. Some animal experiments pertinent to the problem of combining psychotherapy with drug therapy. *Comprehensive Psychiatry,* 7 (February 1966), 1-12.

Miller, S. Use of tranquilizers by city pupils reported increasing. *Baltimore Evening Sun,* October 2, 1970.

Millichap, J. G., Aymat, F., Sturgis, L. H., Larsen, K. W., & Egan, R. A. Hyperkinetic behavior and learning disorders—III: Battery of neuropsychological tests in controlled trial of methylphenidate. *American Journal of Diseases of Children,* 116 (September 1968), 235-244.

Millichap, J. G., & Boldrey, E. E. Studies in hyperkinetic behavior: II. Laboratory and clinical evaluations of drug treatments. *Neurology,* 17 (May 1967), 467-471.

Molitch, M., & Sullivan, J. P. The effect of Benzedrine sulfate on children taking the New Stanford Achievement Test. *American Journal of Orthopsychiatry,* 7 (October 1937), 519-522.

Moore, K. E. Toxicity and catecholamine releasing action of d- and l-amphetamine in isolated and aggregated mice. *Journal of Pharmacology and Experimental Therapeutics,* 142 (October 1963), 6-12.

279

Ney, P. G. Psychosis in a child associated with amphetamine administration. *Canadian Medical Association Journal,* 97 (October 1967), 1026-1029.

Novack, H. S. An educator's view of medication and classroom behavior. *Journal of Learning Disabilities,* 4 (November 1971), 507-508.

Omaha pupils given "behavior" drugs. *Washington Post,* June 29, 1970, 1, 8.

Overton, D. A. State-dependent learning produced by depressant and atropine-like drugs. *Psychopharmacologia (Berlin),* 10 (September 1966), 6-31.

Pasamanick, B. Anticonvulsant drug therapy of behavior problem children with abnormal electroencephalograms. *Archives of Neurology and Psychiatry,* 65 (June 1951), 752-766.

Patterson, G. R., Jones, R., Whittier, J., & Wright, M. A. A behavior modification technique for the hyperactive child. *Behavioral Research and Therapy,* 2 (January 1965), 217-226.

Prechtl, H. F. R., & Stemmer, C. J. The choreiform syndrome in children. *Developmental Medicine and Child Neurology,* 4 (April 1962), 119-127.

Rapoport, R., & Repo, S. The educator as pusher: Drug control in the classroom. *This Magazine is About Schools,* 5 (Fall/Winter, 1971), 87-112.

A report on the use of behavior modification drugs on elementary school children. In M. Yanow (ed.), *Observations from the Treadmill.* Narberth, Pa.: 1970.

Report of the conference on the use of stimulant drugs in the treatment of behaviorally disturbed young school children. Sponsored by the Office of Child Development and the Office of the Assistant Secretary for Health and Scientific Affairs, Department of Health, Education, and Welfare, Washington, D.C. (January 11-12, 1971). Reprinted in *Journal of Learning Disabilities,* 4 (November 1971), 523-530.

Rosvold, H. E., Mirsky, A. F., Sarason, I., Bransome, E. D., & Beck, L. H. A continuous performance test of brain damage. *Journal of Consulting Psychology,* 20 (October 1956), 343-350.

Safer, D., Allen, R., & Barr, E. Depression of growth in hyperactive children on stimulant drugs. *New England Journal of Medicine,* 287 (August 1972), 217-220.

Sanan, S., & Vogt, M. Effects of drugs on the chemotherapy noradrenalin content of brain and peripheral tissues and its significance. *British Journal of Pharmacology,* 18 (February 1962), 109-127.

Satterfield, J. H., Lesser, L. I., Saul, R. E., & Cantwell, D. P. EEG aspects in the diagnosis and treatment of minimal brain dysfunction. *Annals of the New York Academy of Sciences,* 205 (February 1973), 274-282.

Snyder, S. H. Catecholamines in the brain as mediators of amphetamine psychosis. *Archives of General Psychiatry,* 27 (August 1972), 169-179.

Sprague, R. L., Barnes, K. R., & Werry, J. S. Methylphenidate and thioridazine: Learning, reaction time, activity, and classroom behavior in disturbed children. *American Journal of Orthopsychiatry,* 40 (July 1970), 615-628.

Stewart, M. A. Hyperactive children. *Scientific American,* 222 (April 1970), 94-98.

Stewart, M. A., Pitts, F. N., Craig, A. G., & Dierof, N. The hyperactive child syndrome. *American Journal of Orthopsychiatry,* 36 (October 1966), 861-867.

Strauss, A. A., & Kephart, N. C. Psychopathology and education of the brain-injured child: Progress in theory and clinic. Vol. II. New York: Grune & Stratton, 1955.

Strauss, A. A., & Lehtinen, L. E. Psychopathology and education of the brain-injured child. Vol. I. New York: Grune & Stratton, 1947.

Sykes, D. H., Douglas, V. I., Weiss, G., & Minde, K. K. Attention in hyperactive children and the effect of methylphenidate (Ritalin). *Journal of Child Psychology and Psychiatry*, 12 (August 1971), 129-139.

Treatment for fidgety kids? A story of drug use in Omaha kicks up national fuss with some racial overtones. *National Observer*, July, 1970, 1, 5.

Turner, R. K. CNS stimulant drugs and conditioning treatment of nocturnal enuresis: A long-term follow-up study. *Behavioral Research and Therapy*, 4 (August 1966) 225-228.

Vogt, M. The concentration of sympathin in different parts of the central nervous system under normal conditions and after the administration of drugs. *Journal of Physiology*, 123 (March 1954), 451-481.

Weiss, G., Minde, K. K., Werry, J. S., Douglas, V. I., & Nemeth, E. Studies on the hyperactive child—VIII: Five-year follow-up. *Archives of General Psychiatry*, 24 (May 1971), 409-414.

Weiss, G., Werry, J. S., Minde, K. K., Douglas, V. I., & Sykes, D. H. Studies on the hyperactive child—V: The effects of dextroamphetamine and chlorpromazine on behavior and intellectual functioning. *Journal of Child Psychology and Psychiatry*, 9 (December 1968), 145-156.

Weithorn, C. J. Hyperactivity and the CNS: An etiological and diagnostic dilemma. *Journal of Learning Disabilities*, 6 (January 1973), 41-45.

Werry, J. S., & Sprague, R. L. Hyperactivity. In C. G. Costello (Ed.), *Symptoms of psychopathology*. New York: Wiley, 1970.

Werry, J. S., Weiss, G., Douglas, V. I., & Martin, J. Studies on the hyperactive child—III: The effect of chlorpromazine upon behavior and learning ability. *Journal of the American Academy of Child Psychiatry*, 5 (April 1966), 292-312.

Student Classification, Public Policy, and the Courts*

DAVID L. KIRP

University of California at Berkeley

During the past two decades, courts have sought to define with particularity the meaning or, better, meanings of equal educational opportunity. Only recently, however, have courts examined within-school practices—ability grouping, special education placement, exclusion of "ineducable" children—which classify students on the basis of academic performance or potential. In this article, the author examines classification practices in constitutional terms; he assesses both the plausibility of treating student classification issues in equal protection and due process terms, and the policy consequences of such treatment.

Public schools regularly sort students in a variety of ways.[1] They test them when they first arrive at school and at regular intervals thereafter in order to identify aptitude or the capacity to learn.[2] From primary school until graduation, most[3]

---

* A substantially longer and more amply footnoted version of this article, "Schools as Sorters: the Constitutional and Policy Implications of Student Classification," was published in the *University of Pennsylvania Law Review*, 121 (April 1973), pp. 705–797. It is reprinted in edited form with the permission of the *Pennsylvania Law Review*...

[1] This description of typical classification practice is based on survey data reported in Warren Findley and Miriam Bryan, *Ability Grouping* (Athens, Ga.: University of Georgia Press, 1971) and in Christopher Jencks, Marshall Smith, Henry Acland, Mary Jo Bane, David Cohen, Herbert Gintis, Barbara Heyns, Stephan Michelson, *Inequality: A Reassessment of the Effect of Family and Schooling in America* (New York: Basic Books, 1972), p. 250.

[2] Test terminology is tricky. Some tests purport to measure aptitude—capacity to learn—while others test achievement—material mastered. In fact, "all tests measure *both* aptitude and achievement ... [S]uccess on IQ tests, aptitude tests and achievement tests [reveal] varieties of intelligent

Harvard Educational Review Vol. 44 No. 1 February 1974, 27–52

schools group (or track) students on the basis of estimated intellectual ability, both within classrooms[4] and in separate classes.

In primary school grouping, the pace of instruction, but typically not its content, is varied. Grouping decisions may be made for each school subject or a given group may stay intact for the entire curriculum. During the school year, students' grades, taken together with IQ and achievement tests, determine whether children are advanced to the next grade and into which group they are assigned.

In secondary school, placements in educational tracks reflect both interest and ability. There, for the first time in their educational careers, students may be offered choices. In practice, however, prior achievement usually determines program placement: grammar school success means college track or academic high school assignment while mediocre grade school performance frequently leads to placement in a non-college preparatory program. Counselors, not students, frequently make these decisions by matching school offerings to their own estimates of each student's ability and potential.[5] That classification determines both the nature of the secondary school education—Shakespeare, shorthand, or machine shop—and the gross choices—college or work—available after graduation.

Students whom the school cannot classify in this manner are treated as "special" or "exceptional." Such students by no means resemble one another. They may have intellectual, physical, or emotional handicaps; they may not speak English as their native language; they may simply be hungry or unhappy with their particular school situation. The number and variety of differentiating characteristics is large; overlapping among the characteristics (multiple differentnesses) further complicates the pattern. Yet the school, in part because its resources are scarce, cannot tailor individual programs to satisfy individual needs. Instead, it develops classifications which attempt to reconcile the variations among

---

behavior." Jencks *et al.*, pp. 54–57. By school convention, IQ tests are individually administered while aptitude tests are group tests; individual testing is commonly employed only for special class placement.

[3] See Findley and Bryan, pp. 2–18. A 1958–59 survey undertaken by the National Educational Association Research Division reported that among school districts with more than 2,500 pupils, 77.5 percent grouped by ability in the primary grades and 90.5 percent utilized ability grouping in secondary schools. A similar pattern was reported seven years later. Research Division, National Education Association, *Ability Grouping* (Washington, D.C.: NEA Publications, 1968), pp. 12, 15–17.

[4] For a careful study of the rationale and effects of within-class grouping in one ghetto school, see Ray Rist, "Student Social Class and Teacher Expectations: The Self-Fulfilling Prophecy in Ghetto Education," *Harvard Educational Review*, 40 (August 1970), pp. 411–450.

[5] Aaron Cicourel and John Kitsuse, *The Educational Decision-Makers* (New York: Bobbs-Merrill, 1963), describe the counselor as serving the school's and not the child's needs.

exceptional children with the limitations of school resources. Most school districts offer several special programs, differentiating both among levels of retardation (educable, trainable, profound) and between retardation and such other school handicaps as learning disabilities and emotional disturbance. Students unamenable to such special help—either because the school concludes that they are ineducable, i.e., unable to profit from any presently-provided educational program, or because they make life difficult for teachers and classmates—may be excluded from school.

This article examines three of the seemingly infinite range of school classifications: exclusion from publicly-supported schooling, placement in special education programs,[6] and ability grouping.[7] Several factors distinguish these from other school classifications. First, they are each of relatively long duration: exclusion is almost invariably a one-way ticket out of school; movement between special and regular programs or between slow and advanced ability groups is infrequent.[8] Second, their consequences are both significant and difficult to reverse: the child barred from school as "ineducable" becomes more difficult to educate because of his or her exclusion; the student assigned to a slow track, or a special education class, cannot easily return to the schooling mainstream. Third,

[6] Special education refers to classes for students with particular and acute learning disabilities. The disability may be defined in terms of test scores, physical impediments (for example, classes for the blind, deaf, or perceptually handicapped), or psychological disturbances (such as classes for the emotionally disturbed). Special education classes are a relatively recent and increasingly common phenomenon. A recent national estimate of enrollment in special education concludes that 2,106,100 children (35 percent of those who need such help) are enrolled in some special program. Retarded children are somewhat better served than other children in need of special education—based on a prevalence estimate of 2.3 percent, close to one-half of retarded children are in special classes. Romaine Mackie, *Special Education in the United States: Statistics, 1948–1966* (New York: Teachers College Press, 1969), p. 39.

[7] Ability grouping, or tracking, refers to the differential classification of students, ostensibly on the basis of aptitude, for instruction in the regular academic program. See Findley and Bryan, p. 4; NEA Research Division, p. 6.

[8] See James Gallagher, "The Special Education: Contract for Mildly Handicapped Children," *Exceptional Children*, 38 (March 1972), pp. 527–529); "[D]ata collected informally by the Office of Education suggested that special education was *de facto*, a permanent placement. In a number of large city school systems far less than 10 percent of the children placed in special education classes are ever returned to regular education." *Report of the New York State Commission on the Quality, Cost and Financing of Elementary and Secondary Education*, 9B.2 (1972), pp. 9.22–9.39, offers one explanation for this phenomenon: children in special education classes are infrequently reevaluated. In New York City, during the school years 1969–70, 1,603 retarded children had not been evaluated in over three years; 2,028 retarded children had not been evaluated in over five years. See also Jane Mercer, "Sociocultural Factors in the Education of Black and Chicano Children," paper presented at the 10th Annual Conference on Civil and Human Rights of Educators and Students, National Education Association, Washington, D.C., February, 1972; Jane Mercer, "Sociological Perspectives on Mild Mental Retardation," in *Social-Cultural Aspects of Mental Retardation*, ed. Carl Haywood (New York: Appleton-Century-Crofts, 1970), p. 287.

the questionable bases for these sorting decisions suggest that the possibility of mis-classification, and consequent serious injury to the child, is significant. Fourth, these placement decisions (unlike within-class grouping decisions, for instance) are highly visible. Typically, they are made not by classroom teachers but by school or district administrators. Fifth, each of these classifications carries the potential of stigmatizing students. In sum, exclusion, special class assignment, and track placement are of greater moment to the student than, for example, a failing grade on a particular exercise. They are also more obvious candidates for judicial review.

School Classification and School Needs

While, as one testing manual contends, "the original [classification] was when God ... looked at everything he made and saw that it was *very good*,"[9] only during the past sixty years have public schools devoted considerable effort to classifying and sorting students. The prototypal common school, energetically promoted by Horace Mann and Henry Barnard, was designed to provide a shared educational experience for all who could afford to stay in school for an extended period of time. Through most of the nineteenth century, a uniform curriculum was characteristic of schools which, at least in theory, respected neither class nor caste.

The arrival of hundreds of thousands of immigrants from eastern and southern Europe in the late nineteenth century obliged school officials to provide instruction for children who spoke no English, and had little, if any, previous schooling. To professional educators it made little sense to place these students in regular classes; they needed assistance of a kind that common schools had not previously been asked to provide. Urban school systems created "opportunity classes," special programs designed to overcome the students' initial difficulties and to prepare them for regular schoolwork.

Other societal factors served to promote the need for differentiation among students.[10] As the insistence that schools be business-like and efficient was increasingly heard; American educators began to adopt the modern business corporation's complex organizational structure and with it a complex division of labor

[9] William Mehrens and Irwin Lehmann, *Standardized Tests in Education* (New York: Holt, Rinehart & Winston, 1969), p. 3.
[10] For a fuller exposition, see Raymond Callahan, *Education and the Cult of Efficiency* (Chicago: University of Chicago Press, 1952).

analogous to classification. Further, the increasingly industrial American economy seemed to demand a differentiation of skills that a common school education simply could not provide. As Boston's superintendent of schools argued in 1908: "Until very recently [the schools] have offered equal opportunity for all to receive *one kind* of education, but what will make them democratic is to provide opportunity for all to receive such education as will fit them *equally well* for their particular life work."[11] Varied curricula were developed for students of varying ability.

The advent of standardized aptitude testing early in the twentieth century provided a useful means of identifying and placing students. Intelligence tests were increasingly used by American educators because they accorded with the educators' demand for categorization and efficiency. Tests offered scientific justification for the differentiated curriculum, enabling it to function with apparent rationality.[12] By World War I, the use of classification was common practice among American educators. Today, federal and state support has increased the attractiveness to school districts of specialized programs—notably industrial and agricultural trade courses. Differentiated special education programs, also given impetus by state and federal legislation, have expanded with the same speed (if not the same universality) since the 1920's.

Current ability grouping, special education assignment, and exclusion of ineducable children have significant and similar school purposes. They provide mechanisms for differentiating among students, offer rewards and sanctions for school performance, ease the tasks of teachers and administrators by restricting somewhat the range of ability among students in a given classroom, and purportedly improve student achievement.

Interestingly, the first two purposes, sorting and reward-punishment, are seldom mentioned by school officials. The sorting function is self-evident: classification permits the parceling out of students among different educational programs.[13] That certain of these classifications reward and others punish is ap-

---

[11] Brooks, "Twenty-Eighth Annual Report of the Superintendent of Public Schools" in *Documents of the School Committee* (Boston: Boston City School Committee, 1908), p. 53.

[12] See, e.g., Elwood Cubberly, "Foreword to Lewis Terman," in Lewis Terman, *The Measurement of Intelligence: An Explanation of and a Complete Guide for the Use of the Stanford Revision and Extension of the Binet-Simon Intelligence Scale* (Boston: Houghton-Mifflin, 1916).

[13] Certain critics charge that sorting is indeed all that schools do; see Florence Howe and Paul Lauter, "How the School System is Rigged for Failure," *New York Review of Books*, 14 (June 18, 1970), p. 14, or indeed all that they have ever done, Annie Stein, "Strategies for Failure," *Harvard Educational Review*, 41 (May 1971), pp. 158–204. See also Colin Greer, *The Great School Legend: A Revisionist Interpretation of American Public Education* (New York: Basic Books, 1972).

parent from investigations of the effects of grouping on students' self perception.[14] The reward-punishment facet of classification represents one aspect of the schools' stress on intellectual competition, with praise given only for performance that the teacher defines as successful.[15]

It is more commonly asserted that classification eases the tasks of teachers and administrators, and affords educational opportunities tailored to students' needs. These purposes—one emphasizing benefits to teachers and administrators, the other emphasizing benefits to students—permit school officials to view classification as an unmixed blessing. There is little recognition that classification may have decidedly limited educational benefits for school children or that certain sorting practices may even do educational injury.[16] It is the belief that classification helps everyone, and not its questionable empirical foundation, which is significant here. It partially explains the popularity that grouping enjoys among teachers: only 18.4 percent of teachers surveyed by the National Education Association preferred to teach non-grouped classes.[17] It also underscores the problems that reformers unhappy with present classification practices are likely to encounter in seeking to restructure them.

School sorting practices also have their critics. The fashionable educational innovations of the past twenty years—nongraded classes, team teaching, open classrooms—all represent efforts to modify school classifications by introducing elements of flexibility, and to diversify the school program while making any particular classification of more limited duration and significance.

Educational research poses a quite different kind of challenge to present classification practice. It increasingly has undermined one of the essential premises of sorting: that it benefits students. The research concerning the educational effects of ability grouping and special education reveals that classification, as it is typically employed, does not promote individualized student learning, permit

[14] See Joan Lunn and Elsa Ferri, *Streaming in the Primary School* (New York: Fernhill House, 1970); W. Borg, *Ability Grouping in the Public Schools*, 2d Ed. (Madison, Wis.: Dembar Educational Research Services, 1966); Maxine Mann, "What Does Ability Grouping Do to the Self-Concept?" *Childhood Education*, 36 (April 1960), pp. 357–60.

[15] See Jules Henry, *Culture Against Man* (New York: Random House, 1963), pp. 283–322.

[16] A recent study asked school officials why they favored ability grouping. The most common set of answers referred to the needs of teachers and administrators: "improves [teacher] attention to individual [student] needs," "facilitates curriculum planning," and "[makes] instruction easier." The second most frequently mentioned rationales refer to student benefits: "permits students to progress at their own learning rate," and "allows the student to compete on a more equitable basis." Findley and Bryan, p. 15.

[17] Research Division, National Education Association, "Teachers' Opinion Poll: Ability Grouping," *NEA Journal*, 57 (February 1968), p. 53.

more effective teaching to groups of students of relatively similar ability or, indeed, accomplish any of the things it is ostensibly meant to do. Rather, the findings indicate that classification effectively separates students along racial and social class lines, and that such segregation may well cause educational injury to minority groups. They also suggest that adverse classifications stigmatize students, reducing both their self-image and their worth in the eyes of others.[18]

Even those who accept the basic premises of school sorting have reason to question whether schools can adequately do the job. Two recent reappraisals of students assigned to classes for the retarded reveal notable errors. A study done by the Washington, D.C. school system found that two-thirds of the students placed in special classes in fact belonged in the regular program.[19] Retests of 378 educable mentally retarded students from thirty-six school districts in the Philadelphia area revealed that "[t]he diagnosis for 25 percent of the youngsters found in classes for the retarded may be considered erroneous. An additional 43 percent [may be questioned]."[20] The authors of the study were troubled by these results. "One cannot help but be concerned about the consequences of subjecting these children to the 'retarded' curriculum . . . .The stigma of bearing the label 'retarded' is bad enough, but to bear the label when placement is questionable or outright erroneous is an intolerable situation."[21]

Classification on the basis of intellectual ability has also been attacked by those who assert that such distinctions are based on judgments of inherited rather than acquired intelligence, and are therefore undemocratic. Fifty years ago, Walter Lippmann criticized intelligence testing on precisely those grounds, predicting that the use of such tests "could not but lead to an intellectual caste system in which the task of education had given way to the doctrine of predestination and infant damnation."[22] Milton Schwebel, discussing the practice of grouping students, makes a similar charge:

The most direct evidence of a school system's stand on ability is the way it educates the mass of its children. . . . Only the school system which regards the genetic factor as paramount, and the environmental as . . . insignificant [would] rightly subdivide its population

[18] Reginald Jones, "Labels and Stigma in Special Education," *Exceptional Children*, 38 (March 1972), p. 561.

[19] Hobson v. Hansen, 269 F. Supp. 401 (D.D.C. 1967).

[20] Mortimer Garrison, Jr., and Donald Hammill, "Who Are the Retarded?" *Exceptional Children*, 38 (September 1971), pp. 13–18.

[21] Garrison and Hammill, p. 20. One difficulty with the Garrison and Hammill study is that they, unlike the school districts they studied, used five different measures to determine retardation.

[22] Walter Lippman, "The Abuse of Tests," *New Republic*, 32 (November 1922), pp. 297–298.

in accordance with native ability [as] revealed by achievement tests and would proffer a curriculum suitable to the talents of each group. The decision whether it is wise to group children by ability depends upon one's views of the origin of intelligence.[23]

The claim that ability grouping treats intelligence as determined by heredity and not environment[24] is political dynamite. It encourages blacks to view grouping as the pedagogical equivalent of genocide and radical whites to regard it as "not the means of democratization and liberation, but of [class] oppression."[25] This hostility to ability grouping has been translated into varied forms of political pressure. Black psychologists and community groups have demanded, with some success, that intelligence testing be abandoned. Others have urged the abolition of all classifications in which racial minorities are overrepresented relative to their proportion of the school population. Some of these efforts minimize the real differences among children which, whatever their source, do require varied educational programs; their equation of classification and the doctrine of inherited intelligence oversimplifies a complex problem. But whatever the objective merits of such attacks, they have had significant political impact.

These varied criticisms to classification are not couched in legal terms. Yet, as the balance of this article suggests, they do give rise to questions concerning constitutional rights. In that sense, classification is both descriptive of public educational practice and useful as a tool for constitutional analysis.

School Classification and the Courts

Since the 1954 Supreme Court opinion in *Brown v. Board of Education*,[26] courts have increasingly scrutinized decisions once made solely by school administrators and boards of education. Most prominently, racial policies and practices of states and school districts and methods of allocating financial resources among school districts have been subjected to extensive legal analysis and challenge. Such challenges have addressed school policy on the grand scale. They focus on the state, the metropolitan area, or the school district as the entity whose conduct is to be reviewed. That approach implies a model of educational reform which presumes, first, that racial and fiscal inequities ought to be undone (a proposition with

[23] Milton Schwebel, *Who Can Be Educated?* (New York: Grove Press, 1968), pp. 75–76.
[24] See e.g. Arthur Jensen, "How Much Can We Boost IQ and Scholastic Achievement?" *Harvard Educational Review*, 39 (Winter 1969), pp. 1–123.
[25] Howe and Lauter, p. 14.
[26] 47 U.S. 483 (1954).

which there can be little quarrel); and second, that the most effective means of undoing them is to focus on the largest governmental unit that can be haled into court.

For some issues the grand scale approach is demonstrably correct. For example, the problem of inter-district resource inequality can be addressed most cogently only at the state or national level. But in those matters which directly and tangibly affect the quality of children's schooling experiences, the equation of largest with best makes little sense. The school, not the state or even the school district, has primary impact. It is at the school or classroom level that many of the critical decisions about teacher assignment, classroom composition, and curriculum are made.

There are obvious and understandable reasons underlying judicial reluctance to intrude in such matters as student grouping ostensibly based on ability, or student assignment to special programs designed for children with particular disabilities. The minuteness of many within-school (and within-class) decisions makes it difficult to conceive of them as posing legally manageable problems. Such decisions are complex, interrelated, and numerous. For that reason, a court which undertook to review them might well find itself acting as schoolmaster in an uncomfortably literal sense. The necessarily limited capacity for judicial review of within-school policy questions does not, however, foreclose all judicial inquiry. Properly framed, certain aspects of the school classification process can be addressed in intelligible and manageable fashion by courts.[27]

Courts have begun to limit the schools' discretion in the ways they sort students and the categories into which they sort them. Judge J. Skelly Wright's decision in *Hobson v. Hansen*,[28] which abolished tracking in the District of Columbia, is the most famous but not the only case addressing the constitutional propriety of school classification practices. Exclusion of children from school, whether because of asserted ineducability,[29] alien status[30] or pregnancy,[31] has been overturned

[27] This article considers only the constitutional dimension of the classification issue. For a discussion of non-constitutional case law, see Stephen Goldstein, "The Scope and Sources of School Board Authority to Regulate Student Conduct and Status: A Non-constitutional Analysis," *University of Pennsylvania Law Review*, 117 (January 1969), p. 373. See also Elgin v. Silver, 15 Misc. 2d 864, 182 N.Y.S. 2d 669 (Sup. Ct. 1958); Board of Educ. v. State ex. rel. Goldman, 47 Ohio App. 417, 191 N.E. 914 (1934).

[28] Hobson v. Hansen, 269 F. Supp. 401, 513 (D.D.C. 1967).

[29] E.g., Mills v. Board of Education, 348 F. Supp. 866 (D.D.C. 1972) (exclusion of children labeled as behavioral problems, mentally retarded, emotionally disturbed or hyperactive); Pennsylvania Association for Retarded Children v. Pennsylvania, 343 F. Supp. 279 (E.D. Pa. 1972) (consent decree enjoining exclusion of mentally retarded children).

by a number of courts; the manner in which students are assigned to classes for the mildly retarded has been reviewed to determine the rationality of the classification procedures employed[32]; and courts have rejected attempts of formerly *de jure* segregated school districts to employ ability grouping, finding such efforts inconsistent with the obligation to desegregate.[33]

What general constitutional standards underlie these discrete cases? One approach considers the educational harm attributable to exclusion and to assignment to either special education programs or slow ability groups. The assorted ill effects of these classifications render plausible the claim that they deny students an equal educational opportunity. The deprivation represents a real disadvantage given additional significance by virtue of the psychic injury that it occasions.[34]

A second constitutional approach focuses on the fact that minority children are assigned to slow learners' groups and special education classes in numbers far exceeding their proportion of the school population and are thus denied classroom contact with white and middle-class schoolmates. The existence of such racial isolation, coupled with evidence of the racially specific injury it produces, should be sufficient to require a demonstration that these classifications are in fact based on adequate nonracial grounds and that their educational benefits outweigh the racially specific harm of within-school isolation.[35]

The equal educational opportunity and racial analyses both rely on the equal protection clause in challenging the legitimacy of at least some school classifications. A third approach focuses not on the legitimacy of the classifications themselves, but on the procedure by which the school determines how a particular student or class of students should be treated. This due process approach is triggered by two related factors: a significant school-imposed change in educa-

---

[30] Hosier v. Evans, 314 F. Supp. 316 (D.V.I. 1970).

[31] E.g., Ordway v. Hargraves, 323 F. Supp. 1155 (D. Mass. 1971).

[32] See, e.g., Stewart v. Phillips, Civil No. 70–1199–F (D. Mass., February 8, 1971); reprinted in Harvard University Center for Law' and Education, *Classification Materials* (Cambridge, Mass. p. 234 (1972) [hereinafter cited as *Classification Materials*] (denying defendants' motion for summary judgment); Diana v. California State Bd. of Educ., Civil No. 70–37 RFP (N.D.Cal. 1970) [reprinted in *Classification Materials*, p. 292] (consent decree); Spangler v. Pasadena City Bd. of Education, 311 F. Supp. 501, 504, 510–20 (C.D. Cal. 1970) (fact-finding in regard to grouping practices).

[33] E.g., Lemon v. Bossier Parish School Bd. 444 F.2d 1400 (5th Circ. 1971).

[34] See Frank Michelman, "The Supreme Court, 1968 Term-Foreword: On Protecting the Poor Through the Fourteenth Amendment," *Harvard Law Review*, 83 (November 1969), p. 7.

[35] See Frank Goodman, "De Facto School Segregation: A Constitutional and Empirical Analysis," *California Law Review*, 60 (March 1972), p. 275.

tional status and the stigma which invariably attaches to students placed in these programs.

These three legal strategies, assessed in succeeding sections of this article, are at least plausible. Each draws on previous court decisions which have sought to define with particularity the meaning of the equal protection of the laws and due process guarantees of the fourteenth amendment. Yet legal plausibility does not necessarily or automatically yield educationally sound results. This caveat assumes particular importance when courts begin to raise questions about matters as central to the educational enterprise as school classification determinations. In these, as in other issues of educational policy, decisions based on the constitution can have a salutary effect. They can determine the bounds of constitutionally permissible school action, reveal arbitrary conduct, and impose some measure of fairness on school procedure. But the courts can neither revamp the educational system nor improve the quality of those who administer that system.

Equal Educational Opportunity

The Supreme Court declared in *Brown v. Board of Education* that the opportunity for education, where the state has undertaken to provide it, "is a right which must be made available to all on equal terms."[36] While the inequality against which *Brown* inveighed was racial, nonracial educational inequities have been struck down by the lower courts. Those decisions note the constitutional importance of education and view with sympathy the claims of children—a voteless, relatively powerless minority. Is the child's interest in an equal education sufficiently diminished by placement in a slow track or special class, or by exclusion from school, to warrant constitutional scrutiny?

School sorting practices, unlike explicitly racial classifications, cannot be condemned as inherently harmful. Some classification is clearly necessary if schools are to cope with the bewildering variety of talent and interest that characterizes children. Whether particular classifications are harmful, and hence equality-depriving, is essentially an empirical question. Thus, in a lawsuit attacking school sorting practices, demonstration of injury may well be as important as constitutional theory. Adverse school classification may result in two kinds of injury: educational ineffectiveness and stigmatization of students.

[36] 347 U.S. 483, 493 (1954).

Efficacy

What does the evidence concerning the educational efficacy of school sorting demonstrate? Little research has been carried out on the effects of school exclusion, with good reason: excluded children are difficult to locate.[37] Further, the educational effects of exclusion are likely to be inseparable from the impact of other social adversities, making it difficult to isolate the cause of harm. Yet the few studies that do consider the effect of exclusion (or the impact of school shut-downs) on children predictably conclude that the lack of schooling does retard achievement.[38]

While abundant research has been undertaken with respect to internal school classifications,[39] that research is flawed by a host of methodological difficulties: some studies are too abbreviated and thus do not take into account the possibility that children behave differently because they are part of an exciting (or at least novel) experiment; experimental groups, assigned to particular classifications, are not adequately matched with control groups, so that performance variation may be explained by initial student differences; measures of change and growth vary from study to study; responses to questionnaires prove inadequate to reckon with the subtleties of sorting; and, most important, the definition of what constitutes ability grouping or a program for the educable mentally retarded varies from study to study. Despite these problems, the consistency of research findings (particularly among those studies most carefully executed) is impressive. The research indicates that most school classifications have marginal and sometimes adverse impact on both student achievement and psychological development.

The research concerning the efficacy of special education programs is best treated as two sets of data. Studies of programs for children with profound problems—for example, autistic children or those whose IQ is below 25—reveal that

[37] *Wall Street Journal*, March 22, 1972, p. 1, col. 1. Estimates of the number of excluded children range widely. See Task Force on Children Out of School, *The Way We Go To School: The Exclusion of Children in Boston* (Boston, Mass.: Beacon Press, 1971), p. 3 and 118 Cong. Rec. H1257 (daily ed. February 17, 1972; remarks of Congressman Vanik).

[38] See *New York Times*, Feb. 15, 1970, p. 1, col. 1 (children tested after year in which schools were closed for two months due to teachers' strike showed two months' loss in reading achievement); Robert Green and Louis Hofmann, "A Case Study of the Effects of Educational Deprivation on Southern Rural Negro Children," *Journal of Negro Education*, 34 (Summer 1965), pp. 327–341. The children studied by Green and Hofmann had attended school in Prince Edward County, Virginia, which closed its schools to avoid desegregation. Since the effects of school exclusion and the segregation controversy—either of which might have had adverse educational consequences—are inextricably linked, it is difficult to separate the impact of each adversity on achievement.

[39] See, e.g., Borg.

careful intervention can secure substantial benefits.[40] Of course, the measure of benefit differs for these children: the ability to tie one's own shoes or to talk is a major success. But the benefits are real and for the most part unquestioned.

Research concerning classes for children with etiologically more ambiguous handicaps—the educable mentally retarded, mildly emotionally disturbed and perceptually handicapped—reach quite different conclusions. Those programs do not tangibly benefit their students, whose equally handicapped counterparts placed in regular school classes perform at least as well and without apparent detriment to their normal classmates.

It is indeed paradoxical that mentally handicapped children having teachers especially trained, having more money (per capita) spent on their education, and being enrolled in classes with fewer children and a program designed to provide for their unique needs, should be accomplishing the objectives of their education at the same or at a lower level than similar mentally handicapped children who have not had these advantages and have been forced to remain in the regular grades.[41]

The methodological difficulties, noted earlier, suggest one reason for treating these findings with some caution. Where, for example, special education is a euphemism for a day-sitting room staffed by an unqualified teacher, as is too often the case, any benefits it yielded would be remarkable. Yet the philosophy of isolated special class treatment also makes the failure of such ventures understandable. These programs typically adopt a passive-acceptant approach, reflecting the assumption that:

. . . the retarded individual is essentially unmodifiable and, therefore, that his performance level as manifested at a given stage of development is considered as a powerful prediction of his future adaptation. . . . Strategies aiming at helping him to adapt . . . will consist of moulding the requirements and activities of his environment to suit his level of functioning, rather than making the necessary efforts to raise his level of functioning in a significant way. *This, of course, is doomed to perpetuate his low level of performance.*[42] [Emphasis added.]

Thus, even if children perform admirably in the special class, they inevitably fall further behind their counterparts in the regular program. Only an active-modi-

[40] See, e.g., Samuel Kirk, "Research in Education," in *Mental Retardation: A Review of Research*, eds. Harvey Stevens and Rick Heber (Chicago: University of Chicago Press, 1964).

[41] G. Orville Johnson, "Special Education for the Mentally Handicapped—A Paradox," *Exceptional Children*, 29 (October 1962), pp. 62–66.

[42] Reuvin Feuerstein, "A Dynamic Approach to the Causation, Prevention, and Alleviation of Retarded Performance," in *Social-Cultural Aspects of Mental Retardation*, ed. Carl Haywood (New York: Appleton-Century-Crofts, 1970), pp. 341–343.

ficational approach—which rejects the educational isolation and early labeling of retarded children—is likely to reverse this pattern.[43]

In sum, the research conclusion about special education programs is consistent, if modest: programs for the severely handicapped do benefit those children, while classes for the mildly retarded and mildly emotionally disturbed do not serve those children better than regular class placement. Nor, it should be pointed out, do those classes markedly impair academic performance. If the empirical findings are correct, special education assignment has little effect on student achievement.

Studies of ability grouping generally reach a similar conclusion: differentiation on the basis of ability does not improve student achievement. It improves the performance of the brightest only slightly (and only for some academic subjects), while slightly impairing the school performance of average and slow students.[44] William Borg, whose tracking study is perhaps the most careful yet undertaken, found that:

... neither ability grouping with acceleration nor random grouping with enrichment is superior for all ability levels of elementary school pupils. In general, the relative achievement advantages of the two grouping systems were slight, but tended to favor ability grouping for superior pupils and random grouping for slow pupils.[45]

The National Education Association, surveying the tracking literature, concludes: "Despite its increasing popularity, there is a notable lack of empirical evidence to support the use of ability grouping as an instructional arrangement in the public schools."[46]

The premises of ability grouping are in many respects similar to those of special education programs. Both assume the relative immutability of learning capacity; both structure educational offerings to match what is presumed to be the maximum capacity of the child. While students do change tracks, the amount of such movement appears relatively small—prediction of student ability becomes its proof as well. James Coleman has made a similar point:

The idea inherent in the new [ability-grouped] secondary school curriculum appears to have been to take as given the diverse occupational paths into which adolescents will go after sec-

---

[43] Feuerstein, p. 345; cf. Aubrey Yates, *Behavior Therapy*, (New York: John Wiley and Sons, 1970), p. 324.
[44] See, e.g., Findley and Bryan, pp. 23–31.
[45] Borg, p. 30.
[46] NEA Research Division, p. 44.

ondary school, and to say (implicitly): there is greater equality of educational opportunity for a boy who is not going to attend college if he has a specially-designed curriculum than if he must take a curriculum designed for college entrance.

There is only one difficulty with this definition: it takes as *given* what should be problematic—that a given boy is going into a given post-secondary occupational or educational path.[47]

These studies define the effects of school sorting in terms of test-measured achievement. A quite different approach considers the effect of sorting on subtler measures of attitude and outlook, examining the possibility that certain classifications function to stigmatize students.

Stigmatization

Stigma, which Erving Goffman calls "an undesired differentness," is a fact of social life.[48] In American society, no class is officially branded outcast; indeed, the concept of equality which theoretically governs democratic social relations refuses to recognize any class-based traits. Nonetheless, for segments of the society, labels as varied as "blind," "Negro," "homosexual," or "convict" convey broadly accepted social stigmas.

A stigma is not inherently value-laden: the stigmatizing attribute is neither creditable nor discreditable *per se*. Its value lies in how people perceive it—that is, its socially accepted meaning. For example, the polygamist fulfills his traditional Mormon duty, yet he also violates American norms. Stigma is thus properly defined in relational terms.

Stigmatization, whether formal or informal, facilitates interaction with certain types of individuals by prescribing appropriate social strategies for managing encounters with them. Society pities the blind, shuns the criminal, disdains the homosexual, all without reference to the personal qualities which complicate the labeling process. Individual differences are subsumed under the common, negatively perceived attributes.

Even in an egalitarian society, some stigmas are legitimately imposed through official action. The convicted murderer is labeled and punished for a deed which society feels deserving of punishment. His or her stigma is justified as a form of social control. This process, which might be termed just or permissible social stigma-

[47] James Coleman, "The Concept of Equality of Educational Opportunity," *Harvard Educational Review*, 38 (Winter 1968), pp. 7–23.
[48] Erving Goffman, *Stigma: Notes on the Management of Spoiled Identity* (Englewood Cliffs, N.J.: Prentice-Hall, 1963).

tization, is so basic to society that it typically passes unnoticed. Yet there are other more subtle stigmas, equally real and debilitating, which are officially imposed by the state. Many laws classify: they divide the world into classes of people, only some of whom are eligible for or benefit from particular treatment. And many classifications can be said to stigmatize: zoning laws perpetuate a "wrong side of the tracks"; licensing laws separate the qualified from the charlatan. The agency which creates these classifications may well not intend this result. It is more likely to be interested in providing humane treatment or in securing administrative ease. Involuntary confinement in mental hospitals and even the incarceration of criminals, for example, are asserted to be rehabilitative. Yet in understanding stigma, motive matters less than consequences. The relevant inquiry is whether individuals are effectively branded in a manner which they and those with whom they come into contact regard as undesirable.

Many of the classifications that schools impose on students are stigmatizing. However well-motivated or complex the decision leading to a particular classification, the classification lends itself to simplified labels. The slow learner or special student becomes a "dummy." The student excluded from the school system is an outcast, "told . . . that he is unfit to be where society has determined all acceptable citizens of his age should be."[49]

For many children, adverse school classification is particularly painful because it is novel. It represents the first formal revelation of differences between them and other children. The school's inclination to cope with a particular learning or social problem by isolating those who share that problem reinforces children's sense of stigma. Children perceive all too well what the school's label means. Jane Mercer observes that those assigned to special education classes "were ashamed to be seen entering the MR room because they were often teased by other children about being MR . . . [and] dreaded receiving mail that might bear compromising identification."[50]

Differences among children clearly exist, and it would be educational folly to ignore them: to treat everyone in exactly the same fashion benefits no one. Yet the consequence of the schools' classification remains an awesome fact with which the child must cope. Its psychological ramifications extend beyond the child: they reach his family, and others with whom the child has contact. The child

[49] William Buss, "Procedural Due Process for School Discipline: Probing the Constitutional Outline," *University of Pennsylvania Law Review*, 119 (February 1971), pp. 545–577.
[50] Mercer, "Sociocultural Factors."

assigned to a special education class or a slow learners' group discovers that his society is totally altered. His differentness is what matters most to the school.

The stigma is further exacerbated by the school's curriculum. The curriculum offered to the slow or special child is less demanding than that provided for normal children. Even if children assigned to the special class do creditable work, they fall further behind the school norm. The initial assignment becomes a self-fulfilling prophecy[51]: children's belief in their inferiority is reinforced by the knowledge that they are increasingly unable to return to the regular school program. Because classmates and teachers make fewer demands on such children (for by definition less can be expected of the handicapped than the normal), they come to accept others' assessments of their potential. As one student in a slow track said: "All the kids here are victims. They've finally believed it."[52]

The effects of school-imposed stigmas do not cease when the child leaves school, for schools are society's most active labelers. Slow track assignment makes college entrance nearly impossible and may discourage employers from offering jobs; assignment to a special education program forecloses vocational options. While many children labeled retarded by the school do come to lead normal lives, the stigma persists.[53] For the children who cannot escape their past—as by moving from the South to the North to seek employment, leaving all school records except a diploma behind them—the retarded label may stick for life.

Constitutional Standards

The fact that certain school classifications—exclusion, special education, and slow track placement—do not benefit and may well injure students readily evokes the policy conclusion that such sorting is educationally dubious practice. Yet bad policy is not necessarily, or even usually, unconstitutional policy.[54] If the transition

[51] Gallagher.

[52] "Putting the Child in its Place," Unpublished paper, Harvard Center for Law and Education, 1972, p. 41.

[53] See Robert Edgerton, *The Cloak of Competence: Stigma in the Lives of the Mentally Retarded* (Berkeley, Cal.: University of California Press, 1967).

[54] Under the traditional equal protection doctrine, courts uphold legislatively imposed classifications which "bear some rational relationship to a legitimate state end." McDonald v. Board of Election Commissioners 394 U.S. 802, 809 (1969); see "Developments in the Law—Equal Protection," *Harvard Law Review*, 82 (March, 1969), pp. 1976–87. This standard results in near-total deference to legislative discretion. The constitutional safeguard is offended only if the classification rests on grounds wholly irrelevant to the achievement of the state's objective. State legislatures are presumed to have acted within their constitutional power despite the fact that, in practice, their laws result in some inequality. A statutory discrimination will not be set aside if any state of acts reasonably may be conceived to justify it. McGowan v. Maryland, 366 U.S. 420, 425–26 (1961).

could be so effortlessly made, courts would in fact function as super-legislatures. If, however, the interests at stake are closely linked to constitutionally guaranteed rights, or if the class of assertedly injured persons is demonstrably vulnerable to abuse by the majority, then the claim that particular policies operate unequitably becomes more susceptible to judicial analysis. In a challenge to school sorting, the possible bases for such judicial treatment are, first, inequitable deprivation of education—an important, if not a "fundamental" interest[55]—and second, the status of children, a class of individuals who deserve the protection of the courts in securing their rights.

San Antonio Unified School District v. Rodriguez[56] casts considerable doubt on the vitality of constitutional arguments premised on the importance of education. In that case, a closely divided Supreme Court concluded that wealth-based disparities in the financing of public education did not offend the equal protection clause of the Constitution. The Supreme Court affirmed its "historic dedication to public education,"[57] yet could find no constitutional warrant for distinguishing educational inequities from inequities in the provision of any other publicly-supported good or service. Having identified no special status for education explicit or implicit in the Constitution, the Court proceeded to apply the traditional equal protection test—to determine whether the goals implicit in state financing schemes were rational, and whether the means adopted by the state reasonably furthered the state's legislative goal.

The *Rodriguez* analysis is profoundly troubling. Even if education is not of fundamental moment, it clearly bears upon the exercise of constitutionally guaranteed rights. For that reason, in reviewing assertions of inequity the Court should be able to distinguish education from regulation of economic interests, where the lenient standard of rationality historically has been applied. Indeed, in a host of cases—particularly involving state legislation which assertedly diminished the individual's right to privacy—the Court has, under the guise of rationality, applied a more stringent standard of judicial review. That approach does not, as the majority opinion suggests, require the Court "to create substantive con-

---

[55] San Antonio Independent School District v. Rodriguez, 93 S.Ct. 1278 (1973). Where courts have identified an interest as fundamental they have required the state to show: a) that its interest in classifying is "compelling"; b) that the means chosen to effectuate that interest are less onerous than available alternatives. See "Developments in the Law—Equal Protection." The result of applying such a test is predictable; the complainant invariably wins. See, e.g., Shapiro v. Thompson, 394 U.S. 618, 634 (1969); Loving v. Virginia, 388 U.S. 1, 9 (1967).

[56] 93 S. Ct. 1278 (1973).

[57] *Id.* at 1295.

stitutional rights in the name of guaranteeing equal protection of the laws,"[58] or "mark an extraordinary departure from principled adjudication under the Equal Protection Clause of the Fourteenth Amendment."[59] Instead, as Justice Marshall's dissent notes, it calls for a determination of "the extent to which constitutionally guaranteed rights are dependent on interests not mentioned in the Constitution,"[60] requiring the Court to consider "[w]hat legitimate state interest does the classification promote? What fundamental personal rights might the classification endanger?"[61]

In rejecting the claim that education is of fundamental constitutional significance, *Rodriguez* appears to foreclose all challenges to inequities in the provision of education—or, at least, inequities which are neither racial in nature nor represent complete denial of schooling. Yet the analytic formula that the Court adopts is unsatisfactory, at least in part because it *is* a formula. It seems more constitutionally appropriate (if less result-oriented) to review each assertedly adverse educational classification in order to determine whether it suitably furthers an appropriate governmental interest. This approach would "close the wide gap between the strict scrutiny of the new equal protection and the minimal scrutiny of the old not by abandoning the strict but by raising the level of the minimal from virtual abdication to genuine judicial inquiry."[62]

If such an approach were to be adopted by a court considering the constitutionality of school sorting practices, the possibility of successful challenge would be strong. The very factors which link education to rights guaranteed by the Constitution—political participation, the capacity to frame and express individual points of view—seem to be directly affected by school classification. This cause-and-effect relationship between the impact of the injury and the nature of the right is most readily established with respect to school exclusion. Since exclusion represents a total deprivation of schooling, all of education's benefits are necessarily denied the excluded child. Special education or slow learner assignment presumably also affects subsequent opportunities for political participation and intellectual growth, although the link is not so easily fashioned.

That the rights of children are affected by school classification may also be

[58] *Id.* at 1297.

[59] *Id.* at 1310 (Stewart, J., concurring).

[60] *Id.* at 1332 (Marshall, J., dissenting).

[61] Weber v. Aetna Casualty & Surety Co., 406 U.S. 164, 173 (1972).

[62] Gerald Gunther, "The Supreme Court, 1971 Term-Forward: In Search of Evolving Doctrine on a Changing Court: A Model for a Newer Equal Protection," *Harvard Law Review*, 86 (November, 1972), p. 24.

of constitutional significance. There is reason for the courts to treat with special judicial solicitude the constitutional claims of children, requiring a degree of inquiry greater than a determination of mere rationality but less demanding than insistence upon compelling justification for inequalities.

The status of children is unique in the legal system. Because of their age, children cannot pursue their interests through political avenues. Nor can they directly seek redress through the courts; they must be represented by an adult, typically a parent, whom the law presumes will act on their behalf. Their lives are managed and directed to an extent that adults would find intolerable. Educational decisions are routinely made by the state: in almost all states children are compelled to attend school for at least nine years. This initial compulsion serves as a basis for the imposition of further constraints.

Most remarkable has been the ease with which the state has been able to justify its imposition of values on those occasions when its interests and those of children collide. For example, the Supreme Court has held that the distribution of religious literature, fit activity for adults, impairs the health and welfare of children,[63] books suitable for adult consumption cannot be sold to children, whose moral growth might be stunted.[64] In each case, the Court has viewed children's interests in liberty as conflicting with the state's general concern for the well-being of children; in resolving that conflict, children have lost. It is instructive that the Supreme Court only four years ago declared explicitly for the first time that children "are 'persons' under our Constitution."[65] Their rights as persons have been minimal.[66]

Courts have recently begun to recognize the civil rights of children independent of the rights of their parents. *Tinker v. Des Moines Independent Community School District*,[67] which asserted the first amendment rights of children, is of course the leading case. *Weber v. Aetna Casualty & Surety Co.*[68] reveals

---

[63] Prince v. Massachusetts, 321 U.S. 158 (1944).

[64] Ginsberg v. New York, 390 U.S. 629 (1968).

[65] Tinker v. Des Moines Independent Community School District, 393 U.S. 503, 511 (1969).

[66] Even *In re* Gault, 397 U.S. 1 (1967), typically eulogized as protecting children from the excesses of juvenile justice, affords the child only a watered-down version of constitutional procedural protection. Earlier cases dealing with what could have been viewed as the rights of children were instead decided on the basis of the rights of parents or teachers. See, e.g., Pierce v. Society of Sisters, 268 U.S. 510 (1925); Meyer v. Nebraska, 262 U.S. 390 (1923). Even West Virginia State Board of Education v. Barnette, 319 U.S. 624 (1943), which came closest to recognizing an independent right in the child, also involved prosecution of the parents.

[67] 393 U.S. 503 (1969).

[68] 406 U.S. 164 (1972).

judicial concern for the rights of one class of children—those born out of wed-lock. In at least two other kinds of cases, lower courts also have explicitly recog-nized children's personal rights. The Supreme Court of Pennsylvania, in a case involving the right of a Jehovah's Witness to refuse medical treatment for her sixteen-year-old child where the child's life was not in imminent danger, re-manded for a hearing to ascertain the wishes of the child.[69] In *Chandler v. South Bend Community School Corp.*,[70] a federal district court upheld the in-dependent interests of children in education. The district court, which struck down a school policy of suspending students and withholding their report cards unless their parents either paid a textbook fee or established their indigency, declared: "The school fee collection procedure ... conditions [children's] *per-sonal* right to an education upon the vagaries of their parents' conduct, an in-tolerable practice . . . ."[71]

The claim that adverse and harmful school classifications deny equal protec-tion recognizes another interest of children: a concern for educational choice, for securing the maximum liberty possible within the constraints of a compul-sory school system. Children are both too unformed and too precious to be treated arbitrarily by the state. This claim of worth, and the family's interest in securing the child's individuality, has received passing judicial recognition.[72] It underlies the Court's observation in *Tinker* that children may not be viewed as "closed-circuit recipients of only that which the State chooses to communicate."[73] This proposition logically applies with ever greater force to school instruction than to political activities which happen to transpire in the schoolhouse. The pre-sumed equality of all children provides strong basis for contesting actions which threaten that equality by restricting the child's potential for growth.

Applying the Constitutional Standard

Not all school classifications assume equal importance in the life of a child. Exclusion, ability grouping, and assignment to special education have been sin-gled out as the three most consequential sortings, and thus are most likely to warrant judicial inquiry. The important distinctions among these classifications suggest that the application of a constitutional standard should differ for each.

[69] *In re Green*, 448 Pa. 338, 292 A.2d 387 (1972).
[70] Civil No. 71–S–51 (N.D. Ind., October 22, 1971).
[71] *Id.* at 5.
[72] See, e.g., Pierce v. Society of Sisters, 268 U.S. 510 (1925); Meyer v. Nebraska, 262 U.S. 390 (1923).
[73] Tinker v. Des Moines Independent Community School District, 393 U.S. 503, 511 (1969).

School exclusion, the most extreme classification, is the simplest to confront in legal terms. Exclusion represents the complete denial of a service. Even if education plays only a marginal role in shaping opportunities, denial of education is not a trivial matter: without instruction, children are unlikely to reinvent physics or reading. In addition, exclusion based on a judgment of ineducability is likely to cause irreversible harm to both the child's achievement and psyche. Thus, even without a showing of actual injury, courts can hold that exclusion from school is unconstitutional as a denial of equal protection. Several courts appear to have adopted this theory[74]; most prominently, in *Mills v. Board of Education*, the district court ordered that the Washington, D.C. school system readmit all excluded children "regardless of the degree of the child's mental, physical or emotional disability or impairment."[75]

All that excluded children can constitutionally demand is access to some form of publicly supported education and special assistance to permit them to overcome the school-imposed handicap. To insist on more, to require as a matter of constitutional law that the school system make an educationally "correct" placement, calls on the court to treat complex judgments of educational needs in constitutional terms, a position that courts will be justifiably reluctant to adopt. As one federal district court noted, in a somewhat different context, "[T]here are no discoverable and manageable standards by which the court can determine when the Constitution is satisfied and when it is violated."[76] Yet the two district courts which have confronted the issue of exclusion based on asserted ineducability have, in defining a remedy, spoken in terms of individual needs and appropriate placement, leaving those matters in the hands of a court-appointed master or school officials.[77] That remedial approach assures that the educational opportunity that is in fact offered is not meaningless and unusable; it tailors the remedy to fit the constitutionally cognizable harm.

[74] See, e.g., San Antonio Independent School District v. Rodriguez, 93 S. Ct. 1278, 1298–99 (1973) (dictum) (denial of educational service); Shapiro v. Thompson, 394 U.S. 618, 633 (1969) (dictum) (exclusion of indigents); Ordway v. Hargreaves, 323 F. Supp. 1155 (D. Mass. 1971) (exclusion of pregnant students); Hosier v. Evans, 314 F. Supp. 316 (D.V.1, 1970) (exclusion of aliens).

[75] 348 F. Supp. 866, 878 (D.D.C. 1972); *accord*, Wolf v. Legislature. Civil No. 182, 646 (Utah District Court, January 8, 1969) [reprinted in *Classification Materials*, p. 171]; see Harrison v. Michigan, 350 F. Supp. 846 (E.D. Michigan 1972) (dictum).

[76] McInnis v. Shapiro, 293 F. Supp. 327, 335 (N.D. Ill. 1968). aff'd mem. sub. nom. McInnis v. Ogilvie, 394 U.S. 322 (1969). See also Burruss v. Wilkerson, 310 F. Supp. 572 (W.D. Va. 1969), aff'd mem., 397 U.S. 44 (1970).

[77] Mills v. Board of Education, 348 F. Supp. 866 (D.D.C. 1972); Pennsylvania Association for Retarded Children v. Pennsylvania, 343 F. Supp. 279 (E.D. Pa. 1972) (consent order).

Challenges to within-school classifications pose more difficult constitutional problems. They demand that a court weight the different benefits and costs associated with varied educational approaches, a task usually—and quite properly—left to educators. The difficulty is compounded because the balancing process is riddled with ambiguity. If, for example, few students return from special to regular classes, does the explanation lie with the structure of the educational offering or the capacities of the child? As the court of appeals' decision in *Hobson* notes: "In some cases statistics are ineluctably ambiguous in their import—the fact that only a small percentage of pupils are reassigned [from slow to faster programs] may indicate either general adequacy of initial assignments or inadequacy of review."[78] How does a court confronted with two equally plausible, but ambiguous, hypotheses which existing evidence can neither affirm nor reject, resolve the issue?

One easy but unsatisfactory solution to such dilemmas is to treat all within-school sorting decisions similarly, as matters of educational discretion beyond the ambit of judicial review. That approach ignores distinctions between the benefits and harms associated with special education placement, on the one hand, and track assignment on the other; these are differences of degree, to be sure, but differences upon which constitutional distinctions can logically rest.

Special education placement is clearly more onerous than tracking. Even the euphemism "special" conveys a judgment of abnormality, which all the well-intentioned efforts to label both the handicapped and the gifted as exceptional children cannot undo. Students with mild disabilities are isolated from their normal peers. They are not routinely considered as candidates for readmission into the mainstream of the educational program. Furthermore, such programs typically present only scaled-down educational offerings, presuming that children placed in them can never hope to be more than marginal members of the society. And often that presumption becomes fact.

These demonstrable harms—stigmatization, diluted educational offerings, and reduced life chances—suggest that special education placement for the mildly handicapped denies those individuals equal educational opportunity. For that reason, in a suit challenging special class placement, it seems appropriate to shift the burden of proof from parents and children to school officials. Once evidence of harm has been introduced, school officials should be required to show that the special education program accomplishes what it is supposed to do: that

[78] Smuck v. Hobson, 408 F.2d 175, 187 (D.C. Circ. 1969).

it sufficiently benefits students to justify the inevitable stigma that attaches to such placement. If benefit cannot be demonstrated, either for particular students or for all those placed in classes for the mildly retarded or handicapped, it makes constitutional (and pedagogical) sense to reassign those students to regular classes, providing them with supplementary instruction to help recapture lost educational ground. The standard seems both manageable and just. Defining justification in terms of efficacy imposes a burden aptly suited to the problem. It also encourages more frequent evaluation of each student's progress, thus assuring that special classes are not transformed into a "penitentiary where one could be held indefinitely for no convicted offense."[79] The demonstrated ineffectiveness of special education programs for the mildly handicapped indicates that few will survive if obliged to prove their mettle.

A successful challenge to placement in inefficacious programs for the educable mentally retarded or mildly emotionally disturbed has a relatively modest and accomplishable goal: the effective integration of those students into the general life of the school. A challenge to tracking, on the other hand, goes to the heart of the educational enterprise. Tracking decisions—unlike special education assignments—reach all students and are not premised on marked differences in the potential of children. For that reason, a general objection of tracking readily converts into an attack on any educational practice which rewards some students while punishing others. If none of the sorting that schools engage in appears to benefit students, why not discard it? Such a question frames the point too broadly, confusing what educators might do with what courts can legitimately do in order to secure equal protection of the laws. Although phrasing a question as one of educational policy does not render the courts impotent to act, the very facts which render research concerning the efficacy of tracking so unsatisfying—tracking's near-universality, its links with other school differentiations, its varied connotations—counsel for judicial restraint rather than potentially disruptive action.

A challenge to tracking on grounds that it impairs equality of educational opportunity may well be a disguised demand that schools eliminate disparities between student outcomes. The difficulty with that demand is simply that it cannot be accomplished through any educationally sound and administratively feasible remedy presently available. Since individuals' capabilities clearly differ, it would be a cruel hoax, a "deceit of equality,"[80] to premise a challenge to tracking on the

---

[79] Ragsdale v. Overholser, 281 F.2d 943, 950 (D.C. Cir. 1960) (concurring opinion).
[80] Michael Young, *The Rise of the Meritocracy* (New York: Penguin Books, 1961), p. 49.

argument that tracking caused school failure, implicitly promising that the educational differences would vanish if tracking were done away with. The example of Washington, D.C. is instructive here. The holding, in *Hobson v. Hansen*,[81] that tracking as practiced in the District of Columbia must "simply be abolished," has had little if any impact. School officials—relying on the court of appeals decision in *Hobson*, which limited the applicability of the district court order to the existing tracking system while permitting "full scope for . . . ability grouping"[82]—simply changed the label and retained the full panoply of student differentiation.

IQ Tests: the Facilitators of Classification

The fact that tracking should not be judicially abolished unless harm can be empirically demonstrated does not imply that all issues linked with ability grouping should be skirted by the courts. Even if the assumptions underlying tracking prove correct—or, more likely, unverifiable—the mechanisms of sorting may be defective. The resulting risk of mistreating students necessitates a careful examination of sorting devices such as tests, grades, or teacher recommendations.

School systems employ a host of factors in determining how to sort students. Past performance in school, student willingness to adapt to the particular classroom regime laid down by the teacher, or parental intervention—all play some part in determining whether a given student is assigned to a regular or slow class for the coming year.

Yet schools do use more objective measures of ability; IQ tests carry great weight in determining the child's educational future. In many school systems, IQ tests form the primary basis for sorting decisions. Students who score between 55 and 75 are assigned to classes for the educable mentally retarded; students who score between 75 and 90 are placed in slow learners groups; and so on.[83]

---

[81] 269 F. Supp. 401 (D.D.C. 1967).

[82] Smuck v. Hobson, 408 F.2d 175, 189 (D.C. Cir. 1969) (en banc).

[83] The following table, taken from Alfred Baumeister, *Mental Retardation: Appraisal, Education, and Rehabilitation* (Chicago: Aldine, 1967), p. 10, describes a system of classifying retardedness according to scores on two generally accepted IQ tests:

	I.Q. Range	
Level of Retardation	Stanford-Binet Test	Wechsler Test
Borderline	68–83	70–84
Mild	52–67	55–69
Moderate	36–51	40–54
Severe	20–35	25–39
Profound	below 20	below 25

These tests are at least nominally objective: they purport to measure factors other than such admittedly irrelevant ones as teacher prejudice and social class. They are also decent predictors of subsequent school success, better than school grades, teacher recommendations, or parental pressure. IQ tests do measure with considerable accuracy the adaptability of a given student to the school's expectations.[84]

IQ tests and the uses to which they are put have been sharply criticized on varying grounds. Their questions are ambiguous, a trap for those who rightly recognize that more than one answer may be correct. They treat intelligence (or, more accurately, school intelligence) in aggregate terms, failing to recognize that a given student is likely to be competent at some things but not at others, and that combining those strengths and weaknesses into a single score inaccurately describes and oversimplifies the notion of intelligence. They fail to measure "adaptive behavior," the capacity to survive in society. The tests also do not indicate *why* a given student did poorly in a particular subject, and thus provide no basis for educational intervention to improve performance.[85] Finally, these tests define intelligence in static, not dynamic terms: they fail to account for the "uneven growth patterns of individual children."[86]

Those who design IQ tests rightly argue that many of these criticisms are properly directed not at the tests but at those who use them. IQ tests need not be employed in punitive, prophecy-confirming ways; test results can be of some use in developing appropriate educational strategies. Yet too often the tests are misused: a single score becomes the basis for student assignment to a particular track from which there is no escape until the next test is administered. The schools' apparent incapacity to test students accurately makes test administration appear even more dubious.[87]

---

[84] See Anne Anastasi, "Some Implications of Cultural Factors for Test Construction," in *Testing Problems in Perspective,* ed. Anne Anastasi (Washington, D.C.: American Council on Education, 1966), pp. 453–456. The predictive validity of aptitude tests is far from perfect. "[T]he correlation between elementary school test scores and eventual educational attainment [years of schooling completed] seems to have hovered just under 0.60 for some decades." Jencks *et al.,* p. 144.

[85] See, e.g., Banesh Hoffman, *The Tyranny of Testing* (New York: Crowell-Collier Press, 1962); Gerald Lesser, Gordon Fifer, and Donald Clark, "Mental Abilities of Children from Different Social Class and Cultural Groups," *Monographs of the Society for Research in Child Development,* 30, Serial No. 102 (1965).

[86] Jane Franseth and Rose Koury, *Survey of Research on Grouping as Related to Pupil Learning,* (Washington, D.C.: U.S. Office of Education, 1966), p. 36.

[87] In Hobson, school psychologists examined 1272 students assigned to the special education or basic track; almost two-thirds of them had been improperly classified by the school system. Smuck v. Hobson, 408 F. 2d 173, 187 (D.C. Cir. 1969), (en banc).

The criticisms of testing acquire particular force when minority children are disproportionately assigned to slower learner groups and educable mentally retarded classes on the basis of IQ test results. Tests are condemned as culturally biased, confirming white middle-class status rather than measuring intellectual potential. The deficiencies of such tests were the basis on which Judge Wright overturned the Washington, D.C. tracking system. The court viewed the tests as "a most important consideration in making track assignments,"[88] concluding that "standardized aptitude tests. . . produce inaccurate and misleading test scores when given to lower class and Negro students,"[89] and that the school system had not advanced any more culturally neutral sorting alternatives.

For the advocate bent on undoing school classifications, an attack on testing holds considerable appeal. If it can be shown that IQ tests do not measure intelligence, the argument for sorting based primarily on the results of such tests collapses, and the basis for differential treatment becomes simply irrational. The difficulty with that approach rests in its failure to distinguish careful from careless test use. Tests can indicate something about a student's capacity to perform. They do not reveal, but merely remind, that non-middle-class and minority children fare badly in schools as they presently are organized.

When they are abused, testing processes are properly amenable to judicial scrutiny. The practice of administering tests in English to students whose native language is Spanish, and using the results as a measure of ability is simply indefensible; the scores of those students are, at best, only a proxy for acculturation into the dominant culture. Further, when test scores serve as the primary basis for student assignment, their use becomes more suspect.

The importance that is attached to a single test is also constitutionally significant. Achievement tests, which purport to measure subject matter competence and not ability, are appropriately employed to group children in a particular subject for a limited time. But the use of tests to track students for a period of years—prohibiting either cross-tracking (which recognizes the varied abilities of any given student) or limiting egress from slow tracks—should raise considerable judicial suspicion.

Flexibility, test reliance, and the use of tests to identify particular learning difficulties all represent matters of careful and complex judgment. For a court to insist on them requires the elaboration of distinctions between appropriate

---

[88] Hobson v. Hansen, 269 F. Supp. 401, 475 (D.D.C. 1967).
[89] 269 F. Supp. at 514.

and dangerous testing practices, avoiding the easier but inappropriate judicial alternatives of either abolishing IQ testing or treating testing questions as unmanageable. As long as some sorting is to be permitted (and sorting is likely to persist no matter what courts or school administrators might require), judgments about ability will necessarily be difficult to defend with precision. Nevertheless, since classification decisions greatly affect a student's educational career, schools should bear the legal burden of demonstrating that the IQ tests upon which many of those decisions are premised can reliably predict school performance for different types of students.

Racial Over-representation

Few schools sort students explicitly on the basis of race. Classification in large systems is routinely handled by school officials who know nothing about a given student except his or her academic record. When counselors discuss appropriate track placement with their students, their recommendations are premised on estimates of student ability and school needs. The grounds on which school personnel defend sorting reveal no apparent racial motivation.

Yet school sorting does in fact have racially specific consequences. It tends to concentrate minority children in less advanced school programs. While racial disproportionality does not characterize programs for students with readily identifiable handicaps (for example, classes for the trainable mentally retarded or the blind), the proportion of minority students in lower tracks and special education programs is typically two or three times greater than their proportion of the school-age population. Racial disproportionality also appears to have a particularly damaging impact on the attitudes and verbal achievement of minority students. The limited available evidence suggests that overrepresentation in these less advanced programs may be particularly harmful in minority students.[90] Although few studies have examined the racially specific harm of sorting, one

[90] The special education and ability grouping research discussed in the context of equal educational opportunity arguments was carried out either in white or racially unspecified communities, and thus is of limited relevance. Since *Equality of Educational Opportunity* (Washington, D.C.: U.S. Office of Education, 1966), provides student performance information for only one point in time, it is difficult to mine that richest of education data sources for evidence of the consequences of reassigning students from one group to another. Cf., e.g., Marshall Smith, "Equality of Educational Opportunity: The Basic Findings Reconsidered," in *On Equality of Educational Opportunity*, eds. Frederick Mosteller and Daniel Moynihan (New York: Random House, 1972), pp. 69, 239, 313–315. (The report does not tell scholars and policymakers "what will happen if they change the status quo.")

reanalysis of *Equality of Educational Opportunity* did attempt to assess the impact of within-school segregation on the verbal achievement of black students. It concluded that while *school* integration does not benefit blacks, *classroom* integration does. "[C]lassroom desegregation has an apparent beneficial effect on Negro student verbal achievement no matter what the racial enrollment of the school."[91] The United States Civil Rights Commission's re-examination of the Coleman data noted a subtler (and difficult to document) effect of within-school segregation: black students in nominally integrated schools, "accorded separate treatment, with others of their race, . . . felt inferior and stigmatized."[92] Such within-school segregation was perceived as having been based upon personal and pejorative judgments of ability.

The constitutional implications of these racially specific consequences of school sorting are not self-evident. Racial classifications typically run afoul of the Constitution if they result either from explicit legislative mandate[93] (as in the school desegregation cases) or from the discriminatory application of an apparently neutral legislative scheme.[94] The latter can be seen in the efforts of formerly dual school systems to couple desegregation with the adoption of an ability grouping scheme. In those instances, the motivation for initiating tracking is quite probably racial. The fact that segregated schools have typically provided black students with fewer school resources than their white classmates suggests that such discrimination would be likely to recur in an ability-grouped school. Since grouping inhibits school desegregation, it violates those districts' obligation to desegregate "at once."[95]

In most school systems, however, the overrepresentation of minority students in lower tracks stems neither from statutory command nor from discriminatory

[91] James McPartland, "The Relative Influence of School and Classroom Desegregation on the Academic Achievement of Ninth Grade Negro Students," *Journal of Social Issues*, 25 (Summer 1969), p. 102. Tracking decisions also appear to have more significant effects for blacks than whites. While half of all white children assigned to a college track actually enter college, only a third of whites in non-college tracks continue their education beyond high school. For blacks, the likelihood of college attendance is diminished even further by assignment to a non-college track. Jencks *et al.*, pp. 156–58.

[92] *Racial Isolation in the Public Schools* (Washington, D.C.: U.S. Commission on Civil Rights, 1967), pp. 86–87.

[93] See, e.g., Loving v. Virginia, 388 U.S. 1 (1967).

[94] Yick Wo v. Hopkins, 118 U.S. 356 (1886). Cases concerning jury discrimination, see, e.g., Turner v. Fouche, 396 U.S. 346 (1970), and municipal services discrimination, see, e.g., Hawkins v. Town of Shaw, 437 F.2d 1286 (5th Cir. 1971), *aff'd en banc* 461 F.2d 1171 (5th Cir. 1972), have focused on discriminatory application of ostensibly neutral policies.

[95] Alexander v. Holmes County Board of Education, 396 U.S. 19, 20 (1969).

practice. It is, rather, an unintended consequence of a policy whose premises are meritocratic, not racial; the disproportionality is inadvertent.[96] Such unintended disproportionalities have not been recognized by the courts as necessarily stating a valid cause of action under the equal protection clause. In *Jefferson v. Hackney*, the Supreme Court was confronted with the contention that Texas' welfare policy was constitutionally suspect because it provided a less adequate subsidy for the Aid for Dependent Children (AFDC) program, whose beneficiaries were primarily black, than for welfare programs whose recipients were primarily white. The contention was dismissed as a "naked statistical argument."[97]

In many instances, such curt treatment of claims premised solely on disproportionate racial impact seems proper. Except for those rare governmental actions which treat all persons uniformly, every statute classifies on some basis. And in all save the statistically freakish instance, an inadvertent consequence of that classification may be racial: for example, government-subsidized research on the causes of sickle cell anemia is of primary concern to blacks; in a residentially segregated city, some municipal bus routes will attract more black passengers while others carry mostly whites. Surely such effects do not call for the compelling state justification demanded where racial discrimination can be proved.

Yet in considering the racial consequences of school sorting, the *Jefferson* standard is inappropriate for several reasons. Regardless of the presence or absence of racial motivation, the disproportionate impact of school sorting links race with education. Courts have long recognized the harm done by state-mandated school segregation. What differentiates school sorting from the run of desegregation cases is not the fact of harm—indeed, the evidence that within-school desegregation is educationally damaging is, if anything, stronger than the inherent or empirically demonstrated harm upon which *Brown* rests—but the nature of the state's responsibility in the two cases. Yet judicial inquiry involves more than blame-attaching; it also attends to the fact of harm.

The expansive view of state responsibility for school segregation adopted by several northern federal courts may be premised on just such considerations. Those courts have looked at the racial consequences of ostensibly neutral poli-

---

[96] The possibility that tracking might produce such segregation apparently did not concern those who argued *Brown*. As Thurgood Marshall said: "I have no objection to academic segregation, only racial segregation. If they want to put all the dumb ones, white and black, into the same school that is fine, provided they put all the smart ones, white and black, into the same school." Jack Peltason, *Fifty-eight Lonely Men: Southern Federal Judges and School Desegregation* (New York: Harcourt, Brace, Jovanovitch, 1961), p. 112.

[97] 406 U.S. 535, 548 (1972).

cies—school boundary-setting, construction, teacher assignment and the like—and have been willing to infer state action from a finding of racially isolating effect. They suggest that a school district may be held to answer for the foreseeable consequences of its actions (and even its failure to act). What makes these decisions defensible is not the legal legerdemain which converts inaction into action, color blindness into culpability, but the fact that segregation, whatever its source, may inflict real and perceived injury.

The educational harm caused by disproportionate placement of minority students in the least advanced of educational programs is in part racially specific. That proportionately more blacks than whites populate the lower tracks and special education classes has more than statistical significance. If the reanalyses of the *Equality of Educational Opportunity* data are to be credited, such assignments affect blacks more harshly than they do whites; the injury has racial connotations. That fact distinguishes school sorting from such governmental actions as the Texas welfare policy affirmed in *Jefferson* which, while hurting more blacks than whites, hurts the individual black no more than her or his white counterpart.

The argument that minorities deserve special judicial solicitude because of their vulnerability to majoritarian abuse,[98] so frequently advanced in cases involving racial discrimination, assumes particular force in the context of school classifications. Track assignment (unlike, for example, welfare roll-trimming) is not a general, public decision around which the far from voiceless black political leadership can coalesce. It is, in form if not in fact, not a political issue at all but an individual judgment of intellectual worth which the black parent feels particularly powerless to challenge.

These factors—that racially disproportionate sorting does plausible educational harm and affects a vulnerable minority—suggest that judicial attention is appropriate. Once significant racial disproportionality has been shown, a school district should be obliged to demonstrate that its classifications serve substantial independent educational purposes.

[98] The source of this argument remains United States v. Carolene Products Co., 304 U.S. 144, 152–53 n. 4 (1938): "[P]rejudice against discrete and insular minorities may be a special condition, which tends seriously to curtail the operation of those political processes ordinarily to be relied upon to protect minorities, and which may call for a correspondingly more searching judicial inquiry." That the claims of minorities do not always entitle them to such protection is made clear in Whitcomb v. Chavis, 403 U.S. 124, 153 (1971), where the Supreme Court characterized black voters' claims of election district discrimination as embodying the disappointment of political losers, not warranting judicial intervention.

Taken together, however, these factors do not stress discrimination against minority students, but rather speak to the deprivation attributable to racial overrepresentation. This focus on deprivation, not discrimination, has several noteworthy implications. It shifts the analysis from blame-fixing to problem-solving, and thus is less concerned with the causes of injury than with the fact of injury. It limits the utility of the *prima facie* case approach, which fastens on evidence of disproportionate racial impact (with respect to the provision of municipal services, for example) as presumptively demonstrating racial discrimination, substituting an inquiry into the consequences of a school policy which isolates minority students in particular school programs. And it implies that providing identical schooling experiences for minority and white children might be constitutionally appropriate only if such evenhandedness promises to overcome the deprivation upon which the judicial inquiry is premised. The deprivation analysis is, in short, necessarily more fully attentive than traditional approaches to the problem posed by racial overrepresentation in a given school program.

Allegations of disproportionate racial impact in education and employment, couched in deprivation terms, have prompted several courts to shift the burden of demonstrating the efficacy of the classifying device to those responsible for implementing it. However, the analyses set forth in these cases are of limited utility because the courts, while tacitly accepting the deprivation theory for the purpose of shifting the burden of proof, continue to stress discrimination and the traditional equal protection analysis when determining what showing that burden requires.

To Judge J. Skelly Wright, for example, "the fact that those who are being consigned to the lower tracks are the poor and the Negroes" was a "precipitating cause" of the *Hobson v. Hansen* inquiry into the workings of the Washington, D.C. track system.[99] Although the District of Columbia had initiated tracking shortly after it was ordered to dismantle its dual school system, *Hobson* did not treat the grouping scheme as racially motivated. Yet lack of evil motive did not exonerate the school system. As the court declared, "the arbitrary quality of thoughtlessness can be as disastrous and unfair to private rights and the public interest as the perversity of a willful scheme."[100] That black children were most

[99] 269 F. Supp. 401, 513 (D.D.C. 1967).
[100] *Id.* at 497.

likely to be placed in the slowest programs revealed to the court "unmistakable signs of invidious discrimination" which demanded explanation.[101]

While racial overrepresentation provides adequate grounds for judicial scrutiny of school policy, the particular burden imposed in *Hobson* seems inappropriate.

Since by definition the basis of the track system is to classify students according to their ability to learn, the only explanation defendants can legitimately give for the pattern of classification found in the District schools is that it does reflect students' abilities. If the discriminations being made are founded on anything other than that, then the whole premise of tracking collapses and with it any justification for relegating certain students to curricula designed for those of limited abilities.[102]

The critical word here is "ability." If the court is referring to the present level of proficiency, then reliance on IQ tests to classify students might well be rational. *Hobson*, however, equates ability with "innate capacity to learn," and correctly concludes that IQ tests do not reveal such inherited traits.[103] But few school officials would ever claim to base sorting decisions on grounds of innate capacity. The premise of tracking (and classification generally) is that, whatever the source of the differences, students with particular and varied learning styles and abilities require the special assistance that only a differentiated curriculum can offer. That premise does not countenance discrimination, except in the non-pejorative (and non-legal) use of that word. Whether or not classification does serve those varied needs, or indeed has any educational consequences, is the crucial question for one concerned with school-caused deprivation. But the *Hobson* court's analytic misstep—equating ability with innate characteristics, and stressing discrimination rather than deprivation—prevented it from confronting the question. The abolition of tracking remedy which followed from the court's analysis may have been unresponsive to the problem at hand.

Analytic difficulties also plagued *Larry P. v. Riles*,[104] a suit challenging San Francisco's special education assignment policy as racially biased. In that case, the district court asked only that school personnel provide a rational defense of their classification procedure. But the judicial inquiry was far more exacting

---

[101] *Id.* at 513.
[102] Hobson v. Hansen, 269 F. Supp. 401, 513 (D.D.C. 1967).
[103] *Id.* at 514.
[104] 343 F. Supp. 1306 (N.D. Cal. 1972).

than that typically associated with the requirement of mere rationality. The court dismissed the evidence that intelligence tests were but one of several bases on which placement decisions were made, and asserted that they were the primary criteria for placement in classes for the educable mentally retarded.

More significantly, the court rejected school officials' remarkably candid statement that "the tests, although racially biased, are rationally related to the purpose for which they are used because they are the best means of classification currently available."[105] While "the best . . . available" seems readily equatable with rational practice, the court reframed the issue, in effect penalizing the school authorities for their candor. "[T]he absence of any rational means of identifying children in need of such treatment can hardly render acceptable an otherwise concededly irrational means, such as the IQ test as it is presently administered to black students."[106]

Contrary to the court's implication, however, the fact that other bases for grouping students, such as achievement tests, teacher recommendations, and psychological evaluations, exist does not automatically render the measures employed in San Francisco constitutionally irrational. None of these alternatives is self-evidently preferable to intelligence testing. The standard of review adopted in *Larry P.*, then, is both different from and more demanding than the courts' focus on rational school behavior indicates. The decision in fact calls for a demonstration that the classifying device used has real benefits—that it can predict student performance in school—which justify its continued use. Applying this standard to the racially disproportionate classifications themselves, the burden appropriately placed on the school is to show that its classifications actually serve a substantial educational purpose—that they provide real benefits for the affected students.

A challenge to classification which is based on racially specific consequences poses many of the same judicial dilemmas—notably, problems of proof and remedy—that a nonracial challenge to tracking might create. School officials will have a difficult time establishing that placement in a slow track or special class for the mildly retarded or disturbed does in fact make good its promise of improving school performance. Existing evidence simply does not support the proposition. Thus, the benefit that the present system provides is more candidly described in terms of teachers' and school bureaucrats' needs. While these needs

[105] *Id.* at 1313.
[106] *Id.*

must be kept in mind if a court decision is to be implemented, one can readily imagine educationally promising reforms which would produce neither new crises in the classroom nor administrative chaos.

But what can be done to remedy the deprivation? The seeming intractability of what economists term the "education production function"—the manipulation of school resources in a manner which affects student performance—differentiates education from most state-supported activities. Where discrimination in the provision of municipal services or representation on jury rolls has been proved, the problem in effect defines its own remedy: equalize services, assure minority representation on juries. But no such straightforward relationship between problem and resolution exists for school sorting. It is easier to identify the problem than the remedy. That fact argues against the adoption of a remedial approach which limits the school systems' options by seizing upon a single solution as necessarily appropriate. A racial quota system for school classifications or court-ordered abolition of sorting are equally misguided remedies, albeit for different reasons.

In *Larry P.*, plaintiffs proposed that "the percentage of black students in EMR classes could exceed the percentage of black students in the school district as a whole by no more than fifteen percent."[107] Such an approach is undesirable, for although it criticizes the racial implications, it embraces and sustains existing classifications whose pedagogical benefits are at best dubious. To the arbitrariness of existing sorting practice it adds another level of arbitrariness, responding not to real educational differences but to statistical nicety.

To require wholesale randomization of classes seems equally unwise. In a given sixth grade class, the most advanced student may be reading at a ninth grade level, the slowest at a third grade pace; a uniform curriculum could not hope to confront such variation. It is tempting, but incorrect, to jump from the assertion that existing classifications mislabel and miseducate students to the remedy of doing away with all efforts to identify and intelligently address differences among students.

Judicial insistence on a modification of existing classifications, which seeks both to reduce racial overrepresentation in less advanced groups and to secure greater flexibility in grouping, represents a far better approach. That standard leaves the school district free to adopt a variety of grouping alternatives taking account of varied student needs, while not locking students into a tracked strait

[107] 343 F. Supp. 1306, 1314 (N.D. Cal. 1972).

jacket. Given the existing uncertainty concerning the causes and cures of this particular deprivation, the command of reconsideration and flexibility has considerable virtue.

In rethinking and reconstructing its classification system, the school district should focus on three variables, linking remedial efforts in all three areas to develop a more rational and constitutionally justifiable system. First, gross extremes of racial separation should be reduced. Outside of the classroom, in those aspects of school life that are more social than academic (for example, assemblies, athletic events, lunch periods), efforts should be made to promote social mixing.

The second variable is the need for flexibility in the tracking scheme itself. Classification decisions should be based on criteria broader than the usual standardized tests; adaptive behavior, for example, should be taken into account. Placement of students should be reviewed frequently to allow greater mobility. Cross-track integration in those areas that the tests do not measure—music, art, physical education—will increase this flexibility. In the higher grades, testing and tracking by subject, rather than by general ability, will render the structure more rational, while increasing the possibilities of in-class mixing. Larger school systems might consider adopting stratified heterogeneous grouping, which reduces ability disparities within any given classroom, or team teaching with flexible grouping.

Assuming that some classes will remain predominantly segregated, attention should be focused on relieving educational deprivation within the minority-dominated tracks. The most obvious step would be to increase the per student allocation of educational resources in the lower tracks. But the educational benefits of such action remain unclear. Alleviation of racially (or culturally) specific deprivation may require something beyond more resources—the need may be for different resources. Culturally sensitive pedagogical techniques, analogous to the creation of Spanish-language classes for Mexican-Americans, may be employed. The use of pedagogical methods geared to the differences in minority learning patterns and cultural background, if combined with efforts to increase integration and create a more flexible system, should satisfy the valid educational purposes test.

Modification is a vague remedial standard until given substance by a school district plan. It would not necessarily eliminate all instances of racial disproportionality; indeed, it would not be designed to do so. While a modification approach encourages a school system to adopt a sorting scheme which fixes less pronounced labels on students, it does not pretend to remove all stigma. Yet modification of school classifications, if undertaken with an eye to integrating minorities into the life of the school, might well benefit both the school and the minority student on whom the preponderant burden of adverse classification presently falls, thus responding to the problems associated with racial overrepresentation.

Due Process

A third constitutional approach to the inequities caused by classification relies upon the due process clause of the fourteenth amendment, which declares that "no state shall . . . deprive any person of life, liberty, or property, without due process of law." That language, while commanding the government to act fairly, does not define what fairness means in particular situations. As the Supreme Court has observed,

'Due process' is an elusive concept. Its exact boundaries are undefinable, and its content varies according to specific factual contexts. . . . Whether the Constitution requires that a particular right obtain in a specific proceeding depends upon a complexity of factors. The nature of the alleged right involved, the nature of the proceeding, and the possible burden on that proceeding, are all considerations which must be taken into account.[108]

That some procedural safeguards are attached to the provision of public education is by now well-settled law. While much of the case law concerns student discipline, several recent decisions have required that students be afforded procedural protection prior to such basic changes in their status as assignment to slow learner groups, special education programs, or school exclusion. The appropriateness of applying such safeguards is premised on factors discussed earlier in this article: the educational effect of these decisions, the possibility of arbitrary decisionmaking, and the stigma that these adverse classifications convey.

That certain decisions previously left to the discretion of the school are subject to review and challenge should matter considerably to children and their families. Proceduralization makes the school's decision appear more fair—if only because the bases of the decision are shared and not secret[109]—and minimizes the possibility that school discretion will be abused. And proceduralization increases the likelihood of educationally sound decisions, since the exercise of review may

[108] Hannah v. Larche, 363 U.S. 442 (1969).
[109] See, e.g., Warren Seavey, "Dismissal of Students: 'Due Process,'" *Harvard Law Review*, 70 (June 1957), p. 1406.

force school officials to reexamine regularly both the premises and conclusions of sorting.

In this setting, the real significance of due process lies not in the recognition that school sorting is too consequential to be undertaken arbitrarily, but in the scope of procedural protection that the courts conclude is appropriate. The mere existence of a hearing says nothing about the rules governing the inquiry, or the likelihood that a particular showing will yield a given outcome; and it is the latter issues which frame the real points of contention.[110] To praise due process without providing either context or content for the concept risks elevating principled means above just ends.

In determining precisely what due process should mean in this context, courts are obliged to balance the needs and interests of several concerned parties. This balancing exercise is a familiar one, and distinguishes the request for procedural protection from the more novel claim that courts review such substantive educational issues as the efficacy of particular school placements. "[H]owever little courts may know about education ... they do know about factfinding, decision-making, fairness, and procedure."[111] For that reason, the development of procedural safeguards which promote fair classification is an easier task for the judiciary to contemplate than is the development of substantive educational rights doctrines.

Interest Balancing

In school sorting disputes, the contending parties include the child, the family, and the school. The interest of each differs, and each has to be taken into account. The importance of education to the child's future wellbeing has often been recognized by courts. The panegyric to education in *Brown v. Board of Education* has been so often repeated by so many interested parties in support of such varied arguments that its force has been blunted, the language rendered

---

[110] See Henry Foster, "Social Work, the Law and Social Action," *Social Casework*, 45 (July 1964), pp. 383–386. Robert O'Neill, "Justice Delayed and Justice Denied," *Supreme Court Review*, 161 (1970), pp. 184–195, identifies interests and values served by the due process hearing: a) accuracy and fairness, b) accountability, c) visibility and impartiality, d) consistency, and e) administrative integrity. O'Neill notes several governmental interests: a) collegiality and informality, b) flexibility in the dispensation of benefits, c) agency initiative, d) discretion and confidentiality, e) minimization of expense—each of which is at least potentially impaired by the insistence on procedural formality.

[111] Buss, p. 571.

a cliché. But this cliché, like so many others, is rooted in an important truth. Educational performance and educational status do affect life success, even if the nature of the relationship differs from the model that *Brown* had in mind. The child also has an interest in avoiding the unjust imposition of stigma and (to phrase the point in more familiar language) in liberty. School-imposed stigmas bedevil children because children are compelled to submit to them, to surrender at least a decade of their lives to the state. That infringement of liberty itself raises constitutional issues.[112] It also distinguishes school-imposed classifications from those created by governmental agencies whose control over the citizenry is in some sense voluntary.

The child's parents also have a stake in the issue, but their concerns should be distinguished from those of the child. Even if both share the same perception of the school's decision, its consequences will affect them differently. This point assumes particular importance when the school, by assigning a child to a special class or excluding him or her as ineducable, has in effect identified that child as less than normal. That determination may spawn a host of parental reactions: parents may, for example, hire outside experts to supplement the school's program, or they may embrace the school's decision. Parents may be unwilling to endorse the educational program which is objectively best for the child, if the recommended course of action appears to compound parental problems. For those reasons, the distinctions between parents' and children's interests must be kept in mind when framing procedures for reviewing adverse school classification.

The school's interests are equally legitimate, and very different. The school has to concern itself with the aggregate welfare of all children as well as the individual welfare of any given child. It will resist any arrangement, such as the provision of a particular program not previously offered, which demands additional expenditures: the cost of that program, if not subsidized by state categorical assistance, will be borne by the district. And those added costs will require either additional tax dollars or trimming other parts of the budget. The education of an autistic child, for example, costs at least $10,000—twenty times what most school districts annually spend for the average student. Yet the $10,000 investment could possibly enable the autistic person to break through the psychological barriers that cut him or her off from the world. To choose between those two interests poses problems of exquisite difficulty, unanswerable by recourse to such

[112] Wisconsin v. Yoder, 406 U.S. 205 (1972).

judicial formulas as "the [school district's] interest in educating the excluded children clearly must outweigh its interest in preserving its financial resources."[113]

There exist other, more subtle costs to the school: teacher resentment at being obliged to defend a judgment, or unwillingness on the part of school personnel to make any recommendations concerning special treatment for a particular child because of the procedural regime invoked by such decisions. Many of these arguments are recited whenever a student challenges a disciplinary decision of the school in the school board meeting room or the courtroom. In those circumstances, courts have generally concluded that serious infringements on a child's liberty cannot be imposed unless adequate procedural protection is provided.[114] The application of such safeguards to adverse school classifications poses an ostensibly different problem. It questions a judgment couched in education and not disciplinary terms, a decision central to the school's claim of pedagogical competence. For that reason, school officials are likely to resist terming such classifications as stigmatizing. They will also object to the creation of any process which distinguishes the interest of the school from that of the child, claiming that school classifications further both interests.

In reviewing school decisions more obviously punitive in nature than classifications, courts have not been unsympathetic to these assertions. But the distinction between educational and punitive decisions—which has its analog in the claim that juvenile criminal proceedings are intended to help and not punish youngsters, and therefore should be unfettered by procedures—makes little sense in either setting. However the school chooses to describe the enterprise, its consequences vary for the parties at interest; what is best for one may not be suitable for the others. And for the student, the effect of punitive and educational decisions is similar if not identical: exclusion, whether premised on incorrigibility or ineducability, results in absolute educational deprivation; suspension or special class assignment both diminish educational opportunities and stigmatize the affected student.

The school may choose to ease teachers' burdens by separating children into

---

[113] *Id.* at 876; McMillan v. Board of Education, 430 F.2d 1145 (2d Cir. 1970), declares that:
[I]f New York had determined to limit its financing of educational activities at the elementary level to maintaining public schools and to make no grants to further the education of children whose handicaps prevented them from participating in classes there, we would perceive no substantial basis for a claim of denial of equal protection. 430 F.2d at 1140.
[114] Dixon v. Alabama State Board of Education, 294 F.2d 150 (5th Cir.), *cert. denied*, 368 U.S. 930 (1961); Wasson v. Trowbridge, 382 F.2d 807 (2d Cir. 1967): Goldwyn v. Allen, 54 Misc. 2d 94, 281 N.Y.S. 2d 899 (1967).

groups according to tested measures of ability. If the school cannot afford the educational services that a severely retarded child requires, it may attempt to relinquish its obligation to educate the child by labeling him or her ineducable. Teachers who cannot cope with an "acting out" child may propose assignment to a less advanced track or a special education program as a means of tempering behavior. Confronted with the school's statement that a child is ineducable or less educable than others, the child is at the very least entitled to an advocate who can distinguish his or her needs from those of the school and a forum in which to press this contention.

Requirements of Due Process

Characterizing the interests of children, parents, and school officials is essential to comprehending the nature of the potential dispute. It does not, however, define with precision the scope of procedural protection. The mechanical transplanting of procedural protections developed in the school discipline context to issues of school classification ignores differences between the two problems.

In the routine discipline case, the decisive issue is the truthfulness of the accusation: did X threaten the teacher with a knife? The hearing effectively concludes when this determination is made. The facts concerning the wisdom of a school classification are not so readily established. Is Y an educable mentally retarded child? On what basis is that judgment made? What alternative explanations can be suggested for this behavior? The appropriate remedy may also be more difficult to develop. If X did indeed brandish a knife, he or she will be punished by being suspended from school; the only determination that must be made is the duration of the suspension. But the fact of retardation does not warrant punishment. It requires careful and intelligent educational intervention which demonstrates some promise of benefiting the child. The range of plausible alternatives includes institutionalization, assignment to a special program or placement in a regular class coupled with the provision of additional assistance.

Where the justness of diminished educational status is at issue, two critical questions require resolution: the accuracy of the school's classification and the appropriateness of the proposed treatment. The first query (whether the particular assignment is consistent with general guidelines for a given treatment) calls both for clarity and administrative regularity, obliging school personnel to specify the bases upon which they sort children. The second question (whether the particular assignment is likely to benefit the child) demands justification, joining substantive standards with procedural nicety.

It makes sense to place this burden of justification with school officials. Since it is they, not parents or children, who control the information on which a given decision is based, they can most readily answer these questions. School officials also determine the policies which the teachers and counselors carry out. The burden appropriately borne by the school is not satisfied by mere explications of policy. The potential stigma and educational inefficacy of certain treatments—assignment to special classes and exclusion—suggests that placement in a regular school program, supplemented with special help, should be viewed as the norm, inapplicable only when the school can demonstrate that another alternative offers substantially greater promise. As the *Mills* court notes: "placement in a regular public school class with appropriate ancillary services is preferable to placement in a special public school class."[115] Either is to be preferred to institutional care.

Before reclassification or assignment to a special program becomes a fact, the school should inform the family and the child affected, to explain the proposed action and to indicate what alternatives might be available. If such a process actually functioned, the need to secure the more formal protections of due process might well disappear. There is, however, little evidence from past school behavior to justify hope that such wise and preventive measures will be adopted voluntarily. Schools do not encourage parental involvement in any sorting decision. Even where state law requires parental consent before a child is assigned to a special education class, that requirement is often either ignored or satisfied by coercing parental acquiescence. Parents are informed that a particular placement is the only option available and occasionally threatened with criminal sanctions if they reject it. Misunderstanding or intimidation become even more common when parents speak little or no English, and when school officials speak only English. Schools are unwilling to discuss sorting decisions with parents for many of the same reasons that they object to formal procedural review: such discussions take time, they require that educational decisions be rendered in a language comprehensible to laymen, and they necessarily invite challenges over matters that the school treats as its prerogative.

Effective review of a classification decision requires access to the school's records and the opportunity to have the school's determination reviewed by an impartial outside authority. Unless parents can examine test scores, psychological interview writeups, teacher recommendations, and the like, the school's design is not only unchallengeable, it is incomprehensible. And unless the parents can

---

[115] Mills v. Board of Education, 348 F. Supp. 866, 880 (D.D.C. 1972).

obtain the services of a disinterested professional, they may well lack the competence to understand the basis of the school's action. This need for expertise distinguishes classification from discipline cases. The significance and complexity of these adverse classifications, as well as the possibility of professional misjudgment, suggest that parents should be entitled to expert assistance, a right which should not depend on their capacity to pay for the expertise.[116]

If the need for expert help is greater in classification cases than in discipline disputes, the need for legal counsel may be less. A great deal of energy has been expended in deciding whether a child confronted with the possibility of punitive school action is entitled to legal assistance or, to make the point differently, whether lawyers should be barred from such proceedings because they might convert orderly discussions into miniature courtrooms. This energy seems misspent. Although children are likely to need the assistance of someone familiar with their particular problems and willing to represent their interests, that person can be a lawyer or almost any other outsider. While the lawyer may be a particularly useful advocate because of his familiarity with hearing procedures and awareness of the need to negotiate, he is by no means the only person who can effectively discharge the duties of an advocate.

For advocates to function effectively, they must be permitted to question those whose judgments are being reviewed. Such examination may well be both novel and frightening to school teachers and school psychologists. For that reason, there is real need for care and respect in probing and for avoidance of tactics suitable for courtroom confrontations which might increase discomfiture and tension. Such care is also likely to encourage candid conversation, and thus to illuminate the bases for the school's decision.

Several alternatives are conceivable. The school board could act as a reviewing agency. The limited expertise and already substantial agenda of that body, however, make that option unappealing. The school board could create an ad hoc group to make recommendations to the board; such a group might well develop the expertise that review of these decisions and judgments among competing alternatives require. An expert not otherwise connected to the school system might

---

[116] A comparison of the complexity and the importance of discipline and classification cases suggests the greater need of expert assistance—appointed, if necessary—in the latter cases. That retesting has revealed substantial school errors makes the need for such expert assistance all the stronger. *See* Smuck v. Hobson, 408 F.2d 175, 187 (D.C. Cir. 1969) (en banc): Stewart v. Phillips, Civ. No. 70–1199–F (E.D. Mass. 1971). *See, e.g.*, Madera v. Board of Education, 386 F.2d 778 (2d Cir. 1967), *cert, denied*, 390 U.S. 1028 (1968).

be appointed to consider classification matters. Yet another option, possibly linked with one of these three, would leave ultimate review in the hands of a higher education agency (a representative of the county or state department of education, for example) whose ostensible detachment from the school's recommendation would suggest fairness. None of these alternatives is constitutionally required. What is required is a tribunal sufficiently divorced from the initial decision to be capable of unbiased and informed judgment.

For children who have been excluded from school or improperly assigned to the wrong track for a considerable period of time, due process review comes rather late. If the arguments developed here carry any weight, such exclusion or misplacement was legally wrongful because students were not provided with procedural protection. More pertinently, injury has been done: children have been denied some or all of the benefits of an education to which they were entitled. Especially for handicapped or severely retarded children, who can be helped more quickly and more effectively early in life, the injuries are real indeed. For that reason, these children should be entitled to educational assistance equivalent to that which the school has denied them. Equivalency is, to be sure, a difficult concept to implement, since it requires a determination of what education the child has *not* had. In the clearest case—exclusion—requiring the school to make up the amount of schooling lost, measured simply in terms of school days, commends itself primarily because of its ease of application. One federal court, applying just such a standard, ordered periods of remedial work during the school day, after-school tutorial classes, guidance and psychological services, and summer make-up programs to remedy the wrongful exclusion.[117]

The Impact of Procedures

The procedural approach to sorting issues converts matters of substance into matters of form, leaving the critical placement determinations in the hands of assertedly neutral educators. The minimal judicial involvement implicit in the approach has considerable appeal to courts reluctant to make what appear to be educational policy decisions. Yet the ultimate impact of proceduralization on both the school and the student remains a subject for speculation. While hearings may force schools to adopt uniform decision criteria, that very fact may leave the school less willing to make (plausibly better) decisions tailored to specific cases. The possibility that a school might retaliate against a child intrepid enough to

[117] Knight v. Board of Education, 48 F.R.D. 115 (E.D.N.Y. 1969).

demand review of a sorting judgment, in subtle ways that a court could never hope to confront, represents a quite different cost of review. Further, neither the child nor his parents are likely to perceive themselves well-served if a formal hearing reveals that an adverse school classification has in fact been justly imposed. Such a finding denies both child and parent the opportunity to feel wronged, to view the school's action as a misrepresentation of the child's true potential. Process protects against the arbitrary imposition of unjust stigmas; it also reinforces the impact of stigmas found to be properly imposed.

The introduction of procedural niceties into the life of the school may also have unintended but important beneficial consequences. The school required to review each adverse classification may, in the face of that considerable burden, choose to reconsider the process of sorting. It may conclude that children are better served by labels that are less conclusory, and carry with them less pervasive consequences, than those presently in use. In this sense, the claims for procedural and substantive justice share identical aspirations.

One ardently hopes that this aspiration will become reality. Yet even if this hope is misplaced, even if schools continue to develop ever more intricate classifying schemes to sort the students they serve, the application of procedural standards makes public what has hitherto been hidden, and provides a means of contesting particular decisions. That represents at least a step in the right direction.

Conclusion

This article suggests that present classification practices raise three quite different kinds of constitutional questions. First, the exclusion of "ineducable" children and the assignment of other students to inefficacious special education programs may well embody a denial of equal protection. Second, the overrepresentation of minority students in slow learner groups and classes for the mildly handicapped appear to have racially specific harmful effects; unless school officials can demonstrate that the educational benefits somehow outweigh the harm, some modification of present patterns appears constitutionally required. Third, it is constitutionally appropriate to protect students against the possibility of misclassification by affording them (and their parents) the right to a due process review of placement recommendations.

Educators may well fear that these legal arguments, if accepted by the courts, will require substantially uniform treatment of all, thus drastically limiting their capacity to confront the real and bewildering variations in children's needs and abilities. Yet, as the discussions of the scope of appropriate remedies indicate, such an outcome is neither desirable nor likely. If, for example, classes for the mildly handicapped have little pedagogical justification and also stigmatize students, they should be discontinued. But it does not follow that the tailoring of short-term, goal-specific programs for different kinds of students will routinely arouse judicial suspicion. The differential vulnerability of minority students to adverse classification poses both an educational and a political dilemma which can intelligently be addressed through increasingly flexible program offerings. Such rigid remedies as the establishment of a racial quota system seem singularly inappropriate, for they neither respond to the underlying problem nor offer a workable solution to it. Due process hearings, if handled with sensitivity to the real interests of both the school and the child, encourage better individual placements as well as reconsideration of the school's assumptions concerning which classification decisions are useful and necessary. Adherence to procedural regularity does not convert the school into a courtroom.

The ultimate test of the impact of judicial intervention in this realm will occur in the schools themselves. Court cases challenging one or another aspect of classification explicitly call into question the schools' perception of this mission. They threaten time-honored patterns of institutional behavior and demand nothing less than that what Seymour Sarason terms "the culture of the school"[118] undergo convulsive change. For that reason reform will not come quickly or easily whatever the courts ultimately say about these issues.

Yet to state that change will be difficult to accomplish does not imply that currently prevailing school practices will forever persist. Educators have changed their minds and altered their cultures before; they are likely to do so again. And judicial intervention to secure one or another of the constitutional principles discussed in this article may well serve to encourage such changes of mind by insisting upon changes in behavior. In short, the hope that significant school reform will follow judicial decisions is just that—a hope. But every notable consitutional claim embodies the similar expectation that a declaration of rights will lead people to change their lives, to act consistently with what has been held to be just behavior. In the school setting the hope seems at least plausible, and justifies judicial efforts to protect school children against the too often ill-considered, arbitrary, and hurtful distinctions made by their elders.

[118] Seymour Sarason, *The Culture of the School and the Problem of Change* (Boston: Allyn and Bacon, 1971).

A Policy Statement on Assessment Procedures and the Rights of Children

JANE R. MERCER

University of California, Riverside

The author discusses the findings of an eight-year study in which she explored school and agency classification procedures for children based on standardized intelligence tests. Mercer discovered that in the American city she investigated, such procedures resulted in labeling as mentally retarded a disproportionately large number of Chicanos and Blacks. She argues that current classification procedures violate the rights of children to be evaluated within a culturally appropriate normative framework, their right to be assessed as multi-dimensional beings, their right to be fully educated, their right to be free of stigmatizing labels, and their right to cultural identity and respect. Mercer proposes supplementary evaluations which assess an individual's competencies outside of school and suggests that only children scoring in the lowest three percent on standardized IQ tests and adaptive behavior evaluations should be placed in classes for the mentally retarded.

Classification systems based on standardized tests have labeled a disproportionately large number of people from minority groups as intellectually subnormal. The assessment of exceptional children did *not* become an issue because psychologists, educators, and medical practitioners were dissatisfied with the present system. Rather the groups labeled abnormal are challenging standardized tests. Lawyers representing Black and Chicano clients have successfully argued in

Harvard Educational Review Vol. 44 No. 1 February 1974

court that present assessment procedures violate the rights of minority children (Larry P. v. Wilson Riles; Diana v. State Board of Education). They protest the mono-cultural value system most psychologists, educators, and test makers take for granted.

During the past twelve years, we have been studying mental retardation in Riverside, an American city with a population of 130,000.[1] We concluded that present assessment procedures violate certain basic rights of children and that a system of pluralistic, multi-cultural assessment is needed. This system must consider adaptive behavior and sociocultural background when interpreting the meaning of scores on standardized measures. In order to explain clearly the rationale behind the pluralistic assessment procedures which we propose, it is necessary to review the conceptual models and design used in our earlier study.[2]

Social System Perspective

The social system perspective defined mental retardation as an achieved social status some individuals take in some social systems. This aspect of the study focused on the labeling process and the characteristics of persons who achieve the status of mental retardate in various social systems in the community, especially the public school.

We asked 241 organizations in the community for information on each mentally retarded person served by each group. Because we were studying the labeling process, we did not impose one standard definition of mental retardation but asked each organization to use their customary definition. When we studied the number of persons jointly nominated by various types of organizations, we found the public schools labeled more persons as mentally retarded than any other organization.

[1] Data in this paper has been collected under the auspices of the following grants: Public Health Service Grant R01 MH20646–01 from the National Institute of Mental Health, Department of Health, Education and Welfare; Public Health Service General Research support Grant No. 1–S01–FR–05632–02, from the Department of Health, Education and Welfare, Socio-Behavioral Study Center in Mental Retardation, Pacific State Hospital, Pomona, California; Public Health Service Grant No. PH43–67–756; McAteer Grant No. M8–14A and M9–14 from the California State Department of Education, Office of Compensatory Education. The opinions and conclusions stated in this paper by the author are not to be construed as officially reflecting the policy of the funding agencies.

[2] Portions of the material in this paper were presented at the Kennedy International Symposium on Human Rights, Retardation, and Research, Washington, D.C., October 16, 1971; The First Annual Study Conference in School Psychology, Temple University, June, 1972; and The Tenth Annual Conference in Civil and Human Rights of Educators and Students, National Education Association, February, 1972.

We then studied each type of formal organization to see what standards they were using in screening for mental retardation. We found that 46 percent of the persons nominated by the public schools had IQs above 70 and 62 percent had no reported physical disabilities. All other agencies, except law enforcement, used more stringent criteria. For example, only 12 percent of those nominated by the Department of Mental Hygiene had IQs above 70 and only 11 percent were without physical disabilities.

We concluded that the public school system is the primary labeler in the community. Any public policy directed at modifying labeling practices in the community must include modification of public school labeling practices. Any major change in the labeling policies of this single system would have a significant impact on labeling processes in the community as a whole.

Who Is Labeled

We next studied the characteristics of 812 people who held the status of mental retardate in one or more organizations. We found that 72 percent of the persons on the register were five through twenty years of age, only 7 percent were under five years of age, and only 21 percent were over twenty. Compared to their percentage in the general population of the community, school-age children were over-labeled and pre-school children and adults were under-labeled. Before children get to school, only those with the most physical disabilities and lowest IQs are identified. After graduation from school, only the most intellectually and physically subnormal adults continue to be officially labeled.

We classified each person on the case register into ten groups according to the median value of the housing on the block on which she or he lived. We found that persons in the lowest socioeconomic categories were greatly overrepresented on the register and those from higher statuses were underrepresented. When we studied ethnic groups we found substantial disproportions. Chicanos comprise 9 percent of the Riverside population and 38 percent of those labeled retarded. Blacks are 6 percent of the population and 11 percent of those labeled retarded. But Anglo-Americans[3] constitute 85 percent of the population and only 51 per-

---

[3] The term Anglo-American is used to refer to those Caucasians in the population whose primary language is English. Most English-speaking Caucasians are of European descent and the category includes persons of many nationalities and religions. Products of the Americanization process, they now share a common language and tradition which, for the want of a better term, is being referred to as the Anglo-American tradition. The accepted nomenclature for the various ethnic groups varies from one region to another and from time to time as historic events make some designations more acceptable than others. For the purpose of consistency, however, we have de-

cent of those labeled retarded. Because most Chicanos and Blacks in Riverside come from lower socioeconomic backgrounds, ethnic group and socioeconomic status are correlated. When we held socioeconomic status constant, we still found Anglos underrepresented and Chicanos overrepresented in the case register. Blacks appeared in their proper proportion.

Ethnic disproportions were especially marked among public school nominees. When we compared Riverside school data with data from other school districts in the state of California, we found that this overrepresentation of Chicano and Black children in classes for the educable mentally retarded was a statewide pattern.

Clinical Perspective

The clinical perspective tends to use two definitions of normal simultaneously and interchangeably: the pathological model and the statistical model. The pathological model categorizes a person as abnormal when symptoms are present and normal when pathological signs are absent. The statistical model defines abnormality according to the extent an individual varies from the average of the population on a particular trait.

In the second phase of our study we adopted the clinical perspective and used the definition of mental retardation used by the American Association for Mental Deficiency (AAMD). "Mental retardation refers to subaverage general intellectual functioning which originates during the developmental period and is associated with impairment in adaptive behavior" (Heber, 1961).

This is a two-dimensional definition. Before a person may be diagnosed as mentally retarded, he or she must be subnormal in both intellectual performance and adaptive behavior. Evidence of organic dysfunction or biological anomalies is not required.

In the same document, subnormal is defined as performance on a standard measure of intellectual functioning greater than one standard deviation below the population mean, the lowest 16 percent of the population (Heber, 1961).[4]

---

cided to use the terms Black and Chicano rather than other more or less popular forms of ethnic identification.

[4] The field work for this study was conducted in 1963. At that time, the American Association on Mental Deficiency definition of mental retardation was "subaverage intellectual functioning" defined as "performance on a measure of general intellectual functioning that is greater than one standard deviation below the population mean" (Heber, 1961). In 1973, the definition was revised to read as follows, "Mental retardation refers to significantly subaverage general intellectual

Educational practice generally places the dividing line somewhat lower. The highest IQ test score for placement in a class for the educable mentally retarded ranges between 75 and 79, depending upon local usage.[5] This cutoff includes approximately the lowest 9 percent of the population. Test designers suggest an IQ cutoff below 70, approximately 3 percent of the population (Wechsler, 1958; Terman & Merrill, 1960). In the clinical epidemiology, all three cutoffs were used and the results compared.

Intellectual adequacy was measured by using standardized measures of intelligence, primarily the Stanford-Binet LM and the Kuhlman-Binet.[6] We conceptualized adaptive behavior as an individual's ability to play ever more complex roles in a progressively widening circle of social systems. Because there are not generally accepted measures of adaptive behavior, we developed a series of 28 age-graded scales, drawing heavily on the work of Doll (1965) and Gesell (1948a, 1956), especially for the younger years.[7] Questions were answered by a respondent related to the person being evaluated (Mercer, 1973a).

We used measures of subnormality in intellectual performance and subnormality in adaptive behavior to constitute our working typology for mental retardation. Combinations of these two dimensions produce four major types of

---

functioning existing concurrently with deficits in adaptive behavior, and manifested during the developmental period . . . significantly subaverage refers to performance which is two or more standard deviations from the mean or average of the test" (Grossman, 1973, p. 11).

[5] Some states are redefining standards for placement in special classes. For example, the 1971 California Legislature lowered the general cutoff for placement to two or more standard deviations below the mean while allowing psychologists some discretionary power in placing persons with IQ test scores above 70 (Senate Bill 33, California Legislature, 1971).

[6] The research design called for a first-stage screening of a large sample of the population of the community using the adaptive behavior scales and then a second-stage testing of a subsample using standardized IQ tests. The first-stage sample was a stratified area probability sample of 3,198 housing units in the City of Riverside, California, selected so that all geographic areas and socioeconomic levels in the city were represented in their proper proportion. In each household, one adult member, usually the mother was interviewed about all other members of the household to whom she was related. Interviews were completed in 2,661 of the 2,923 occupied housing units, an overall response rate of 90.7 percent. In all, 6,907 persons under 50 years of age were screened.

A disproportionate and random sample of 483 persons were selected for individual intelligence testing. Tests were completed on 423 persons for an overall response rate of 87.6 percent. Intelligence test scores were also secured from other sources for an additional 241 persons, making a total of 664 scores available. Each person in the tested subsample was assigned a weight according to the number of persons he represented in the larger, screened sample.

[7] Mercer (1973a) provides examples of items used for measuring the adaptive behavior but she cautions: "The questions in the Adaptive Behavior and Physical Disability Scales were designed for field screening in a survey research project. Although they proved adequate for that purpose, they are not sufficiently reliable or adequately normed for use in a clinical setting" (p. 287). A clinically appropriate Adaptive Behavior Inventory for Children (ABIC) designed for children ages 5–7 should be available in 1975.

persons: the clinically retarded, the quasi-retarded, the behaviorally maladjusted, and the normal. The clinically retarded are those who are subnormal in both IQ and adaptive behavior. The quasi-retarded are those who are subnormal in IQ but normal in adaptive behavior. The behaviorally maladjusted are those who have normal IQs but are subnormal in adaptive behavior while the normal are those who pass both dimensions.

Conclusions from the Study of Mental Retardation Assessment

Cutoff Level for Subnormality Should be Lowest 3 Percent (IQ below 70)
The behavioral characteristics of the adults in our sample who failed the traditional criterion, the lowest three percent, were compared to adults who failed only the educational or the AAMD criteria. We found that the majority of the adults who were failing at a 9 percent or the 16 percent criterion were, in fact, filling the usual complement of social roles for persons of their age and sex: 83.6 percent had completed eight grades or more in school; 64.9 percent had a semi-skilled or higher occupation, 80.2 percent were financially independent, almost 100 percent were able to do their own shopping and travel alone. Differences between their performance and that of persons failing the traditional criterion differed at the .001 level of significance on 21 out of 26 of the comparisons made. It is clear that most adults who appear in the borderline category were managing their own affairs and did not appear to require supervision, control, or care for their own welfare. Their role performance appeared neither subnormal nor particularly unusual.

We concluded that the three percent cutoff, in IQ and adaptive behavior, was the criterion most likely to identify those in need of special assistance and supervision and least likely to mislabel those able to fill a normal complement of social roles as adults. Persons scoring in the so-called borderline category should be regarded as low normal rather than clinically retarded.

Both IQ and Adaptive Behavior Should be Evaluated in Making Diagnoses
We compared the social role performance of the quasi-retarded (IQ below 70, normal adaptive behavior) with the clinically retarded school-aged child (IQ below 70, subnormal adaptive behavior). Clinical retardates are reported to have had more trouble learning, are more frequently behind the school grade expected for their age, have repeated more grades, and are more likely to be en-

rolled in special education classes. Quasi-retardates, in spite of their low IQ test scores, have avoided falling behind their age mates or being placed in special programs. We found that 80 percent of the quasi-retarded adults had graduated from high school; they all read books, magazines, and newspapers; all held jobs; 65 percent had white-collar positions; 19 percent had skilled or semi-skilled positions while 15.7 percent were unskilled laborers. All of them were able to work without supervision; participated in sports; traveled alone, went to the store by themselves; and participated in informal visiting with co-workers, friends, and neighbors. Their social role performance tended to be indistinguishable from that of other adults in the community. We concluded that clinicians should develop a systematic method for assessing adaptive behavior as well as intelligence in making clinical assessments of ability.

Sociocultural Factors Should be Systematically Considered in Interpreting Clinical Scores

Our third major conclusion was that the IQ tests now being used by psychologists are Anglocentric. They tend to measure the extent to which an individual's background is similar to that of the modal cultural configuration of American society. Because a significant amount of the variance in IQ test scores is related to sociocultural characteristics, we concluded that sociocultural factors must be considered in interpreting the meaning of any individual score.

Specifically, we studied two different samples to determine the amount of variance in IQ test scores which could be attributed to sociocultural factors. One hundred Chicanos, 47 Blacks, and 556 Anglos constituted the first sample. Eighteen sociocultural characteristics were dichotomized so that one category corresponded to the modal Angloculture and the other category was non-Anglo. IQ was used as the dependent variable in a stepwise multiple regression in which the sociocultural characteristics were entered as independent variables. The multiple correlation coefficient for this large heterogeneous sample was .50 ($p < .001$), indicating that 25 percent of the variance in the IQs of the 703 culturally and ethnically heterogeneous individuals in this group could be attributed to sociocultural differences.

In a similar analysis, 1,513 elementary school children in the public schools of Riverside were studied using 13 sociocultural characteristics of their families as independent variables and the Full Scale WISC IQ as the dependent variable. The 598 Chicanos and 339 Black children in the sample included the total school population of the three segregated elementary schools which then existed in the district. The 576 Anglo children were randomly selected from 11 predominantly Anglo elementary schools. The multiple correlation coefficient was .57, indicating that 32 percent of the variance in the IQs of this socioculturally heterogeneous group of elementary school children could be accounted for by differences in family background factors (Mercer & Brown, 1973).

Psychological Assessment Procedures and Rights of Children

We believe that psychological assessment procedures have become a civil rights issue because present assessment and educational practices violate at least five rights of children: a) their right to be evaluated within a culturally appropriate normative framework; b) their right to be assessed as multi-dimensional, many-faceted human beings; c) their right to be fully educated; d) their right to be free of stigmatizing labels; and e) their right to cultural identity and respect.

The Right to be Evaluated within a Culturally Appropriate Normative Framework

Binet and Simon developed their original test of "intelligence" to identify those French children who would not benefit from the regular school program and should be placed in special schools (Binet & Simon, 1905). Items for the test were selected from those aspects of French culture which Binet and Simon believed all French children would have had an opportunity to learn. When the testing movement spread to the United States, the content of intelligence tests was drawn from the Anglo-American cultural tradition and the criterion for testing the validity of these measures was their ability to predict performance in an Anglocentric public school system.

In our studies we found marked ethnic disproportions, both among those labeled by community agencies and among those screened as having the symptoms of mental retardation in the field survey. Ethnic disproportions were especially marked in the public schools. Our analysis indicated that these disproportions first occurred when an intelligence test was administered (Mercer, 1971a, 1971b). Rates of labeling were negatively correlated with the extent to which the sociocultural characteristics of the family conformed to the Anglo-American mode. Scores on "intelligence" tests were positively correlated with the anglicization of the family.

Another characteristic of present assessment procedures which reinforces and legitimates a monocultural value system is that all standardized assessment procedures are based on a statistical definition of normal which uses a *single* normative framework for interpreting the scores of all children. This framework carries five implications for children's rights.

1. The clinical perspective assumes that there is *one* normal curve and this single distribution can be used to classify the behavior of all children, regardless of cultural background.

2. The statistical model generates its own abnormals. If there is any variability in the population measured, some persons will be at the top and others at the bottom of the distribution. By definition, a normal curve will always classify approximately 2.5 percent of its norming population as abnormally high and 2.5 percent as abnormally low.

3. The type of behavior which will be regarded as normal or abnormal depends upon the typical behavior of the population used to establish the norms. Because all but the simplest behavior is learned in a socio-cultural setting, the characteristics of normal behavior will vary with the culture. Before the performance of individuals on a test of learned behavior can be compared, they must have had equal opportunity to acquire the knowledge and learn the skills covered in the test. They must have been equally motivated to learn those skills and be equally familiar with and comfortable in the test situation. Children from different cultural heritages in American society are not identical. Their scores on so-called intelligence and achievement tests were statistically different ($p < .001$). This finding has been reported in virtually every similar study (Mercer & Smith, 1972). Children from different cultural heritages do not meet the assumptions of the inferential model on which diagnostic conclusions are based. We cannot assume that they are from the same population.

4. Including a proportionate number of non-Anglo children in the norming sample does *not* solve the problem. The statistical model assumes that the behavioral characteristics being measured are normally distributed. If this is not the case, a statistically defined normal is misleading. In a skewed distribution, the mean moves in the direction of the skew. In a bimodal or trimodal distribution, the mean does not adequately represent the behavior of any of the subgroups making up the distribution. When two or more cultural groups are included in a norming population, as happens in the standardization of many tests, the largest subgroup has the greatest influence in establishing the behavioral norms. Cultural groups which differ systematically from the majority group will be defined as abnormal (Mercer, 1972a).

5. Establishing separate norms for an entire racial/ethnic group or devel-

oping culture-specific tests for each racial/ethnic group is not the solution. Important socio-cultural differences exist not only between but within racial/ethnic groups. In the sample of Black and Chicano children mentioned earlier, we were able to identify five levels of socio-cultural modality, ranging from a group completely assimilated into the Anglo-American culture to a group having little contact with modern industrial America (Mercer, 1972b). Such cultural heterogeneity must somehow be recognized in psychological assessment.

The problems mentioned above have been clearly documented by numerous investigators (Eells, 1951; Darcy, 1963). Unfortunately findings confirming cultural bias have had minimal impact on the training of psychologists or the practice of psychological testing in the public schools. We found little evidence that clinicians consider cultural factors in interpreting standardized test scores. We believe that each child has a right to be evaluated within a culturally appropriate normative framework. Children should not be classified as abnormals because they have been socialized into a non-Anglo cultural tradition.

The Right to be Assessed as a Multi-Dimensional Human Being

We found that most community agencies, especially the public schools, relied on measures of intelligence in diagnosing mental retardation. Ninety-nine percent of the labeled retardates nominated by the public schools had been given an intelligence test but only 13 percent had received a medical diagnosis. The only measure of adaptability was implicit. If a child's behavior violated the norms of the teacher, she or he was judged to be maladapted and was referred for psychological evaluation (Mercer, 1971c). No community agency systematically assessed the child's ability to perform complex non-academic tasks in the home, neighborhood, and community. Assessment focused only on the narrow band of behavior sampled in the psychometric situation.

As mentioned earlier, the field survey used a series of scales to measure adaptive behavior. We found that a multi-dimensional assessment was particularly important in understanding the human potential of people from non-Anglo backgrounds. We estimated that 60 percent of the Chicano and 90 percent of the Black adults who scored below 70 on standardized IQ tests, were performing adequately in their occupational, parental, and community roles. When we interviewed the mothers of children labeled as mentally retarded by the schools, we found many were situationally retarded. Their retardation was confined to the six hours in school. In the eyes of their family and friends, they were normal. Some were carrying a heavy load of responsibility in the home. Others were known in their neighborhoods for their mechanical aptitude and ability to solve problems (Mercer, 1971a).

Our studies convinced us that a child has a right to be assessed as a multi-faceted person playing roles in many social systems. Children who succeed in non-academic roles are *not* comprehensively retarded even though they may score as subnormal on a standardized intelligence test. In our study we classified those who scored below 70 on an IQ test but had normal adaptive behavior as the quasi-retarded. We believe that a systematic multi-dimensional assessment of children's adaptive behavior in non-school settings would provide information on their competencies. This approach would assist the school in understanding and appreciating them as human beings and would provide information for planning educational programs. Such a program could build on individual assets and accomplishments rather than classifying by deficits.

The Right to be Fully Educated

There are a few children, we estimated less than 1 percent of the population, who have suffered biological damage and have a very low ceiling on their learning ability (Mercer, 1973b). Such children need special education programs geared to their needs. However, there are other children, we estimated as many as 75 percent of those in public school programs for educable mental retardates, who perform poorly on intelligence tests but are not comprehensively retarded. Many are in the borderline category—IQ scores 70-84. They will escape the retarded label when they leave the school and begin to function as adults. Some are quasi-retardates who have school specific problems but are performing adequately in other social systems. Others are from non-Anglo families and have difficulty coping with the Anglocentric style and program of the school. Such children cannot be educated to the limit of their potential in classes designed for the mentally retarded.

One of the most persistent complaints we heard from parents of children inappropriately placed in classes for the mentally retarded was their concern about the limited and repetitious nature of the educational program. For example, one Black mother in our study said, "Bill is being retarded in special education. . . . We have to make Bill go to school because the class does not offer a challenge to him. What they do is repetitious—the same thing over and over. . . . He does not like school."

Many of these children, given prompt assistance early in their educational career, would eventually be able to progress without special help. Placed in a special education class for the mentally retarded, they will never be fully educated.

The Right to be Free of Stigmatizing Labels

There are children whose physical anomalies and behavioral deficits are so visible that they deviate from the normative expectations of every social system in which they participate. When such children are formally labeled as mentally retarded and placed in special programs, they do not acquire a new stigma. There is convergence between social system definitions and clinical definitions of abnormality (Mercer, 1972a, Chap. 15).

However, many of the children in special programs have no physical anomalies. Sixty-seven percent of the children in special classes in our labeling study were not viewed as subnormal by other social systems. This disparity was especially marked for minority children. Forty-eight percent of the children labeled as mentally retarded in the public school were Anglo-American, while 36.5 percent were Chicano and 11.9 percent were Black. Conversely, the ethnic proportion for those labeled mentally retarded in all social systems in which they participated were 78 percent Anglo-American, 13 percent Chicano, and 5 percent Black. This closely approximates the ethnic proportions in the general population. Minority children were particularly burdened with school-specific stigmatizing labels.

As early as 1905, Binet expressed his concern with stigmatization. "It will never be to one's credit to have attended a special school. We should at the least spare from this mark those who do not deserve it. Mistakes are excusable, especially at the beginning. But if they become too gross, they could injure the name of these new institutions" (Binet & Simon, 1905). Sixty-five years later we are no longer at the beginning in psychological assessment. Mistakes are no longer excusable. We believe that children have a right to be free of stigmatizing labels.

Yet the recognition of this right for quasi-retardates is complicated by their need for supplemental help to remain in regular educational programs. The provision of tutorial assistance, speech therapy, or remedial reading may result in the exchange of one label for another, if learning environments are not carefully structured to avoid negative stereotyping.

The Right to Ethnic Identity and Respect

The violation of this final right to ethnic identity and respect is more elusive and difficult to document.

Achievement and intelligence tests are designed to predict a child's probability of success in American public schools which are culture-bearers for the Anglo-American tradition. The public schools have been a mechanism for the Americanization of non-Anglo migrants to the United States. Speaking a language other than English has been consistently discouraged. For example, 32 percent of the 5,800 schools surveyed recently in five southwestern states opposed the use of Spanish in classrooms. Schools having the higher percentage of Chicano children and the highest percentage of children from lower socio-economic levels were the *most* likely to discourage the use of Spanish. Children from Spanish-speaking homes are expected to learn English with no special assistance from the schools. In 1970 there were only 131 bilingual programs in public schools to serve the entire Spanish-speaking population in the United States (U.S. Commission on Civil Rights, 1972).

When some parents protested that present psychological assessment procedures were "a conspiracy to keep minorities down" and were "most unfair," they were expressing feelings of systematic exclusion from the dominant society. Intelligence testing perpetuates the subordinate position of non-Anglos in American society. Standardized testing provides a mechanism for blaming children and their families when the educational program of the school fails.

In our interviews with non-Anglo parents, we found some who accept the Americanization process. They wish their children to assimilate into Anglo-American society and to relinquish all other linguistic and cultural ties. There were a few cultural separatists at the opposite pole who did not want their children to adopt an Anglo-American life style. The third group, probably the majority, wish their children to be bi-cultural. They want their children to be able to speak standard English, to secure good jobs, and to share in the benefits and resources available in modern, industrial American society. They also want their children to be literate in their native language and to perpetuate its cultural traditions. Present classification systems and measurement procedures implement Anglo conformity.

We believe that psychological assessment and public educational policy should recognize the integrity and value of different cultural traditions. People with multi-cultural backgrounds have a richer experiential world than people who know only one culture. If such an ideal were valued, minority and majority children would be encouraged to become multi-cultural.

A multi-cultural, pluralistic approach to assessment can not affect public education unless other aspects of the educational system and the larger social structure change in a multi-cultural direction. Our system of multi-cultural assessment has a more modest goal—to develop a comprehensive view of the child's performance and to consider the child's environment in planning her or his educational program.

Policy Implications: A System of Multi-cultural Pluralistic Assessment

The annual ethnic survey of California schools substantiates our findings of disproportionate placement of minority children in programs for the mentally retarded. Evidence indicates that such disproportions are a national pattern. In June, 1970, the San Francisco Board of Education discontinued the use of group mental ability tests and recommended a moratorium on the use of individual tests of intelligence with Black children unless specifically requested by the parents (San Francisco Board of Education, 1970). Other cities have taken similar action. In October 1970, the Bay Area Association of Black Psychologists proposed a moratorium on tests of intelligence and scholastic ability in the assessment of Black children. The Association of Psychologists of *La Raza* has petitioned the American Psychological Association and various governmental agencies to remedy inequalities in job placement and educational opportunities resulting from the misinterpretation of IQ tests given to persons of Chicano heritage. They have charged that standardized tests were used in the misplacement of Chicano children in classes for the mentally retarded.

The California Legislature recently deleted group mental abilities tests from the list of tests required under the state mandated testing program. Assemblyman Willie Brown introduced a bill in both the 1972 and 1973 California Legislatures which "prohibits school districts from administering to pupils in the district any test which measures or attempts to measure the scholastic aptitude of pupils" (Assembly Bill, Number 483). This bill was passed by an overwhelming majority in both the House and Senate but was twice vetoed by Governor Reagan.

In 1971, the California Legislature amended the Education Code to provide a legal framework for pluralistic assessment. The following quotation contains some of the salient provisions of that bill.

The legislature . . . declares . . . that pupils should not be assigned to special classes . . . for the mentally retarded if they can be served in regular classes.

Before any minor is admitted to a special education program for mentally retarded minors . . . the minor shall be given verbal or nonverbal individual intelligence tests in the primary home language in which the minor is most fluent and has the best speaking ability and capacity to understand.

... No minor shall be placed in a special education class for the mentally retarded if he scores higher than two standard deviations below the norm. . . . No minor may be placed in a special education program for the mentally retarded unless a complete psychological examination by a credentialed school psychologist investigating such factors as developmental history, cultural background, and school achievement substantiates the retarded intellectual development indicated by the individual test scores. This examination shall include estimates of adaptive behavior . . . . such adaptability testing shall include but is not limited to a visit, with the consent of the parent or guardian, to the minor's home by the school psychologist or a person designated by the chief administrator of the district . . . . (California Legislature, Senate Bill No. 33, 1971).

This legislation provides a legal framework for multicultural pluralistic assessment in the public schools. We are currently involved in developing a method for operationalizing the concepts contained in this legislation.

Our assessment procedure includes identification of the socialization milieu in which the child is being reared; assessment of the child's academic readiness in relation to the general public school population and in relation to his own sociocultural milieu; assessment of the child's adaptive behavior in non-academic activities; an inventory of the child's health history; and screening for physical impairments. Information on the socialization milieu, the child's adaptive behavior, and the child's health history are secured in a structured interview with the mother or principal caretaker. Information on the child's general academic readiness and screening for physical impairments is secured during an assessment session with the child.

We have tested a representative sample of 2,100 California public school children, five through eleven years of age (700 Anglo-American, 700 Black, and 700 Chicano children) and have interviewed their mothers. From this data, we are developing a series of measures and an interpretive framework which we hope will recognize the cultural identity of all children; locate them within a culturally relevant framework; describe them as multi-dimensional individuals playing roles in many social systems; and, ultimately, lead to the development of educational programs that will allow full functioning in a pluralistic society.

References

Binet, A., & Simon, T. Sur la nécessité d'établir un diagnostic scientifique des états inferieurs de l'intelligence. *Année Psychologique,* 11 (1905), 1–28.

California State Legislature, Assembly Bill No. 483. 1972, Regular Session. Introduced by Assemblyman Brown, February 18, 1972.

California State Legislature, Senate Bill No. 33. Approved by Governor, May 18, 1971.

Darcy, N. T. Bilingualism and the measurement of intelligence: Review of a decade of research. *Journal of Genetic Psychology,* 103 (September 1963), 259–282.

Diana v. State Board of Education, NO. C–70–37 (N.D.Cal., 1970).

Doll, E. A. Vineland Social Maturity Scale, condensed (Rev. ed.). *Manual of direction.* Minneapolis: American Guidance Service, 1965.

Eells, K. *et al. Intelligence and cultural differences.* Chicago: University of Chicago Press, 1951.

Gesell, A. L. *The first five years of life.* New York: Harper & Bros., 1948 (a).

Gesell, A. L. *Studies in child development.* New York: Harper & Bros., 1948 (b).

Gesell, A. L. *Youth: The years from ten to sixteen.* New York: Harper & Bros., 1956.

Grossman, H. *et al. Manual on terminology and classification in mental retardation.* Special Publication Series No. 2, 1973, American Association on Mental Deficiency.

Heber, R. F. A manual on terminology and classification in mental retardation. *American Journal of Mental Deficiency,* 64. Monograph Supplement (2nd ed.), 1961.

Mercer, J. R. Institutionalized Anglocentrism: Labeling mental retardates in the public schools. In P. Orleans & W. R. Eliss (Ed.), Race, change, and urban society. *Urban Affairs Annual Review.* Vol. V. Los Angeles: Sage Publications, 1971 (a).

Mercer, J. R. Sociocultural factors in labeling mental retardates. *Peabody Journal of Education,* 48 (April 1971), 188–203. (b)

Mercer, J. R. The meaning of mental retardation. In R. Koch & J. Dobson (Ed.), *The mentally retarded child and his family: A multidisciplinary handbook.* New York: Brunner/Mazel, 1971. (c)

Mercer, J. R. Who is normal? Two perspectives on mild mental retardation. In E. G. Jaco (Ed.), *Patients, physicians and illness.* (Rev. ed.) Glencoe, Ill.: Free Press, 1972. (a)

Mercer, J. R. The lethal label. *Psychology Today,* Vol. 44 (September 1972) (b).

Mercer, J. R. *Labeling the mentally retarded.* Berkeley: University of California Press, 1972. (a)

Mercer, J. R. The myth of the 3% prevalence. In G. Tarjan, R. Eyman & C. E. Meyers (Ed.), Socio-behavioral studies in mental retardation: Papers in honor of Harvey L. Dingman. *American Association on Mental Deficiency Monograph Series,* 1973, No. 1. (b)

Mercer, J. R., & Smith, J. M. Subtest estimates of the WISC Full Scale I.Q.'s for children. *Vital and Health Statistics,* Series 2, No. 47. U.S. Department of Health, Education and Welfare, Public Health Service. (DHEW Publication No. (HSM) 72–1047), March, 1972.

Mercer, J. R., & Brown, W. C. Racial differences in I.Q.: Fact or artifact? C. Senna (Ed.), *The fallacy of I.Q.* New York: The Third Press, 1973.

P. v. Riles, 343 F. Supp. 1306 (N.D. Cal., 1972). Northern District of California, Filed June 21, 1972.

San Francisco Board of Education. Minutes of the special meeting. June 16, 1970.

Terman, L. M., & Merrill, M. A. *Stanford Binet intelligence scale.* Boston: Houghton-Mifflin, 1960.

United States Commission on Civil Rights. *The excluded student: Educational practices affecting Mexican-Americans in the Southwest.* Report III, Washington, D. C.: U. S. Government Printing Office, May, 1972.

Wechsler, D. *The measurement and appraisal of adult intelligence.* (4th Ed.) Baltimore: Williams & Wilkins, 1958.

On Education

He always.
He always wanted to explain things.
But no one cared.
So he drew.
Sometimes he would draw and it wasn't anything.
He wanted to carve it in a stone or write it in the sky.
And it would be only the sky and him and
   the things inside him that needed saying.
And it was after that he drew the picture.
He kept it under his pillow and let no one see it.
And he would look at it every night and think about it.
And when it was dark and his eyes were closed, he
   could still see it.
And it was all of him.
And he loved it.
When he went to school he brought it with him.
Not to show to anyone, but just to have it with him
   like a friend.
It was funny about school.
He sat in a square brown desk.
Like all the other square brown desks.
And he thought it should be red.
And his room was a square brown room,
   like all the other rooms.
And it was tight and close.
And stiff.
He hated to hold the pencil and chalk,
   with his arms stiff and his feet flat on the floor.
STIFF.

With the teacher watching and watching.
The teacher came and spoke to him
She told him to wear a tie like all the other boys.
He said he didn't like them.
And she said that it didn't matter.
After that they drew.
And he drew all yellow and that was the way he felt about the
    morning.
And it was beautiful.
The teacher came and smiled at him.
"What's this?" she said. "Why don't you draw
    something like Ken is drawing?"
"Isn't that beautiful."
After that his mother brought him a tie.
And he always drew airplanes and rocketships
    like everyone else.
And he threw the old picture away.
And when he lay out alone looking at the sky
    it was big and blue and all of everything.
But he wasn't anymore.
He was square inside and brown.
And his hands were stiff
And he was like everyone else.
And all the things inside him
    that needed saying, didn't need it anymore.
It had stopped pushing
It was crushed
STIFF
Like everything else.

This poem was given to a grade 12 English teacher in Illinois. Two weeks later, the student committed suicide. Reprinted by permission from *Scholastic Scope*, © 1970 by Scholastic Magazines, Inc.

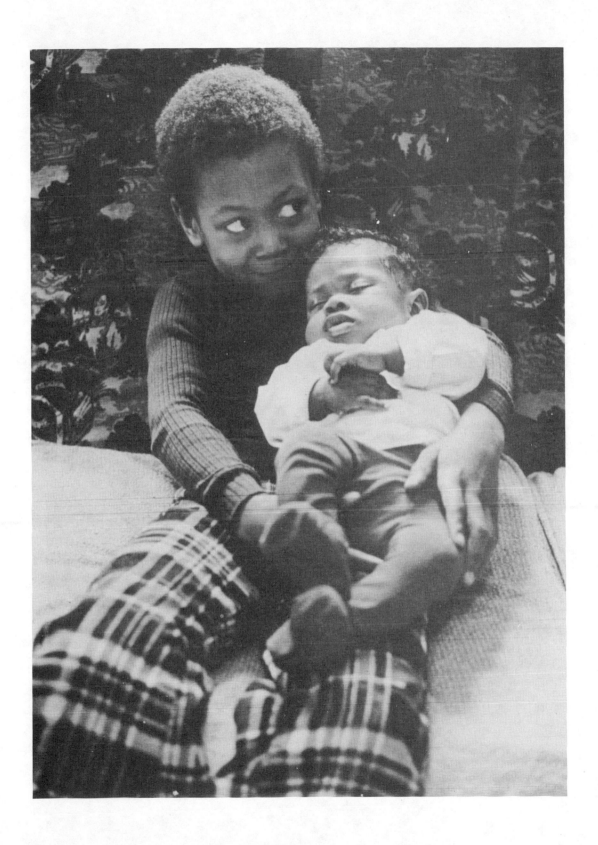

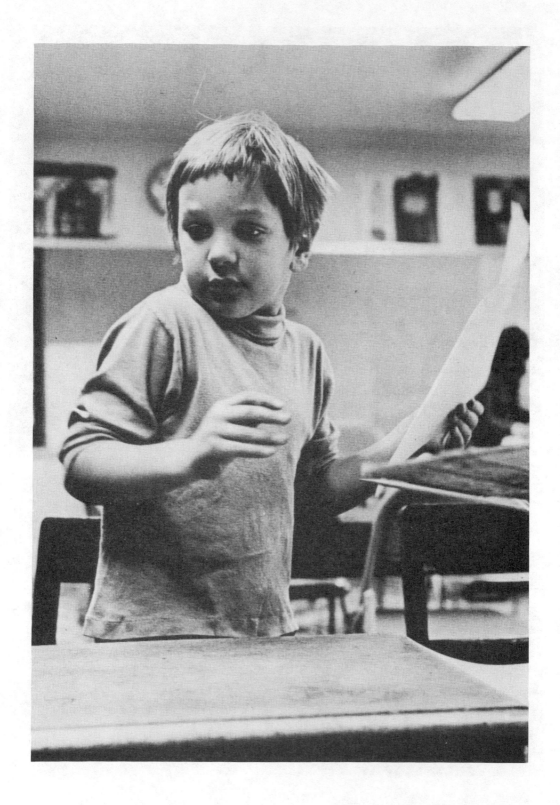

Book Reviews

CHILDREN AND YOUTH IN AMERICA: A
DOCUMENTARY HISTORY VOL. 1 (1600–
1865) AND VOL. 2 (1866–1932), ed. by
Robert H. Bremner *et al.*
*Cambridge, Mass.: Harvard University
Press, 1971. 1,522 pp. $10.00 (Vol. 1)
and $20.00 (Vol. 2).*

The lives of children, a subject almost
wholly neglected by historians, get a
full measure of attention in the excellent documentary collection, *Children and
Youth in America*. The rich material in
these two volumes is superbly organized
and imaginatively selected. When the third
and final volume is published, it will add
immensely to such valuable collections as
Grace Abbott's *The Child and the State*.[1]
Just as a literary anthology cannot help
but be a work of literary criticism, collections of this sort are exercises in historical
judgment and interpretation; in this case
the result is a comprehensive and often
somber presentation of the place of childhood in our national life—far and away
the best chronicle of public policy toward
children we now have.

Volume I deals with the nine generations of American children between the
founding of the English colonies and the
end of the Civil War. It is divided into

[1] Chicago: University of Chicago Press, 1938.

three periods, each representing a stage in
the development of policy toward children. In the first, 1600-1735, the documents
reveal a concern for defining the nature of
public authority over children who were
subjects—not citizens—of private family
governments. In the second, 1735-1820,
they indicate a quest for the proper public
response to children in an ideological climate stressing self-help, individualism, and
self-interest. In the third period, 1820-1865,
the documents demonstrate the growing
complexity of public concern for children.
A sense of crisis over the future of children
and the family produced waves of reform
and institution-building. We hear voices
from the past discussing issues by no means
settled today. How should the state and the
adult public regard children in a society
marked by turbulent political, social, and
economic change and a high degree of geographic and social mobility? What should
adults expect of children? What should
they do for them? What should they deny
them? Bremner and his colleagues illuminate the answers to these questions through
a vast selection of materials, ranging from
legislative debates and newspaper clip-
pings to private diaries and memoirs.

Volume II, covering the period from the
end of the Civil War to the beginning of
the New Deal, reveals a more institutionalized, increasingly professional set of con-

cerns, and therefore is less humanly vivid. It documents the remarkable rise in the status of children in American society, which Richard Titmuss, speaking of Britain, rightly has called the revolution in child care standards since the nineteenth century.[2] Selections show how the renewed emphasis on the distinctiveness of childhood channeled reform and philanthropic energy into the provision of special facilities for children, and how an earlier generation's institutional answers to social problems became part of the problem for succeeding generations. There was state and federal legislation forbidding child labor, compelling children to spend more and more time in schools. With the approach of the New Deal, there was a growing, yet skittish and fearful, acceptance of the notion that the federal government has a responsibility for the health and welfare of the young.

Like the ancient Romans they admired so much, Americans during this period had a special passion for building institutions. The institutions were meant to mediate between older values and the tumultuous consequences of unchecked economic and technological growth. Institutions such as the public schools, prisons, insane asylums, and reformatories were supposed to shore up what were conceived of as declining older institutions such as the family, the village community, and the church. They often ended up as mechanisms for imposing an Anglo-Saxon, Protestant consensus on alien newcomers to society.

Living as we do in a world of ailing institutions inherited from this past, we are likely to look with jaundiced eyes on the

[2] Titmuss, *Gift Relationship* (New York: Pantheon Books, 1970), p. 11-12.

consequences of institutionalization. We tend to see the ambiguities of particular reforms for special groups—children, blacks, the insane, juvenile delinquents. At the very least, the group in need has often ended up isolated from the rest of society; at the worst, institutions have become human dumping bins. It is difficult for a skeptical age to listen patiently to the evangelical rhetoric of so many figures in the American reform tradition. Reform ideology is often the same, the grandiose promises are similar, and the resulting cycles of disillusionment, repression, budget cuts, and reaction, are all too familiar. Out of the reformers' mix of fears and hopes emerge the coral reefs of bureaucracies and unresponsive professions. But to point out these results is not to subscribe to the current anarchist mood of hostility to all institutions, reformers, and professions. Our revulsion against pathological professionalism and institutional arthritis is quite natural, but it need not follow that our main social problem is that we are overorganized, or that we can do without a reformed professionalism. Proponents of total deschooling and a dismantling of our social service institutions should take a hard look at Volume I of *Children and Youth in America*. In the seventeenth and eighteenth century many Americans lived in a relatively deschooled and deinstitutionalized society; Bremner's grim documents do not suggest that children were better off under this arrangement. Decent environments for people require institutions—pluralistic, voluntaristic, and on a human scale—but institutions nonetheless. And true professional standards to guide them.

The material in Volume II often is drab in comparison with Volume I, yet it has the same comprehensiveness and intelligent organization, and it is impossible in this short space to do justice to the many topics it deals with: the legal status of children, children's health, schooling, blacks, Indians, and other minorities, immigrant children, child labor, birth control, abortion, juvenile delinquency, developments in pediatrics, the fight against infant and maternal mortality, professionalization and the growth of bureaucracy, the Depression, the advent of the high school as a mass institution. Both volumes of *Children and Youth in America* are strong in two areas that have been neglected up to recent years: the history of education and the history of children's health. The material on education clearly profits from the current revival of interest in that subject which revisionist historians of education have sparked by their suspicions about the actual function of public schooling. The very welcome interest in children's health derives, in part, from the fact that this whole project is sponsored by the American Public Health Association. It suggests an understanding of the importance of children's health that continues to elude schools and legislatures.

Given the sources, it is inevitable that documents relating to childhood should record adult attitudes toward children; this is not the only realm in which our historical knowledge is limited to the beliefs of the articulate and the privileged. Nonetheless one would like to see ways around this. Perhaps Volume III could include material from some of the growing oral history archives, although no one, to my knowledge, has been following Robert Coles' lead in interviewing children and transcribing the results. Certainly it would be possible to include more material from

literary sources, which Bremner and his colleagues tend to neglect. Images of childhood fashioned by artists and writers are important sources because they sometimes influence and reflect popular thought and because they often constitute profound, imaginative explorations of unacknowledged cultural dilemmas and tensions. Considering the wealth of photographs available, particularly for the period following the 1880's, the illustrations in Volume II are disappointing; one hopes for more and better selections for Volume III.

No one expects wholly novel ideas from a documentary collection of this sort. Its chief virtue, perhaps, is its potential for giving concrete examples of great historical abstractions. Leafing through these pages, one can see how the shift from farming village to industrial city altered the American sense of community. Children were moved from a world in which the family was the main economic unit to one in which work took place in factories. As labor rose in value we see the consequences of industrialization for the new work force of women and children. Side by side with the new romantic and religious interest in the estate of childhood came the exploitation of the factory system. Stephen Knight, for example, describes his youth in a Rhode Island cotton mill:

My work was to put in the roving on a pair of mules containing 256 spindles. . . . The running time for that mill, on an average, was about fourteen hours per day. In the summer months we went in as early as we could see, worked about an hour and a half, and then had a half hour for breakfast. At twelve o'clock we had another half hour for dinner, and then we worked until the stars were out. . . . For my services I was allowed forty-two cents per week. . . . The proprietor of that mill was accustomed to make a contract with his help on the first day of April, for the coming year. . . . On one of these anniversaries, a mother with several children suggested to the proprietor that the pay seemed small. The proprietor replied, 'You get enough to eat, don't you?' The mother said, 'Just enough to keep the wolf from the door.' He then remarked, 'You get enough clothes to wear, don't you?' to which she answered, 'Barely enough to cover our nakedness.' 'Well,' said the proprietor, 'we want the rest.' (pp. 606-607)

Through Bremner's materials on family life, we see the rise in the esteem for children in middle-class homes, and how this was connected with increased privacy, more property, and a keen sense of social divisions. The quick eye for class, ethnic, and racial differences seems to have been one of the by-products of a relatively egalitarian, competitive order. Foreign visitors document changes in the conception of authority, the declining power of fathers to decide the future of their children, and the slow extension of egalitarian and democratic ideas into every sphere of life. Bremner's visitors note the precocity of American youth throughout the nineteenth century; it is clear that the American youth cult had its roots in nineteenth century America's emphasis on equality. Certain themes seem perennial: the pervasive assumption that each new generation faces wholly different circumstances, that each American life has to be, as Henry Adams put it, an education, because nobody can look to the experience of their parents for guidance. Also—and this grows more common as the immigrants arrive—children, being more at home in the new surroundings, come to act as cultural guides for their puzzled parents.

One finishes these 1,522 absorbing pages with several thoughts. These volumes remind us that our pervasive sense of crisis concerning children and the family is quite traditional, being part of a worried national conversation that began in the 1820's and has continued to the present. They remind us, too, that concepts such as childhood itself, or youth, or adolescence, have evolved under specific historical circumstances and are not timeless universal truths about the human condition in every age and place. Children were adults in miniature until society perceived their distinct needs, set up specific institutions to cater to them, and developed a body of thought to account for their peculiarities. We can trace the glacial, yet sure, transition of children from perverse creatures whose will must be broken to souls fit for redemption then to being valuable enough to care for, unique and precious beings. Volume I, in particular reminds us of the remoteness of much of the American past from our present existence. A nostalgia for what Marx called "rural idiocy" persists, but we are a civilization in which children, far from being the economic asset they once were for so much of American history, are a distinct luxury. We see how defining childhood as a special stage of existence has had both good and bad consequences: the recognition of children's needs has often resulted in measures that cut them off from life. What was once a direct initiation into the world of adults, reality, and work, no longer holds. Along with our other ghettoes we have created age ghettoes where peers speak only to peers, and few young people learn what it is like to raise children, do productive work, or grow old.

The documents also make it clear that substantial gains have been made for children's welfare, despite well-warranted criticisms of our inadequate social service system. While it is fashionable to question the motives of many of our reformers—and they were a mixed lot—there is no doubt that without their efforts American life would be much more of a jungle than it is. At the same time, few readers will miss seeing the tenacious historical roots of America's public neglect of its children, at least compared with other industrially advanced societies. Even the relatively large sums of money spent on education seem to some extent to have been compensations for neglect in other areas, such as health. Throughout our history, children's welfare has been subordinated to economic goals, and institutions for children, operating in a context of market priorities and social inequality, have too often turned into scrap heaps. Social control of the alien poor has amounted to an obsession. Richard Titmuss has insisted that the central issue of public policy is the sort of treatment we are willing to give to strangers.[3] In America it seems that the problem of strangers and their children has been unusually hard, for they have been not only from a different social class, but from another people, and, often enough, another race. In this light, even proud and valuable American traditions of voluntaristic philanthropy can take on a sinister quality as one notes the systematic way in which private services have historically excluded the

[3] Titmuss.

alien and the marginal. Individualism, the pervasiveness of the entrepreneurial and capitalist outlook, the lack of a social democratic tradition, the limitations of the reform mentality, the divisiveness of race and ethnicity, the rigid and self-serving nature of our bureaucracies and professions—have all worked against a public commitment to meeting the needs of every child.

Children and Youth in America is the sort of work we need to add substance to our current interest in children and the family, for it is a curious fact that these topics are now of enormous interest. The reasons for this are complex and partly historical. As a nation we have long—too long, perhaps—thought of ourselves as young, an identification which has often blinded us to the old, settled nature of many of our social arrangements. America's profoundly Romantic literary traditions have led many of our best writers to explore the world through the child's eyes; in recent decades what were the concerns of a handful of nineteenth century intellectuals have become part of the general cultural property of masses of educated people. For the Romantics, new and old, childhood often stands, in Proust's phrase, for a return to the unanalyzed. It represents a complex of attitudes: hostility to logical analysis, a contempt for form, a suspicion of intellect, and a reluctance to develop a complicated reaction to society and life. It is an intensely private and solitary outlook. These are its vices. Its virtues are its integrity, its sense of wonder, its compassion, its humor, its refusal to be complacent. All this is part of the present cultural mood. For some Americans, childhood has become a kind of ideology, the last hope for the future, after successive creeds and intellectual idols have fallen. As William Kessen puts it, the child, once at the margin of society's concerns, is now something of a culture hero.[4]

Our absorption in childhood also reflects the fact that large numbers of middle-class Americans are wealthy enough and have time enough to devote themselves to the rearing of their children. The death of a child is no longer common. Perhaps this is the biggest difference between childhood in the past and childhood now, just as the reduction in the ravages of childbirth may be the biggest change in the lives of women. The reduction of the infantile death rate from 300 or 400 per 1,000 births to less than 25 is an astonishing demographic fact, notwithstanding the persistence of disgracefully high rates among minorities and the poor. Before 1750 the odds against a child's completing five years of life may have been as high as three to one. We are apt to think of the nineteenth century's preoccupation with death and funerals, widows and orphans, as morbid sentimentality; but it also mirrored social reality. One would like to see more study of the psychological consequences of these facts; what we see as the callousness toward very small children of earlier times may reflect a simple reality: parents in a culture in which child mortality is high may not be able to invest much feeling in very young children.

The growing interest in the family and children is linked with a growing interest in recording the history of ordinary people. Since ordinary people do not usually leave impressive documentation of their lives, there has been a tendency to mine quan-

titative sources—parish records, birth and census data—in an attempt to make the numbers speak for the forgotten. An excellent example of this is Stephen Thernstrom's *The Other Bostonians* which documents the degree to which the supposedly stable and placid America of the past was a vast arena of men, women, and children on the move, geographically and socially.[5] Michael Katz and his colleagues are exploring class and family issues in nineteenth century Canada. Until recently the terrain of the family has been barren of work except for a few imposing monuments such as Arthur Calhoun's *A Social History of the Family*[6] and Oscar Handlin's classic, *The Uprooted*.[7] For a good sampling of recent work in this area of social history, see Tomara Hareven (ed.), *Anonymous Americans*[8] and Michael Gordon (ed.), *The American Family in Social-Historical Perspective*[9] and Oscar and Mary Handlin, *Facing Life*.[10]

Philippe Aries' famous work, *Centuries of Childhood*,[11] has provoked a series of debates which have made us realize how blinkered and parochial our ideas about childhood may be. Aries argues that child-

[4] Kessen, *The Child* (New York: John Wiley and Sons, 1965).

[5] Thernstrom, *The Other Bostonians: Poverty and Progress in the American Metropolis, 1880-1900* (Cambridge, Mass.: Harvard University Press, 1973).
[6] New York: Barnes and Noble, 1966.
[7] Boston: Atlantic, Little Brown, 1973.
[8] Hareven, ed., *Anonymous Americans: Explorations in Nineteenth Century Social History* (Englewood Cliffs, N. J.: Prentice Hall, 1971).
[9] New York: St. Martin's Press, 1973.
[10] Oscar and Mary Handlin, *Facing Life: Youth and the Family in American History* (Boston: Atlantic, Little Brown, 1971).
[11] Philippe Aries, *Centuries of Childhood: A Social History of Family Life* (New York: Alfred A. Knopf, 1962).

hood, conceived of as a separate stage of life, is a creation of Western society in the last three centuries; adults in previous ages saw children as tiny adults, not as beings with distinct needs and ways of thinking and feeling. Some of the new historical works, including Bremner, remind us, too, that adolescence and youth as we now understand them did not really exist before the latter part of the nineteenth century.

Historians like John Demos and Philip Greven are widening our understanding of the colonial family by careful work in the local history of families and the interplay of generations.[12] Demos has made some interesting, if speculative, attempts to apply the psychoanalytic insights of Erik Erikson to the inhabitants of colonial Plymouth. Under the influence of French demographers, Peter Laslett and a polygot set of colleagues are starting to overturn persistent legends about the types of family structure that prevailed in past times.[13] Many of us carry in our heads a group portrait of our ancestors clustered in extended families, grandfathers, aunts, uncles, all sitting around a fire with grandchildren and cousins under the gaze of a patriarchal family head. Yet in England and other countries now under study it seems that the nuclear family—husband, wife, children— was the norm at least two centuries before industrialization. Anthropologists and soci-

ologists grow indignant at Laslett, accusing him of demolishing straw men; nevertheless what William Goode has called the "classical family of Western nostalgia"[14] has profoundly influenced both academic and popular ideas on the family. Certainly it colors our attitude toward present issues, as when many critics see the isolated nuclear family as a historical novelty, and a pathological one at that. This is another instance of a more general nostalgia for the past—the assumption that past societies were more stable, more communal, and more harmonious than ours. It makes it very difficult to draw up what has to be a very complex balance sheet of the losses and gains in the whole process of modernization.

The increased interest in children is not limited to historians. It is plainly one important reason why the intense interest in educational reform of the 1960's has not died out; for all the budget cuts and racial tension, there is probably more change— both creative and faddish—in American schools today than ever before, and more public and parental involvement in school issues. What might be called the developmental approach to children's learning— emphasizing the stages in children's physical, emotional, and intellectual growth, the active nature of the child as learner, and the profound variations among individual children—has never received a more respectful hearing by American teachers, although it can scarcely be said to dominate classroom practice. William Kessen's *The Child*,[15] a brilliant historical

[12] John Demos, *Little Commonwealth: Family Life in Plymouth Colony* (Oxford: Oxford University Press, 1971); and Phillip J. Greven, Jr., *Four Generations: Population, Land and Family in Colonial Andover, Massachusetts* (Ithaca, N. Y.: Cornell University Press, 1970).

[13] Peter Laslett and Robert Wall, ed., *Household and Family in Past Time* (Cambridge, England: Cambridge University Press, 1972).

[14] Goode, "The Theory of Measurement of Family Change," E. H. Sheldon and E. Moore, eds., *Indicators of Social Change* (New York: Russell Sage Foundation, 1968), p. 386.

[15] Kessen.

anthology of psychology's interest in the child, shows a growing—if scarcely dominant—recognition in that behaviorist-ridden field of the diversity among children and the uniqueness of each child. In the law, the movement for public interest advocacy has an articulate wing exploring possible extensions of children's basic constitutional and legal rights, examining, for example, the implications of labeling and tracking in classrooms. In medicine and psychiatry, stirrings toward public health and community medicine are focusing on children's health and family practice. Sociologists and anthropologists are taking a new look at the family, although they have yet to produce studies to compare with Oscar Lewis' family portraits[16] or Robert Coles's magnificent three volumes, *Children of Crisis*.[17] Commissions of inquiry are already at work trying to knit together these disparate efforts, although one doubts that good synthetic scholarship will suffice to produce compassionate social policy. All one can safely predict is a flood of literature of mixed quality on the young and their families.

This literature reflects the general testing of values and institutions that began in the chaotic 1960's and is continuing, in more muted, scholarly, and restrained form, into the 1970's. Once again, Americans feel that their distance from old certitudes is uncomfortably great. There is much concern that public policy has weakened the family instead of strengthening it and, at the same time, that the family as an institution is under heavy attack. The women's movement is important in all this, but the women's movement itself is only part of an intellectual process that has been in motion at least since the time of the Progressive reformers like Jane Addams and John Dewey: a widening of social sympathies among intellectuals and professionals to include historic outsiders —immigrants, women, children, the old. While American institutions have neglected outsiders and discriminated against them, American intellectuals have often been drawn to their communal values, using them to criticize American economic institutions.

In his book, *The Coming of Post-Industrial Society*,[18] Daniel Bell suggests that concern for communal values is part of a broader point of view that he calls the sociologizing mode of thinking, which he contrasts to the economic outlook. The economic outlook assumes that individual choice in the free market is the best mechanism for establishing social priorities, and that economic growth and private consumption are the chief social goals. On the other hand, the sociologizing mode sets wider, non-economic goals when considering such matters as national economic

[16] Oscar Lewis, *Children of Sanchez* (New York: Random House, 1961); Lewis, *Death in the Sanchez Family* (New York: Random House, 1969); Lewis, *Five Families* (New York: New American Library, 1971); Lewis, *Five Families: Mexican Case Studies in the Culture of Poverty* (New York: Basic Books, 1965); Lewis, *Pedro Martinez: A Mexican Peasant and his Family* (New York: Random House, 1964); Lewis, *La Vida: A Puerto Rican Family in the Culture of Poverty, San Juan and New York* (New York: Random House, 1966).

[17] Robert Coles, *Children of Crisis*. Vol. 1: *A Study of Courage and Fear* (Boston: Atlantic, Little, Brown, 1967); Vol. 2: *Migrants, Mountaineers and Sharecroppers* (Boston: At-

lantic, Little Brown, 1972); Vol. 3: *The South Goes North* (Boston: Atlantic, Little Brown, 1972).

[18] New York: Basic Books, 1973.

planning, the environment, good medical care, decent schools, the general quality of life. Bell forecasts a society wracked by competing demands on the political order to redress the present imbalance to include more communal values: to admit previously excluded groups, to distribute income more equally, to readjust the relative size of the public and private sectors, to balance individual and social goals, to square demands for greater participation with a greater degree of meritocracy, professionalism, and expertise.

Bell is far too sanguine about the ease with which private corporate power will submit to public control. Even in intellectual circles, after all, the status quo has many articulate defenders. Along with the widening of social sympathies has grown a literature of learned reaction. Scholars like Arthur Jensen and Edward Banfield have recast old and enduring ideas into new academic form, proclaiming that heredity is destiny, or that the poor are poor because of defects of character, or that all is as it must be in this most necessary of worlds. At bottom, of course, these responses are a defense of what exists: a society in which private interests set the major social priorities. Even in intellectual circles, therefore, let alone in politics or the economy, Bell's sociologizing mode is hardly triumphant.

But Bell is probably right when he predicts an impending series of battles between cultural and economic perspectives on social policy. And if he is, then I think families and children will receive even more attention, for the family may emerge as a pre-eminent symbol of non-economic values. Nineteenth century Americans were sentimental about families: the realm of work was supposed to be a Darwinian jungle in which only the fittest survived, whereas the family home was supposed to be a haven for harmony, morality, and good manners. Americans today are not free from this sort of sentimentality. The family is still widely regarded as a refuge for non-economic and pre-industrial values, a kind of pastoral realm of human feeling to hold up against a world of conflict, minutely-divided labor, and rationalized bureaucracies. Yet for all our sentimentality, and our general reluctance to observe the interaction of the family with other social institutions, it may be a fact of some political consequence that family values are more deeply rooted in American life than entrepreneurial, economic values. In the coming battles over national priorities and a new social policy, children and their families may be more important as symbols than ever.

JOSEPH FEATHERSTONE
Harvard University

A Review of Child Care Books

PREGNANCY, BIRTH AND THE NEWBORN BABY, by The Boston Children's Medical Center.
New York: Delacorte Press, 1972. 474 pp. $10.00.

I'M RUNNING AWAY FROM HOME, BUT I'M NOT ALLOWED TO CROSS THE STREET, by Gabrielle Burton.
Pittsburgh: Know, 1972. 206 pp. $4.50.

THE MAGIC YEARS, by Selma H Fraiberg.
New York: Charles Scribner's Sons, 1959. 305 pp. $2.45.

THE EMERGING PERSONALITY, by George E. Gardner.
New York: Delacorte Press, 1970. 292 pp. $6.95.

HAVE YOU HAD IT IN THE KITCHEN?, by Teddi Levison and Mickie Silverstein.
New York: Grosset and Dunlop, 1971. 149 pp. $5.95.

THE GROWTH AND DEVELOPMENT OF MOTHERS, by Angela Barron McBride.
New York: Harper and Row, 1973. 167 pp. $6.95.

BABY AND CHILD CARE, by Benjamin Spock.
New York: Pocket Books, 1968. 620 pp. $.95.

INFANT CARE, by U.S. Department of Health, Education, and Welfare, Office of Child Development.
Washington, D. C.: U.S. Government Printing Office, 1962. 98 pp. $.20.

YOUR CHILD FROM ONE TO SIX, by U.S. Department of Health, Education, and Welfare, Office of Child Development.
Washington, D. C.: U.S. Government Printing Office, 1962. 98 pp. $.20.

EXPERIENCE AND ENVIRONMENT, by Burton L. White and Jean Carew Watts.
Englewood Cliffs, N. J.: Prentice Hall, 1973. 552 pp. $14.50.

Fifty-nine million copies of the government's pamphlet on *Infant Care* have been distributed since its first printing in 1916. Twenty-two million copies of Dr. Benjamin Spock's *Baby and Child Care* have been sold since it was written in 1946. In other words, one copy of each book has been sold for almost *every* first child born to an American family during the relevant time period. No other child care books have been nearly so popular, although the sheer volume of published titles on the subject is imposing. Bookstores are filled with books on pregnancy and birth; physical, emotional, social and cognitive devel-

opment; management of young children and children's special problems.

Child care books obviously respond to the needs of parents; if they did not, people would stop buying them and writers would stop producing them. How well they respond depends on the accuracy of their perceptions of the needs of parents and the astuteness of their assessment of parents' physical and psychological situations. Their advice is useful if it answers real questions and if it is possible to carry out. One can also ask, of course, how well the books respond to the needs of children. In this review, I will assume that the needs of

Harvard Educational Review Vol. 43 No. 4 November 1973, 669–680

children are best served when the needs of their parents are served as well. Most parents, at least most parents who buy books on child care, are eager to do a good job of raising their children. They will do the best job if they themselves are happy and secure, are able to create an environment of love, growth, and mutual respect for their children, and are productive and joyful. I assume that children develop best when they are independent members, to the extent of their capabilities, of a functioning community, however small. It is true there is no scientific evidence that such environments are best for children or that unhappy environments necessarily produce damaged children. But it is hard to imagine a situation which is bad for adults being good for children. The converse, situations which are good for adults but bad for children, is unfortunately all too conceivable. In this review, however, I will not discuss the problems of parents who do not like their children and are indifferent to their welfare. That is another problem, and one outside the purview of child rearing manuals.

Child care books are most useful to parents raising their first child, and the books tend logically to focus on first children.[1] The books respond to new parents' needs for two kinds of advice. The first is advice on physical care. That babies are completely dependent on adults is obvious. Some adult responses to babies seem to come instinctively, but most information on how to care for these small dependent creatures must be learned. Few people in our society have intimate long-term contact with babies before they have one of their own. Few are enough older than their siblings to have been entrusted with their care, even if baby care were com-

monly required of older children. Teenage girls often have baby-sitting experience, but it is seldom intense enough to teach them the innumerable details of the job. Young parents, then, need to quickly learn all sorts of information: what to feed babies, what to do about mysterious rashes, what might be wrong when a baby cries. They also need to learn when they should worry and when their baby's behavior is a normal part of his development. Since few people learn these things from their own experience or from older members of the community, they turn to books.

Parents also look for advice on training children, on teaching them how to do things and teaching what to do and not do in specific situations. Although parents know vaguely that they want their children to learn certain things—to go to the bathroom in the conventional manner, for example, and to keep their natural aggressive and exploratory urges within bounds—they are understandably confused about appropriate timing and tactics for teaching them. Concern about training children has existed among parents in this country since colonial days, though the approved procedures have changed considerably over time.[2] Early child rearing advice was based on the Calvinist notion of inherent evil which has to be controlled in the

[1] Over the last twenty years, between thirty and forty per cent of all children have been first children. If fertility patterns continue as they are tending now, more and more families will have only two children, and the percentage of first children should rise to a bit over forty.

[2] For a historical examination of child-rearing advice in the 19th century, see Bernard Wishy, *The Child and the Republic* (Philadelphia: University of Pennsylvania Press, 1968).

growing child by firm discipline. The late nineteenth century saw a change to the notion of the child as a blank slate to be shaped by the parents. Today's parents are heirs of a long tradition of child study, clinical observation of children, and attempts to understand the uniqueness of child hood.

Contemporary culture sees childhood as a special time, and parents have come to believe that children must be understood, taught, and generally dealt with differently than adults. They have been told that socialization does not happen naturally, and that certain techniques are more effective than others in adjusting children to family life and helping them develop desirable adult characteristics. Most parents, like most researchers, are probably dubious about the alleged links between child rearing practices and the presence or absence of adult neuroses. They do feel, however, and they are probably right, that some ways of training children are less painful and disruptive to both parents and children than others. Parents realize that fashions in child rearing come and go, but they still need advice (preferably the latest advice) on what to do. Books are expected to fill this need.

Parents, like everybody else, also need reassurance and support. They need to be told that they are right or at least normal in what they are doing with their lives and their children's lives. They need books that respond to their own anxieties and worries, that support what their impulses tell them is sensible and right, and that accurately assess their own capabilities and limitations. Books which gloss over parental anxieties make those who do worry feel deviant and guilty. Books which assume that parents can easily do things which in fact many find difficult engender feelings of incompetence and resentment. Parents instead need books which make them feel confident, competent, and pleased with themselves. To perform this function, books must recognize the difficult situation of contemporary parents. The average first baby is born fourteen months after his parents' marriage, and seventy-five percent are born within the first two years of marriage. The majority of mothers work between marriage and the birth of their first child; the average mother has only a short time to adjust to her new job of housewife before the baby arrives. Typically she is also adjusting to a new home. Most families move at least once during the first few years of marriage, often probably motivated by the birth of the baby.[3]

Thus the new mother also has a new job and a new home. She probably expects her new status to be extremely satisfying. Even though the typical woman now spends more than half her adult life in the labor force, motherhood is still considered the ultimate vocation of American women.[4]

[3] Data on childspacing from: U.S. Bureau of the Census, *Current Population Reports*, Series P-20, No. 186. "Marriage, Fertility and Childspacing: June 1965," (Washington, D.C.: U. S. Government Printing Office, 1969). Labor force participation data from: U.S. Department of Labor, *Dual Careers: A Longitudinal Study of the Labor Market Experience of Women*, Vol. 1, Manpower Administration, Manpower Research Monograph No. 21 (Washington, D.C.: U.S. Government Printing Office, 1970). Mobility data from U.S. Bureau of the Census, *Current Population Reports*, Series P-20, No. 235, "Mobility of the Population of the United States: March 1970 to March 1971" (Washington, D.C.: U.S. Government Printing Office, 1972).

[4] On a 1971 Harris poll only sixteen per cent of the women and thirteen per cent of the men

The new mother has high expectations, an acute sense of responsibility, and little appreciation of what lies ahead. She often has no life of her own to substitute for the job she has so recently left, and few friends or activities in the neighborhood she has so recently moved into.

Child care manuals cannot, of course, be expected to cure parents' personal problems. Books can, however, recognize their existence. The situation of many young parents may make it difficult for them to raise their children according to the advice of the child care manuals. Parents need books which recognize their difficulties; books which do not only make their lives harder.

Spock, *Infant Care, and Your Child From 1 to 6* do a fine job of meeting the needs of parents, a fact which probably accounts for their tremendous popularity. All three deal with both physical care and socialization. Spock, for example, devotes 107 of the 350 pages dealing with children between birth and three to feeding and physical care. One hundred and fifty-four additional pages of the 600 page book, relevant to all ages, cover disease, first aid, and special physical problems. The remaining pages on young children deal with such topics as organizing the child's day, weaning, and toilet training. A 38 page chapter on "Managing Young Children" contains the following sub-headings: play

---

disagreed with the statement: Taking care of a home and raising children is more rewarding for a woman than having a job.

[5] In this review, I focus only on books and sections of books which talk about children between birth and age three. Books on older children deal with an entirely different range of problems, and one must somehow limit comments to a specific age group.

and outgoingness, early childhood, the father as companion, going to bed, duties, discipline, and jealousy and rivalry. *Infant Care* devotes most of its 70 pages to physical care but also covers " 'difficult' babies" and "discipline and teaching." *Your Child From 1 to 6* covers development, toilet training, physical care, "Managing a toddler," and "Your babysitter."

The three books give sensible and reassuring advice with regard to both physical care and training. The health and safety of the baby is emphasized but not overdone. The latest edition of *Infant Care,* for example, says nothing about sterilizing bottles, though it does emphasize that the bottles must be clean and the formula fresh. With regard to training, both books encourage parents to be "firm but friendly," to reward rather than punish, and to admit their own feelings of anger and frustration. *Infant Care,* after a section on how babies respond to attention and love, has the following paragraphs on punishment:

What about punishment? Will a baby stop doing something if he is constantly punished for it? It should work that way, but actually punishment doesn't work well in the first years of life. The baby usually can't figure out just what behavior is being punished. If you slap him when he throws a spoonful of food on the floor, he may not know whether he is being punished for eating, for trying to feed himself, or for something else. He may stop eating or trying to feed himself rather than start to become a neat eater. Then too, punishment is a form of attention. Some babies may enjoy attention more than they dislike the punishment. If the child who threw a spoonful of food on the floor saw just a slight frown on his mother's face and was rewarded with a smile for many of the times he got the spoon in his mouth, he would soon give up any purposeful spilling.

Of course, the baby sooner or later must learn that some of the things he does makes people around him irritated or angry. You don't have to be always calm, smile or hold your temper. But, the fact that his behavior is something irritating and that you show your irritation in natural ways at times is quite different from trying to teach him how to behave through punishment. (pp. 34-35)

The three books do a good job in letting parents know what to expect from their children and in reassuring them about common worries. They describe normal physical development with plenty of allowance for normal variation. They describe social and emotional problems at various ages, both warning and reassuring parents about such stages as the terrible twos. *Infant Care* has a fine section on temperamental differences between babies, explaining that some are active and some passive, some regular and some not, some gregarious and some withdrawn, and so on. It also has a reassuring section on "difficult" babies which begins:

While no single trait of temperament makes a baby much more difficult, babies with certain combinations of traits are certainly harder to care for. If you have such a child it may be a great comfort to know that you really have a much harder job than do most other mothers. (p. 27)

The books also have a healthy view of children in the family. Children are to be cared for and enjoyed, but they are also members of a larger society. Spock especially implies that children should not be objects for parents to lavish attention on or shape in their own images, but small human beings who are part of a family and a community.

In spite of their strengths, however, the books seem to make a number of assumptions about mothers of first babies which are largely wrong and probably anxiety-producing. The situation of most young mothers, faced with a new baby, a new job, and often a new home, is confusing, lonely, and somewhat frightening.

Neither Spock's book nor the government books speak to the inevitable frustration and resentment which arise in such situations. Their emphasis on maternal instincts and natural behavior implies that mothers invariably enjoy their babies and feel continually loving and nurturant. Though they admit that mothers will occasionally feel irritable and depressed, they never discuss the feelings of resentment followed by guilt of mothers who expect fulfillment and joy in their new lives and find instead a very mixed bag. Nor do they admit, either implicitly or explicitly, that mothers might have difficulty in maintaining a satisfying personal life. Spock seems to assume, in his discussions of how to manage the baby, that mothers have household routines to keep them productively occupied near their children, and that they have neighbors and friends to be with in the recommended two or three hours a day outside. *Infant Care* says, "Plan to get out without him for at least several hours a week after the first month" (p. 53) without realizing that doing so may be a formidable problem, both socially and psychologically.

By not identifying these common problems of resentment and loneliness, while being so conscientious about identifying others, the books may contribute to the anxiety of women who read them. This in turn may contribute to a maternal attitude which sees the child as the focus of the mother's life and the sole source of her emotional satisfaction and feeling of self-worth. This attitude places enormous demands on the child, who undoubtedly picks up the concerns of his mother. It may also make it harder for the child to become independent of the mother, and to live and grow in his own right. Thus even though the explicit stance of the books encourages independent growth of the child, their implicit assumptions may encourage precisely the opposite attitudes.

The books are also remiss in their insensitivity to the problems of mothers who work, whether out of need or out of concern for their own mental health. About thirty percent of the mothers of children under six now work outside the home. Spock actively disapproves of this large number of working mothers, implying that psychological damage to the children is bound to occur (an implication not supported by empirical research). The latest edition of *Infant Care* is more neutral, saying simply, "Many mothers return to full-time or part-time work after the baby is born" (p. 54). This is followed by some helpful advice about choosing a babysitter or day care center. Neither book deals with the special problems of working mothers.

Advice on how much time to spend with children and how to spend it, for example, could be extremely useful to working mothers. Most mothers actually spend very little time interacting with their children,[6] but Spock's advice can be read as implying much more. Mothers often hesitate to make their own lives because they assume that their children ought to be given all of their time. This is clearly false, but it is a guilt-producing imperative for many mothers. Advice on how to spend the time which is available for children is also important. Realistic, practical advice on what other parents have found to be the most satisfying ways of spending time with their children would be helpful to many parents. Working mothers also need advice on how to help their children, and probably themselves as well, to get through the transition period, a difficult one for many families. Both books devote elaborate attention to the problem of preparing a child for a new sibling, but none to preparing him for a new caretaker. Since the situation is so common, such advice would be a welcome addition to the books.

No other books, among the vast quantity available, approach the popularity of Spock or the government pamphlets. Those books which represent the thinking of "experts," however, may have influence beyond their own sales. The ideas contained in the four books discussed here, for example, can be expected to make their way into popular magazines and eventually into the more popular manuals. Two

[6] One survey found that nonworking mothers average seventy-four minutes a day. See John P. Robinson, "Historical Changes in How People Spend Their Time," in *Family Issues of Employed Women in Europe and America*, ed. Andree Michel (Leiden: E. J. Brill, 1971). White and Watts' observational data imply a bit more, twenty-five or thirty per cent of waking hours.

are publications of the Boston Children's Medical Center, one a literate popularization of psychoanalytic thinking, and the fourth a Harvard research report which has already been reported in the *Times* and is in the process of being rewritten into a manual for parents.

Two themes, nearly absent in Spock, appear in the newer books. The first is a focus on pregnancy and birth. *Pregnancy, Birth and the Newborn Baby*, by the Boston Children's Medical Center, devotes one chapter to newborn babies, focusing on physical care, feeding, and disease. Two-thirds of the book deals with pregnancy and birth, with emphasis on the physical and emotional reaction of the mother to the strange changes taking place in her body and her life. It looks at pregnancy as a special and uniquely satisfying time in the life of a woman and encourages extensive physical and mental self-examination. We can probably expect this emphasis on pregnancy and birth to become more and more common in books on child rearing.

The focus on pregnancy and birth may have mixed effects on mothers. Calling attention to the transition is an appropriate response to a new stage in a woman's life. On the other hand, romanticizing the occasion probably contributes to the development of unreasonable expectations about the joys of motherhood. Encouraging women to focus on pregnancy reinforces the cultural tendency to see motherhood as women's ultimate fulfillment. Moreover, the focus on pregnancy may encourage the tendency to see the child as an extension, even a possession of the mother.

A second theme in the newer books emphasizes the cognitive and emotional development of the child. *The Emerging Personality* by George Gardner, another publication of the Boston Children's Medical Center, is a good example. It talks of the "developmental tasks" of young children, and advises parents on how to help their children carry out their developmental tasks. The book stresses the importance of early stimulation, and advises parents to talk and play a lot with their babies. Gardner says:

How much stimulation the child gets from his environment will influence the rate at which he will progress along the several ladders of development: physical, interpersonal, intellectual, and moral. Often when a particular child appears to be retarded in his development, we question his innate ability to succeed. In fact, we find the real lag has been in the amount of stimulation he has received from those around him. (p. 38)

He goes on to discuss the importance of building the child's vocabulary, and introducing him to varied ideas and objects before he goes to school.

Gardner also stresses the solving of psychological problems, for example, those dealing with abandonment and the development of a sense of basic trust. Again, he emphasizes the later importance of solving these problems effectively, and advises parents to devote considerable effort to building a sense of trust in their children. In his discussion of toilet training, Gardner emphasizes the symbolic significance to the child of "holding on" to his feces as a part of himself and gradually learning to relinquish them. He says:

Our image of ourselves—that is, our feelings about the kind of people we are, the value we place on ourselves or feel others place on us—may have its roots in our early training experience. It will depend on whether our response to those demands was a succession of failures attended by punishment or derogation and leaving a sense of loss of prestige or "goodness" in the eyes of our parents. (p. 78)

In short, the gist of Gardner's advice is that parents should actively encourage the cognitive and emotional development of their children by using certain specified techniques of verbal teaching and psychologically appropriate training. Although he reassures parents in the introduction that their own intuitions and common sense are the best guides to raising children, his later chapters clearly belie this advice. Reading Gardner is bound to be a guilt-producing experience for most parents, especially for mothers who are already ambivalent about spending part of their time on their own lives. There is, of course, no research evidence on the efficacy of these particular techniques, so parental guilt is likely to be as unnecessary as it is damaging.

The Magic Years is a more humorous and humane approach to the same general topic. Fraiberg's descriptions of what goes on in a child's mind are delightful, whether or not they are accurate, and are bound to increase parental understanding of their children's behaviors:

His mother first "introduces" him to the potty, sometimes to the toilet with a little seat. The word "introduces" is a euphemism since at thirteen or fourteen months he is not pleased to make its acquaintance and little cares whether he meets it again. But he loves his mommy and for reasons which he cannot divine she would like him to sit on the little chair with the hole or the big toilet with the little seat with the hole. So he does. It's a bore and there are lots of other things he'd rather do, but he good naturedly agrees to sit on the hole. One day, partly by clever design and quickness on his mother's part, largely by accident, he produces a b.m. in the pot or on the toilet. His mother's face registers delight and surprise and she makes approving sounds and little cries of "good" and "big-boy." He is not sure just what he has done to bring forth such a demonstration from his mother but now he finds out. In the bottom of the pot rests an object, one that is familiar to him from another context, let us say, and which is apparently the cause of this accolade. He joins in the congratulatory noises just to be sociable, but it is not yet clear to him just how this object got there and why it has created such joy in his mother. (pp. 92-93)

Fraiberg is also sensitive to the difficulties of parents, though she assumes enormous amounts of good will and understanding. Her advice perhaps demands more time and energy than most people have, and thus unwittingly contributes to parental anxiety and guilt. For example, her discussion of separation anxiety in the last half of the first year implies serious consequences when the child is frightened by the absence of the parent. She reports on a child who developed serious sleeping problems, waking up screaming every night and not going back to sleep for several hours. Fraiberg traces the disturbance to an incident when the child woke in the middle of the night and was cared for by a strange babysitter, which made the child

371

extremely anxious about the possibility that the mother would never return. She says, "From the standpoint of prevention of such a sleep disturbance we can see that it is not advisable to bring unfamiliar persons in for baby care if we can help it" (p. 83).

The odds of such an accident causing severe problems for a baby are, of course, quite low. But Fraiberg's description may make it even harder than usual for parents to break away from their children or lead their own lives.

Experience and Environment is a research report, but its findings have important implications for parental behavior.[7] *Experience and Environment* describes the behavior of "competent" and "incompetent" children and their mothers. Since its findings are presented with more assurance than is common in research reports (or than is justified in this one) it should prove popular with commentators; it also uses a relatively clear definition of success (mainly success in school) which is appealing. White and Watts find that mothers of competent children spend more time interacting with their children than mothers of incompetent children. More of the competent mothers' interaction is "highly intellectual" —that is, direct teaching or explanation. In discussing "Best Guesses About Most Effective Child-Rearing Practices" they say:

> Our A mothers (mothers of the most competent children) talk a great deal to their children, and usually at a level the child can handle. They make them feel as though whatever they are doing is usually interesting. They provide access to many objects and diverse situations. They lead the child to believe that he can expect help and encouragement most, but *not all,* the time. They demonstrate and explain things to the child, but mostly on the child's instigation rather than their own. They prohibit certain activities, and they do so consistently and firmly.... They are imaginative, so that they make interesting associations and suggestions to the child when opportunities present themselves. They very skillfully and naturally strengthen the child's intrinsic motiva- to learn. They also give him a sense of task orientation, a notion that it is desirable to do things well and completely. They make the child feel secure. (pp. 242-243)

[7] A real review of *Experience and Environment,* which this is not, would focus on its strengths and weaknesses as a research report, rather than on the quality of its advice to parents. It may be worth making a few comments here about the research, if only to emphasize that in discussing the book's practical implications I am not testifying to the validity of its findings. The study is a report on intensive observations of thirty-one children, twenty-two of whom were predicted on the basis of their siblings' performance, to be especially "competent" and nine of whom were predicted to be incompetent. The point of the study was to identify the behavioral characteristics which distinguish competent from incompetent children at a very young age, and to describe the home environments which produce competence. The strengths of the study lie in its descriptive material on what children and their mothers do; there is a lot of variety in the sample, and the results should be reassuring to many parents. The weaknesses bear on the distinctions made between competent and incompetent children: the definitions are dubious, the sample extremely small and confounded with social class, and the strength of the findings is difficult to assess since categorical variables and no controls were employed.

They also say, "These effective mothers seem to be people with high levels of energy" (p. 244). Indeed, it will be interesting to see if translations of the White and Watts supermothers into practical advice to parents will deal with the difficulties of the task. One predicts, however, that the book will only add to the problems noted earlier.

Accounts of mothers who have confronted and coped with the need to define new patterns of family life can be really helpful to children and their families. *The Growth and Development of Mothers* is a lovely example. McBride recounts not only her own experience but also the results of an extensive reading of child rearing and family literature. Her first chapters, "The Motherhood Mystique" and "Why Have Babies?" document our cultural expectations about the jobs and responsibilities of motherhood. She says:

I began to think more and more about the warm, soft, tactile world of childhood. Having a baby would be my chance for self-renewal. How wonderful it would be to unhook my bra and have the baby suck. I could feel those happy hormones tugging at my womb, confirming my lustiness, while I gave my husband a loving look, part earth mother, part Madonna. I would finally be a complete woman. My love affair with my child would be a pure, beautiful, holy relationship. Every day would brim over with bright colors and lullabies, cuddling and snuggling, balloons and gurgling sounds. Oh, how we would sing and dance—even though I cannot carry a tune and am self-conscious about expressing the rhythm I feel. In my reverie, the waves would play hide-and-seek with my toes as I put the dandelion flag

on the tower of the sand castle. My child and I would lazily comb the beach for seashell soldiers to guard the princess's home. (p. 20)

She goes on the describe the "anger-depression-guilt-go-round" which arises when actually being a mother fails to live up to its advance billing:

'I love you.' (Caress.) 'I am furious with you.' (Spanking. Tears.) 'I'm sorry.' Sounds like the script of a B movie, but this is no paperback pulp; this is the language and movement of real life. There are days when all of us, and especially parents, go around in emotional circles, riding the anger-depression-guilt-go-round. One moment you admire your child's prowess on the monkey bars; then you get furious (and I mean furious) because she yelled and stomped her feet and demanded ten cookies for a midmorning snack. She cries and flails her arms like an angry windmill. You respond with a mean wallop to her behind, then join in the crying because the day that looked so sunny and promising has been ruined. (p. 37)

You consider the virtues of reading a book titled *Parent Effectiveness Training: The "No-Lose" Program for Raising Responsible Children* and decide to scream instead. Scream. I regularly feel like screaming to protest all those "oughts" that choke me with guilt and that Janus-like god, anger-depression, who makes me feel like an emotional volcano. First, I get mad at myself, then I spill over, and the boiling inside scorches everyone around me. How galling it is to think of those social scientists sitting quietly behind their desks telling me to keep calm, not let the noisy confusion get to me. Those pontifical sentences like "If you're not a good person, chances are you may not be a good parent" make me wonder if I am not the newest incarnation of the evil mother. In my more sane moments, however, I have come to realize that my feelings are normal. (pp. 38-39)

McBride goes on to describe in detail how she translated her new understanding into a more satisfying life for the whole family. She went back to part-time work, which she defended expertly from family demands, and again felt good about her own productivity. She started demanding that other family members share the housework. She let everybody know when she was angry and expected them to understand and do likewise—which they did. She speculates on what the world would be like if all family members shared fully in the home, in outside work, and in the community; and if families shared with each other. She presents her speculations as a blueprint for both her family and her readers.

Books like McBride's are good antidotes to the popular child rearing manuals, even though they don't go very far in actually helping people decide what to do. *Have You Had It In The Kitchen,* written by two mothers who returned to full time work while their children were still young, offers some practical suggestions. In a section entitled "The Grey Flannel Apron," they advise working mothers to get organized, get help, and above all stop feeling guilty. Their suggestions sometimes verge on superwoman fantasies, they do not talk about really young children, and they seem much less willing than I would like to challenge their chauvinist husbands.

Nonetheless, some of their suggestions may be useful.

I'm Running Away from Home But I'm Not Allowed to Cross The Street is a woman's liberation book written by a most unlikely candidate, a practicing Catholic with five children. She offers humorous and sensible advice on how women can live their own lives within happy functioning families.

Then I fumbled and mumbled something like this:

'The house is there for the benefit of everyone in the family. The responsibility for it should be divided. At one time in my life, I volunteered to assume everyone's responsibility. It's time for me to be moving on. This will necessitate everyone reassuming his personal responsibility for the functioning of the house.

At this point, you explain that you're going back to school to become a brain surgeon, or write full-time (that's me, saying that), or you're going to raise the kids REALLY without cluttering it up with diverse other full-time gardening, cleaning or maintenance jobs. If your husband says, 'Yeah! And who's gonna pay for all this, sister?' you might point out that a large Eastern bank estimates your annual services are worth $10,000 and you'll deduct your tuition from back wages. But this kind of tit for tat is a dead end route. Either he thinks you're making a contribution and have some personal rights or he doesn't. You might as well find out how the wind blows.

Roger agreed:
— that the house does benefit all of us;
— that a benefit implies a responsibility;

— that if I didn't want to be a Queen of the Castle any more, I should have a right to abdicate;

— that I hadn't shown any great aptitude for housework and eight years was a reasonable trial;

— that I had a right to try something else. (pp. 59-60)

Even very useful books like these are inevitably limited by the social and economic context in which today's families find themselves. It is a world in which work hours and locations are inflexible, there is no easy moving back and forth between work in the home and work outside, and child rearing is private rather than social. A different sort of work and community structure could alleviate many of the discontinuities and tensions which impinge on contemporary families. Perhaps the most useful how-to books for parents would help them design more livable communities. But even in the absence of a better society, we can demand child care books which deal with the realities rather than the myths of the society we have.

MARY JO BANE
Harvard University

Marriage, Parenthood and Family: Separate Domains of Change?

THE FUTURE OF MARRIAGE, by Jessie Bernard.
New York: World Publishing, 1972. 367 pp. $9.95.

WOMEN AND CHILDCARE IN CHINA: A FIRSTHAND REPORT, by Ruth Sidel.
New York: Hill and Wang, 1972. 207 pp. $6.95.

THE CHANGING FAMILY, by Betty Yorburg.
New York: Columbia University Press, 1973. 230 pp. $9.00, $2.95 (paper).

Most of us can contemplate the prospect of major social change only in bits and scraps. Although we acknowledge that our economic, political, educational, and familial structures are interlocked, we find it difficult to plan change in one system taking into account all the others. Even within a single system—in this case, the family—it stretches the imagination to consider the interrelated processes of change.

Family structure and function comprise the elementary basis of social organization, and therefore the keystone of both *status quo* and radical revolution. Both change and resistance to change are rooted in our personal lives; we all come from, and live in relation to, families. Even if our own options in the lives of our present families are limited, we can, must, look forward to the adult family lives of our children. Prediction thus becomes a preoccupation: can we rear our children so that their own options will be different from ours? Must we impose on them, as an implicit undertow

to our well-intentioned training, the same priorities and prejudices of our own past experience?

Two of these books offer us partial visions of truly radical prospects for the lives of our families; the third, by contrast, predicts no real change, only more of the same. All three present views of the future that seem tantalizingly incomplete.

Ruth Sidel's *Women and Childcare in China* presents a rich survey of childcare centers, at the parents' place of work and in their communities, for children between early infancy and the early school years. Children are treasured in China: in public they are magnets for admiration and delight. Childcare centers are important and essential units in the new society that is being constructed with self-conscious care. Sidel describes these in detail. Her emphasis is on the children who are cared for, the routines of care, and the caretakers who are almost exclusively women. Sidel emphasizes the advantages for child and caretaker alike of the consistency of childcare philosophy in centers and homes; the occasional exception (as when grandmothers delay toilet training for their grandchildren) are gently corrected at the first opportunity. As a counterpoint to the story of childcare we learn something about the lives of women, especially mothers; the focus is on the reasons women now live as they do in China: the availability of non-kinship nurturance for children, and the policies of government with respect to women.

Perhaps it is only because of the limited information sources available to Sidel as a visitor on a brief tour, but there is little sense in this book of how husbands, wives, and children talk to, love, and take care of each other. What we do learn about the lives of women seems for the most part to be impersonal and doctrinaire, public policy instead of real life. Although the role of women in Chinese society is greatly changed from what it was in the "bitter past," Sidel implies that women are approaching economic equality and political power without relinquishing (or being relieved of) the principal responsibility for nurturance. The picture is that of "superwoman" who can, and will, fill *all* roles in society. One wonders: do those fathers really not want to spend time caring for children? By what myths do Chinese men rationalize their restriction to non-nurturant jobs?

In *The Future of Marriage,* Jessie Bernard carefully documents the past, present, and projected future of spouse relations in marriage. She summarizes the many reports about the interaction between sex and marital status with regard to happiness and good mental health. In a number of comparisons, married men are ranked as the most fortunately situated and married women the least, with single women and men ranked in between. She proposes that "there is . . . no longer any reason why the costs of marriage should be so excessive for wives" (p. 247). Bernard examines and highlights the differences between male and female prophecies about the future of marriage, and discusses several alternative options in spouse relations varying along the two independent continua of permanence and exclusiveness.

Again, one is struck by the selectivity: here children are incidental to family life. Marriages without children (of which, Bernard predicts, there will be exponentially more) are treated as almost insignificantly different from marriages with children, except that the latter must survive a period—twenty years or so—during which the marital relationship undergoes severe and hazardous stress as a consequence of the childrearing responsibility. Negotiations between spouses about their shared family responsibilities include childcare among their topics; Bernard alludes to out-of-family childcare both as already in existence (leading to changes in spouse relations as a consequence), and as a hope for the future of those who would intentionally explore an innovative marital style. But there is little in this book that conveys a sense of interdependence between spouse relations and the conduct of childcare. The paired questions of "who will care for the children?" and "what will they become?" are noticeably minimized in Bernard's book.

Betty Yorburg attempts to consider everything about families but gains completeness at the expense of closeness to living, breathing reality. Her method in *The Changing Family* is to stand back, portraying families that hardly seem to be peopled by real human beings. This is a least-common-denominator brand of sociology. She argues first that the multiplicity of options for families is a source of confusion and pain. But then she adds that because we are becoming increasingly rational and materialistic and decreasingly superstitious and religious, our choices are not so great after all. She predicts that the exclusive and permanent nuclear family will endure, on the rather circular argument that small children *must* have exclusive one-to-one care (scant mention of the strong published evidence in support of the advantages of multiple parenting) and that adults so conditioned cannot adapt to any form of marriage except that of the exclusive one-on-one relationship. Although she devotes chapters to ethnic and class differences in family style, she emphasizes an idealized middle-class nuclear family as a "melting pot" outcome, and discounts enduring pluralism. The last sentence of Yorburg's book illustrates both the generality of her writing, and the sense that individuals are helpless in the current of social-political-economic forces: "Government will have to render much more help to the American nuclear family for the realization of this goal [the eternal human need for the fulfilled life] and it will have to do so soon. It will either plan more effectively, or both the nation and the family will perish—because their ultimate fates are inseparable" (p. 204).

Perhaps the lesson is that the future of the family can, for now, be contemplated only as through a kaleidoscope, examining first one plane and then the next. Sidel and Bernard taken together remind us that the modern family has a dual heritage. Human adults first bonded together with some commitment to permanence and exclusiveness in order to bring their children safely through the relatively long period of human immaturity and dependency. We can and often do think of the purpose of family life as childrearing.

The second line of inheritance for the present-day family is represented by our expectations with regard to spouse relations. Lasting or not, exclusive or outreaching, the family of husband and wife stands as a voluntary kin relationship; all the usual kin obligations and rights are reinforced by expectations for something not unlike the attachment bonds that we see as universal and essential in the first two years of life. In this latter sense we look to the family as the locus of adult caretaking —we take care of each other there, and are taken care of.

Each view of the family inherits a wealth, or a burden, from past history, custom, and law. The heritage tells us what is right and what is wrong, and thus offers a certain security. But a strong heritage also inhibits adaptational change, as we find ourselves recapitulating patterns of behavior we thought we knew were maladaptive. There is, for instance, no bloodier ground than the family to try to undo sex-role stereotypy, no matter how firmly we might determine to do so.

Can we separate the family as a base for childrearing from the family as the essential home for adults, and gain more than we lose in understanding family structure and function? If we move toward different patterns of childcare than those of our recent past, must not spouse relations also inevitably change as a consequence? Alternatively, if spouse relations vary (as in permanence or exclusiveness), can we avoid thinking about the outcomes for the children? Can we hold in our heads so much complexity of prediction, or must we simplify away from reality in order to manage the problem?

Yorburg deals with the dilemma by simplification. She contemplates change only in terms of more or less of this or that; her vision of the future is a distinctly nonradical extension of the present. In the interests of generalization she formulates one prediction for families that subsumes all classes, all ethnic groups, all personal philosophies.

Sidel simply shows us how things are, in a contemporary society quite different from our own, where childrearing is managed in a way that we have not tried. She suggests some parallel possibilities in our future without positing any outcomes.

Bernard, whose last chapter epitomizes her intentionally personalized style (distinctly different from traditional academic sociology), tells us what some individuals are now dreaming, planning, or trying to live out in their families. Her catalogue of options (and their imagined consequences) seems to be based on the reality of actual lives. It is a selective reality: Bernard proposes that we can get a glimpse of the future only by looking to those who are now free enough to have options.

Perhaps it is unfair to criticize these authors for giving us only small pieces of a large puzzle: those pieces are in fact very carefully examined. But at least for this reader there is a strong wish for a glimpse at the whole puzzle assembled. I would like to ask Sidel, when sharing child care is ap proved and modal behavior for parents, and when women are expected to participate in productive work in the service of society, what happens to spouse relations? to the balance of power in the sexual partnership? to the post-parental depression common in so many American marriages? And, of Bernard, if spouses could participate interdependently in the family re-

sponsibilities of caring for each other, cleaning and cooking, and producing income, would their children identify with both parents? grow to value caretaking activities as much as product-oriented work? want to work and play in mixed-sex groups throughout childhood? And, of Yorburg, if the relatively isolated, sex-role stereotyped nuclear family is to continue as our most probable choice, what will evolve from the anger and despair that many—spouses, parents, and older children—are now voicing and acting out in protest to families that cannot meet the demands made on them?

The future of our families is so important for ourselves, our children, and our nation, that it is tempting to wish for a prophet to illumine the alternate ways. Until that future can be convincingly foretold, we shall have to live out our days as if we knew where we were going.

MARY C. HOWELL
Harvard University

Student Rights

MAKING SCHOOL WORK: AN EDUCATION
HANDBOOK FOR STUDENTS, PARENTS AND
PROFESSIONALS, by Larry Brown and
Tim Spofford.
Boston: Massachusetts Advocacy Cen-
ter and Massachusetts Law Reform In-
stitute, 1973. 99 pp. $3.95.

THE RIGHTS OF STUDENTS: THE BASIC
ACLU GUIDE TO A STUDENT'S RIGHTS,
by Alan Levine with Eve Cary and
Diane Divoky.
New York: Discus Books, 1973. 160 pp.
95¢.

In recent years there has been a dramatic
upsurge in activity to promote student
rights in public elementary and secondary
schools. An unprecedented number of
court decisions have been rendered[1];
countless local school boards have adopted
codes outlining student rights and responsibilities[2]; commissioners and state school
boards in many states have handed down
rulings and regulations favorable to students[3]; several legislatures have enacted
statutes to protect student rights[4]; and
handbooks on student rights proliferate.
These events, particularly the court decisions, prompted one commentator to suggest that school administrators are now
under unprecedented restrictions in their
efforts to control student behavior.[5]

Yet beneath this flurry of activity are
indications that students dare not rest on
past victories. Several observations contribute to this cautionary note. One is the
increasing realization that the highly
touted Supreme Court decision in *Tinker*
v. *Des Moines Independent School Dis-*
trict[6] provides little protection against
school officials intent on punishing students for exercising First Amendment
rights. In *Tinker* the Court held that students could not be suspended for the non-

---

[1] An extreme example of the increase in
student rights litigation is over the question
of whether school boards can regulate the
length of a student's hair. A leading treatise
on school law published in 1969 listed three
reported cases, all decided in favor of the
board. Leroy Peterson, Richard Rossmiller,
and Marlin Volz, *The Law and Public School*
Operation (New York: Harper and Row,
1969), p. 422. A more recent compilation lists
131 cases, 57 of which can be described as supporting the students' position, 74 in support
of the school board. National Organization on
Legal Problems of Education, *Nolpe Notes*
(Topeka, Kan., 1970-1973).

[2] As an indicator of this trend, the National
School Boards Association has an office which
collects and disseminates information to its
constituents about drafting codes of student
discipline.

[3] The State Commissioners of Education in
New York and New Jersey, for example, have
the authority to review decisions of local
school boards and frequently reverse local actions against students. In addition, it has been
noted that nineteen states have or are in the
process of releasing policy statements on student rights. See John C. Pittenger, *Policy and*
Guidelines on Student Rights and Responsi-
bilities in Pennsylvania (Unpublished paper,
Harrisburg, Pa.: 1973), p. 2.

[4] An example is Indiana's "Student Due
Process Law" enacted in 1972, which describes
in considerable detail the grounds for and the
procedure by which students may be suspended or expelled. *Burns Indiana Statutes*
Annotated, §§ 28-5354 through 28-5369.

[5] Edward T. Ladd, "Regulating Student Behavior without Ending Up in Court," *Phi*
Delta Kappan, 54 (January 1973), p. 304.

[6] 393 U.S. 503 (1969).

Harvard Educational Review Vol. 44 No. 1 February 1974, 172–177

disruptive wearing of armbands. But the Court added the proviso that conduct by the student which "materially disrupts classwork or involves substantial disorder or invasion of the rights of others, is, of course, not immunized by the constitutional guarantee of freedom of speech."[7] Some courts have seized on this proviso and been quick to sanction the curtailment of student expression in situations where the disruption was not substantial. One court approved suspensions to punish distribution of literature because administrators thought the handout "could conceivably cause an eruption."[8] Another court affirmed the suspension of a student for wearing an emblem which had been the source of school tension the previous year.[9] Other courts justified similar suspensions on the ground that some student behavior, while essentially free speech, shows defiance to school officials.[10]

The student rights movement also has placed excessive reliance on challenges to the *way* in which decisions about students are made rather than the *validity* of those decisions or the *authority* of administrators to make them. For example, it is now well settled in most states that students may not be expelled or suspended for long intervals without notice of the charges and a hearing to test the truth of the charges. Yet suspensions and expulsions continue, perhaps with increased frequency in some

sections of the country.[11] And the power of administrators to determine the length of exclusions, even if grossly out of proportion with the alleged offense, has gone virtually unchallenged.[12] Impatience with procedural reform is also surfacing in the area of student classification and tracking. A leading commentator on this subject has pointed out that merely because a student has been provided with notice and a hearing prior to placement in a slow track does not mean that the classification is valid or ultimately in the best interest of the student.[13]

Additional caution in assessing the accomplishments of the student rights movement is dictated by a series of setbacks on

[11] Data on the frequency of suspensions and expulsions are very difficult to find. One excellent report on the problem is *The Student Pushout: Victim of Continued Resistance to Desegregation* (Atlanta: Southern Regional Council, 1973) in which the Southern Regional Council documents the growing frequency of exclusions, particularly of black students, in the South.

[12] In a recent Massachusetts case, a state court found that it was unreasonable for a public school system to permanently exclude a twelve-year-old boy for misconduct. Even though the boy admitted to smoking cigarettes in the washroom, teasing girls, and unexcused absences, the court held that permanent exclusion "cannot be justified upon the record." Tavano v. Crowell, Equity No. 32699 (Barnstable Superior Ct. Aug. 31, 1973).

[13] "The major problem with (procedural reform) is that it does not raise the substantive question of the validity of the practice itself. Even if the classifying process is 'fairly' administered, what convincing justification does the school have for a practice which stigmatizes and isolates children and narrows their occupational options." Merle McClung, "School Classification: Some Legal Approaches to Labels." *Inequality in Education*, 14 (July 1973), p. 24.

[7] *Id.* at 513.
[8] Norton v. Discipline Committee of East Tennessee State University, 419 F.2d 195 (6th Cir. 1969) *cert. denied*, 399 U.S. 906 (1970).
[9] Melton v. Young, 465 F.2d 1332 (6th Cir. 1972).
[10] Schwartz v. Shuber, 298 F.Supp. 238 (E.D.N.Y. 1969); Sullivan v. Houston Independent School District, 475 F.2d 1071 (5th Cir. 1973).

the issue of administrators' authority to search students and their lockers without a warrant. Courts in recent years have used a number of arguments to authorize unannounced searches by school officials and police. One court approved a personal search of a high school boy mainly because of "the omnipresent evil of drug and narcotic abuse among young people of this nation."[14] A locker search was sanctioned by another court on the somewhat dubious ground that the school official was not acting for the state in this situation but stood *in loco parentis* (in the place of the parents) to the student.[15] Still another court stressed that student lockers are not protected by the constitution because they are owned by the school, not by the students.[16] Until advances are made in these very important areas of privacy, students may have to resign themselves to the role of second-class citizens.

The Supreme Court itself gave a signal last spring that educational reform through the law may have a difficult future. In *San Antonio Independent School District* v. *Rodriguez*,[17] the Court held that the method by which Texas finances its schools does not violate the Equal Protection clause of the Fourteenth Amendment. In the process, the Court found that although education plays a "vital role in a free society,"[18] it "is not among the rights afforded explicit protection under the Federal Constitution."[19] The actual constitu-

tional ramifications of this holding are quite narrow,[20] but there are efforts to expand its influence to educational litigation unrelated to the *Rodriguez* suit. For example, in an appeal to the Supreme Court, the Columbus, Ohio, Board of Education argued that *Rodriguez* bars a student challenge to an Ohio law authorizing school officials to suspend students for up to ten days without a hearing.[21] Although this argument is likely to fail, one observer has noted that *Rodriguez* might give "a judge hostile to student rights [a] feeling that he can rule against students without fear of repudiation."[22]

The final point in this litany of doom regarding student rights involves the public perception of schools. In a 1973 Gallup poll, "lack of Discipline" was rated by the general public as the number one problem in education. In fact, discipline has ranked first in this annual poll for four of the last five years.[23] Attitudes so persistent and widespread frequently influence public policy. Indeed, there are signs that pre-

[20] Because education was not found to be a fundamental interest and because plaintiffs failed to make out a case of economic discrimination, the Court required only that the Texas school finance scheme "bear some rational relationship to legitimate state purposes." *Id.* at 1300. Presumably, if the Court had accepted plaintiff's arguments pertaining to fundamental interest and economic discrimination, it would have struck down the Texas law unless it could be shown to be fulfilling a compelling state interest.
[21] Jurisdictional statement of Appellants at 6-9, Williams v. Lopez, —— U.S. —— (1974).
[22] Peter Roos, "The Impact of Rodriguez on Other School Reform Litigation," *Law and Contemporary Problems,* 38 (Winter-Spring, 1974), forthcoming.
[23] George Gallup, "Fifth Annual Gallup Poll of Public Attitudes Toward Education," *Phi Delta Kappan,* 55 (September 1973), 39.

[14] In re Thomas G., 11 Cal. App. 3rd 1193 (1970).
[15] In re Donaldson, 269 Cal. App. 2d 509 (1969).
[16] People v. Overton, 24 N.Y. 2d 522 (1969).
[17] 93 S.Ct. 1278 (1973).
[18] *Id.* at 1295.
[19] *Id.* at 1297.

occupation with discipline is having a damaging effect on student rights.[24]

It is within this context of uncertainty about the accomplishments and prospects of the student rights movement that the handbooks under review must be examined. *Making School Work* is written for use only in Massachusetts. This limitation in the application of the handbook is also the principal reason for its effectiveness. By limiting its focus to Massachusetts, *Making School Work* is able to provide the kind of concrete information, such as names, addresses, and telephone numbers, that a handbook designed for national application cannot. In addition, it imparts a sense of familiarity with local bureaucratic tendencies that can be of immense value to a parent or student trying to work through established channels.

Above all, *Making School Work* is a manual to help parents and students get results when dealing with the schools. Its advice is eminently practical whether the recommended tactic is massaging local administrators, forming parent and student groups, or retaining an attorney. It utilizes the experience of the Massachusetts Advocacy Center[25] to identify the types of problems students and parents are likely to confront and then presents courses of action that promise the best results. For example, if a parent or student is dissatisfied

with a track in which the student has been placed, several approaches are recommended. First, school officials should be quizzed about the procedure used to track kids in the school system. If the proper procedure was followed, the next step is to meet with teachers and counselors to examine the validity of the data that went into the decision. If still dissatisfied, then a parent or student can arrange an independent assessment of the student's abilities. Parents are also reminded that a 1973 Massachusetts law allows them to inspect all records on the student kept by the school. These specific remedies are buttressed by general advice to make notes and keep copies of all conversation and correspondence with school officials. The appendix also contains a useful array of sample letters that will aid students and parents when writing teachers or administrators.

The approach taken by *Making School Work* is appropriate for another reason. Massachusetts has recently passed a number of important and novel pieces of educational legislation.[26] Most prominent are the Special Education Act and the Transitional Bilingual Education Act. The ultimate impact of these laws will largely depend on their implementation in the next few years. The release of *Making School Work* at this time should help ensure that the needed adjustments in the administration of these laws will occur before state regulations become scripture and bureaucratic patterns become rigid.

Making School Work is not only limited

[24] For example, in 1973 Indiana amended its "Student Due Process" law to provide pre-expulsion hearings only on request. See footnote 4. Also, there are reports that the Philadelphia Board of Education suspended a previously adopted ban on corporal punishment in the city's schools.

[25] See Peter Edelman, "The Massachusetts Task Force Reports: Advocacy for Children," *Harvard Educational Review*, 43 (November 1973), p. 639.

[26] This should not be interpreted to mean that Massachusetts is a progressive education state. The passage of reform legislation in the area of education can largely be attributed to a particularly effective legislative aide and several dedicated legislators.

geographically but is also limited in the issues addressed. No mention is made of some of the most visible student rights issues of recent years, such as freedom of expression, grooming, literature distribution, or religious exercises. Why? We are not told, but it is reasonable to assume that the authors perceived civil liberties as issues about which the law is in a constant state of flux; consequently, they are difficult to describe to most parents and students. But a more important reason probably lay in the authors' inclination to view these issues as peripheral to the core questions about the scope and quality of education.

This neglect of civil liberties in the schools is in sharp contrast to the approach of *The Rights of Students*. A substantial portion of this handbook is devoted to these issues. Considerable attention is given to free expression, and the majority opinion in *Tinker* is set out in full in the appendix. But the scope of this volume exceeds civil liberties. Corporal punishment, tracking, school records, and other areas are discussed in some detail. The material is presented in a question-answer format which is useful in focusing issues and allowing readers with a particular problem to find an answer quickly. Moreover, with some qualifications discussed below, the research is sound and up-to-date—qualities not always found in student rights materials.

The Rights of Students was written for national consumption. As a result it bears some of the characteristics of any short treatise on law in a nation with fifty-one separate court systems. One is a tendency to stress court opinions supporting the authors' predilections and to ignore unfavorable rulings. For example, the authors note that one court has required a hearing

prior to a suspension lasting two days, another prior to a five-day suspension, and a third prior to a ten-day suspension (p. 59). Yet they neglect decisions specifically upholding five-, seven-, ten- and twenty-five-day summary suspensions.[27] Selective citation in materials designed for lawyers is probably excusable because lawyers are expected to do their own legal research. But materials for students ought to convey that courts are hardly unanimous even if there are a couple of very favorable decisions in a particular area. The danger is, of course, that students will assume that the favorable opinions represent the law in their district.

Another problem stemming from the scope and format of *The Rights of Students* is a tendency to ask a question and then base a response on cases which do not raise that precise issue. At one point the authors ask, "Do you have a right to bring a witness to a disciplinary hearing?" The answer: "Yes, if you are granted a hearing, you have the right to witnesses" (p. 65). It is true that the cases cited to support this principle held that a student can have witnesses at a disciplinary hearing. But it does not follow as a matter of due process jurisprudence that a student is entitled to have witnesses at every hearing. In two recent and favorable decisions, courts required hearings prior to short suspensions but made no provision for witnesses for the student.[28]

[27] Jackson v. Hepinstall, 328 F. Supp. 1104 (W.D.N.Y. 1971); Linwood v. Board of Education, 463 F.2d 763 (7th Cir. 1972), *cert. denied* 93 S.Ct. 475; Farrell v. Joel, 437 F.2d 160 (2nd Cir. 1971); Hernandez v. School District No. One, Denver, 315 F. Supp. 289 (D. Colo. 1970).

[28] Vail v. Board of Education of Portsmouth School District, 354 F.Supp. 592, 603 (D.N.H.

The student rights movement is at a critical crossroads. And, to a degree, the handbooks reviewed here might represent the divergent paths open to students. *Making School Work* is principally concerned with using existing law (statutes, administrative regulations, and court decisions) and established channels to make schools conform to their legal obligations. Its underlying theme is the consolidation of past gains so that the performance of schools measures up to the promise of the hard-won legal victories. *The Rights of Students,* on the other hand, encourages further legal reform and the spread of favorable decisions to all states.

Perhaps there is enough energy left in the student rights movement to pursue both goals. Student-oriented groups in every state should take a hard look at their existing rights and draft strategies to enforce those rights locally using *Making School Work* as a model. At the same time, there ought to be some students willing to be on the cutting edge of the law defining new rights and striving to pull the Constitution, kicking and dragging, in through the schoolhouse door.

THOMAS J. FLYGARE
Harvard University

1973); Lopez v. Williams, C.A. 71-67 (E.D. Ohio, Sept. 12, 1973).

Notes on Contributors

MARY JO BANE is Associate Professor of Public Policy at the John F. Kennedy School of Government, Harvard University. Formerly Associate Professor of Education and Associate Director of the Center for Research on Women at Wellesley College, she is the author of *Here to Stay: American Families in the Twentieth Century* (1976) and (with George Masnick) *The Nation's Families, 1960–1990* (1980).

ROCHELLE BECK was Program Director and Director of Public Affairs for the Children's Defense Fund in Washington, D.C., writing and editing a range of books and articles on domestic policy issues affecting children and families. Since 1981, she has been traveling in Latin America and writing about U.S. policies toward Hispanics at home and abroad.

ROBERT B. COATES is Associate Professor in the School of Social Service Administration of the University of Chicago. Formerly a Research Associate at the Center for Criminal Justice, Harvard Law School, his present professional interests are juvenile justice and child advocacy. He is the author of *Advocacy in Juvenile Justice: Concept and Practice* (1981).

MARIAN WRIGHT EDELMAN is President of the Children's Defense Fund in Washington, D.C. She has served previously as Director of the NAACP Legal and Education Fund in Jackson, Mississippi, and Director of the Center for Law and Education, Harvard University. Dr. Edelman is the author of many articles on the rights of children and has been the recipient of numerous academic honors and awards for public service. In 1979 she was a member of the National Commission on the International Year of the Child and the President's Commission for a National Agenda for the Eighties.

PETER B. EDELMAN is Professor of Law at Georgetown University. He has served as Director of the New York State Division of Youth, Vice President for University Policy, University of Massachusetts, and as Legislative Assistant to Senator Robert F. Kennedy.

JOSEPH FEATHERSTONE is Headmaster, The Commonwealth School, Boston, Massachusetts, and Lecturer in Education at Harvard University. His most recent book is *What Schools Can Do* (1976).

THOMAS J. FLYGARE is General Counsel of the University System of New Hampshire and also writes the monthly column, "De Jure," in *Phi Delta Kappan*. His current primary professional focus is equal employment opportunity and the application of antidiscrimination laws to higher education. He is the author of a Phi Delta Kappa pamphlet, *Legal Rights of Teachers* (1976).

LESTER GRINSPOON is Professor of Psychiatry, Harvard Medical School, at the Massachusetts Mental Health Center. His major professional interest is general psychiatry. A frequent contributor to the medical and scientific literature, he is the author of *Cocaine: A Drug and Its Social*

Evolution (1976) and *Psychedelic Drugs Reconsidered* (1979). He is also the editor of *Psychiatry 1982: The American Psychiatric Association Annual Review*.

MARY C. HOWELL is a pediatrician and development psychologist. Her professional interests are the integration of work and family life, child-rearing alternatives, professionalization, and sex-role stereotyping.

DAVID L. KIRP is Professor of Public Policy and Lecturer in Law, University of California, Berkeley, and Director of the Law Program, Institute for the Study of Educational Finance and Governance, Stanford University. His publications include *Doing Good by Doing Little* (1979), *Educational Policy and the Law* (2nd ed., 1982), *Just Schools: The Idea of Racial Equality in American Education* (1982), and *Gender Justice* (forthcoming).

RICHARD J. LIGHT is Professor of Education and Public Policy at Harvard University. His present areas of major interest are quantitative methods for program evaluation and synthesizing outcomes across several research studies. He is coauthor with Jeffrey Travers of *Learning from Experience* (1982) and, with David Hoaglin, Bucknam McPeek, Frederick Mosteller, and Michael Stoto, of *Date for Decisions* (1982).

JANE R. MERCER is Professor of Sociology, University of California, Riverside. Among her many professional concerns are the sociology of education, racially and culturally nondiscriminatory assessments, and the development of transnational procedures for bilingual students. She has served as Principal Investigator for the National Institute of Mental Health into various aspects of integrated multiethnic education and the desegregation process. She has written widely on mental retardation and multicultural pluralistic assessments. Forthcoming in 1982 is her most recent article, "What Is a Racially and Culturally Non-discriminatory Test? A Response to Jensen's *Bias in Mental Testing*," to be published in *Perspectives on Bias in Mental Testing*.

ALDEN D. MILLER, formerly of the Center for Criminal Justice at the Harvard Law School, is Associate Professor, Institute of Criminal Justice and Criminology, University of Maryland. His current interests are in youth opportunity and social control in communities. Professor Miller has written in the areas of social change and methods of causal analysis.

ROBERT H. MNOOKIN is Professor of Law at Stanford University Law School. The former Director of the Childhood and Government Project at Berkeley, he is concerned with the legal and economic problems of children and the analysis of the distribution of power and responsibility for the child among the child, the family, and the state. He is the author of *Child, Family, State: Cases and Materials on Children and the Law* (1978) and is presently completing a book on test-case litigation on behalf of children.

WALTER F. MONDALE, presently counsel with Winstron & Strawn, Washington, D.C., served as Vice-President of the United States (1977–1981) and United States Senator from Minnesota (1964–1976). He has been a leading governmental spokesperson for children and has served as chairman of the Senate Subcommittee on Children and Youth and has been a member of the Senate Subcommittees on Education, on Poverty, and on Health.

LLOYD E. OHLIN is Toureff-Glueck Professor, Emeritus, at Harvard Law School, where he was Director of the Center for Criminal Justice and Roscoe Pound Professor of Criminology. Professor Ohlin has written extensively in the areas of delinquency and corrections.

JUSTINE WISE POLIER is President of the Field Foundation, New York City. She served as Justice of the New York Family Court from 1935 to 1972 and cites the law and social science as her major professional interests. Among her writings are *Back to What Woodshed?* (1956) and *A View from the Bench* (1964).

HILLARY RODHAM, a practicing lawyer and member of the Rose Law Firm in Little Rock, Arkansas, is on the Board of Directors of the Children's Defense Fund, President of Arkansas Advocates for Children and Families, and former Chairman of the Legal Services Corporation. Her present professional interests are children's needs, legal sources, and commercial litigation. Her recent writings include "Children's Policies: Abandonment and Neglect," *Yale Law Journal* (1977), and "Children's Rights: A Legal Perspective," in *Children's Rights* (ed. Patricia Vardin and Ilene Brody, 1979).

SUSAN B. SINGER is a psychotherapist at the Family Service of Greater Lowell, Lowell, Massachusetts, working with adults, children, and families. She was formerly a social worker in the Neurology Department of Boston University Medical Center and a Research Assistant at the Massachusetts Mental Health Center.

VICTOR L. WORSFOLD is Associate Professor of Philosophy and Education and Associate Dean for the Arts of the University of Texas at Dallas. Rights in education and theories of personhood are subjects of special interest to Professor Worsfold, who has written on students' rights and ethics of educational administration.